Continual Lessons

Continual Lessons

THE JOURNALS OF

Glenway Wescott

1937 · 1955

EDITED BY ROBERT PHELPS

WITH JERRY ROSCO

Farrar Straus Giroux

NEW YORK

Library of Congress Cataloging-in-Publication Data
Wescott, Glenway.
Continual lessons: the journals of Glenway Wescott, 1937–1955 /
edited by Robert Phelps with Jerry Rosco. — 1st ed.
1. Wescott, Glenway. —Diaries.   2. Authors,
American—20th century—Diaries.   3. Gay men—United States—
Diaries.   I. Phelps, Robert, 1922–89.   II. Rosco, Jerry.
III. Title.
PS3545.E827Z464   1990   818'.5203—dc20   90-3303
[B]

Grateful acknowledgment is made for permission to reproduce the
following: four portraits of Glenway Wescott, the Estate of George
Platt Lynes; portrait of Glenway Wescott and Monroe Wheeler (last
page of second photo insert, top), Nancy Rica Schiff. All other pho-
tos courtesy of John Connolly, Anatole Pohorilenko,
and Lloyd Wescott

INTRODUCTION

BY ROBERT PHELPS

Well over a century ago, Emerson predicted that "novels will give way, by and by, to diaries or autobiographies—captivating books, if only a man knew . . . how to record truth truly."

This volume is perhaps best described as an attempt to make the sort of book Emerson dreamed of, to use the form, the appearance, of a diary to try to tell one man's "truth truly." The author is Glenway Wescott, for decades a shining name in American literature, and the text begins in 1937, in the middle of the author's life, "nel mezzo del cammin." Wescott had known precocious prestige as the author of *The Grandmothers* and *Goodbye, Wisconsin*, and after nearly a decade abroad, he had returned to his native country to live in New York and on a spacious cattle-breeding ranch in western New Jersey. A novel in progress, *The Dream of Mrs. Cleveland*, had run aground, and the author by way of a lifeline began to keep a journal. The result is an intimately personal book, exploring the daily activity of a man who loves the making of literature and the living of life almost equally well and who, like Stendhal, might have given as his profession "Observer of the Human Heart."

There are fascinating friendships—with Somerset Maugham, Katherine Anne Porter, Jean Cocteau, Janet Flanner, Alfred Kinsey. There is a dense, multifarious family ferment. There is gossip—worldly, homintern, literary—and though a few of the names are necessarily coded, there is no loss of all-too-human interest thereby. There is a protracted and nearly destructive love affair with a young, alcoholic journalist. There is everywhere a Virgilian reverence for nature, and at the heart of it all, there is a ménage à trois all the more extraordinary for being composed of three honorable, gifted, and very passionate males.

The tone varies—witty, grave, desperate, elegiac, sardonic, comic—but the voice we hear throughout is that of Glenway Wescott, one of the most subtle and sober in American literature. Closer at first glimpse to the majestic French tradition that includes Montaigne and Jules Renard and André Gide and Paul Léautaud, *Continual Lessons* is at the same time a peculiarly American book: American in its obstinate, necessary aloneness, in its air of being not so much a book as Notes in a Bottle, secret marginalia, one man's evidence in his self-defense.

If Glenway may be said to have held any aesthetic belief, I think it would have had to do with his preference for images over ideas. He had a vigorous mind, but one which always preferred the concrete image to even the most supple of ideas. He never kept a pet, unless you count the human ones, but the sight of a sparrow hawk planing above his neighbor's meadow or the housekeeper's cat watching and waiting could fill him with rapture. He was especially partial to squirrels and their capacity for aerial flight. He once telephoned me at 6 a.m. to describe the joyful antics of a red squirrel leaping from branch to branch.

In a letter to a young French writer whom he had met in 1938, he declared, "Voilà . . . I dread intellect; I mistrust love but have faith in intelligence." And a little further on he was more explicit in this admonition: "Write about work and landscapes and incidents, and about sex and money and health; not just thoughts."

The best view of Glenway Wescott I can offer is in the form of three miniature portraits.

After lunching at the Lambertville Inn in New Jersey one day, we emerged to find ourselves in a heavy downpour and found refuge in the local bookstore. Immediately Glenway took charge. "Hold out your arms," he ordered, and stacked them with orange letter files from the counter nearest us. We moved on to the typewriter paper—blue, pink, magenta. With hardly a pause he pounced on the pens, among them a beautiful fat-nibbed Parker, the kind he particularly liked: "Excellent for the final draft of a book review." He continued weaving among the counters, his rosy boyish face agleam, from paper clips to rubber bands, from Elmer's glue to colored inks, from spiral notebooks to staple guns. Momentarily sated, he paused. "If anyone should ever ask me to participate in a writers' conference I would want my course to be called Desk Method."

Nonetheless, my actual memory of Glenway's desk methods sees him as I did on many occasions, not officially behind any real desk, but at the kitchen table turning over his material while an omelette is browning on the stove and a Bach cantata sings from the hi-fi.

As for credos, Monroe Wheeler, Glenway, and I were once walking along the gentle ridge above his house and I asked how each would summarize his philosophy. Monroe's answer was straightforward, prompt: "I never want to be left out of the dance." After a slow, foxy smile, Glenway reached down and picked up a stone. "I believe everything breathes; even this stone must utter a blissful sigh every millennium."

On another such day, Glenway was seen trundling his suitcase to a taxi waiting to take him to the train station in Trenton. He had a heavy date that weekend in New York. It was early May, the weather was crisp, the day was bright. As he stood with his luggage, he noticed the place on his acreage reserved for the cutting garden. "Wait," he directed the driver. Rushing into the house, he fetched the garden shears. And while the driver watched, astonished, but not as astonished as he would become presently, Glenway went about his task so effectively that two hours later his host, a young poet named Mark Pagano, opened the door to a literal shower of two hundred daffodils.

Unlike Gide's journals, or Virginia Woolf's, or those of Marcel Jouhandeau, this collection never had an Ur-life of its own, that is, in a series of numbered notebooks with placed and dated entries. It originated in the contents of literally hundreds of ring binders, into whose pages its author had pasted every sort of memo, newspaper clipping, letter carbon, etc. There are, of course, journal entries as well, but the text offered here is a mélange. In preparing it for publication, I have chosen to simulate the conventional diary, though in substance as well as appearance it is closer to a scrapbook. The relatively few footnotes are selective and subjective.

A CHRONOLOGY

GLENWAY WESCOTT

1901 – 1987

1901–16 Glenway Gordon Wescott was born in Washington County, near Kewaskum, Wisconsin, the first of six children, on April 11, 1901. His family's hundred-acre farm was humble; the runoff from hills kept a lower field useless with stagnant water, and Bruce Wescott couldn't afford horses or livestock and instead bred pigs. The father felt additionally unlucky when his first son proved too sensitive for the more difficult farm work.

Glenway attended Orchard Grove Country School from 1906 to 1912. As a young boy he had a high-pitched soprano voice, took lessons, and was paid three dollars to sing at funerals. He knew an elderly neighbor woman who recalled the danger of Indian attacks in her youth. He discovered his first "shocking and controversial reading" in Leviticus and Deuteronomy, and his first adult fiction in serialized Hall Caine novels.

He attended West Bend High School from 1913 to 1915, living with his uncle and others and thus escaping the difficulties with his father at home. In 1914, the school periodical, *The Tatler*, published his little essay "King David and His Court." That same year, thirteen-year-old Glenway began a two-year relationship with a fifteen-year-old named Carl. Years later, a short story, "Adolescence" (1928), recalled that secret childhood romance. He attended Wanheska High School from 1915 to 1917. A short story, "The Dare," appeared in the school publication *The Megaphone* in 1915.

1917–20 At the age of sixteen, Wescott entered the University of Chicago, where he joined the Poetry Club and was quickly elected its president. The poet and critic Yvor Winters recalled of the club: "This was a very intelligent group, worth more than most courses in literature; among the members was Glenway Wescott, a year younger than myself, who, like myself, had discovered most of the unknown moderns in high school, and Elizabeth Madox Roberts, about twenty years our elder." A dozen years later, Roberts, a Southern novelist, would dedicate her masterwork, *The Great Meadow*, to Wescott.

Although influenced in the direction of Imagist poetry by Winters, Wescott started work on a long story in 1918. That year he also began a well-intentioned but half-serious engagement with a Chicago-area young woman who had lost her fiancé in the war. The sympathetic friendship ended two years later.

Wescott was hospitalized with the Spanish flu in 1919, the year he met Monroe Wheeler, a bright and ambitious young man who would soon become his lifelong companion. Wescott withdrew from the university after his third semester and took his only conventional job ever—as a department store clerk for Hart, Schaffner and Marx—a disaster that ended after only two weeks. That November, when he didn't know which way to turn, he was invited by the father of Yvor Winters to be a secretary and companion for his son, who was then recuperating from tuberculosis in Santa Fe. The happy restful months that followed restored his own health and his still-unfocused love for literature.

After a visit to his family in Wisconsin, he returned to Chicago in the fall of 1920. He and Monroe Wheeler lived first in Evanston, then in a downtown boardinghouse. One day, as they sat together on the campus of Northwestern University, Wescott's new friend proposed a solution to the problem of being homosexual. "They will let you alone," Wheeler said, "if they believe you are a poet."

Indeed, Wescott had been president of the Poetry Club at sixteen. At seventeen he had been friends with Janet Lewis, who soon married Winters. Vachel Lindsay gave him a gift of cuff links for his first dress shirt when he turned eighteen. By nineteen he'd met Carl Sandburg and Edgar Lee Masters. And all along he'd been writing scores of poems in the Imagist style of Winters, Lewis, H. D. (Hilda Doolittle), Mina Loy, and others.

Wheeler used his small savings to publish a series of chapbooks. Among these were *Marriage*, a long poem by Marianne Moore, and *The Bitterns*, twelve poems by Wescott. Wallace Stevens wrote to Wescott: "It is difficult to make poetry as sophisticated as this fly. But you certainly make it tremble and shake. I will watch your work with the greatest interest."

1921–24 Through the spring of 1921, Wescott worked as an office boy at *Poetry* magazine, and his poems and reviews began to appear in *Poetry* and *The Dial*. That summer, he and Wheeler were guests at the West Cummington, Massachusetts, property of Mrs. William Vaughan Moody, a Chicago literary hostess and widow of the poet and playwright. Near the large log cabin where they stayed was a two-room cottage, the birthplace of William Cullen Bryant. Glenway used it as his studio and resumed work on the long fiction he had started in Chicago. He also visited the MacDowell Colony in Peterborough, New Hampshire, and met Edwin Arlington Robinson, Maxwell Bodenheim, and Robert Frost.

Living in New York City that fall, the twenty-year-old summoned the courage to visit the St. Luke's Place apartment of the poet he most admired, Marianne Moore. She and her mother soon became friends of Wescott and Wheeler.

The two men embarked by ocean liner for England, traveling in steerage berths alongside the propeller—sleeping not on mattresses but on sacks filled with corn husks. In England, with only a few letters of introduction from *Poetry* editor Harriet Monroe, the Wisconsin farmboy met Sir John Lavery and Lady Lavery and writers R. B. Cunninghame Graham, Raymond Mortimer, Osbert Sitwell, and the colorful Ford Madox Ford and his third wife, artist Stella Bowen. Ford—who was better respected by the American expatriates than by his British contemporaries—later wrote: ". . . if Mr. Wescott had not paid me a visit of some duration, I do not think that I should have taken seriously again to writing."

After a long stay in Germany, where they were struck by the shocking poverty in the postwar nation, they returned to New York City in 1922. To ease their own poverty, Marianne Moore brought homemade soup to their basement studio at Lexington Avenue and Eighteenth Street. Later in the year, Wescott returned to Germany as personal secretary to the financier and art collector Henry Goldman.

He made a third trip to Europe in 1923, commissioned by the family of the famed vocalist Elena Gerhardt. When he returned to New York he was introduced by Mina Loy to Ezra Pound and continued to publish poems and reviews in *The Dial* and *Poetry*, as well as in *The New Republic, Transatlantic Review, Broom, Contact, The Little Review,* and *Manikin*. More important, he made the transition from poet and small-journal reviewer to fiction writer and Midwest prodigy. The long story he had been returning to for years was serialized as "Bad Han" in the January and February 1924 issues of *The Dial*. Working in his two-room apartment at 17 Christopher Street, and influenced by D. H. Lawrence's *Sons and Lovers*, he expanded the story into his first novel, *The Apple of the Eye*, published that year by Dial Press. Sinclair Lewis offered the book-jacket comment: "It seems to me to have something curiously like genius."

The Dial also printed "In a Thicket," which was chosen for *The Best Short Stories of 1924*.

1925–28 With a thousand-dollar advance from Dial Press and a three-thousand-dollar gift from patron and friend Frances Robbins, he and Wheeler set out to join the expatriates in France in February of 1925. Worried about getting to work on his second novel, however, he found Paris too filled with distractions. Ford Madox Ford suggested that they move south to Villefranche, a coastal suburb of Nice, where they settled into two large rooms in the Hôtel Welcome. Their neighbor and new friend was the flamboyant artist, writer, and filmmaker Jean Cocteau. Suddenly their social world included Isadora Duncan, Mary Butts, Christian Bérard, Georges Hugnet, Sir Francis Rose, Paul Robeson, Rebecca West, Igor Stravinsky, Pablo Picasso, Allen Tate, and Caroline Gordon. Despite the social activity, the young writer learned to work with the discipline of his new friends and fellow artists. "We lived as the Victorians wrote," Glenway said; "what should have taken months we did in weeks."

In 1925, while working on his second novel, he regularly published reviews and essays in *The Dial*. A story in *Collier's National Weekly* was selected for *The Best Short Stories of 1925*. His book *Natives of Rock*, a beautifully printed, privately published volume of twenty poems, was well received. The following year, a Wescott story was published in a deluxe edition, *Like a Lover*, by Monroe Wheeler. New editions of his first novel were published in New York and London.

When, that same year, Ernest Hemingway's *The Sun Also Rises* appeared, Glenway realized he had an enemy. Scribner's editor Maxwell Perkins had forced Hemingway to change the name of an unattractive character in Chapter 3 from Roger Prescott to Prentiss. But the depiction of "a rising new novelist" from New York "by way of Chicago" was unmistakable.

Hemingway had first met Wescott and Wheeler at a game of bridge arranged by Ford Madox Ford. Although Wescott had once ignored F. Scott Fitzgerald's request to help get Hemingway published, he believed it was his friendship with Duff Twysden, the Brett Ashley of the novel, that had annoyed Hemingway. When Wescott's second novel was published to wide acclaim in 1927, Hemingway told an American reporter, "Every word was written with the intention of making Glenway Wescott immortal."

The Grandmothers, a Midwestern classic and a model of the chronicle novel, won the prestigious Harper Prize and swept through twenty-six printings in six months. In it Wescott used for the first time the character Alwyn Tower as his narrative voice. Novelist and critic Louis Bromfield called the work "one of the most beautiful books I have ever read," while a *New York Herald Tribune* review headline proclaimed Wescott "A Celebrity at Twenty-seven." Wescott met W. Somerset Maugham, who applauded his rapid success, and in 1928, when the new Pulitzer Prize laureate Thornton Wilder visited Villefranche, he took long walks with the young literary star. He congratulated Wescott but warned him that critical acclaim and big-city sales were not enough: he needed somehow to get his name on the news pages. Over the decades, however, Wescott was more likely to land on the society pages.

But for a time he was clearly among the top four or five American expatriate writers. The appreciative reception for *Goodbye, Wisconsin*—ten stories and the title essay—sustained his reputation, and individual selections appeared in a number of magazines and journals, as well as in *The Best Short Stories of 1928*. He and Wheeler traveled to Spain and Morocco, then moved that summer to the rue des Eaux in Paris.

At the time, Wescott did not see the value of keeping a journal. Writer Julien Green noted in his own journal that December: "Lunch yesterday with Wescott. He told me that it did not seem possible to keep an absolutely sincere and truthful journal. But sincerity is a gift like any other. One cannot choose to be sincere."

1929–33 In Paris, Wescott and Wheeler established artistic and social liaisons that set a pattern for the rest of their lives. Since the Chicago days, Wheeler had designed and published seven attractive small books by respected writers. Now he joined forces with a California millionaire, Barbara Harrison, in producing Harrison of Paris deluxe-edition books. In four years they produced thirteen beautiful Paris editions, including works by Shakespeare, Lord Byron, Dostoevsky, Thomas Mann, Bret Harte, Wescott, and Katherine Anne Porter. The endeavor would end in 1934, but Barbara Harrison was to become the sister-in-law of Wescott, and he would never again write without being somewhat mindful of her support and her position in society. Her approval and friendship were actually much more important to Wheeler, but Wheeler's happiness was everything to Wescott.

Wheeler had developed a relationship with a young photographer, George Platt Lynes, who would be a part of the Wescott clan into the fifties. In his remaining Paris years, Wescott was involved with Jacques Guérin, a young man from a distinguished family. Through the rest of their lives Wescott and Wheeler would have a substantial number of separate friends and lovers, while remaining lifelong companions.

The Babe's Bed, Wescott's final Midwestern work, appeared in 1930 in a slipcased Harrison of Paris edition of under four hundred copies. Wescott had made summer visits to Wisconsin from 1926 through 1929, and this Alwyn Tower work fictionalizes an expatriate author's visit to his troubled family's farm in the Midwest.

In 1932, he published *Fear and Trembling*, a large book of essays inspired by a two-month motor trip through prewar Germany. Although prophetic, the book was too abstract and mannered for popular taste. A harsh *New York Journal* review was headlined "Wescott Worries in Fine Words About Us." Wescott himself said, "I tried in a much too soft and elegant way to alarm the United States about the intentions of Germany." Within a year, Harper & Brothers pulped most of the edition. *A Calendar of Saints for Unbelievers*, published in 1932 and 1933 by Harrison and Harper's respectively, was a humorous chronicle of failed and foiled "saints"—with attractive illustrations by Wescott and Wheeler's friend Pavel Tchelitchew.

In 1932, Wescott met Katherine Anne Porter, eleven years his elder, at Barbara's lavish Paris house. The meeting started a lifelong friendship and correspondence, usually supportive and intimate but sometimes negative and angry. Gertrude Stein wrote of Wescott in her *Autobiography of Alice B. Toklas* (1933): "He has a certain syrup but it does not pour." Nearly forty years later he responded in an essay: "There was truth to this: more and more peculiar truth as the years have passed."

1934–39 During the troubling first years back in America, Wescott struggled as a writer. In France, his friends, his reading, his speech had been French. "I came back not only thinking but dreaming in French," he said. There was a *Hound and Horn* essay on Henry James. A few new stories appeared, but they'd been written in France. And serious, admirable attempts at new novels were abandoned.

As Wheeler and he settled into their new home at 48 East 89 Street, Wheeler's career in the arts took prominence. In Europe he'd befriended Renoir and many of the modern painters, including Picasso and Chagall, and now, in New York, he joined the staff of the Museum of Modern Art. Wescott wrote several pieces for exhibits and galleries.

Barbara Harrison married Lloyd Wescott in 1935, and Glenway accompanied them to Europe, visiting Cocteau and other friends. In 1937, they gave him, Wheeler, and George Platt Lynes a country home, Stone-blossom, on their large western New Jersey farm. This was the year Wescott finally began to keep a journal.

During 1938, he made a solitary trip to Paris and London, seeking old friends and new inspiration. That summer, after a visit to Maine, he wrote a fifty-page story with an erotic theme. Although he was always pleased with "A Visit to Priapus," he reluctantly withheld it from publication throughout his life.

Some of his old Imagist work appeared in a 1938 anthology of Wisconsin poets; a powerful new poem, "Summer Ending," was published in *Poetry* in 1939. There was a critical essay on Katherine Anne Porter in *Southern Review*. Then, recalling the twenties in Paris and an afternoon at Barbara's 32 rue de Vaugirard home, Wescott produced a remarkable new work of fiction.

1940 *The Pilgrim Hawk*, a short novel fusing reality and symbol, external and internal storytelling, lyrical tone and sober clarity, was published by Harper & Brothers and serialized in *Harper's* magazine. Over the years, *The Pilgrim Hawk* would be critically acclaimed, published in four languages, and selected for major anthologies. The (London) *Times*, forty-seven years later, suggested that it was as perfect a literary work as anything in the English language. In 1940, the book's sales were modest and the reaction moderate, but Wescott felt vindicated for the unsuccessful years of the thirties.

Also in 1940, "The Dream of Audubon," a libretto of a ballet in three scenes, appeared in *Dance* magazine, and later in *The Best One-Act Plays of 1940*.

1941–44 Klaus Mann wrote in his autobiography, *The Turning Point* (1941): "As for Glenway Wescott, he now appears almost as conspicuously European in America as he used to be conspicuously American in Europe. As a writer and a character, he is just as suave and subtle. Being highly fond of civilized people, I always relished his company."

Somerset Maugham, who barely remembered meeting him in the late twenties, now became a permanent friend of Wescott and Wheeler. Wescott made two long visits to Maugham's temporary American home, Parker's Ferry, in South Carolina.

Among Wescott's essays and reviews was the 1941 *New Republic* piece "The Moral of F. Scott Fitzgerald," later included in Edmund Wilson's 1945 anthology on Fitzgerald, *The Crack-Up*. Two 1942 stories in *Harper's Bazaar*, "Mr. Auerbach in Paris" and "The Frenchman Six Foot Three," suggested the World War II novel that was forthcoming.

1945 *Apartment in Athens*, a skillful suspense novel that fell totally outside his Alwyn Tower fiction, was a Book-of-the-Month Club selection and a best-seller. Praised by Maugham, Porter, Janet Flanner, and Eudora Welty, the novel—with its unstinting depiction of the German occupation of Greece—was as big a popular success as his 1932 anti-German essays, *Fear and Trembling*, had been a crushing failure. An abridged version was serialized in *McCall's*, and the book appeared internationally in five languages. It was to be his last work of fiction.

1946—49 Five aborted novels, totaling over one thousand pages—*The Dream of Mrs. Cleveland*, *A Fortune in Jewels*, *The Little Ocean Liner*, *A Year of Love*, and *The Deadly Friend*—are among Wescott's unpublished work. There were other false starts as well. In 1946, an angry Maugham scolded him by letter: ". . . don't tell me that you have fallen back into your old, neurasthenic, detestable habit of leaving a work unfinished just because what you have written doesn't come up to what you saw in your mind's eye before you began to write. It never does," not even for Tolstoy or Flaubert, Maugham reasoned. But Wescott, though struggling, simply could not finish another major work of fiction. "Every time I wrote a book, I thought I could do another like it," he said, "until I tried."

The second half of his career was marked by public service to the arts, complementing the interests of Wheeler, who had become director of exhibitions and publications for the Museum of Modern Art in 1941. Wheeler revolutionized the production of museum publications, and over the years would supervise over 350 books on the visual arts.

In 1947, Wescott was elected to the American Academy–Institute of Arts and Letters. For nearly forty years he would champion causes, secure grants for worthy writers, plan proceedings, and address the prestigious group at its grand upper Manhattan headquarters. In the late forties, he also volunteered his time for UNESCO and the International Copyright Convention. In 1949, he befriended Alfred C. Kinsey and became involved in the Institute for Sex Research at the University of Indiana, Bloomington.

Meanwhile, the Wheeler-Wescott apartment, now at 410 Park Avenue, remained a unique meeting place for artists and celebrities. At a

February 1949 party, Maugham felt upstaged by the arrival of the hosts' neighbor Marlene Dietrich. Novelist Frederic Prokosch in his memoirs recalled another party at which Edmund Wilson accidentally dropped a shrimp into the coif of an unsuspecting Edith Sitwell, while the polite gathering pretended not to notice.

In the spring of 1949, Wescott had a euphoric reunion with Thornton Wilder. At Wilder's hotel they sat in facing armchairs, each with a separate bottle of whiskey in a bucket of ice, and spoke half the night about how a mature writer might plan a new major work. Also that year, E. M. Forster paid a visit to the Stone-blossom farm. Over the next few years, Wescott and Christopher Isherwood would encourage Forster to plan for the posthumous publication of his long-suppressed novel, *Maurice.*

1950—59 While still attempting new works of fiction, Wescott devoted most of his time to the American Academy—Institute of Arts and Letters. In 1957, he was elected president, a position he would hold until 1961. He wrote some essays and major introductions for volumes of Maugham and Colette. Published in 1954, his "newly narrated" *Twelve Fables of Aesop,* a Museum of Modern Art book illustrated by Antonio Frasconi, remained a popular work for over twenty years.

Trips to Europe included visits to Maugham at his famous Villa Mauresque and to Jean Cocteau and Colette in Paris.

In 1953, his father died. In 1955, he was stunned by the sudden illness and death of George Platt Lynes.

The poet Louise Bogan, in a collection of her letters, *What the Woman Lived,* recalled a 1955 visit to Stone-blossom. She found Wescott's house a blinding disarray of paintings, books, art objects, records, flowers. Wheeler was off to Europe on behalf of the museum. When Bogan was escorted across the farm to visit Lloyd and Barbara, she expected to find simple country folk, dependent on Glenway. Instead, she found a lively, refined couple who had just bought a $30,000 Renoir. "The whole situation deserves the pen of a Chekhov or a Gogol," she wrote, delighted and surprised by "what can come out of a Wisconsin hayloft." In 1957, however, the state of New Jersey was forced to flood the entire valley in that area, because a reservoir was desperately needed. The Wescott clan found a new and permanent home nearby, the 400-acre farm they named Haymeadows.

1960—69 Wescott's beloved mother died in 1960. On his sixtieth birthday, in 1961, Academy—Institute president Wescott introduced Robert Frost to the assembled group. In his speech, the poet recalled their first meeting, at the MacDowell Colony forty years earlier. Glenway was struck by the moment: "I stood as though all soul, alone upon one of the great divides of my life."

In 1962, he published *Images of Truth*, his remembrances and criticism of Porter, Maugham, Colette, Isak Dinesen, Thomas Mann, and Thornton Wilder. There followed a successful nationwide lecture tour. That year, Porter's long-awaited *Ship of Fools* was published, and he reviewed the novel and appeared with her on a WNBC radio program.

In 1963, Wescott, who had often referred to the expatriate years as his real education, received an honorary doctorate in literature from Rutgers University.

"The Valley Submerged," an essay about the last days of Stone-blossom, rich in Wescott double meaning and images, appeared in the summer 1965 issue of *Southern Review*.

Although several of his books were republished over the years, he was especially moved by Harper's 1966 edition of *The Pilgrim Hawk* and poet Howard Moss's review of it in *The New Yorker*.

In 1967, Wheeler was elected to the Museum of Modern Art's Board of Trustees.

1970—79 A number of Glenway's essays appeared in the early seventies. These included remembrances of the twenties and thirties in three issues of *Prose*, of Forster and his posthumous novel, *Maurice*, in *The New York Times Book Review*, and of Stone-blossom in a Doubleday *Works in Progress* anthology.

Since the late fifties, he'd planned to release one or more collections of new essays and old fiction, but he kept turning to other ideas or Academy–Institute projects. Finally he committed himself to the publication of his journals. He wrote to editor Robert Phelps in June 1971: "I know that suddenly the work as a whole has become real to me." But for a number of reasons the journals were destined for posthumous publication.

In January of 1975, the New York Public Library purchased a number of his manuscripts and typescripts. At his New York apartment, he still gave parties and readings. including readings of his journals.

At Haymeadows, visitors were shocked by the four grown tigers that lived close to his stone house. Raised by his brother's troublesome son-in-law, the tigers were kept in a one-acre fenced enclosure for years. Wescott imagined the newspaper headline: "Writer Eaten by Tigers!"

Although a lover of classical music, he once attended a Rolling

Stones concert, arriving by limousine. When a young friend gave him a David Bowie album, he admitted dancing to the song "Fame."

In October 1976, Wescott and Wheeler escorted eighty-five-year-old Katherine Anne Porter to the 92nd Street Poetry Center. The occasion was her last visit to her old friends. In August 1977, Barbara Harrison died. Late that year, the two men took a trip to London.

1980–87 Through the early eighties Wescott maintained his full active schedule. In 1980, he took a last trip to Europe with Wheeler, who continued to travel for the rest of his life.

A small section of these journals appeared in the Fall 1981 *Grand Street*. An essay on Marianne Moore and other poets was in *Partisan Review* in 1983, and Wescott wrote the introduction to Hugh Ford's *Four Lives in Paris*, a book about the expatriates.

By 1985, Glenway had begun to live permanently at Haymeadows. On his eighty-fifth birthday, in April 1986, two young friends brought him a boxful of *The Grandmothers*, newly published only days earlier. "I had nothing to do with it," he said of the new Arbor House edition. "It came through the trees, looking for me."

Months after surviving a stroke, he died at home on February 22, 1987. Eighteen months later, Wheeler died in New York, just two weeks after making a final trip abroad.

The Museum of Modern Art dedicated a reading room to Wheeler. The vast Wescott archive at Haymeadows was acquired by Yale University. The ashes of both men were scattered at a tiny, centuries-old farmers' graveyard at Haymeadows.

—J.R.

Continual Lessons

1 9 3 7

And for clarity's sake, let us often use, and sanc-
tion the use of, words of one syllable. The short-
est and most potent is the personal pronoun: I.
—"The Moral of F. Scott Fitzgerald"

June 14

Dinner last night with George and Monroe at Katherine Anne's*
apartment in Perry Street. Her table handsomely set; raffia cloth and
turkey-red napkins, wooden plates, and four silver goblets, and her new
Russian forks of nugget silver, the handles enameled with dark flowers
by some Muscovite William Morris.

After dinner, George drove us to Coney Island. We had been there
just a year ago, but with Cecil Beaton, Marcel Khill, and Cocteau,†
when of course I listened and talked back more than I looked. Portals
and towers in a fog are all I remember, and long wet wreaths of light
bulbs. We arrived after closing time, therefore could only go up and
down the street of games and freaks, where I find nothing surprising.
No one ever told me of the elegance and infant splendor inside the
enclosures, particularly the one called Luna Park.

Last night we saw this at its best, almost empty; it was about to
rain. Clean cement esplanades; *gloriettas* and pagodas and *giraldas*: the
electricity thickly dotted on the wood, which resembles paper. A child's
idea of palaces, never having seen anything but tenements; or an artist's

---

* George Platt Lynes (1907–55), fashion photographer and an intimate of the G.W. household
from the late twenties until his death; Monroe Wheeler (1899–1988), Director of Exhibitions and
Publications at the Museum of Modern Art and G.W.'s closest friend. Their relationship is best
evoked by the dedication in G.W.'s 1962 book, *Images of Truth* "To Monroe Wheeler, life long",
Katherine Anne Porter (1890–1980): G.W. met the distinguished American short-story writer and
novelist in 1932 at the Paris home of his future sister-in-law, Barbara Harrison, a close friend of
Porter's.

† Cecil Beaton (1904–80), photographer, stage designer, and author; Marcel Khill (1912–
40), Jean Cocteau's Algerian lover and secretary in the mid-thirties, a Resistance fighter who was
killed in the battle of Sedan; Jean Cocteau (1889–1963), French author, artist, and filmmaker,
whom G.W. met in 1925, when they had rooms at the Hôtel Welcome in Villefranche. G.W. was
one of his New York hosts when Cocteau made his voyage around the world in June 1936.

concept of what he will do, before art has begun to deflate and reform and perpetuate it.

The Chutes: a cascade drawn with a ruler; water thinly and decoratively draped over planks. The flat-bottomed boats rush down it, under a bridge, and out on the glassy pool, with stiff rapid ribbons of wash and gashes of shadow. How handsome my friends looked to me, profile against profile in the prow!

The Shooting Gallery with its tightly packed targets: clay pipes, revolving white stars, a large resonant pendulum, burning candles, and ducks incessantly sliding across and ducking and returning. Crude and pretty color schemes: one of those sour blues with purple in it, and sky-blue and blotter-green. A bit of charge from Monroe's rifle, or Katherine Anne's, glances back and strikes my forehead, just hard enough to appeal to my imagination.

As we skirted the side shows Monroe took my arm and said, "It reminds me of 'The Runaways.' " My first, no, my second short story, written in Wiesbaden in 1922. Characteristic reminder, with his piety about writing and particular cult of what I had done and could still do. Where literature has been at work is holy ground to him; even Coney Island.

Characteristic also: a nostalgic recourse to our early experience together, whether or not we were happy at the time he happens to think of. I wasn't happy in Wiesbaden. A constant recoil of his mind toward his youth, when indeed, until his love of me began to impose penalties, alarms and fatigues, he had the happiest nature I have ever encountered.

His fanatic persistence in a stand once taken, in a hypothesis once stated: for example, that "The Runaways" is excellent. Rather rigid strength of character which makes it difficult to extricate him from any false position; such as, at present, his dubious economics, his flattered worldliness. Strength and weakness coupled; I suppose they always are. His loyalty and his inspiring willpower depend somewhat upon the fact that his grasp of present realities is not very precise or keen. Presbyopic and noble.

As a rule, a given man or woman's life is like a work of fiction that does not end when it should; thousands of pages of boring realism follow. Whatever mystic idea and meaningful pain and dramatic action there may be all occurs in a month or a year or so, immediately digging a rut, setting up a treadmill; thenceforth the hero must plod and reiterate and deteriorate, oh, how slowly!

* * *

Pavlik's dealer urges me not to consult the artist himself about framing the *Lion-Boy*, as he will want silk moiré, and there is too much silk moiré about his work anyway; it is funny, and I wish I knew who said it first . . .*

June 17

Over the weekend Paul Cadmus† made a large pen drawing of me. A good likeness, I think, at least psychologically like—my sweet-sour expression, spoiled but virtuous, voluptuous but tough, heartbroken but happy. In only two photographs have I ever recognized this mood, to me most natural: one taken by the little Englewood professional who gave George lessons, the other by George himself, at my ease propped up on pillows on the daybed in the rue de Vaugirard, flattering to my profile, with my forefinger touching my upper lip.

My intimacy with Charles Rain‡ is waning rapidly; soon I shall need someone to take his place. I must not rest long in my present equanimity and indifference about this. I know what will happen if I do, what has always happened. As I love George, I should think it wicked as well as imprudent to depend tranquilly upon his tenderness. Therefore, cheerfully, although with the usual anxieties, and resolutely, or irresolutely, I cannot tell—time will tell—I take stock of my acquaintance; try to feel some sufficient excitement about this one and that; urge myself to hurry up and make some amorous (pseudo-amorous) attempt, No matter which or what, before I get caught again by my fever and misbehavior and shame and hopelessness . . .

I have come upon a poet unknown to me, James Agee,** *Permit Me Voyage*; enjoyable, orderly, rather Italianate. But it is Auden (*On This Island*) who has chiefly delighted all spring: as brilliant and glamorous as Eliot, and less vexing.

* Pavlik (Pavel) Tchelitchew (1898–1957). Russian-born neo-Romantic painter who illustrated G.W.'s *A Calendar of Saints for Unbelievers* (1932). Tchelitchew's painting *The Lion Boy* was one of G.W.'s favorite personal possessions throughout his life. On the back of it he wrote, "The model for this picture (Pavlik told us) was a boy he encountered on the beach in Santa Margherita Ligure in the summer of 1936. It was not quite finished when he brought it back to New York. Barbara Wescott and I saw it in his studio, unfinished, and she bought it for me. After that, Ury Cabell posed for the hands" (see photo insert after page 140).

† Paul Cadmus (1904–   ). Distinguished portrait painter.

‡ Charles Rain. Companion of G.W.

** James Agee (1909–55). Poet, film critic, novelist, and author of *Let Us Now Praise Famous Men* and *A Death in the Family*.

The night of the Braddock–Louis bout in Chicago. George and I dined uptown at Jimmie [Daniels's]*: chile con carne, upon which he prides himself (and well he may). Edna Thomas, with whom he lives, a project supervisor of the Federal Theatre in Harlem, came home most melancholy, having had to lay off actors all day long as ordered by the administration: all destitute, the young ones enraged, the old in feeble desperation.

After dinner, as usual, friends wandered in to eat and drink a little, and to hear the broadcast from Chicago. A typical assembly: lovely, plumper and plumper Blanche Dunn (courtesan), in whose bed my brother spent the wee hours of certain of those delectable foolish Harlem nights in 1934–35? She had put $100 of her old white keeper's money on the white boxer, since these people believe that prizefights are all framed and scarcely care who seems the best boxer.

Alonzo Thayer, jolly and dejected, alcoholic and who knows what else? He may have been in love with someone (presumably Jimmie) all these years; and if so, doubtless has never said a word, and perhaps has kept from knowing it himself. Thus under cover (I suppose) grand passions are much commoner and unhealthier than you might think. Part-Jewish mulatto, fine-boned and getting fat; makeshift lover of mine in 1933, half a dozen nights: humble of me, and indeed I knew that then . . .

Old Caska Barnes had got one of those pink slips of Edna's (dismissal from the theater), and been presented with a consoling bottle of gin by someone, and drunk it all; therefore was irritatingly affectionate and pompous.

Feral Benga, the Dakar dancer (*vide* Cocteau's film and Gorer's book and Pavlik's portraits): the finest middle-aged physique in the world, heart-shaped chest, smoothly tapering legs like Josephine Bacaire's . . . Round-eyed: the whites of his eyes circularly showing as if in ceaseless apprehension or fury; nevertheless a beguiling worldly personage, and good company. During the winter he took Kenneth McPherson away from Jimmie. Then his established Austrian favorite came over from Paris, and Jimmie aptly but spontaneously seduced this one. Which flank attack threw Feral into a confused and unattractive temper; so Jimmie got his lord and master back, although on poorer terms, I fear. Not a trace of bad manners on either rival's part now. In this raffish society people really do bury the hatchet.

* Jimmie Daniels. Black singer who performed at his own club in Greenwich Village, as well as in Europe.

While we waited for the fight to begin, Jimmie played records which he has been studying with a view to some foreign engagement, such as Massary's prewar waltzes and Yvonne Printemps's* Martini and Messager. Then, with his characteristic shrill giggles, Feral for our amusement attacked Sacha Guitry's† reputation as a ladies' man. Occasionally Guitry engages pretty boys to parade naked up and down his salon after dinner (visual chamber music); and, cocking that big Thespian head of his, views them with expert though inactive appreciation—so Feral said.

During certain rounds of the broadcast Jimmie slept, his perfect hands carefully clasped on his gin-and-ginger-ale. George rolling his eyes in voluptuous admiration of him; then how gently winking at me! But luckily or otherwise, this vapid, languorously stoic, bittersweet Harlem atmosphere now has a sobering effect upon me.

The instant Louis knocked Braddock out, we hastened through the flat to the Seventh Avenue window to see the rejoicing. For an hour or so Harlem had seemed deserted: every building, as it were, talking in its sleep with a plurality of soft wireless voices; everyone indoors in parties around the radio, determined to have a good time whether or not the black protagonist should make good; even the main streets silent except for police cars coming and going with sinister although motherly cry . . . Now instantly all the young and the youthful sprang from every doorway, faintly shouting, running nowhere in particular. Proudly a man drew a woman into the shadow between two parked cars and so kissed her that she was swept off her feet, between his legs. Flimsy-looking children boxed as they ran. The less foolish and less energetic (like our party) made fun of the others, but in intimate manner, delegating their feelings.

The strangest sight was this: Just below Edna's window out of an alley or a casement came five or six youngsters with a small slot machine which they threw down on the sidewalk. One carried and wielded a cast-iron café table, hammering the slot machine as hard as he could. The sort out of which you get handfuls of peanuts, which presently we could see sprinkled over the pavement . . . One took it and slammed it down again, one kicked it; and the others danced worriedly around, in each other's way, almost fighting, waiting for the pennies—which finally came. Then they stooped and shoved and grabbed; one threw himself flat on his stomach, thrusting both hands under himself to collect what he was able to cover; and soon everyone ran away.

I could not quite understand it; still cannot. It happened within a

---

* Yvonne Printemps. French café singer of the thirties.
† Sacha Guitry (1885–1957). French playwright and actor.

minute after the Negro boxer's triumph. Had that instantly given all of them at once courage to commit petty larceny, unabashed, in public? Had the stealing been done at an earlier hour, the division of the spoils interrupted by the broadcast, and was this the mere resumption of their normal evening's work or play? Or had they deliberately kept the slot machine to celebrate with?

We saw no other bad behavior of any kind. During the afternoon I had heard a little thoroughbred German haranguing some others in a shop in our neighborhood (Yorkville); who maintained that if Louis won, no white man would be safe above 110th Street.

June 23

The younger generation. Charles is being visited by a friend from Chicago, a tall strong young man who teaches swimming at Northwestern. This one is allowing himself to be in love with another, somewhat older, who prefers intercourse with women; and C. is all alarmed and incensed about it. Without cracking a smile; rather, wringing his hands, he relates that one night (perhaps it was the first night) the swimming teacher took the other in his mouth; the other then offered or consented to do likewise, and, after certain odd fumbling caresses, did. Later C.'s friend discovered what the fumbling had been: his he-man surreptitiously had outfitted him with a French letter.

Dinner with Paul Cadmus in the Village. He showed me a hundred drawings or more; the nakedest and least disinterested are the best, particularly those of Jared French.* Until lately they have shared this apartment, an oddly un-American interior; good shabby antiques; a quantity of books and music, charming evidence of self-education. Late in the evening a youth named Lloyd Goff, who was Paul's assistant on a government job of mural painting, wandered in, at his ease, sleepy, perhaps tipsy. Paul paid the least possible attention to him. Soon he threw himself on a bed or couch and fell asleep. With no plan, yet somehow amorous or something, I waited for him to be gone. Paul and I still sat and talked and talked, reminiscence and theory, in that peculiar mood of ours or of his: smiling relaxation, solemn boyish idealism, who knows what else . . . Goff then woke up and undertook to say good night; but the next thing I knew, there he lay again, sprawled face down on another couch, his head underneath two pillows, his clothes all drawn on the bias and tight upon his very fine little back and buttocks. At last

---

* Jared French (1905–87). Neorealist-Romantic painter.

I gave up whatever impulse it was that had kept me so late. Paul fondly (I may say) accompanied me to the subway. Perhaps, he said, he would make a drawing or two before he went to bed; our talk had been so stimulating, and a sleeping model suits him . . .

Since I can't think when, I have wanted to give some account of myself as a lover and a loved one, of the plot of my life replete with coincidences and influences, Monroe's influence especially but not solely, and now of that triumvirate in which I figure in third place, perhaps more governed than governing; who knows? Surely it constitutes a theme or a set of themes less hackneyed and possibly more significant than any other thing experienced or observed by me. But how, how, can it be dealt with clearly and interestingly and enjoyably except in an entire autobiography, painfully encroaching upon others' lives?

I came back to this thought the other day when Monroe inquired about my novel supposedly in progress, and I had to confess my despondency about it. Once more, as it appears, having imagined and promised a full-length novel, I am gradually ceasing to take a sufficient interest in its devised happenings and composite characters. Little by little a chilly complexity of form and style develops and fills the vacuum without advancing the work, slowing me up. Episode after episode, chapter after chapter, grows cold and insincere and unmalleable before I can complete it. Faithfully I sit at my desk for a certain number of hours daily, or almost daily, resisting my natural distractions and overcoming my amorous melancholy for the most part, but slower and slower, and with worse and worse skepticism.

In the course of this conversation, *in re* my amorousness, I quoted to Monroe a part of a letter that I wrote George last week, comparing him to a falconer, myself to a falcon. This impressed him as a revelation of my psychology and fate, and he said, "You must be modest and write what you can, without too much art and ambition. When personal passion interests you more than anything else, that must be your subject matter."

I should see Jack B. again and put down some of his anecdotes: of sailor-prostitutes who pretend to be doing for pay what they also evidently enjoy. The one who, having taken some active part in their intercourse or perhaps merely manifested some enthusiasm, begged Jack not to tell any of his colleagues, who would not respect him if they knew, etc. An odd and (I fancy) a new morality: commercialization of one's sex more respectable than the free gift of it. Europeans, as a rule most money-loving, would appreciate this as evidence of our love of money, but mistakenly. They never understand that with us profit is more a matter of religion or superstition than of desire. We are less avaricious (I think) than greedy, morally greedy: determined to feel free to indulge, somewhat, in every possible pleasure, without having to renounce our claim, upon occasion, to every conceivable virtue. Hence all sorts of disorderly motivation. The intimacies of true lovers of men with men who merely let themselves be loved are particularly distressing and interesting. The unsophisticated virile beloved goes to extremes of sophistry without a qualm; and the lover's docile disrespect for himself as he countenances this seems scarcely less wrong.

June 29

After dinner George sat in the blue armchair and kept falling asleep, until bedtime; and I sat in the yellow armchair and contemplated him fondly, and contemplated myself with due discomfort and dislike. For I had allowed myself to entertain the most imprudent hope of love. I fancy I played my poor part decently; surely I was afraid not to, lest George forbid me to assume it any longer. For no doubt the old hopelessness was worse than such disappointment. I tried not to make too pathetic or antipathetic a face. I said nothing spiteful, nothing ominous. Nevertheless, at last George said that it was high time I discovered for myself some new substitute lover. Of course I could not fail to appreciate what prompted him: his inability, embarrassment, compassion; and of course I agreed.

So the falconer plucks off the falcon's dark hood, and sharply exclaims, and urgently points across the plain where, somewhere, there may or may not be wily partridge, banal rabbit. But the falcon, blinded by its dream in the darkness, cannot see much; and infatuated with the master's hand upon which it sits, by which in the past it has been fed ideally, it cannot care much; and with the tight pain in its gut from long fasting and yearning, it cannot fly very well.

Paul Cadmus is one of the favorite young painters here now. He held a successful exhibition this spring; has been given a second government commission, for a post-office mural; and has had any amount of notice in the magazines. For one thing his subject matter is popular: YMCA locker rooms, sailors having fun, aging Venus and dumb Adonis up to date, etc. Also he has notable virtuosity of the classic order, real draftsmanship, sculptural modeling, interlocking composition—which our countrymen, when they have the courage to be out of the French fashion, naturally enjoy. A color reproduction of his painting of two bicyclists having appeared in *Esquire*, that rich amorous little man Cole Porter bought it. But Paul's candid romanticism about strong and sportive men is such as to appeal to the normal unsophisticated American taste as well.

Paul's mother was an immigrant Basque; and he has the bizarre, distinguished north Spanish look. Wonderful bright eyes: and he fixes them on one (on George and me) with the oddest ardor; and listens quietly, fondly; and smiles and smiles, though not exactly humorously. His teeth protrude and his gums show, consciousness of which has caused some habitual tension of his lips, as usual; but it is not nervous or ugly in his case. He has a pleasing, moderately strong body, not (I should think) of perfectly masculine measurements, yet not at all womanish either; pure-looking, also proud-looking, although he himself thinks it deplorable in every aspect. His coarse suave skin he determinedly sunburns on the sooty roof of his Greenwich Village flat.

For a number of years, here and in Mallorca, he has lived with and passionately loved one Jared French, also a painter, and of bisexual habit. Their relation has not, however, been one-sided; no sort of stylized contrast of virility and effeminacy has developed—although basically Paul is more feminine than most of us, I think. All his thought is somehow relative, partial, anti-selfish, in the way of the noblest, fondest women; his moods, as it were, atmospheric, like the weather, and mysterious, even to himself. Evidently Jared French has exercised extreme influence in the forming of his principal habits of mind: quiet disdain of society; study of literature and music; cult of the normal young man of the people, that is, of the lower classes—whom they both must think Jared resembles. Paul is frankly given to the phallic passion, and idealistic and indeed religious about it; his friend likewise, I understand. Which grand perversity I approve, indeed; the grander the better.

Some of Jared's painting is pleasanter than Paul's, though less original and less soundly skillful: scenes of rather soft abandoned baseball, homosexual *fêtes-galantes*, like Watteau or Renoir. I wish I knew him. I have met him: a commonly handsome man of my age, with a small eye and a tough little blond mustache; with a certain stolidity that highly sexed men often have, somehow lackluster, as if daydreaming of effect upon others. He has kept having relations with women. Paul has admired him all the more for this, according to a concept of ideal manhood which perhaps he has inculcated upon Paul in his own honor. Naturally the admirer and idealist has suffered: the waiting and waiting, the wanting worse and worse, the corrupt curiosity, the dreadful effort to be polite, the wanting to die, with jealousy perhaps at last a habitual stimulant—Jared coming unabashed and not exhausted from a female bed to his bed, and going likewise again. Nevertheless they have been wonderfully happy. This spring Jared decided to marry the mistress whom he has loved best. Paul doubted whether he would ever be happy again; but now that it is done, I see no indication of tragic disorder. The beloved husband still spends much time with him; and I suppose that the roles of spouse and adulterous darling have simply been reversed. In any case Paul would have borne the loss decently; for his chief strength is suppleness and a sort of deep-seated courtesy—courtesy even in his introspective dealings with himself. (How unlike me!) If he were unbearably hurt he would have to fall ill somehow and never say, perhaps never know, why. No indignation. There is not much in his art either.

The decadence of curse words; ancient meanings wasted away:

For instance, *golly* is a reduced, collapsed form of "God love me!" Go'lo'me et seq.

Jiminy means "By the Gemini"—the twins, Castor and Pollux, sons of Leda and the god-swan.

Great things that have slipped the world's mind . . .

July 2

Open-air *Salome*, Smallens conducting, one Erika Darbo, of Swedish origin and German experience, singing. As played by the good-looking imported Miss Darbo, Salome reminded me of that girl we used to meet at Jimmie Daniels's parties, who wouldn't go out and get her poor old mother some cocaine . . .

Stone-blossom
July 3

This morning George returned from the farmhouse with news of Lloyd* and Barbara's† financial worries: for example, the fact that she has to pay a gift tax on every cent of the increasing cost of the farm because it is in his name. I suppose his pride is such that he was unwilling to administer it simply in hers. Also it appears that Monroe's

---

* Lloyd Wescott (1907–   ). G. W.'s younger brother. A gentleman farmer and award-winning cattle breeder; contributed significant time and effort to the local medical center and a women's reformatory. In later years, a friend to the New Jersey Democratic Party.

† Barbara Harrison Wescott (1904–77). A wealthy patron of the arts who, in Paris in the early thirties, collaborated with Monroe Wheeler in producing deluxe-edition books under the Harrison of Paris imprint. Married Lloyd Wescott in 1935, becoming a strong matriarch of the Wescott clan. A friend of Katherine Anne Porter, and the dedicatee of *Ship of Fools*.

office space in her building is no longer available rent-free. This led us into a discussion of Harrison of Paris, from the beginning and from now on. Monroe wishes to continue to make use of his position as its director to keep people from knowing that he wants a job; more of his imprudent salesmanship in respect to himself. Needless to say, he spoke fantastically of the ethics and the economics involved. As to his advising Barbara to throw good money (rent, secretary's salary, etc.) after bad, in the hope of selling all their stock of books little by little, he elaborated in dollars and cents a policy that I quite fail to understand or believe. In the end, in his way, to put a stop to my criticism and George's, he made an unkind unlovable remark. I did not say too much, but felt exceedingly out of patience and somewhat out of love. George a little later remarked that I always have been, periodically, and always will be. I reminded him how much less other bother there was for me in the past, and greater reward, and sweeter consolation. It is the thirsty overloaded camel that gets panic-stricken at the sight of a straw.

Less rain, so the threatened wheat is all in the granary. Lloyd is as proud as if it had not in fact been raised at a loss. Even his liver having responded to the hypothesis, he is playful, bright-eyed, handsome.

Barbara still resolved to have a baby, went to Trenton for another gynecological operation, a forcing of air through the Fallopian tubes; it was not necessary; they were open, which cheers her. An elderly Anglicized cousin of hers has come who boasts some historic early American ancestors, and who evidently always has been "stopping" with people, and has all the necessary manners.

July 4

Supper at Elizabeth's* with our parents. I must correct my social procedure with my family; seek new subjects of conversation with them; restrict my detailed gossip with this one and that about the others' conduct; and make less comment on Lloyd's administration policy: sighing anxiety, sputtering dissent . . . Over and again in this kind of domestic conference I appear (to myself at least) somehow feebly boastful and pseudo-angry; mildly, as it were *pour épater les bourgeois.*

Twenty-two years ago I broke off my first love relationship, by letter to E.R.K.† Because it happened to be dated Independence Day I have

---

* Elizabeth Wescott Hotchkiss (1904–88). Third eldest of G.W.'s four sisters.
† E.R.K. [Carl Rixkuelthau]. The Wisconsin farmboy who, as G.W. said, "relieved me of my virginity at the age of thirteen."

not forgotten and can indulge in mild anniversary emotion. So old, how
young!

As a writing board I use a shabby old picture book, one Moritz
Retzch's engraved illustrations of *Romeo and Juliet*, 1836; Alfred de
Vigny's copy bearing his superb angular signature; Jacques* gave it to
me. Some years ago there appeared on the market a love letter addressed
by de Vigny to his mistress Marie Dorval, upon which, by way of exasperated greeting and complaint and promise, he had splashed a few
drops of his sperm. Parisian bibliophiles were charmed; but the pro-
prietor of le Gaulois, Arthur Meyer, a little gentleman with some re-
semblance to a poodle, outbid the rest and burned it, boasting of his
hero worship and his service to public morals.

De Vigny left to posterity an intimate journal; his friend and
literary executor piously destroyed most of it. Alfred de Vigny, *ora pro
nobis* . . .

July 6

Return to town. Image of American summer: the way the drivers
of long-distance trucks hang their sleek biceps and golden forearms,
relaxed, out the windows of the hot little coops in which they sit.

July 7

Amorous and wretched, pacing the town as if it were all one vacuous
bedroom, but still patiently pacing. Newsreel theater, a most unpleasant
program: The Braddock–Louis fight. A broken-toothed old clubwoman
opining that, instead of banning dogs from Manhattan, we should get
rid of three hundred thousand "useless humans." The new bobsled run
at Palisades Park, seventy-two miles an hour on ballbearings. The club-
bing and killing of irritating picketers by huge serene policemen in
Chicago on Decoration Day: the reel that was suppressed for a while.
Then dreamy views of places in Virginia associated with George Washington, with accompaniment of "Carry Me Back" and "My Country 'Tis
of Thee"—from which I fled.

How lamely and affectedly humans fight; how dully they kill! Think
of cats, horses, snakes, mongooses.

* Jacques Guérin. A distinguished bibliophile and collector—he owned Proust's desk—
who, as a young man in the early thirties, was an intimate friend of G.W., not long after Monroe
Wheeler met George Platt Lynes.

July 8

And again last night, George as falconer urged me as falcon to get after some ordinary prey, pigeon, rabbit. As there is nothing much in sight—except the too unattractive, the ill-omened, or the obviously unattainable—I have kept thinking of Eugene Loring* as desirously as I could. So we asked him to hear José Iturbi play Mozart at the Stadium with us; and we both found his company pleasant.

When we returned and George retired, I simply told him that it was my intention to try to induce him to come to bed with me. Then we spent half an hour uninhibitedly though not very gaily arguing the point by word of mouth and the usual dumbshow. I was not able to have my own way. It was odd: he was somewhat excited, pleasingly potent, but resolutely unwilling; whereas I was cold and feeble but ardently aggressive. He kept assuring me of his appreciation of me in every respect; of course this might have been half vain gratification and half tact; it seemed sincere. Needless to add, I was indifferent to it by virtue of my own insincerity. So I let him go, with some little show of malice and some of sentiment.

Surely he did not mean me to think his refusal final. I fancy it had to do with something definite in his life at the moment, perhaps another amorous engagement last night. He expressed the usual doubts of my respect for him, that is, his self-respect, if I were able to have him upon such short notice. Like most such young people, alas, he is much less inclined to desire me than to aspire to my friendship.

Without any corroboration or approval of my intellect, my instinct, as it were, with faithful whisper does assure me that there is heaven and that I will go there, upon certain conditions: (a) if I do not commit suicide, and (b) if I do not go insane. An odd and, I believe, a blessed feature of my instinctive morality is this feeling that insanity is rather a crime than a misfortune: the evil heart's rape and mutilation of the imprudent brain.

July 12

George Gershwin is dead of a tumor of the brain, diagnosed too late. For several years the noted Zilbourg has been (so to speak) psychoanalyzing him for so-called imaginary headaches. Zilbourg is a White Russian who translated *He Who Gets Slapped*; then directed some little theater in Greenwich Village, where Katherine Anne knew him; then worked out a psychotherapy all his own, and has made a good thing of

* Eugene Loring (1914–82). A ballet dancer with Balanchine's company in the late thirties and later a choreographer.

it. A social fellow, dear friends with his patients, he has groups of them weekend with him in Connecticut; and he goes traveling about in the way of an abbé or an augur, father-confessor, entrail-interpreter. This summer he was to have gone to Java, to dissuade the Javanese from killing themselves; Zilbourg is president of an international anti-suicide society.

All the above is gossip, but from fairly close quarters. Bernadine* went weekending in Connecticut, and as one would send a suitable little present to one's host, she urged Barbara to induce me to get myself reformed by him.

She also insistently and enthusiastically conveyed Russell Davenport's† periodic invitation to me to write for *Fortune*. Indeed she was sincere and affectionate in this, if not very subtle. Of course I understand her anxiety, and in my way share it.

July 12

Names: of a Negro actor in a recent British film: Ecce Homo Toto.

Of a sallow, softly burly taxi driver in our part of town: Solly Lo Piccolo. Of another taxi driver: Giovanni Mule.

Of a dressmaking firm from which garments come to George to be photographed: Mutual Rosenbloom.

Of a bassoonist: Stephen Macymciw—or, as I came across it, printed in capital letters, like a date in a bad dream: MACYMCIW.

Pavlik's mimicry of Helena Rubinstein, the beautician, so good and memorable that we have all tried to do it after him: Like a disgusted owl she keeps arching her neck back over her shoulder with a little jerk, squinting forcefully; and in those doleful tones of hers she confides to Alice Halicka her determination to marry a title. They probably speak Polish; Pavlik reports it in an international baby-talk, pigeon-Jewish. "The name Rubinstein means nothing, only business, business. Lots of money now; can have good title, French. Old bachelor, maybe widower, nice (you know): never married Jew'sh before." A realist, stoically scornful of herself, she hastens to be the first to point out that in any case it could be only for her money. Around over her bosom studded with a selection of her famed hoard of jewels, and over the silken sackful of her old body as a whole, she, rigidly agitated, waves her dark hand to

---

* Bernadine Szold. A socialite and longtime friend of G.W. He dedicated his 1925 poetry collection, *Natives of Rock*, to her.

† Russell Davenport. Editor of and writer for *Fortune* magazine.

emphasize this point: oh, not for her looks, not now anymore! She admits
having in mind, for example, the Duc de Vendôme.

July 13

Monroe still urges me to write about myself.

It may be wise or it may not. For one thing, I am not sure that the
old stimulus of wishing to please him will still have effect. But I may
as well try it, during my failure to write fiction. It should at least somewhat
prevent his little comments upon my failure, his mildly goading humor,
and his hints of hopelessness about me, or pseudo-hopelessness. I do
perfectly understand his goodwill and unspoken instinct in the matter.
He touches upon my soreness of conscience in hopes of quickening it.
In the old days when he hurt me I usually tried twice as hard, while
my fit of resentment lasted. Now I react less well. Day after day my
melancholy seizes upon some pessimistic remark of his as its excuse,
and feeds upon it. There is no use appealing to him to be more kind or
more cunning; for he neither plans what he will say nor listens to himself
closely.

Jimmie Daniels dined with George and me, and we saw the Dietrich
film *Knight Without Armour*. The work of Feyder and his scenic expert,
Meerson, is excellent, especially in the last half: nightmare of flight into
exile, trains never on time, false passports, hysterical policemen, familiar faces here and there. That in all probability is what revolution
would amount to for us. Wonderful insane stationmaster marching up
the platform to meet an invisible express train . . . A small tragic role
is played by an actor named Clements who extraordinarily resembles
Col. Lawrence: small overworked body; profile like a meat ax deeply
nicked with strong painful features.

July 15

Genre picture. I sat on the toilet seat idly turning the pages of
Yeats's anthology; and George came stumbling in half asleep, with a
large hanging half-erection, to urinate; I got out of his way, still reading;
and he kissed me good night, sleepily stooping and brushing my shoulder
blade with his lips as he passed; and how happy I was! Although quite
dissatisfied with what I had written all day . . . How luxurious and
strange a life!

Trucks: one inscribed in large letters, AROMATIC ESSENTIALS;
presumably full of same. The driver's seats of two others (belonging to
different trucking companies) entirely enclosed in a grille of heavy wire,

painted white, and solidly bolted to the windshield and the doors—through which those two drivers peered like two important lunatics, out for an airing, caged. Why? Do people throw things at them?

July 20

Last spring, in late April or early May, I weekended in a nineteenth-century farmhouse in Connecticut with two close friends, one still young, one very young. At the head of the stairs in that house, it so happened, the old door of their bedroom failed to meet the worn threshold under it by an inch or so. The house was on two levels; the floor of that bedroom was about two feet below that of the upstairs hallway; therefore that considerable crack or aperture corresponded almost exactly with their adjoining beds. My hosts had chanced to mention this, with reference to the drafts in winter, even in early spring; but it hadn't occurred to me how I might be taken by surprise by means of it, through it.

Katherine Anne was also staying with them, and after lunch on Sunday she and they retired for a siesta. I too went up to my room but found myself not sleepy, and presently, quite serene, without a thought, I started back downstairs; and just as my foot descended to the step that brought my eye in line with the crack or aperture and with the (so to speak) marriage bed beyond, I happened to glance just right and so saw the two friends. Both their naked bodies in ideal appearance, in inter-course, and well under way . . .

Doubtless I was in a frame of mind most apt to delight in frag-mentary, momentary erotic beauty such as this, between the inadequate door and the outworn threshold, delimited and separated from me: what might have been a portion of Greek vase in graceful agitation. Do I exaggerate? I think not, or not much. In spite of loneliness and pent-up feeling, self-pitying in a way, my very admiration rose so that it amounted to thanksgiving, thanksgiving for this mishap, this miracle. There between floors in my absurd improper position, on tiptoe and weak in the knees, I might have been kneeling somewhere, in a fit of prayer or vision, far removed from ordinary human circumstances, actual in-dividuals, social respectabilities. As it happened, I could not see any sexual organ or even erogenous zone, and both faces were turned away; which may explain why I let myself loiter there for perhaps two minutes, phenomenally full minutes.

Not ashamed, trying and failing to be ashamed, and yet afraid; like a malefactor, afraid of being found out. Even such a psyche as mine, stubborn and predestined, can be taught—and at that time, in my per-haps immature middle age, had been taught—by appropriate literature, moral treatise, precept, if not experience. I knew better than to interrupt my friends, by opening their door or knocking on it, or by calling their names. Furthermore, physically, I was not in a state at all uncontrollable or even difficult to control; no excessive energy or extreme fantasy, such as might conceivably lead to intrusion or other rape-like tyrannousness. I wasn't in the least afraid of myself. All was gentle and indeed weak— except in my own mind and heart.

Truly, what I wanted to happen had happened, was happening; *their* delight and my proximity. But changes were taking place in me; some safety valve would have to develop for me, inner or outer, some outlet and free play for my several relevant senses—so that I should not seem to myself so crazy, so silly, so morbid, so solitary. If I couldn't find or conceive any such change or escape, I might just continue like this, worshipful and, as it were, disembodied, in an inexhaustible con- templation of my lost love, my love unattainable, until I died; or perhaps die immediately, and be out of their way and the way of other such lovemakers, and out of harm's way. Death! I murmured to myself, as one often does in climaxes of the amorous life: the one and only effi- cacious and final form of self-control . . .

I trembled from head to foot, I failed to breathe properly, I could feel the pulse in my wrists and hear it softly surging in my ears, or at least in one ear; but, alas, not for a second did I fail to enjoy or to suffer. Sixty or a hundred seconds. Finally I dragged myself the rest of the way downstairs. What was I to do with myself? To my shame, be it said, I went back upstairs and came back past the aperture once more; luckier or (you may say) less lucky—I must have moved too fast, or my loving couple had shifted across the bed—tolerating my behavior less and less.

Intolerantly then, without a plan or idea, I crept out of doors, quite quietly, and hurried up the road to a small tumbledown barn—it seemed to me that I had not seen it until that instant—and I clambered up into the loft, which was not boarded up on one side; and from that safe distance I could still gaze upon my friends' pretty, dread dwelling, against its background of small hills, amid its modest trees. How white it was! I thought; white as an egg, out of which what in God's name was hatching? Pandora's box, utterly open and swarming.

There was a heap of fodder in the loft, dry and delicate, the fragrance of which might have blown unmixed all the way from the Wisconsin of my precocious boyhood. I lay down and undid my trousers and, in a second, simply pressed out of my scarcely tumescent, not very sensitive penis its ready drops. There was no necessity of my doing this; it didn't correspond in any real sense to my trouble. I did it deliberately, to weaken myself, to stupefy myself, as one might gulp down a small undangerous sedative drug. Then I climbed down from the loft, and pulled myself over a gate, and walked across a rather large meadow, up hill. I tore my sticky handkerchief into bits and hid it in a hollow stump. I wandered up and down the meadow, and in due time, just safely tired and humorous and dejected, reappeared at my friends' house.

We dined outdoors, on the sunset side of the house, with the hills in profile; and after dinner I talked at some length with Katherine Anne about our respective literary accomplishments to date and future prospects, in a somewhat high-flown way, vying with each other, like a couple of geniuses; with what concealed dismay and skepticism only I could know.

I couldn't wait to get back to Stone-blossom, and did in fact return next day, with my usual introspection and anxiety about myself as a writer, and about my Self, more than usual. That of course underlay my talk with Katherine Anne, and she aggravated it without intending to. I was anxious for Monroe and George to join me there, two or three days later. Perhaps my habit of never putting restraints on love, and of entering into any state of rapture which I found available, had gone too now. Might I now have to admit that my three-cornered relationship with them was untenable, destructive, or at least unconstructive; and with that admission, might it not worsen? Might I not find myself duty-bound to leave them? The duty was not only the matter of their right to love and happiness untroubled by me, but of my literary vocation; which meant as much to Monroe, in his way, as it did to me in my way. I couldn't just stay there and go to pieces before his eyes; innocent and pitying and sometimes incorrect eyes. From early manhood on, he has been a believer in willpower, especially my willpower. Whereas I felt sure that if I expended too much of my strength in self-discipline, or dissipated it too much in bouts of toxic sensibility, I might never write well again. That would disappoint dear friend number one, and disgust dear friend number two, and convict me in my own opinion of entire unworthiness of my destiny and present assignment in life, this peculiar predicament, at once blessedly included in love and wretchedly left out, with psychological miracles still apt to happen to me; no miracle more ridiculous than the weekend's epiphany in Connecticut: myself as Peeping Tom.

By the time my dear ones arrived, finally, I had decided to keep all of this to myself. Little ecstasy, followed by little disaffection and letdown and subsequent bitter humor and coarse thought, had done me good. I then noted to my amusement that the doors of two rooms in

Stone-blossom also gaped a little at the base; and as a reminder and as a rite, purgatorial, pretexting my foreknowledge of the drafts of winter-time, though winter was far off, I sent for the carpenter and had the thresholds replaced.

Country details: When our housekeeper, Mrs. Smith, lived at Stone-blossom thirty years ago, there was such a plague of rats at the barn that they gnawed the horses' feet just above the hoof, until the blood ran. Not every horse, however: "There's something different about some that draws them."

Lately calves in the pasture ate off the tail of Dr. Case's spotted riding horse, so that he has had to crop it close, like a mule's.

Charles Rain is a type of young artist from out West. His father is a urologist who sends him a sufficient monthly allowance. He attended the Art Institute, then went to Germany for a year or so, then came here to practice painting and rise in the world. He has talent but no individuality except that incident to amateurishness, no subject matter except that suggested by the Old Masters and Frenchmen in fashion, whose methods he aspires to imitate. He enjoys working hard, probably does work hard, but absentmindedly; his automatic phonograph going all the time, Forsythe and Fats Waller. He has exhibited his work at Julien Levy's at his own expense and sold a little to or through friends. He is a celebrity worshipper, perhaps not more so than other Western boys on the make, but so far he has passed the time here on a deplorable social level, the best he could get onto, I suppose: tittle-tattling queens, etc. The main outlines of his history are ordinary: mother preferred to father, irresistible naughtiness as a small boy, a hypocritical clergyman in Chicago, then the Kurfürstendamm, and around town here in the usual way. He has paired off with a number of our acquaintances, very briefly. According to him he yielded because he had accepted favors or expenditures, and was made to feel under an obligation.

There is a sister who has a beautiful head of hair cut like a sixteenth-century young man's, and pop-eyes wicked-looking or crazy-looking; she and Charles exchange confidences shamelessly. There is also a boyhood friend who also paints, less amateurishly but more imitatively; and they live and work in one large room, decorated in ordinary stylish decorator's style, as neat as can be: their paintings fussily framed and hung, their little sculptures well placed amid luxuriant bouquets.

In a fit of the worst nerves last December, out of a clear sky, and with erotic malice aforethought, and because Monroe had suggested it,

I invited Charles to dinner; and he merely, as it were, could not resist me; and I was delighted by his enthusiasm and his physical fitness. So now I have enjoyed him some twenty-five times, that is, weekly. This absurdly exact count I happen to have kept in my appointment book; my referring to it is indicative of my pessimism and sense of humor about him at this point. On the other hand, I am not quite unwilling to resume this peaceful healthful intercourse upon his return from Vermont in the autumn; only my impression is that it will hardly be possible.

Our intellectual or, I should say, social relations have been artificial and tedious always. Monroe and George rather enjoy having him about because they find him comical; neither he nor I have resented this; but it was not conducive to my fooling myself in any fashion. About his hope and his hopelessness as a painter he is intense, tearful, which is hard to endure; he needs the most patient educating and he wants a constant gush of encouragement; but he stubbornly or stupidly fails to take advice; however, I have endured and been patient and somewhat quashed. Lately Pavlik consented to criticize his work, harshly of course; and for me this started a fresh series of pitiful long talks, before fornication or after it or *instead* of it.

Thus on two occasions his fine young sex has quite failed to function; and his sad embarrassment, and his long unsuccessful self-manipulation, and the prospect of more of the same, have had a chilling influence upon me too. Instead of behaving cleverly I talked wisely. Let us stop while all is still proud and easy, I said, and so on. Apparently he has no notion how he might blame me. It seems to him that he involuntarily is rejecting me, and (poor vain youth) he is glad of that, and so am I. Indeed I may not be as entirely to blame as I suppose; some other amorousness may have occurred, as night after night I have left him to himself. I know that he is apt to lie, and shame would unnerve him. Let that pass; the above is all true, whether or not it is the whole truth.

He is a good boy, on his humble level: he is tactful, generous, modest, credulous. He is discreet: for instance, he destroys everyone's letters and even tears out the pages of his date book as the days pass, explaining that he might be involved in some scandal and will not incriminate his friends. I should not, however, expect him to behave well in anger or in panic. His great fault is basic shame, childish fright, as the look in his eyes indicates: flickering away to the right and the left and almost back over his shoulder, as if some bully or detective were always at his heels. This apartment of ours is, he thinks, a social foothold and stronghold; my insolent humor, a bracing soothing remedy; my arms, armor. He has been so much snubbed, and so often taken by night, rebuffed by day, etc.: our easy essentially selfish courtesy, my selfish and therefore careful use of him, may well have seemed to him heavenly. Besides his experience of mean homosexual society, and dread of the hard heterosexual world, he suffers from other little self-indulgent terrors: for instance, he cannot read or sit still alone without scratching himself, raising red welts on his arms and breast, and often hopelessly acknowledges this, remarking at the same time that his mother died of cancer.

His very tall and slim figure is like that of one of the acrobats of Picasso's early manner, with strong hands and heavy feet and sexual organs of noble outline. In the bedroom, in my arms, with a blissful grimace, his face is beautiful—not at any other time, to my taste; nor has he ever seemed to me exciting until he is in potent condition and begins to act excitedly; and my failure to be thrilled at once, my evasions, my postponements, must retard his potency.

Of course, looking back upon the relationship as a whole, convenient intercourse, sufficient substitute for a love relationship, I do wish to get it back in working order. I am not as spoiled as one might expect. In my exorbitant mind, my not in the least widowed heart, my busy New York day, perhaps there is not room for much more than Charles has to offer. Then too I know the tedious mess of the search for a successor; the rarity of playmates as inexpensive and amiable and physically acceptable as he; the dangers of another stretch of celibacy, a sort of psychic scurvy, hysteria in the home, etc. I do come to the proper conclusion. Yet I am glad and say that it probably is too late.

When I have finished any such research as the above, I feel that it is shameful, petty, marginal; but I did not, it was not, at the start; what I have learned by it makes it seem so. For all this is not so much self-expression or reminiscence as laboratory experiment; literary art here is intended to be chiefly scientific, that is, exploratory, also therapeutic, God willing. If I can carry on, patient and industrious, if I can check my evil sense of humor and endure my occasional shame, something may come of it.

July 24

By the swimming hole.

Lovely peculiar color, colors, of George's sex in bright sunlight: half its length is very tawny, even sallow. Then on the tissue laid bare by circumcision (delayed until his late adolescence) there are little odd markings, like faded bloodstains, and others like stains of grape. The glans is a gray sort of pink, softly freckled, and its flange or corona vivid pink. Under which the scrotal skin, too delicate and lax and weighted, has a cold bloom and silveriness of wrinkles.

Thus his beauty gives me a great and real satisfaction, along with the impossible, constant, too keen stimulus. I told him so as we lay there on the harsh fine gravel, sunbathing. I must keep telling myself so; it helps me to content myself with my inadequate share of amorous reality . . . "That's good," he said. So he rested, his (perhaps) umber eyelids descending. I could not rest, gazing at him in my bewitched way instead, and trying to sort out a palette of adjectives for the above difficult bit of word-painting, difficult to the point of futility.

Aphrodisiac sun soaking through the colorful drooping organ meanwhile, strengthening it . . . Indeed, not only that but all his exceptionally pale flesh is fraught with many little tints: in every slender part a suffusion of veins, lightest blue; and his armpits faintly golden; and the least scratch or bruise anywhere bright, and his waistline stained by his belt all summer; and on his heavy upper eyelid a little plum-colored crescent, as if painted, and a lesser steely crescent above that when his eyes are shut; and his shaved cheeks and chin, shadowy iron.

Presently he opened his eyes, found me still looking at him, and said, "Look at something else now. You make me nervous."

Instantly ashamed, angry and sorry and sorry for myself, I wanted to cry like a baby. I retired to a log that lies there across a little backwater with minute mud-colored fish in it, and did cry, inactively, *in petto*. Cramp of face; eyes burning and blurring (the school of fish a-jitter); mind full of little panic and contradictory protest . . . Reduced to so little love; learning to do with so little; suddenly requested to do with somewhat less. Lovemaking with my eyes, and with my nouns and adjectives; nothing but that for weeks at a time . . .

If this was self-pity, it was so mixed with sense of humor as to give no comfort, not even ignoble comfort. It was not resentment. The little deprivations must follow the same rule as the great, which no one intended. George's allowance of my glances must occur or not occur like his other greater bounty, irresponsible, unpredictable. I did not lose my sense of proportion or think of this as tragedy. Indeed I was not thinking at all, I was experiencing; and what I was experiencing was a kind of reflexive psychic sob, a retching, an exhaustion.

George soon noticed my mournful posture on the log, looking down at the little dingy fish instead of at him, and complained of my having misunderstood.

Oh no, I understood aplenty: familiar truths about myself, and this and that surely to the point about him, respectfully. All morning, as it happened, I had been aware of his touchiness, kindly controlled, and

I knew it was because he was tired, and I thought it was because he needed his beloved.

He went on to remark that he often finds my fixed blank look at him uncomfortable, and to express some uncertainty of the sense of it.

I have sometimes pointed out that it is like Cupid's—the dog, not the god; Cupid in his lap adoring. But I did not have the courage to repeat that bitter witticism. Also this time there must have been a sharper glance of laborious brain, vexed by my poor series of definitions of color (above). But I did not give that as an excuse, since I myself thought of it as a substitute for love; therefore it must have been subject to the same repugnance. I simply let him apologize and scold me and cheer me. And with no great delay I began to resume my better manner. Then Elizabeth and the children came down to the river.

From Edgar Allan Poe's *Marginalia*: "If any ambitious man have a fancy to revolutionize, at one effort, the universal world of human thought, human opinion, and human sentiment, the opportunity is his own—the road to immortal renown lies straight open, and unencumbered before him. All that he has to do is to write and publish a very little book. Its title should be simple—a few plain words—*My Heart Laid Bare*. But this little book must be *true to its title*.

"Now, is it not very singular that, with the rabid thirst for notoriety which distinguishes so many of mankind—so many, too, who care not a fig for what is thought of them after death, there should not be found one man having sufficient hardihood to write this little book? To *write*, I say. There are ten thousand men who, if the book were once written, would laugh at the notion of being disturbed by its publication during their life, and who could not even conceive *why* they should object to its being published after their death. But to write it—*there* is the rub. No man *could* write it, even if he dared. The paper would shrivel and blaze at every touch of the fiery pen."

I first came upon this passage in an edition of Baudelaire's tragic notebook, *Mon Coeur Mis à Nu*; for years it has kept appealing to my imagination in its strange way. I may say that I am not too much in sympathy with the first sentence. How characteristic of this plainly inspired but often vulgar master! I fancy sometimes that it was Poe who first evolved the prose of the press agent's release. But there is another more perturbing note, that of impotence or at least inactivity. Here speaks the man who has not done the thing he advocates: thus timorous men incite others to assassinate, penniless men advise others to invest their cash, and stay-at-homes describe world cruises.

By virtue of my own diary—this manuscript, such as it is, a poor thing but of my own heart, and, as far as it goes, bare as backside—I am in a position not only to doubt Poe's promise of *eternal renown* but to deny his hopeless (perhaps self-indulgent) conclusion. I was indeed one of the ten thousand of whom he speaks, shameless, willing. The rub does come in the writing rather than the daring to write; I am impressed by his having guessed that; I did not. When he says that the paper *shrivels*, he means the mind, of course—O nineteenth-century style! In fact it rather shrinks than shrivels, and grows lean, turns pale, gets cold, gets tired. It gets so tired of its appearance in the mirror that it wildly clamors to put on some mask, to hide in some fancy dress, to frolic no matter how; so tired that it seems almost willing to go mad; which willingness frightens one. There is no *blaze*, only a cruel brightness, like that of klieg lights from which movie actors' eyes get inflamed; only a vacuity and disgust and numbness. As to *the fiery pen*: so far as I know, in this connection or any other, it is good for nothing except quickly jotting down lies. The minute my pen starts to heat up I quit work; or next morning I have to revise what I have done. But in fact it is not hard to keep it cool. The mind of itself distills a little steady trickle and puddle of a sort of ice water—cold tears and cold ichor and cold sweat—in which to dip and sober and temper one's nib.

An odd one, Poe—not really Israfel, not naturally winged. It was never a quite powerful or secure or smooth flight. Think how few his perfect lyrics are. Consider his prose style, how so often conceitedly ambling, ill-cadenced; and disfigured by oratorical italics and bits of foreign language; and laden with conscious scholarship. Re-examine his criticism, at times pretentious, at times foolish; the grandest theory intermingled with snap judgments in the fashion then, and so old-fashioned now! Mesdames Browning and Hemans enchanted him, Byron shocked him, etc. Yet, even without appreciation of his writings, anyone can see by his effect upon the life and letters of the century since, anyone can see that he had heavenly talent.

What is most striking in his case is a desperate insistence up and up in the literary scale, a constant itch for poetic and intellectual flight. Therefore he rigged himself up with artificial wings, rhetorical devices, highfalutin ideas and ideals, and kept on the lookout for every possible difficulty, every kind of aesthetic eminence, and kept clambering up and jumping off, come what might. Furthermore, as he was the damnedest of literary hacks, the hungriest and thirstiest, he had to earn a living by this wild amateurish attempt at virtuosity, this trying to fly or seeming to fly. Journalism in America then was all rather like holiday in small towns, itinerant carnival; and year after year Poe appeared everywhere: what upon our present circuits of summer festivity is called an "attraction." Not much like an angel, not much like a bird: an aerial acrobat. Icarus of our American culture, Icarus at the county fair! Whatever happened, always imperturbably he would spread himself in midair, auto-parachute, and come down somehow, and presently start up again. Whenever his attempt was not really unique or difficult, he prefaced it by some little alarmist address to the audience. And from this daredevil's insecure improvised pinions every now and then an odd bit fell, inspirational feather, fabulous in the eyes of the youngsters of the century, even foreign youngsters. Here and there this bird picked up seeds, and in the way of not fastidious nature, down they all came somewhere else, droppings, which sprouted and grew—stimulated by the change of scene and soil, as vegetable species are—and flowered and bore fruit incalculably, superbly. Which accounts for a great many things, familiar now: modern French verse (Baudelaire, Mallarmé, Valéry), the prose poem, the abstract style of literary criticism, the detective story, etc. . . .

Wondering about him, I often think of a silly etching by Félicien Rops: the devil with great worn crow's wings, high up in a dirty sky, in a squatting posture. It is entitled *Satan jettant à la terre la pâture qu'elle attend*, Satan casting upon earth the nourishment it is waiting for. He stares down ferociously, and with a terrible fist presses out of his coarse virile organ splashes of sperm. Decidedly this corrupt and trashy Rops was one of our high-minded poet's descendants. I fancy that, in his cups, and far from the ladies, Poe might have been flattered by my facetious analogy. If I had been Longfellow or Emerson, how I would have fought him! Even now that he is dead, a blessed disinfected classic, I rather hate to pay tribute to his pretentious deviltry. But it did its work divinely.

July 25

One of the Scottsboro boys, acquitted after six years of imprisonment and various trials for rape, shouts, "Hallelujah! Gee! I feel as happy as when I was two years old." How happy is that?

In a tornado, take refuge in the southwest corner of a basement, for the house will be blown down toward the northeast . . . a poetical thing to know . . .

1 9 3 8

. . . As a rule, the development of talent into mastery, or even genius, is not a matter of studying to write or training to write, but of exercising as greatly as possible the entire being, senses, nerves, excitements, emotions, thoughts; only two or three habits of mind making the difference, leading on specifically to literature: the recollective faculty, conversational power, including the power of making others talk, and of course studiousness of the classics of literature and the other arts.

—*"An Introduction to Colette"*

S.S. President Harding
March 22

Lonesome all the way, though humorously and willingly so.

I've changed, changed, for I was seasick for almost two days. The pressure in the pit of the stomach, the vacuous belching, the hot and cold, the stupidity, the exhaustion. But it wasn't bad in bed, and I slept a great deal.

Elegant sturdy little captain who loves puzzles; nice Garden Club lady from East Orange; nice spinster from Detroit; immense beautiful young English farmer who can't quite like me, alas; and an aged elegant expatriate named Mrs. Hughes, tottering, with pretty blue hair, who knew D. H. Lawrence.

Soft sunshine all afternoon; tonight the foghorn.

Strangely, and rightly, Monroe's roses are still strong and round, full blown, pale from the damp, happy.

Paris
March 26

The first thirty-six hours: Jacques Guérin at the Gare St.-Lazare at midnight, as always, holding bulky white gloves, wearing tight loud British suit. His affectionate inquiries about Monroe *et al.*, *grosso modo*; and his account of his affairs, René Paulhan's death, etc., and his love affair. Lunch the next day with him and his mother and Jean Boy. Eardley's arrival. Dinner with Jacques, and the evening looking at his books, to which he has been adding superbly. This week, the Balzac that King Charles I had in prison. Marie Antoinette's *Manon Lescaut.* Balzac's *Curé de Village* dedicated to Lamartine. A letter addressed to Lafayette by Benjamin Constant's concierge just after his death, enclosing a lock of his hair. The great Montaigne first in black morocco sprinkled with carnations. Etc. Nothing shabby, nothing thoughtless.

More and more Proust, packages and packages, including letters of childhood and adolescence. The strangest of the latter is addressed to his grandfather Nathan Weill, a request for thirteen francs. He explains that his father had given him ten francs to go to a brothel, so as to put a stop to his masturbation. In his excitement young Marcel broke a chamber pot and then could not get an erection again. Therefore, ten francs for another chance, three francs for another chamber pot. He had consulted his mother about it, and it was she who advised him to appeal to his grandfather instead of to his father!

I've never known finer or more French weather, but I freeze. Rooms smell of French winter, stale; so all the windows are kept open. Everyone sits on the café terraces because "it makes so beautiful"; and so do I, shivering. The sky is large chunks of ice-blue and snow-white, slowly alternating and drifting. Under my balcony the chestnuts hold up their little flapping leaves and sticky buds as if it were time. Perhaps my chills are somewhat psychological, effect of an impulse to run away to the Midi immediately.

March 28

Another of these evenings allsoulalone that I so dislike. Françoise Rosay was very fine, the film too long and slow. I must admit that Jacques and Jean Boy invited me to see *Le Chapeau de Paille* with them, and I said I was engaged.

Then I went to the Boeuf and made friends with Jules Monk's baron! It's the limit.

Places mean little to me; like air and treetops, all very well; but I have to live in nests. I do delight in landscape and cityscape; but it seems that what delights me I make up anyway: words. Literature would do as well as travel. I need those I must love, those I can make love to—the rest is superfluity, practically.

As for Tito,* he is in love; he told me all about it, which took an hour or so. He looks older, which pleases me, but he thinks that he may have something the matter with his insides. He has a delightful funny studio, a good ways up the rue Lepic.

Jean Boy is Jacques's lover. It started arbitrarily, unenthusiastically; it has lasted three years; and it seems very substantial still. A singular creature, a Basque, driven away from home by his father because of his pederasty. Here he starved off and on for several years, really starved, slept under bridges. No one would give him a job without some sexy involvement; he is too proud for that. Someone absconded with some money. He joined the Salvation Army, and that lasted two years. Now he makes hats; has a smart little shop next door to this hotel; is coming into fashion. Tall, and gaunt, beurre-noir complexion—ugly, I think—with a whipped sort of carriage, an ashamed look. Jacques makes him unhappy; he admits it. But he is very pleasant to talk to and seems to like me.

Jacques has rented a little no-account house in Port-Royal, where they spend every weekend. Of course he asked me to go with them. They also all expect me to go to Villefranche for the Easter holiday. I am afraid of it. Surely I'm right. I shouldn't mind their relationship in the least; but oh, the languors and the autocracies and the one-track subjects of conversation. I should in any event insist upon stopping at the Welcome.

March 29

I wrote Jean Petin a note, and Sunday morning Michel Girard† called me to say that he is doing his three weeks of reserve military service, would be in town only that day, and wanted to see me. So after the picture dealers' luncheon I went there. Wonderful flats in the aristocratic quarter, one *rez-de-chaussée* and the other *au 5-ième*, overlooking Mme Philippe Berthelot's pavilion and modest parqueted flowers. Lots of fine bibelots, but also lots of room: with Aubusson, eighteenth-century moquette, seventeenth-century black and brass cupboards, Chopin's hand in bronze, etc. Jean Petin offered me his spare room! Of course I

---

* Tito Valdez. Barbara Harrison Wescott's nephew.
   † Michel Girard. Appears in G.W.'s short story "The Frenchman Six Foot Three," published in *Harper's Magazine*, July 1942.

didn't dare; heavens, what behavior for a Frenchman. Michel has grown too homely for words, but was very cordial, even amorous; is there perhaps a connection?

I tagged along with them to the Gare de l'Est—Michel without an overcoat because the French Army doesn't issue one his size, and all the rest of his uniform paralyzingly tight and comic. Nothing could have been more to my taste than the crowd there; indeed I think it has made me feel better about being here. Soldiers returning to Metz by the thousand, soldiers as always, ideal (that is, if you have a French ideal): luminous complexions, brilliant eyes, harum-scarum individuality, no two alike, bodies almost all of ugly shape, like bulbs, like roots—mandrake men—with here and there a detail of real beauty: chapped lips Romanly chiseled, perfectly rounded nape of neck, cavalryman's hand, bit of Rheims or Chartres. When it came time for the train to whistle, half of them stood on the platform, each with his girl, face to face, knee to knee, but quite immobile, blank-faced, not saying a word, and now and then taking long careful kisses, and still standing there, belly to belly, dreaming solemnly together. After the whistle the sweethearts and kid brothers and parents all seemed to sag, to shrink: the mass of them so suddenly deprived of so much sexy youth. As the train pulled out, a thousand hands were flung up, very white and ominous and gay.

Tito came while I was out; and the funny feeling he had in his side is only a strained muscle, from his ballet lessons.

Effect of the passport photo George sent me out in the world with: At Le Havre one of the passport men, a tough cheerful young one, grinned and nudged the other and said, "*Hein, qu'il est beau, celui là!*" And *la politesse française* consisted only in their not looking up at me . . .

Marcel Khill sent me an eager message by Tito; and I wrote Cocteau, a little grudgingly, but after all, if not now, when; what's the good of being bored to death? He has not answered. I stopped in at his hotel, and the concierge was very mysterious; he is *en voyage*; perhaps it would be best for me to write his secretary?

Janet Flanner* telephoned and complained at length in her grand commonsense fashion: the world, the wickedness, Spain, the recession in America; dear little old cold volcano that she is. Today I took her to

---

* Janet Flanner (1892–1978). Journalist who wrote the "Paris Letter" for *The New Yorker* for fifty years under the pseudonym Genêt.

lunch; but oh, we're not as much alike or in agreement as she seems to think. She has no sense of mystery. Solita Solano* and Nancy Cunard† came, and dated us up for tomorrow night, 10:30 in some café. Janet and I talked about the Semitic problem. (I remember that when Jean-Michel Frank had his nose fixed, she said she thought circumcision should be local.) She also reported that Diana Sheean, planning an expedition to Madrid or Barcelona, told her, "You see, I've never been invited to a war before. I felt that I ought to accept, don't you think? I might never get another chance."

Janet seemed to think this charming. It scandalizes me.

Tito is the only person so far who has taken any interest in my presence and purpose and need here, and the only one who has told me anything I haven't heard before. Or so it seems—perhaps, because I am lonely and chaste, I take in things without enjoyment which I may enjoy in retrospect.

What is surprising, in fact, is that I take so little delight in the city itself, the Seine, the spring. It seems that I remember better than I see, and refeel too much with the memory. I think when I am alone— I *feel* only with someone I love; is it that?

I haven't even written Barbara or Lloyd yet. My homesickness has seemed ungrateful. Although it does them, and their Mulhocaway,‡ some honor. Also they took no responsibility for my having a good time here. And what I am grateful to them for is their having wished to help me, to indulge me in my perhaps morbid love of liberty, envy of the past, cramp of my severe loves, weariness of myself—so generously and trustfully. Like holding the falcon overhead when it "breaks." Which did me incomparable good before I set foot on the ship. When I left, in truth, I was happier than I had been for a long time—more loving and family-loving, more peaceful, less foolish, more resolute.

April 2

Last Saturday I went to the casino alone without dining, settled in my nice expensive armchair no. 9—tired businessman of what a business! skeptical, humorous, and recklessly hopeful, and willingly reck-

---

* Solita Solano. A writer and longtime friend of Janet Flanner, whom she met in 1921.

† Nancy Cunard. Daughter of London socialite Lady Maud "Emerald" Cunard, she was a writer and poet and an expatriate publisher in the twenties, operating Hours Press in Paris.

‡ Mulhocaway. The farm in the vicinity of the Mulhocaway River in New Jersey where Lloyd and Barbara settled in 1933. Usually referred to as Stone-blossom, it was part of a valley that would be submerged by the state in 1957 because of water-level problems. From 1957 on, the Wescotts lived at Haymeadows, another farm in the same area.

less. Tito's principal number comes almost at once, to pass the time while old Mistinguett* dresses, finale of the usual series of evocations of different parts of Paris: Au Bois de Boulogne. The stage is all a leafy alcove in which two big white merry-go-round swans not very merrily go round and round; and on an incline of imitation-glass water several big toe dancers with black swans stitched on their skirts perform a bit. Then a third swan is rolled in. Tito's partner enters and undresses, a pale girl with a hooked nose and frail breasts. Tito gets up out of the third swan's behind, bare except for a pouch of lamé, and dances with her: stylized hugging, energetic undulation of shoulder, thrusting of the lamé pouch, until at last he has her flattened out on the floor and gracefully descends on her, amid heartfelt but shy applause.

I enjoyed it a lot, and what I enjoyed most was certainly surprising and comic—being there expensively alone, with a couple of provincial Britishers on my left and a plump young Marseillais with painted mistress on my right, and a profusion of empty armchairs—concupiscent tingling warming cooling smiling sighing, desire at a distance, in public; what one is supposed to feel in one of those armchairs, what myriad old bachelors with respect to myriad ballerinas dead and gone have felt. I think I've never felt it before, never more than the idea or the anticipation, nothing physical. Of course I could scarcely have been more elaborately prepared to feel it; overpreparation and disillusionment due, I should have thought; so it must be somewhat to Tito's credit—as an "artist."

Then the rest of the show: Mistinguett, who has been taking lessons and sings better, Mistinguett and nothing else, except now and then a less impressive turn by Tito: Hindu hands fluttering over his head, and Etruscan grin, and *physique de Proud'hon*, and *mentalité de Paul et Virginie*. At one point his partner wears a rose as *cache-sexe*, and Tito passionately stoops and removes it between his teeth. Nothing else, except a showgirl named La Splendide Ambarina; never have I seen one more splendid: very tall, idle, with slow-burning sidelong glances, important legs, long delicate nose, and apparently no talent at all, not even the exhibitionistic.

By the time it was over, and having waited half an hour on the pavement with the crowd around Mistinguett's little automobile, I was tired, and tired of my intention, and starved. Tito seems much older, he is thinner, and he needed a shave—all of which I liked the look of.

---

* Mistinguett (1875–1956). The popular star of Parisian music halls and cabarets was a longtime friend of Cocteau.

But he felt ill, he said. His muscles have never quite matured, infantile, which of course is pretty; some doctor has warned him that they may pull apart, rupture, etc.; and he was afraid it had happened.

We went to La Cloche d'Or and ate well and drank a couple of bottles of Riesling. Probably I beamed indiscreetly; perhaps my several notes to him were as romantic as I intended, or more so. Anyway it was he who soon brought up the subject of desire, first by shameless pleasing reminiscences of George and so on with the history of his life, and so on rapidly to a grand finale, as if in reply to the question that I had not had time to propose: he has decided to give up homosexuality. He doesn't favor theories or generalizations or shortcuts; he told me the whole story; it took hours. Ever since his flight from T. he has expected to fall in love again, and nothing has happened, nothing but friendship, friendship plus playfulness, and what he calls "convenience." Then there are his early religious scruples, and his ideal mother, and T.'s misery in the end, and his love of the country and even of *The Apple of the Eye* and of children, and therefore back to the land, back to the womb, pell-mell, at least a pell-mell conversation. I tranquilly inquired if he had simply fallen in love with a particular woman; yes, indeed.

None other than La Splendide Ambarina, who is Miss Spain 1937, though not in the least Spanish-looking; Miss Visigoth 1937. At the same time, his partner Alba is madly in love with him—no wonder, dancing in that improvised fashion—and she is horrid about it. She and Ambarina share a dressing room and it was the contrast between their behavior that first attracted him. One night at some *partouse* Ambarina fell to his lot, and he was impotent; still she behaved ideally. Then she made him a declaration. In due time he was not impotent, and so it went, so it goes, so it is supposed to go to the end of the story, the living happily ever after, which is to be, as far as I can make out, on a chicken farm in Spain with numerous offspring. But it is all brand new. There is some mystery about her. He does not intend to have his heart broken. He has an idea that she may be a spy of Franco's, which he doesn't mind, and he hopes that's all . . .

Well, of course it looked as if my goose were cooked, but I was enjoying myself immensely. By that time it was toward morning, and he asked me to take him home; and he invited me to come up and see his studio, which is charming, where he willingly kissed me a good bit, and I played problem child a good bit, but (I think) gracefully, or humorously; and goodbyes were said, with "yes" and "perhaps" and "not tonight" and all that; and I stumbled down the rue Lepic more dead than alive but living at last—Paris, Paris, and very grateful.

There was really nothing discouraging about all this, even the next day, *à froid*, except perhaps his kindly bossy suggestions: that I might try Iolas Coudoudis, that I ought to go to Monte Carlo and see a friend of his in the ballet, that I must go to Smith's tearoom! But I was homesick, I didn't feel well, perhaps I was scared. God knows, I did not wish to settle into a real regular old-fashioned love affair, unrequited; and the stage seemed all set—that is, it wasn't set for anything else.

I didn't hear from him again for several days. Then he called on me here, when I was out, and left a note asking me to tea on Wednesday. His residence in Montmartre seemed more attractive than ever . . . He was taking a violin lesson and I waited, hanging out the window as everyone does in Montmartre: a vacant lot, budding ailanthus and some other tufted shrub. A little mulatto schoolboy in a horrid old-rose smock and gray cotton jacket, carrying a briefcase, dolorously contemplating a group of noisy natives. A little girl, also miscegenate, tossing a head of the handsomest water-spaniel curls I ever saw. A workman painting postwar Utrillo colors over prewar colors of same . . .

That afternoon Tito told me about the Russian prince madly in love, who therefore does all his dusting and mopping. He also told me what he thinks about venality in love; he has never put a price on himself; he believes in presents, even in promises of presents; and indeed he has found that sexual adventure is more profitable if it is all left like that—it made me laugh a good deal. Pleasant unpromising talk . . . I gathered that he had a rendezvous with Miss Visigoth that night. Yet he asked me to come for breakfast the next morning.

As I had a date with Janet and Nancy after dinner I accompanied him to the casino and stood up for his swan number. I thought it best to view him a little less subjectively; to study a little how, let us say, to fall out of, let us say, love, if I should happen to fall in and be very uncomfortable. I thought it would not be difficult. I thought it not at all likely that he can ever become a real dancer; he has no ear, I guess. I may add also that I had begun to be generally in better humor. I had wandered around the Tuileries in the afternoon, writing notes like Gide on scraps of paper; and I had discovered the Goya nudes . . .

I suppose that what happened at breakfast would somewhat depend on what had happened at Tito's rendezvous with Ambarina; it seemed unpropitious. But I thoroughly played my role of foolish rich stylish American madly-in-love; that is, I got up early and took a taxi and went to Creplet's for butter, to Hédiard's for breakfast food and fruit, to the bakery in the rue du Havre for brioches, and to Granger & Moreau for cheese and sweet cream; and so arrived and woke Tito up. He woke

well, good-natured. He requested his fez and put it on. He began by
eating African grapes, and fed me some. It all went as simply and sweetly
as could be. I banqueted before he breakfasted, that was all. He has
the sharpest nipples in the world. That odor of makeup is indeed extraordinary, like Fez, like poison. He did not want to take off the bathrobe
George gave him (was that simply *pudeur de danseur nu*, or was it in
G.'s honor?). He did not get around to the way of intercourse at which
I am amateurish, and which I should have sufficiently welcomed. He
complimented me upon my not-amateurish way, attributing it, according
to his present romanticism, to the fact that I was a farmboy . . . Having
had my way, with my familiar willingness to be neglected, I sprang out
of bed; but he followed me and threw his arms around me from behind,
and at the touch of his hand I swooned and fell on the floor, really
swooned, in a softly whirling darkness with little stars like forget-me-
nots, which was lovely.

Whereupon we breakfasted. My sweet cream from Granger & Moreau wasn't sweet at all, but the regular *fraises-des-bois* stuff. Somewhat
to my dismay he announced that he had accepted an invitation to lunch
with two friends of his, one of them madly-in-love; and he begged me
to charm them if possible, and suggested that I take them a couple of
bottles of wine. One of those merry-melancholy fellows with little chuckles all the time, little double chins from head to foot; and a kind pock-
marked woman, the daughter of Marguerite Carré, the niece of the man
who wrote the libretto of Gounod's *Faust*; they do the décor and costumes
for the casino and half the other such shows . . .

April 4

Still no answer from Cocteau. And I haven't got up courage to beg
for audiences with Gide, Bérard, *et al.*

I realized promptly that the exchange of old intimacy with Jacques
would be nil. So it has been; I have seen him alone only a couple of
times; indeed it is evident that he prudently or lazily avoids it. I cannot
honestly say that I mind. For a few hours of the first twenty-four I did
feel a certain plain pleasant indecent longing; there were reasons
a-plenty, both historical and momentary, both physical and fictitious.
But without transition that and indeed all the rest turned to sense of
humor; and to observing how he has changed, and also failed to change;
to playing my role to perfection. So it has been chiefly an exchange of
a good many free meals at Mme G.'s for a good deal of patient boredom
before and after . . . I shouldn't be surprised if he has been trying to
draw me back closer, as he did last time; and I hope I shouldn't be such

a fool as to refuse, now that I am invulnerable. But he would have done so only if he had vaguely, excitingly sensed that it would make trouble; and it would not have made trouble. So he is simply happy to have me here. And on the whole he is still bored by the happiness he so ably arranges.

April 6

Superb weather, not a drop of rain since I arrived, and all in blossom, but my room has been so cold that I have hated sitting up and typing at my uncomfortable table. So I have been scribbling notes in bed, half-letter, half-journal . . .

Whereupon Cocteau summons me, and Marcel Khill gets his fiancée and her family packed off to the country, so that he can devote himself entirely to me, etc. I like Marcel better than anyone here; that is, I enjoy him more. I really don't like Cocteau much, in his present set of circumstances, but he is hard to resist, in mine. The frequentation of rich French bourgeoisie—Jacques, Michel, Jean Petin, etc.—has a terrible effect. Today it is my duty to lunch at Mme Monteux's with Blaise Cendrars, who has been making trouble between her and Jean. I think seriously of moving to Marcel's charming, no doubt sinister hotel; it is half the price of this.

The fact is, I have been a godsend to all these French; psychoanalyst, fortune-teller, fata morgana, curé, troubadour. To say nothing of the money I spend, monstrous. All futile and frustrating, it is one of the strangest adventures of my entire life, I shall never be the same again.

As to Tito's change of sex: Very likely a woman's body and a woman's action would suit him as well as a man's or better. But the sort of woman whom he will suit, I am afraid, may not prove flattering or dependable. When he is working he has little opportunity to seek out and actively woo good-enough men; whereas he is in a position to be continuously wooed by the pathetic. So women seem less attainable, more imaginary—even he, little realist though he is, not free from the ideal.

April 13

The night before my birthday I had pleasantly but futilely supped and romped in Montmartre with sentimental Tito. All morning I loitered in bed, scribbled, tried to make up my multiple mind about the little practical things, went to the British consulate too late, and arrived at Mme M.'s for lunch. The fine bulldog that Ralph gave her has gone blind and now is losing other faculties. It still plays bravely, barging into the furniture, etc., a loving foolish thing; but at last the vet and others have persuaded her that it is cruel to keep it. Today was the day. She had been weeping all morning, and wore dark glasses to hide her eyes. I think that settled it for me, as to Villefranche; altogether too much kind bored playacting for me.

After lunch, I picked up Marcel, bought Jean some grapes, did an errand or two, called at the Castille. Jean was very ill yesterday, unable to eat, even unable to smoke, crazy-sad; the new boys, new secretary, and new lover–leading man badly scared. He can't go on much longer, surely. But there was Jean Desbordes,* strangely changed, with pop eyes and hair like a wig, there as a *"cher confrère"* for Jean's help and dangerous advice. Edouard Bourdet,† who now runs the Comédie Française, accepted a play of his (Desbordes) and rehearsed it with Bovy, Madeleine Renaud, etc., then suddenly called it off. Today Cocteau is also taking his own play away from Jouvet, with an elaborate absurd letter . . . So everyone talked at once. Barbette is paralyzed in both legs. Moyse is dying. Cocteau has signed a contract to be the president of a company to renew Salzburg at Blois, he is going to drape all the balconies with great colored cloths, etc. Marianne Oswald, the singer, then arrived, grown stout and wholesome after her attempted suicide; she took an instant fancy to me of course, as a potential connection in N.Y. I had to give up being photographed in the ruins of the exposition, because Gertrude Stein kept Cecil [Beaton] too long, and I couldn't cut Tito's birthday party for me. Meanwhile Jean started by telephone a furious altercation with Bourdet, which lasted three-quarters of an hour (literally), while Cecil waited, furious.

A large birthday party, to my surprise: a good many friendly souls whom I insincerely promised to see again. Beatrice Wanger of course; a Nautch girl from Harlem, a Dutch boy who dances Spanish, an American woman who dances Hawaiian (all this literally really), Anton Dolin; and the most attractive young man I've met here, who is Mistinguett's singing teacher; and Mistinguett herself, in whom I delighted. It was grand, that is, luxurious, with champagne and petits fours; I think the ex-Minister of Education paid for it. There was a little Butte boy, seven or eight years old, dressed up as an Arab, who timidly served, and who asked Mistinguett if she was Josephine Baker. Dolin told me that Mary

---

* Jean Desbordes (1906–44). Cocteau's protégé-lover in the late twenties. He died under torture by Gestapo agents during the Paris Occupation.

† Edouard Bourdet (1887–1944). French playwright (*La Prisonnière*) and, in 1938, director of the Comédie Française.

Butts's husband has died, soon after she did. I'm sorry to say that the splendid Ambarina disappointed me without footlights: too coarse features and teeth not even, and flagrantly not ladylike, which has an effect of making Tito seem a little common; no matter. For I bless them with real enthusiasm. Have I made it clear why?—the hopeless, scornful, or despairing mentality of almost everyone else . . . Everyone else except the devils.

Back at the Castille we found Jean and Cecil, who had had a good time, and there was some more uproar. Charles Trenet, the new Chevalier, came to call, big, common, admirable creature, excellent little artist, with his uncle or perhaps "uncle." Jean and the boys were going to the Mogador to see Dolin dance; so Marcel and I pretended to be dining with Katherine Dudley, and hid in his hotel while he made some tracings of Jean's drawings for me. Whereupon in walked Jean Bourgoint,* in better shape than I expected, but how ugly: his great ill-kept hands jerky at the end of his long thin arms; his teeth wide apart and gray; only his pallid eyes blazing. He assured me that now he is a model youth; he is absurdly resentful of and mystified by my long neglect; and rather more affectionately interested in news of Monroe than of me, which touched my heart.

Later poor Marcel went to bed, and slept instantly, and for an hour I lay there beside him, by the light of the dread little lamp, idealistic in squalor, praying for him, as it were, thinking for myself; and I couldn't wake him up, not even to say good night.

New York—Stone-blossom
Summer

Consider the giant anteater. I did, last night at the Fifth Avenue zoo, on my way to the dancing on the Mall. It has one superb marking from shoulder to shoulder, which is a charred shade of white, as if it had been struck by lightning. And the shape of it in its entirety is indeed one that—you might say, as the church says of certain sins—*cries to heaven for vengeance.* Its tail is an integral continuation of its backbone, flexibly stuck out and curving to the ground and sparsely set with long bristle; which reminded me of some very big Fuller brush especially designed to dust behind a radiator or to unclog a part of the plumbing. What it has for a face is little and elongated and of a rubbery-firm substance, like the penis of a pony: a lean penis with tiny eyeballs and

* Jean Bourgoint (1906–66). He and his twin sister were Cocteau's models for *Les Enfants Terribles*. He was also G.W.'s model for Timothy in *The Grandmothers*. Later joined a monastery.

air ducts in it, shorn of its testicles. It also walks fabulously, upon bowlegs, sliding around, all of a piece.

Productions of nightmarish art, the composite devils of such a one as Hieronymus Bosch, the pukey teratology of Salvador Dalí and his followers, are all very well; but they have less style than such a plaything of nature. Yesterday Monroe presented me with a fat illustrated book, *Gynecology and Obstetrics*, by one Dr. Davis. Wherein I observe that in the way of human irregularity also, the compositions of Almighty God beat all.

But there is nothing in nature that sounds like Racine's verse; no color scheme like Piero's. Here is a fine and moot point in aesthetics. Evidently what we call beauty is rarer than its opposite; therefore perhaps beautification is a better artistic policy in art.

Social scene, N.Y.: At a party here one night Preston, the party-butler, remarked to our Anna* that he felt no disapproval of drinking, even heavy drinking; but he thought she might be interested to hear that among our guests there was one young man to whom he had served twenty-one drinks. Which, said he, was gluttonous. So Anna reported; she used the word *glouton*; I should have asked her what his English word was. I wonder who. Duly discounting the figure, how impressive!—the kind of nocturnal good cheer for which N.Y. is famous.

In a village called Chesapeake City there is an important elevator bridge—absurdly important, it seems; the inlet it lies across is modest, dotted with little fishing boats and weekend boats. Homeward bound at twilight we found it elevated and had to line up with a jam of cars. Suddenly, from the east, there came a transatlantic freighter seemingly across the weedy fields, filling the inlet channel as in a groove, and looming above it, then above us; one of the American Export Lines liners which go to Greece and Egypt. It was more or less empty; a great deal of its red belly showed, and a third of the propeller revolved out of the water. The sailors leaning over the rail looked somewhat astonished themselves, as if indeed it had run away with them, across country—little fellows' little apparitions aboard a big one. I have looked at our up-to-date road map; and as there is no such channel, it must be one of the wonders wrought by our lavish President overnight.

* * *

* Anna Brakke. G.W.'s housekeeper.

Sid, my brother's herdsman, has a characteristic dreamy cadence in his speech: he is a Guernseyman—of a cow: "I've got an idea she's carryin' a little heat. She's just comin' off her heat."

I took a sunbath, and during it tried to translate a poem of Goethe's from memory, humming the Schubert tune, concentrating with my eyes tight shut; which gives the oddest impression of being infinitely lost and disembodied. Try it. *"Nähe des Geliebte"*: so far as I remember, the only poem that ever made me weep.

Mother and Elizabeth, despairing of Santa Claus, went to Easton and bought a piano, $60 worth of piano, of the period *Félix-Fauré-Américaine* (as the French reckon), with some jigsawing on it. Not a good piano; like a big banjo with tonsillitis. Beulah* and I must endeavor to keep Mother in ignorance of our opinion . . . So we had a musical Sunday night. Beulah now sings the first two *Gesänge des Harfners* well, with her tart sweetness and cold ardor. Then our sister got Lloyd to render "The Sweetheart of Sigma Chi," which, I think, somewhat scandalized his wife. Then we all sang hymns. George says that we sang them badly, which seems odd—did we? Or is that just his impression as parson's son perverted; the devil and holy water? He made Beulah repeat her three best lieder to clear the air.

I think snobbism is the ridiculous aspect of a very important kind of imaginative faculty . . . For certain purposes you have to get up on a certain level of worldliness; if you are merely snobbish on it, why, more's the pity. But to be subsnobbish is grave—like subtropical, or subnormal.

George's gardener, Louis, has discovered that we are on the verge of an interesting catastrophe. It seems that whenever the pump is at work, it is pouring half of its capacity, by way of the little overflow pipe, into the ground, under the sod. There is already an impressive hole, leading to a sort of cavern, who knows how great. So that in due course the lawn would cave in. One of us, strolling forth for conversation or a sunbath, might find himself underground—like the rape of Persephone.

I returned to town alone by a slow uncomfortable train in which there were as many passengers as possible, and a troubling odor, and

---

* Beulah Wescott (1902–   ). G.W.'s oldest sister, who worked at Harper's.

an audible sprinkling of cinders. I sat facing a lovely couple: it was the maximum of young man, swarthy, with crooked bright glances and a little snowy grin; and under his arm, the minimum of young woman, absolutely blond, hair and skin and dress all alike, no color at all except her little blue eyes in continuous adoration of him. The dirty electric light from the top of the coach shook and gleamed down upon his burned nose and sweaty brow. Ideal Adam and Eve; and she nestled against his side, passive, adjunctive, as if indeed she were a rib just detached . . . They got off at Brooklyn. I shall always remember them with pleasant regret. I thought—and it made me smile to think—that if I were a rich old gentleman I should accost them and engage Paul Cadmus to paint their portrait.

The years of my life are hurried, more and more so. Yet I still remember a boy prostitute with features of ivory, haunches like a cat's, who tried to pick me up one night in 1925, in Florence. M. had gone to bed early, and I had come out alone to the terrace of a café in the Piazza del Popolo. Up and down that boy paced for me, up and down, with anxious but shameless glances. And somewhat hiding my head in an open newspaper, slow to desire, and too timorous and proud, I endured it—until he shrugged his shoulders angrily and disappeared down the dark side street toward the evil part of town.

Also I remember a boy in a cinema in St.-Tropez, still more desirable, and of the opposite inclination about it. We had come a quarter of an hour early, the lights had not yet been lowered, and I could not help simply staring at him. But the extraordinary beauty of his face, upon previous occasions, perhaps all his life, must have brought him nothing but bad luck. For suddenly with a grimace and a gesture of embarrassment, almost of hatred, he covered it with both his hands. I felt so sorry and so put to shame that I got up and returned to our hotel, before the film started.

I was coming up Central Park West in a taxi, and we were stopped by a traffic light. Then the taxi driver turned toward me and said in a loud but mild and philosophic tone, "Well, hell! I suppose she has, she must have, pink underpants on." I was absorbed in some worry, so he startled me, and I hurriedly gazed around to see what he was talking about. There indeed, at a little distance, on one of the benches spaced along in the shadow of a little cliff of primeval Manhattan, sat a fine blonde with her legs crossed in such a way as to show us the end of her suntan stockings and her strong thighs of summery complexion, right

up to the bifurcation. We could even see, as it were, a bit of depilated
Venus mount, which I too supposed to be in fact a fold of pink underpants. As the traffic light changed and we moved, my young hearty-eyed
and bristle-chinned driver turned again and gave me a little glance of
sincere comradeship.

A young Italian in a crosstown bus: His figure was too delicate to
show much through his shabby suit, but he had the sort of head that
attracts and holds attention: hair in a wiry, curly, doubtless dirty tangle,
pressed down square upon his brow; the lower lip half as wide and twice
as thick as the upper; the eyebrows fleshy; the soft eyes with bristling
lashes set rather far back on each side of his face, with a wall of nose
between . . . When he turned toward me there appeared in his pout, in
his gaze, a not happy although not unfriendly disturbance of some kind.
One eye crossed a little.

This type of beauty is out of fashion. Because of the universal habit
of the movies and the almost worldwide interest in spectator sports, the
American juvenile with four-square torso and heavy limbs and little
astute eyes and infant nose and thin lips—also the runner, the skier,
the very Nordic figure put together like a dart or a kite—have taken its
place. Neither of these new types has much to gain or anything at all
to lose by taking his clothes off; therefore nudity is much more familiar
than it was, and perhaps less consequential.

Boyish or girlish forms modestly unwrapped and tantalizing in large
garments, such as this boy's in the bus: how they made all hearts beat,
especially in Europe, before the war. Not much fuss is made over them
today. I think it must occur to almost everyone now how they are subject
to the coarsening and sagging of middle age. The Mediterranean sort of
head is too big to begin with. The tender Italian waistline seems certain
to become paunch in time; at very first glance it makes that suggestion.
The contemporary spirit is above all anxious, prophetic, even in minor
unintellectual matters. Fear of the future affects even taste, even sex
appeal. One turns with the liveliest pleasure to what seems most likely
to last.

Certainly I abominate the new notions of *race*. I am skeptical and
fearful of the concept of *the nation*, even the democratic nation. What
I do naturally believe in is *country*—scenery, climate, diet, and the
peculiarities of work and play that develop geographically; the charm
and anti-charm of places upon people. I believe in the physiology as
well as the morality and politics of this: the continuous tribute that
humanity must pay to nature: Neapolitans in America, such as this boy

in the bus; will they in a generation or two of our *régime* grow tall and broad-shouldered and great of leg? I think they tend to, even without intermarriage; and the general American appearance is bound to be improved, beautified by such importation and innovation.

The glance of the hundred-percent American is somewhat too obvious and rational; and as a rule he needs more feature, more muzzle and beak. I like to see and foresee what I call beauties of the future, the stranger the better, the more the merrier. A hybrid humanity, as it were, human nectarines, human loganberries, human king oranges and pink grapefruit—fruits of the grafting of Helsingfors upon Naples, Gold Coast upon Cornwall, Bucharest upon Texas. Gimlet eyes of Ireland, looking down sensual nose of Armenia, in seeming contradiction to sentimental pouting of the Tyrol. Straw-blond locks tousled over eyes of Persian miniature, eyes of Levantine bride. Opaque pallor of octoroon's child or grandchild, with fingernails perhaps still shadowy like petals of stale gardenia . . . I should like to see what would come of breeding one of my kinswomen, for example, to Ignoto Corrubias, blunt-boned Mayan. One of the silliest things in the statute books is the rejection of the Japanese: cutting off all those delicately broad little noses to spite our national face, which is and always has been a composite face anyway. One of the handsomest men I know is Isamu Noguchi, Scot and Japanese mixed.

Also I think of Elizabeth Welch, the singer, who is Scot and black; and Cecil Born, Basque and British; and Paul Cadmus, Basque and Dutch; and there is a wonderful handsome dancer in Nancy Hamilton's revue, a big Trinidadian youth of a Negroid cast of feature but blond complexion.

Miss Ferragut is an oddly stoic and energetic old person. For many years she has had a bad left leg; it gives under her like rubber, and recently it has had to be enclosed in a sort of skeleton pegleg of nickel-plated steel. There is a hinge at the knee, which locks; she cannot sit down without releasing this; and to do so she must find and press a button or catch somewhere up under her skirt in back. It makes her life difficult. But she is stubborn; she has always been very active in clubs and on committees, providing for crippled veterans, patronizing young artists, etc.; and unless actually in a plaster cast, she refuses to give any of this up. Proud and excitable, she dislikes your noticing her grotesque and admirable exertions. Her maid and chauffeur are trained to give her a hand. Getting into her car is the worst ordeal. She will not or cannot be lifted. Her own delicately flabby, blue-veined arms have to do all the work. When she has pulled herself up to a sufficient height on the running board, she aims her backside at the seat and falls into place with a flounce and a gasp. Her walk also is fantastic: she vigorously swings the limp right leg two or three times, for momentum; then swiftly kicks the reinforced left leg forward, and lands on it, balances on it, with a jerking of her entire frail form and a terrible, strained, peaceful expression.

The night I arrived in Eastwater she and Pauly took me to see *Arms and the Man*, trashy play that it is and poorly performed. She was ready to depart, in one of her baggy beflowered frocks and a selection of the late Mrs. Abel's precious stones, when a little thunderstorm blew in from the shore. While we waited a few minutes for the violence of this to pass, Miss Ferragut did not think it worthwhile to unlock her leg and sit down; but presently she decided to rest her weight upon the arm of a large pseudo-Chippendale chair, which neither Pauly nor I noticed. The floor was highly varnished and there happened not to be a rug under this chair. Suddenly it flew out from under, hurling her in a little heap, down between the legs of an adjacent pseudo-Chippendale table. I gathered her in my arms and stood her up. She had no idea at first whether or not another of her rare bones was broken. None was, in fact, and it did not even cause her much pain; but she was painfully angry at herself.

In due time the thunderstorm abated, and the three of us in a flutter, as if we had been just slightly struck by lightning without any injury, got into the car and arrived at the stylish little playhouse and got out, and slowly worked our way in amid the assembled summer neighbors, down to the fauteuil on the aisle reserved for Miss Ferragut because of its accessibility. There with refined stealth she began to feel around in her rear ruffles for the button which would enable her to bend and be seated. But, well-meaning and slyly helpful, her brother without warning came up behind her unexpectedly and pushed the fauteuil down for her, which struck her into a sort of seated position, with a worse flounce and gasp than ever. The rubbery leg lay under the row of seats in front of her, which was all right; but the nickel-plated leg struck out in the aisle almost at a right angle to it, unbendable, and seemingly irretrievable, for she was sitting on the button. She would have to stand up again to get at it. For years she had not even tried to stand up on the rubber leg; and how could she get out in the aisle where the other leg lay? Half frantic with her fatigue, her vexation, her fortitude, there she sat, in a hush which was (I said to myself) more impressive than any hollering of Valkyrie, more mournful than any cry of whippoorwill. And beads of sweat appeared on her forehead, to match her string of pearls. Poor

Pauly went down the aisle a way and stood with averted eyes, lest she grimace at him or give an opinion of his bungling solicitude. Then she began twisting from head to foot; tugging at the independent member; straining to reach the button on which she sat, and all in vain. It was a perfect image of the petty individual fussing against great fate, or of the intellect endeavoring to quell a revolt of the subconscious. Meanwhile the theater began to fill up, and many fine friends stopped to say good evening. Accustomed to see those poor legs of hers at the oddest angles and taught by her to take no notice, they were very hard to shoo along out of the way. At last a very fat and tall friend turned her back so as to hide us from a couple of short friends; whereupon I suddenly squatted, braced my toe against the toe of metal, grasped the little encased shin, and gradually shoved it toward her and toward the perpendicular. This enabled her to get it under control and to rise upon it and to let herself fall into place again, normally, but too tired even to gasp or sigh.

At that instant the light died out of the chandelier overhead, and the curtain went up on Shaw's celebrated comedy. How inferior it seemed to the scene of slapstick I had just witnessed—everything underlined, yet less clear in the specification of the nature of courage, which is its subject; all its examples of humanity quite common, yet less revelatory of universal human nature. But alas, I reminded myself, I could not publish any praise of my little old friend, or analysis of her uncommon strength of character, without hurting her feelings badly. She and her kind have no real discrimination; so any attempt to honor her as she deserved would seem to her insult and punishment. Thus in every walk of life, I think, a great deal of our most heroic subject matter is being suppressed or censored—by compassion if not by shame . . . For now as a rule very intelligent men are very kind; and very sensual men, decent; and original men, inactive. The more violent our collective society grows, the less willing the worthy individual is to war against it with any scandalous or sharp weapon. Think of the filial reticence of Forster, the conjugal reticence of Gide, the patriotic reticence of Lawrence of Arabia! *Noblesse oblige* may be the doom of this civilization, at least of the literature of this age.

One night during the Munich crisis, I dined with the playwright Russel Crouse and his wife. She was a newspaperwoman in her youth, well informed about international matters, idealistic; a little rosy person with a neat face and hands always a-flutter. Naturally there was talk of the terms upon which Chamberlain secured what he entitled peace-in-our-time. "Oh dear," said Mrs. Crouse, "oh dear, it's got to come sooner or later. We'll have to fight. The suspense is terrible. They've only post-poned it."

I remarked that even postponement seemed to me much better than war at once.

"But, heavens," she cried, "it couldn't be worse than this waiting and waiting. I remember the world war, perhaps you don't. The suspense, the suspense! It makes us all so nervous, we can't do a thing. You know, it's like listening to the man in the flat upstairs getting undressed, and he drops one shoe—it's like waiting for him to drop the other shoe!"

On the whole, to be a writer these days feels like an atavism or mania or hobby. I have had a little of the privilege of fraternizing with, that is, of filializing at the feet of, Thomas Mann. But he is much more political than literary now; preoccupied with his exile as Victor Hugo never was. A great man, yes, but not a great brain; I keep wishing I could lend him some of mine, as I surely am not in a position to need it all. And at a certain distance the bark of Frau Mann sounds like Hitler's. The indomitable German outcry, which for years was a great painful solo, now a great horrible duet . . . She wants an expeditionary force organized at once, to dethrone that bluffer, that robber, that lunatic; and incidentally to restore to her the second-best set of real linen sheets, which the washwoman had when she left, and great-aunt's silver candle-sticks, which stood on the mantelpiece in the guest bedroom . . .

I suppose that keeping a diary would be unwholesome were it not for the thought of the eventual reader. A certain concern with clarity and the willingness to simplify also follow upon that thought. In my old notebooks I find that whatever I have set down just for my benefit has become tedious even to me; sometimes I cannot figure out what I meant. But the shadow of an unknown future person over one's shoulder may put one too much upon one's honor in some way. The thing is never to forget him, but never be unwilling to run the risk of disappointing or disgusting him. Now an unpleasant little fact, as also a difficult idea or a seemingly inexpressible emotion, has a particular attraction for me. Literary skill, as I am inclined to think of it, as I most enjoy it, has to do with the adroit handling of such difficulty, in detail after detail. But of course I am nonetheless subject to self-consciousness: if not shame, at least an anxious elegance, a longing to rise above the petty or pitiful level of myself. But I must not rise too high. For introspection of the secret shameful order, and with real reference to the commonplaces which cause it, is most important in a text of this kind.

1 9 3 9

*For alcohol is a god, as the Greeks decided when
it was first introduced from the East, although a
god of vengeance.*
—The Pilgrim Hawk

I remember my emotion a good many years ago in the Kronprinz-
enpalais in Berlin when I first saw the great Kröller-Müller collection
of Van Goghs arranged in chronological order. In room after room, all
was dingy, moody, amateurish, with a little political or sociological by-
play; the immature Dutchman holding himself back, postponing his
lifework, and somewhat stingily preserving, you might say, his pictorial
virginity—until the room in which his first attempts at Impressionism
hung, the work of the year he went to live with his brother in Paris. It
was an old story, but a very thrilling and freshly instructive thing to
see. I could see just when and where the Muse of painting had arrived
on the scene, to take possession of her man. I even fancied that she
was there still, in widow's weeds, boasting as widows boast, of what she
had done to him and to art thereafter.

But I cannot really love the art of Van Gogh; I am too American,
that is, a believer in good fortune and good temper and good looks; a
lover of the calm and definite kind of form set apart somehow in brilliant
uncluttered space; a lover of the deliberate pose, the steady brush, the
third (not the fourth) dimension. That, roughly speaking, always has
been the style of our American painting when it has been very good:
the farm pictures of Homer, before he began splashing watercolor about
like Sargent; the scenes of shooting and sculling by Eakins which have
a background of dewy field or geometrically rippled water. You can
always tell that we are a people very empiric and sportive, not overeducated and not really religious, not maniacal, not even logical; and
that our continent is not narrow, our atmosphere not opalescent or shadowy. Even our "primitives," and odds and ends not consciously artistic,
have it: a certain insolent or childish simplicity, very neat, very spacious,

almost vacuous; a little look of constant sensuality without much moral trend one way or the other. Even the aquatints of old Audubon, intended to be merely informative of the native birdlife, seem now emblematic of what kind of native art we are apt to have, if any.

Half the time it appears that we are most apt to have not any. Who can write of American painting without a note of hellfire and jeremiad? Think how much artwork we import! Think of the selection we exhibited in Paris last year! Evidently our idea was to conciliate the French as much as possible by showing how humbly we have gone to school to them; and in the mood of conceited schoolmaster thereby induced, of course they gave us a good critical spanking. Think what prices a few exceptional American artists fetch! Impressive American pictures as rarely come into the market as Gothic sculpture or Coptic cloth; and it is their rarity rather than their excellence which counts. All this is enough to make one picket the art schools, and go in for wallpaper or photography, and pine away with repressed patriotism. It is a bad state of mind, particularly bad for those who have some creative aptitude or purpose. The less art there has been, the less likelihood of any: so it has gone, in a vicious circle.

January 28

I bought a newspaper to read on top of the Fifth Avenue bus, and therein came upon the news of the death of Yeats, and to my astonishment experienced an auditory illusion: two or three claps of thunder, not loud, at a distance, but awe-inspiring on that bright winter day.

February 8

Auden is in N.Y. and dined here last night, very energetic and amiable—he greatly resembles Vachel Lindsay!

March 3

Monroe is a man with, as it were, a good deal of nothing about him; a creature decidedly *not* this and *not* that, but of great mysterious significance and adjunctive effect; a sort of cipher.

I do not mean to say that Tom, Dick, and Harry think nothing of him or underestimate him; oh no. Upon casual acquaintance and in worldly contact they usually hold a more generous opinion of his talents and traits of character than those who know him best, those who love him. Chief of the latter, I always have to quibble over point after point; yet on the whole he is the most extraordinary man I have encountered. How strange a mixture of strength and weakness; and what strength

apparently based on weakness. He is not at all unselfish, though un-
ambitious and tireless in others' service. He gives a poor account of
himself, by word of mouth; eloquent, but with a tendency to misstatement, loose enthusiasm, or unjust disdain. I cannot call him very intelligent, for he is unrealistic in retrospect, and never looks very far
ahead in any visionary sense. An eager listener and quick understander,
even in this receptivity of intellect he tires easily, he turns apathetic,
or restlessly changes the subject. His culture is not only conventional
but indolent and inexact.

In fact, let us say, he is a man of heart rather than head. But here
again we come upon discrepancies, mysteries. Even his loyalty is somewhat circumstantial. If a discord or a dispute arises between you and
some lesser friend—and if he is sure of your devotion, and at the time
you happen not to need his championship badly—he never hesitates to
side against you, keeping the balance of power. As I have been most
dependable and worshipful, I have been much sinned against in this
way; and occasionally it has been bitter. His greater or less friendship
depends upon how you fit into his egocentric idealism and various proud
scheming; and those who fit in nowhere do not count. There is also
something that might be called political in his sense of justice; his
judgments are always according to his pride, his affiliation, and his
interest; and those who do not promptly appreciate him he soon dislikes
or forgets.

As I have suggested above, he esteems works of art above all.
Evidently he himself has no artistic talent of any kind. Also he does not
discriminate between this work and that work as he ought. Art with a
capital A is his preoccupation, and especially what, without talent, he
can do about it or have to do with it. Almost everyone's talent or taste
is somewhat corrupted by personal contact with an artist; but in his
case, the yielding is especially quick and shameless. All his appreciation
is a kind of advertisement; and his own sales resistance to whatever he
happens to say himself is nil. Furthermore, in practice, in his little daily
decisions and actions, his sense of relative values, with Art at the top,
does not hold up as it should. For he lives in an excitement and a
confusion. His intense worldly curiosity, and his interest in wealth and
power and in ripe old age, cause him to waste time, to be promiscuous
of his energy, and to seem frivolous or unfaithful occasionally. He never
forgets his principle; he never loses sight of the wood, but he keeps
seeing the trees one by one; and the momentary tree overexcites him.

In every sort of relationship he is at first as ardent and flattering
as if it were love and he the lover; but his pride appears little by little,
and casts the opposite spell; in the long run he always becomes the

beloved—beloved or nothing! Perhaps he really has an insufficient sense of his own ego, and therefore suffers a kind of alienation unless he can see himself mirrored in others' eyes. Or perhaps he feels a certain deadness or coldness in life itself, and therefore must keep warming himself where he can; and certainly the various hearths of others' appreciation of him always have been convenient. I think his choice of friends as a rule has been according to their good opinion of him rather than his opinion of them; that is to say, they have chosen him.

As I say, he is a cipher: the point of my joke is to be found in the dictionary: *Arithmetical symbol (0) of no value in itself but multiplying number it is placed after.* The character of his friendships is a little miscellaneous, as it depends upon the merit and the aim in life of those who have happened to be attracted to him; and his intellectual interests and worldly ambitions also seem to have come up by accident. In any case, he immediately intensifies, he exaggerates, he amplifies, he multiplies by ten, whomever or whatever it is. If you are a low number, a 2 or a 3, he will make 20 or 30 of you; but if you fortunately are 9 in some way, the combination with him is the way to become 90. His happening to meet me when we were young, and my happening to have a little knowledge and talent for literature, in which he saw a correspondence to his love of art and a compensation for his lack of talent and an opportunity for us both to get on in the world—this gave his life the shape it has had.

March 23

Lloyd and Barbara returned from England on the *Queen Mary* this morning, and their talk was as usual: bitter dislike of stepmother, passion for the Suffolk horse, intense affection for us all *grosso modo*. And France is full of black soldiers, even the villages; and the sky over Suffolk is black with planes, mysterious with (one hopes) anti-bomber inventions . . .

Louis MacNeice* also arrived this a.m.; I caught a glimpse of him on the pier; beauteous Celt, with bluish-black hair and delicate beak. I am working with a certain peace of mind at least about the work itself, page by page. I wrote two great hunks of fictionesque autobiography, reminiscent of *recherche du temps perdu mais à peine passé*, strict tough naked stuff no doubt unprintable.

What has New York amounted to this past winter, goodness knows. Lowbrow on the whole. Except for Auden and Isherwood; they raise the

---

* Louis MacNeice (1907–63). Irish poet and man of letters, friend of W. H. Auden.

tone, but I'm afraid my tone as they have raised it has bored them just a bit; they do see a great deal more of Lincoln* than of me. George is about to begin a tapestry to cover the Louis XIII daybed in the Dutch oven room: ten years' work; a design by Jared French, Adam and Eve amid rumpled bedclothes and a good deal of mattress ticking showing— and he expects me to read to him all the time he stitches it. Which reminds me, one major cultural experience: a complete reading and practically an adoration of Forster.

April 3

My grudge arose from Nelson's† saying that "homosexual men have no guts" and our interchange of remarks after that. As for myself, I do not know whether or not I have "guts." It does sometimes seem to me that I have not; not enough. Anyway I understand that Nelson did not mean to impeach my morality. And as I talked back, I thought of half a dozen homosexual men who are dear old friends of mine who have what I regard as the highest and strongest manly character—not to mention the dean of English literature; and the greatest living French writer; and (they tell me) Sibelius; and the late Lord Kitchener, etc.

Stone-blossom
April 30

Out of a den in the side of a hill, Father has dug seven young foxes about the size of cats. They are of the red breed, but haven't turned red yet; rather a dirty blond, like schoolboys' camel's-hair overcoats. Very mild and at ease they seem, pretending not to be afraid: foxy.

Father keeps them in chicken crates in the granary, enjoying the problems they raise, and never deciding whether to turn them over to the game warden to be killed for a bounty, or to sell them to some fox hunt in another state, or to keep them until they amount to a fine fur jacket for Mother, or simply to set them free! Everything of this kind is a game for him.

In the den, there were innumerable bits of hen and pheasant and rabbit; it is going to be expensive to feed them, and Father cheerfully complains of this, too.

* * *

* Lincoln Kirstein (1907–   ). Poet and patron of the arts, who founded *Hound and Horn* in the early thirties (to which G.W. contributed an essay on Henry James) and financed George Balanchine's succession of ballet companies. Husband of Paul Cadmus's sister, Fidelma.

† Henry Nelson Lansdale (1915[?]–64). Dedicatee of *The Pilgrim Hawk*. An art and music critic and, for about two years, an intimate of G.W.'s.

I have a brook and a small old outbuilding of stone in which generations of farmwomen have done their washing in the brook water.

The previous resident here was a poor solitary woman, who could not take proper care of things. Upon our arrival this washhouse, for example, was full of malodorous mud and, embedded in it, a dead hen and a dead rat and other unpleasantness. My resourceful brother altered the course of the brook to flow through it for twenty-four hours; and this constituted the first charm of the place for me, corresponding as it did to the fifth labor of Hercules, the cleaning of the stables of the farmer-king Augeas.

June 27

As for amorous matters in general: Credo: Love-plus-lust is divine; and if one is lucky, it constitutes the central section of one's experience. The rest is marginal, before and after; but it does not follow that it is necessarily ignoble. Love-minus-lust is the noblest part of mature human behavior. Lust also may be a good thing, and some people can't keep in good health and good spirits without it. It is a food; it is an exercise; it is a sunbath—and it may or may not be a waste of time; that depends on one's temperament and management and good luck or bad luck.

This week I stayed on at Stone-blossom by myself Monday and Tuesday. I love it so, even when it signifies family fuss more than anything else; even when it makes me all emotional and fidgety, as Wisconsin did in my boyhood. Now there are thirty young eunuchs of the Hereford breed in the big meadow across the road; they are blood-red, and they graze with a dreamy, rolling sort of rhythm, all crowded together. All Monday it rained a fine spray, which varnished the picture wonderfully. There are no flowers that I like in George's garden now, only some small, formless, watercolorish things; but the lilies are swelling. So far we have turned out six nestfuls of birds on the lawn: two of robin, one of oriole, one of a yellowish warbler, one of wren, and one of I don't know what, in a little cavity toward the top of the crab apple; and there are swallows' eggs in the garage. The orioles made almost as much noise as human babies; and just before they flew, a fool tribe of tent caterpillars encamped in their bough, enfolding the lower part of their nest; and they hung off the edge and gobbled some.

I am often tempted to try to earn a living by other efforts than mothering and brothering and in-lawing and talking and cooking and playing poker. But how silly! I will not write for pay; and everything else would be from frying pan into fire; and I couldn't reside in Mother Hubbard's shoe if I had to work; and probably I should die of love if I left my two loves. That's all; it's enough.

I have been wondering about a new thing that has developed along our brook: tall, gracile, and earnest-looking, with a very odd odor. Now it seems to me that it may be one of the frightful hemlocks, not the tree but the killer—"Hemlock is the shortcut to Hades" (Aristophanes); that one. There is "a mousy reek" that is supposed to warn one; was what I smelled mousy? It starts by a coldness of the head . . . Or it may be something that I translate as "the hedge vomitmav."

But even impressionistic landscape is better when the painter has learned to draw. A neglect of drawing seems to me as unfortunate for the pictorial art as a lack of candor in literature . . .

Just now Surrealism is very much the fad. I remember how Dalí, hanging on to a fur-lined bathrobe, leapt or fell through Bonwit Teller's window. The result was that his exhibition was crowded for weeks, and for the first time he sold all his pictures. Eight or nine out of every ten persons in that crowd surely thought that Bonwit Teller performance very cheap and false. But six or seven out of ten would not have come to the exhibition at all if there had been no performance. We hate cheap publicity—we also hate alarm clocks, but they wake us up . . .

Now Dalí has a sideshow at the World's Fair; and the personal history of it, behind the scenes, is more fantastic than the rubber piano and the underwater burlesque queens. Edward James is financing and managing it; and our little Ruth Ford,* to whom he has proposed marriage nine times, is acting in it, and her mother as well. Charles Ford† and Pavlik are in Paris; and Ruth's play fell through; and they have been literally hungry for several months. So they were not in a position to refuse to play Edward's little game, though of course they are of Pavlik's persuasion in matters of art, not Dalí's. The sideshow has a great crazy plaster façade with a dragon coiled all over it; and dear Mrs. Ford sits up in the midst of that as the head of the dragon, which is fed three times a day.

I have suggested to George that the next time an interview is required of him, he might pose as a much misunderstood, unmodern, even

---

* Ruth Ford. Actress for whom William Faulkner wrote the play *Requiem for a Nun*.

† Charles Henri Ford (1913–   ). Poet, lover of Tchelitchew, and coauthor, with Parker Tyler, of the 1933 novel *The Young and Evil*.

stuffy character, chiefly interested in boxer puppies and tulip bulbs. Thus a reputation is built up, zigzag.

A hex on my letters.
This one I addressed
"Place de la Concorde New York N.Y."
So it came back.

July 13

The drought abated somewhat this weekend, with a little tropical drizzle now and then; and now it's hot again, hot still. The lawn is plush once more; and we're both improving at croquet. When we arrived, Thursday night, we took the flashlight to see how the lilies were doing, and what increase of water there was in the brook; and lo, right on the verge of the dam sat a great fascinated bullfrog.

The tiger lilies themselves are a triumph. The Japanese beetles did not touch them, having chauvinistically eaten the Japanese lily buds to the right and left; *tigrinum* is Chinese. Those we brought in a week ago are still presentable, having adorned the garden almost two weeks before being cut. The leaves wither and stink, but they go on blossoming to the last bud. We brought in another armful last night, shoulder-high in the vase. Ideal for our purposes, except that they are hard work: you need an ax to freshen the stems; you can scarcely get the vaseful through a doorway; the pollen daubs you like an Indian and stains the sink so that it has to be scrubbed with Dutch Cleanser. I've just done all this.

July 19

It's been a hell of a week. First, Monroe's departure, in a grand atmosphere of recalcitrant dry cleaners and lost wristwatches and in-synchronous palpitations. Second, the semiannual family crisis, with my mother in tears, my sister in a temper, my brother in a dumb melancholy. Third, a financial crisis: I have had to open a bank account of my own, how I hate banks, and this bank won't give me a cent until it has sat down and written pompous letters to the oddest people inquiring if my celebrated signature really is by me; so, lo and behold, the great parasite in a pickle! Fourth, my mother came to town and wore me all out at the World's Fair Monday. She is an indestructible witch, made of India rubber; all charm and loquacity and good cheer all day yesterday; and we kept going at the fair from noon until nine-thirty . . .

We saw the Masterpieces; and *The Hot Mikado*; and a species of grasshopper that enjoys being petted, and a tarantula like a small, very mangy puppy; and shovelsful of dull diamonds in a crypt by R. Loewy; and an ideal sunset—eight hours of it. Having put her to bed, I joined George and Agnes at the Ruban, to hear Billy Haywood, who has improved, and the best guitarist ever, better than Segovia.

Tuesday night George and I dined with Messrs. Carson and Guy where they are summering, at Sneedens' Landing in Oliver Jennings's hideaway. A little bit of old Ile-de-France: *pierre-de-moulin* adhering to almost perpendicular palisade amid impenetrable thicket, full of damp Breton furniture, amateurish art. Sociability also a bit Ile-de-French, I thought, as we just sat after dinner, tabby-catty and sourpussy, and came home at 10:20.

August 3

Wescott-hypersensibility: We mocked Father for complaining of his health upon the occasion of Mother's departure. He went on, worse and worse; but she bravely went anyway, Tuesday p.m. But before Elizabeth got back from Trenton he was rolling on the floor in unmistakable plain pain, and Lloyd rushed him to the Easton Hospital, where they found an infection of the prostate and bladder and performed a very serious operation that night. They think it quite successful. I shall go there tomorrow morning.

August 15

There is a young Russian named Ury Cabell who looks like enlarged Nijinsky and has a poetical mind, good-for-nothing perhaps, and 'tis pity, etc. I enjoyed seeing him here last winter; but he soon began to resent my being so aware of not having a quite good influence on him. Don't I sound smug? Well, Klaus Mann,* suffering from no such smugness, took him to Hollywood; wherefrom he wrote me a letter yesterday. Incredible place: they all breathe Chartreuse and drink tuberose and eat hearty meals of maxrheinhardt and lie down upon the softest fritzlangs, etc. Even Auden has arrived there now; and there are Aldous H. and Gerald Heard and Geoffrey [Grigson] and our Christopher and John Collier and John Van Druten† and all the other Johns. They'd better all look out. There must be the devil in it, and/or Kundry and/or Dorian Gray . . .

*   *   *

* Klaus Mann (1906–49). Writer, and son of novelist Thomas Mann.
† Aldous Huxley (1894–1963), novelist and poet; Gerald Heard (1889–1971), writer; Geoffrey Grigson, poet; Christopher Isherwood (1904–86), novelist; John Collier (1901–80), poet; and John Van Druten (1901–57), playwright and screenwriter.

At least I *have* found *one* worthwhile book by Maugham—*The Gentleman in the Parlour*—rich with the reward of literary virtue, beautifully written in the hard way, but not, I am amused to observe, ever exactly beautiful. His lack of talent is so basic; it must be in the very cerebral tissue, like ophthalmic migraine. There is something minutely wrong with not only every sentence but every idea, something one is half ashamed of minding, something in the nature of mispunctuation or misspelling. And how often, when he has hit any sort of high spot, he is inspired to say that same thing doggedly over again, but more flatly; and other such tricks, cussed and contrary. The naturally ugly man, having done three hundred and sixty-five daily dozens a year for years and years; or the naturally slovenly women dressed by, oh, certainly not Chanel or Schiap, but let us say Callot Soeurs . . . Yet it is wonderfully good reading, this one, with really fine miniatures, short-short stories; and a kind of arrangement throughout, chapter-sequence, etc., that I might well have studied before beginning my ill-starred *Fear and Trembling.*

Ford Madox Ford* once said that *The Apple of the Eye* was "harrowing" rather than tragic, and explained it in the classic or Aristotelian way. He also pointed out that the Middle West was really an unimportant, uninteresting part of the world *per se*; so therefore . . . I did choose to be edified by both these opinions, but indeed it was poor pickings, slow going. And it was not simply that my art happened not to be the kind of art that he happened to like—I am afraid that, by nature, he was really ungenerous. And he did not have what we today can call "taste," no more than he had what we can consent to in the way of morality. Therefore out of the window more or less his criticism must go . . . Even in his best fiction the main thing is either apologia (hence the long-windedness) or paean of anglophobia. But I did and still do like *Some Do Not* and its sequels; and *The Good Soldier*; and (perhaps) *The Marsden Case*; and (as I remember) *Joseph Conrad*, which I take to be a kind of novel.

November

Monroe is right about my self-indulgence, in a way. I would be pathetic, if I couldn't, and weren't supposed to, and didn't wish to, be a writer. On the other hand, if I weren't a writer, I shouldn't have any trouble. So it seems.

* * *

* Ford Madox Ford (1873–1939). The British novelist and man of letters was an early influence on G.W.

George brought our huge white puppy to town last night. I myself, *boeuf d'amour*, now view it somewhat resentfully, which, I think, I hope, no one notices. But in truth the only laboriousness which really interferes with my literary labor is that within me, in consequence of my emotional instability and extreme awareness of others' emotions. Having puppy will cheer George for a while and thus lighten my life in that respect. Last night at half past one I found the hallway turned to latrine from end to end, and I scrubbed it on hands and knees. Monroe arose sniffing, and sniffed nothing, and therefore expressed a slight benevolence toward it. Its name is Peter.

A Georgia dish of cornmeal and fish is called "hushpuppy." In the Southwest, "jerky" and "sowbelly" . . .
Harlem song:

> *What did I do*
> *To be so black and blue?*

In a study of the superstitions of 11,000 high-school seniors, college freshmen, and adults, Dr. H. F. Kilander found that nearly a third of the first two groups believed that illness of the eye may result from wearing rubbers indoors; 13 percent of the adults are of this opinion also. One out of twenty said that excessive thinking causes baldness.

I have grown very skeptical of psychoanalysis and all that. In fact, in the way of healing or making happy, it must be that I am skeptical of everything except love and work. By love I must mean LOVE, but by work I mean what almost anybody can do. It must be that I believe that, in the psyche, always, there is a great deal of essential evil, essential and natural and incurable. The thing to do is to distract one's attention from it. Love and work are distractions.

As I walked down Madison Avenue with Herbert Long he asked if I had ever noticed what a certain jeweler displays in his window. I had not, so across the street he led me to have a look. One of those Russian dealers who first went into business to relieve their compatriots of what they had hid about their person when they fled from the Revolution. A dozen trays of miscellany: Muscovite ornaments in sets, lapis and amber, signet rings, bulbous brooches, elderly watch fobs. At first I could discover nothing extraordinary. Two or three other strollers paused beside us, excited by the pointing of Herbert's finger. In a large tray full of tiny charms, all those in the third row from the top were obscene: pigs in intercourse, a monkey masturbating, etc., and two very realistic male sexual organs, gilded. One was hinged, so that it could be made to stand up amid its little golden curls above its nicely wrinkled little scrotum. Later Herbert telephoned to inquire the price of this odd merchandise: ten to fifteen dollars, according to the size and workmanship.

The past is my true love, and the future no doubt must be my bride; and can it be new love or must it be *mariage de convenance*? Either way I make no objection. And in any case the present is my enemy. It and I sit rolling dice all day, every day; and the stakes seem to be high. But because it is a game, or, more exactly, because it is *like* a game, I am inclined to speak of it in the sheepish way or in the mocking style. And perhaps that is worse than not speaking of it at all.

Once upon a time there was a young man named Denham Fouts, who looked like Cléo de Merode and came from Georgia, name and all (there was a "von" in it in those days). He earned a living wrapping up packages for General Foods, Inc. He would call on me—I was living on Murray Hill with Lloyd—whenever he was hungry or felt like asking questions about how to get on in the world, which I would answer, all purely Socratic. The outcome was that in due time he went abroad and became as you might say a *grande cocotte*, which is a rare thing. He got chucked into a Nazi concentration camp, and obscurely escaped, which appealed to people's imaginations. He also went around the world with a royal Greek. He also went around the world with Peter Watson. Perhaps all this might have made me ashamed of my teaching, but it did not. Pure Socratism, I believe, is a type of education that always misses its mark, though it may hit something else, sideways . . . All this is prefatory. Yesterday I got a letter from this young man in London, asking me to contribute and to solicit contributions to a magazine, *Horizon*. Peter Watson is financing it; and it is to be monthly, from December 1 on; and it is to be purely literary. Cyril Connolly is editing it, as he should; and the assistant editor is Stephen Spender; and the associate editor is this young man. I swear, I do believe that it will be a good magazine if possible. But just think of it: the founding in London, England, as of December 1, 1939, of a new literary magazine entitled *Horizon*.

During the ten days we kept George's white boxer puppy, we were able to accomplish, in the matter of housebreaking it, just nothing. At last, without a word of consultation, George gave it away; and he seems to have no regrets. I heaved a sigh of relief, along with other sighs of course. I think this is a sort of parable.

We dined at the Gate Friday night and Saturday night. Of course Jared isn't capable of poker, and indeed we got sleepy or pretended to soon after dinner, which was ungenerous to Barbara, I'm afraid. But she was in her extreme exuberance. We lunched at St.-bl. [Stone-blossom] both days and dined there Saturday, on omelette and endive, on mushrooms and romaine, on bitki and beets, and variety of expensive fruit. I posed for Jared all Saturday p.m., Sunday a.m. and p.m., and again early this a.m.—we came back on the noon train.

Paul and Margaret French washed all the dishes, and went walking. The first time they found a hepatica in bloom, a dwarfed colorless flower upon red leaves. The second time Barbara forcefully joined them, and they put out thirty or forty feet of brushfire up in the hills. The third time they took a bath towel and waded through the Mulhocaway to visit Lloyd's bulls but saw no indecencies. Before and after his working hours Jared was, with infinite sweetness, at what might be called his worst: half Arthur Frank and half Alice in Wonderland. Margaret kept happily blushing and quite silently guffawing, in her way. I happened upon a large package of my early unpublished verse; I had no idea there was so much of it; and she read it hour after hour, Germanly. Perhaps no one else ever will; and it seems to me fine that someone should have formed an opinion of it, especially one so unlikely to give it out. The secret of Midas's ears.

Jared's picture of me is in the new medium, which means a complete delicate grisaille underneath, upon which later the color is put in little dryish dabs, mixed with egg yolk; and it should be from the egg of a city (not a country) hen. It is truthful enough, that is, very explicit as to my concavity and my pregnancy and my genital minginess, but also somewhat flattering, as you might say "powerful," with my legs planted farther apart than I was inclined to plant them, a bit Michelangelesque. He got it ready for the dabs, or very nearly. But now he must finish his picture for the Whitney show, which has a nice daffy title: *Washing the White Blood off Daniel Boone.*

Thanksgiving

What a life, always a little as it were Midsummer's Night. This dull morning, for instance, when I fancied that only Nelson knew I was in town, Margaret sent me a dozen carnations with an extraordinary letter about my juvenile verse and her husband. Flemish-looking carnations, yellow, that yellow that is like a time-stained white . . .

Also Miss Wetmore telephoned. Speaking English of course, but scarcely; English with her most decided dachshund accent. There she was *in medias res* the instant I took up the receiver, the cart already well before the horse, not even deigning to say who she was—that accent serves a useful purpose. For ten minutes she vigorously scolded me for not accepting some invitation which she did not even specify until the ten minutes were up and we were both tired out. Then on the rebound I was asked to *Boris* next Friday night.

Goldwasser, the drink of Danzig, is an orange liqueur flavored with caraway and containing particles of real gold.

1 9 4 0

In order to last a novel must be functional. To be
sure, it must entertain, and it must convince, and
it must thrill somehow; but it must also help.
—"Fiction Writing in a Time of Troubles"

January 7

Stravinsky, in his coarse, schoolmaster manner, is conducting the
Polish Symphony of Tchaikovsky. It is fine blue and brown weather; I
should be taking a healthful walk, with Monroe and George. Instead I
have been remembering Isadora Duncan as I knew her at the end of her
life in the South of France. The very last time I saw her she complained
bitterly of her dissatisfaction with the autobiography she had written,
and she asked me to help her with it. I refused, assuring her that it did
not matter, it would be all right; the less apparent literary art there was
about it the better. She told me that it was the only thing she had ever
done just for money, and she was ashamed, and having spent the money
she could not give it up. It was worse than I knew, she said. Not only
was the style poor and stilted, there was bad grammar in it. There had
been many objections to her dancing, but there had been no bad grammar
in that; and she wept. So I promised to come on the next Wednesday
or Thursday to have a look. But when that day came she was dead, in
the strangest automobile accident I ever heard of. With her friend Marie
Desti and our friend Monroe Wheeler I sat up all night beside her glorious
beheaded body in a kind of wake. I think Mrs. Desti was Irish. Half
the night she told us tales of Isadora's great days; and sometimes she
keened, like the bereaved heroines of the plays of John Millington Synge
. . . There was also an American woman whose name I have forgotten,
who went to the garage where the fatal automobile was and bought a bit
of the fringe of the shawl Isadora was wearing, and thrust it inside her
dress and hastened to Monte Carlo to gamble, thinking it would bring
her luck.

February 7

The town seemed very literary last night, which amused me: the Manns were in Lloyd and Barbara's car, very very *boche*, I'm sorry to say; and in the midst of Times Square I saw the Colums, Padraic* with his look of a quack, poor man, and Molly pounding the pavement with her large legs . . . George was dining at home, with Fred Herrick, and as I felt dreary, I walked for a long time in the wet night and crept into my bedroom unnoticed. But Fred, it appears, did nothing but complain of his troubles: vicissitudes of the theater, and should he or should he not marry a pupil of Ouspenskaya's,† would that or would that not be good for his acting, etc. As George remarked later, "After all, I have been complained to by experts . . ."

I think a great deal about my writing, I reread my old mss, and make notes. Certainly I used to talk my books to death; but now I am sure that I have been going to the other extreme, hushing them to death. *The Dream of Mrs. Cleveland* is extraordinary stuff, very exciting. But the trouble is that it is two books—and I never really got to the one which the title covers; I kept floundering in what went before—the previous history of the Clevelands, the Dorsets, the Dergoes, all those deathbeds of millionaires; necrological history of the nineteenth century in the U.S.A.

My checkbook prompts me or reprompts me however to rewrite the story of *The Pilgrim Hawk* for George Davis‡—but indeed I do not trust him to take it.

What a difference between Brahms's Fourth and the other three. The First is a crusade, or even (to bring it up to date) an invasion. This is rather a kind of bacchanal. How the stag-like basses shake their violin-antlers: I'll show you the several places. And the woodwinds crying concupiscence, or crying absence . . .

Poor Wagner: his bacchanal makes such a fuss, and in fancy dress; the protagonists (I feel) all so little, with little sex; only their pining and outbreaking sense of sin, and blasphemy for fun. Whereas the music of Brahms generally, and in this Fourth especially, is as plump as flesh, and as clean as flesh can be. And above all (I think) Wagner intended to express insatiability, and very proud he was to have that to express, furthermore. And what the hell is insatiability after all: just failure to be satisfied. "What the hell is scientific sex . . ."

---

* Padraic Colum (1881–1972). Irish-American man of letters.
† Maria Ouspenskaya (1876–1949). Actress.
‡ George Davis. Literary editor of *Harper's Bazaar*.

February 20

I have never written Monroe so little during any of his absences. But as I have just come from a good performance of *Figaro* I should remind him that he has always been the Mozartian one; that I have loved him without question or artificiality or tedium all these years. For it seems that our life together began with performances of Mozart, which is not fact, yet . . .

I asked George—not altogether playfully—what I should do; which of five jobs new and old to concentrate on. George with his good practical vision said *The Pilgrim Hawk*—and it seems workable.

From a letter to W. H. Auden

Let me apologize for not having even thanked you for the loan of the ms. of "The Prolific and the Devourer"—which I reread with a various interest, amusement, astonishment, edification, emotion, *et seq*. In fact I forbade myself to write you about it. There was so much to say, and none of it to be casually said; it would have taken a whole day or two or three.

I have just received *Another Time*. As you know I have delighted in many of these poems all winter, and now begin the rest—poetry gives such a long pleasure. (May I protest against the non-appearance of "Ganymede"? . . .)

This bit of comic literary history, from Sam Barber*: Mrs. Yeats will not consent to anything until she has had an occult message from her husband, and it takes months. Therefore Macmillan's haven't been able to publish his last poems. Also she insists on being paid twopence on each copy of his works, BUT she does not wish to be paid at all for every seventh copy, which of course maddens the bookkeepers. Sam has written magic to a certain poem, and Schirmer's have been waiting months for the great man to knock right.

Leap Year's Day

Thanks to Mozart, I did more work on the hawk story than I have been able to do at one sitting for a long time. By evening I knew that I had had enough for one day; and Auden and Chester Kallman† came to dinner, a dinner of roast pork as it happened. It was George who had been urging me to ask them; but of course that did not mean that I could

---

* Samuel Barber (1910–81). American composer.
† Chester Kallman (1921–75). Poet and beloved of Auden.

sit back and take it easy; and anyway I guess it makes me nervous to
be with my literary confreres when they are steamed up . . . So I vomited
a good deal during that night; and all day yesterday I had a splitting
headache. Last night we dined alone, and I began to read aloud
S. Benson's *Tobit Transplanted*. (It won't do; it is too precious, etc.—
in all those books delectable in the twenties and disappointing now, I
observe particularly one common trait: remarkable epithets that as you
might say "jump" or jerk in the sentence, distracting you from the
cumulative effect which must be a novel's greatest effect; an extraor-
dinariness of expression which makes the characters seem as odd as the
writer, and therefore obscure, so long as the life story of the writer is
left out; and excess of images, just for fun . . .) This morning I feel
better, still sore all through, but uncongested in my upper story—I think
it was, and still somewhat is, my liver.

This morning I turned away from peregrine hawk and my peregrine
people, and read the first section of my journal a long while, 1937, and
removed some poor stuff. What a pathetic thing subjectivity is, for a
mind like mine. You'd think I should have known better. But still, with
the inevitable polishing up, there will be a little text to keep. It made
me terribly sad, but proud of the great love I have been given, through
thick and thin, turgid and limpid. Like music in due time leading me
again out of swamp . . .

Paul Cadmus came back to the flat with me, but he was so worn
out and impassioned and self-conscious that I was glad to send him
home soon. He has been bewitched, really bewitched, by a new young
man who he says is exactly like Stephen in *The Longest Journey* [Forster]:
characteristic of him to find a precedent in art instantly, and to be rather
inflamed than sobered by it.

Figaro again, as fine and festive as could be. A somewhat better,
that is smoother, performance; good enough; the best, and perhaps the
most successful, thing they've done this year. Even Ezio Pinza was able
to sing at least one big aria with no help from the prompter . . . Nelson,
with my expert whispering about the plot, delighted in it; and he was
so proud of himself therefore that it practically exorcised his usual
tiresome devil. George had had practically nothing to eat and somewhat
too much to drink, and came home loud, grandiosely fond, absurdly
lovable. We hobnobbed with Paul and the Frenches all sweetly cooing,
a dovecot in tweeds. And with Paul, we followed Mrs. Geo. Washington

Kavanagh around—the reconstruction of her face really is interesting at close range.

And it was not *Deh! vieni*, although little Bidú [Sayāo] sang it more nearly in Schumann's way than I would believe possible; it was not *Dove sono* although for note after note Rethberg sounded youthful in it, and in her youth I suppose her voice was the most beautiful in the world; it was not *Or via sortite*, more beautiful than any string quartet, and (I think) the human voice is more moving than any string—no, it was *Pace, pace; Friede, Friede* as always, and *Perdono! più docile io sono*, love on its knees asking forgiveness for its misunderstanding and for its impotence, that brought the tears to my eyes . . .

March 4

That handsome Mrs. Ekstrom* whom Monroe met in the Orient has very ardently welcomed me to the ballet competition. Her first name is Parmenia!

George and I were alone at St.-bl., and the weather was fit only for the fireside, rain and sleet and pools amid the snow, bluish pattern all over the yellowish grasses like Pavlik's picture: the one with the tiger face which is also a likeness of Pavlik's father. We read Richard Hughes's *In Hazard*, beautifully written in the virile straight way that so pleases me now; but there is somewhat too much mechanism of the ship and the hurricane; not enough personages, not enough dreams. The dreams were splendid in *A High Wind in Jamaica*.

March 17

Here I sit by the fire, on sunny Palm Sunday—alone listening to the Emperor Concerto, Monroe's concerto. I should hate not being alone.

I feel that I never saw such a wealth of the immortal things as that represented around me, on the putty-colored bearded sofa. I have Yeats's *Last Poems*, which George gave me for farewell. The Roman kind of courage while dying which I think the Romans themselves never expressed at all: lust, and scorn of whoever appeared to have been his enemy, gay and versified to perfection.

I also keep rereading Stephen [Spender]'s journal: None of us of today has done anything better. It is wise enough, though very personal, and it is exciting. As it is a journal, it marks a kind of defeat for me; but I don't mind. For mine has been, I conclude, a lesson rather than a production. But who am I to quarrel with the Teacher? And if I produce

* Parmenia Ekstrom. Earliest biographer of Isak Dinesen.

something else, will anyone care what it has cost? This is odd; for example: I do believe that by writing so much in the first person, I have learned to write dialogue.

Nelson has had to take to his bed with poor digestion. He says it is caused by excess of orange juice; I say, beer on top of Barbara's Calvados. But it may in fact be the bug everyone has been undone by.

An odd weekend anyway. Friday evening we dined with Barbara alone—Lloyd had to attend some county-fair politics in Trenton. Though she is having the curse, she was in lovely form. Nelson aroused her to a great outburst against journalism; and it's the only time I've known indignation to improve her style. Subtle as a snake, kind, vengeful . . .

I wept during the Emperor Concerto—time in its flight, and love, and Monroe's absence, and my interminable industrious failure; also the tedium of so much that seems requisite to my ordinary welfare . . .

I have just read Maurice Baring's *Darby and Joan*, very odd. Perhaps I'll try reading something by him to George, *The Passing Show*, or "*O.*" Unable to think of anything else I began Trollope's Barchester novels. George enjoys them, but I am afraid I won't be able to bear their prolixity: fifteen volumes. Baring is not unlike that, but cut to the bone.

I don't think I'll risk sending Monroe a portion of *The Pilgrim Hawk*. For one thing, I am trying to draft it all the way through, or almost, before stopping to refine it. I think there won't be much fine writing anyway; I am striving for simplicity and reticence. Also, if it turns out as I hope, it should not "interest" any of *us* very much; that is, I am portraying Rambouillet and Barbara and those Irish very much as they would have appeared to an outsider. Influence of Maugham? I may be riding for a fine and indeed a funny fall; or I may be becoming a storyteller.

April 4

Last night's banquet, the bemedaling of Katherine Anne Porter, couldn't have been more boring while it went on; it couldn't be more amusing to recollect and interpret. As Maurice Baring wrote on the first page of his autobiography, "Memory is the great artist." (I am sorry to say that on the whole that book does not illustrate the point very well . . .)

"Even when I was a small child," said Porter, "I knew that youth was not for me." The sense of this, I think, is important; her lifelong mild foreboding and great patience from start to finish. Also the sentence as such is characteristic: the vague speedy first phrase, and little or no middle, and the coming to the point or the end with a kind of little swoop and bump. Any sketch of her character or account of her life would have to start with or start from statements of her own about herself like this. I at least, after a good many years of friendship, never feel that I can estimate her altogether from my own point of view, from the outside, irrespective of her self-opinion. What she thinks is wonderfully combined with what she is.

Insofar as she and I are wits, it is not at all in the same way. For example, when someone mentioned Pearl Buck, Katherine Anne said, "Oh, poor Pearl Buck! She has no more bounce than a baked potato." How different from my own workmanlike wounding style; tattooing all over the surface of my subject with, I'm afraid, a somewhat smug air of undoubtedly doing good.

We talk a great deal of our literary art of course, each of us laudatory of the other and self-critical. It is not that we are inclined to esteem other writers more highly than ourselves, except the few great old men. A careless listener might think us conceited. Yet she often seems to need definite praise to cheer her up; and she seems to think that I need it. Perhaps I do, in the last analysis. But when there is definitely question of that, I cannot give it to myself much, or accept it from others without quibbling. Certainly most contemporary writing is merely synthetic, re-hashed, canned stuff, easy to digest but not nourishing. We at least take our subject matter fresh from our experience; thus, and in some other ways, we are entitled to feel superior.

But so far, you might add, Katherine Anne has become just the best biscuit-maker in the country. And I am just an expert on sauces, various and suitable and subtle sauces, and a side dish or two. Neither of us has really undertaken the *pièces de résistance*.

Here is another example of her style; naturally it delighted me. "You remain, after all, the councilor of virtue." I had been somewhat apologizing for my sharp criticisms of my dearest friends. "If possible, you are going to smack them into goodness."

April 5

I dreaded telephoning Marianne* so I wrote her a letter, very painstaking and self-conscious (I suppose she never gets a not-self-conscious letter?)—and asked her to telephone me. Which she did this morning, in her usual high and long and not straight vein . . . Her

---

* Marianne Moore (1887–1972). The renowned American poet befriended G.W. and M.W. in Greenwich Village in the early twenties.

mother has had shingles, but seems better; and as her mother, sitting there beside the telephone, insisted on my being told, they have great confidence in their doctors. "And we feel that we must remember," said Marianne, "that one does often *outgrow* such ailments." She has been writing, but her confidence in herself is much shaken by the fact that both *The Atlantic* and *The New Yorker* have rejected her offerings; on the other hand, the *Kenyon Review* has written very encouragingly.

April 9

Spring so far has been as troublesome and histrionic as winter. There have been good days, such as Sunday, when we had summer sunshine and it seemed to be making fun of the fields, which were still sleeping like the dead. But Monday there was dark wind again with an infinite amount of biting water in it.

These last few days, with the increasing wretchedness of Monroe's absence and the invasion of Norway, really have seemed maddening. But I have worked, hacking "Audubon" into shape for the Ballet Guild prize, and it goes fast and I enjoy it. Also my health feels better. Tuesday night I took Porter to the ballet: *Seventh Symphony*, thank heavens, perfect for us two; and after it George bought her a bottle of champagne; and next morning she started home.

My birthday turns out to be practically Nelson's. George photographed him for me, by which I had the grace to be surprised as well as delighted. Meanwhile Paul Cadmus drew him; and George regards the result of that with indignation as a weak piece of flattery. Certainly his pen, always either a little too fond or too hateful, did shrink from that size and asymmetry of nose which is Nelson's most striking feature. In another sense, however, as a moral likeness, it is quite unflattering and interesting, to me. For in the eyes and mouth there is that accursed or haunted expression, and sad and loving and perhaps consequential determination to keep doing better: in every way. The soul of man, which may be a booby trap, I know . . .

April 12

Last night we heard Bernard Herrmann's cantata *Moby Dick*, tremendously touted in advance. He is CBS's staff genius; and let me assure you, he is just one of those frauds. A score for a Walt Disney film without the film. Not even very loud, in spite of the CBS thunderdrum. Of course he is only a kid. Paul tries to make me ashamed of my fit of interest in American composers; but needless to say I am rather proud of it. To hell with Mozart quartets arranged for four hands on an upright piano out of tune, etc. To hell also with Debussy, an entire evening of which by Toscanini I am to hear tomorrow, at NBC. Nelson gave me the Roy Harris Third Symphony recorded by Koussevitzky— he hated it when Toscanini played it, I delighted in it, and was very mean to him about it. I remember Elly's discovery of him years ago in Missouri or somewhere when, as I believe, he still had a milk route or something . . .*

George's photographs of Nelson are brilliant. Flattering him and at the same time showing him up; what a good photographer. Everything there except the Byronic eyes, which he squinted. As to the birthday business, I knew he was going off the deep end but I didn't know how deep: for example, he gave me the two-volume Kenneth Clark *Leonardo* catalogue, ruinous.

Margaret French gave me a reading of my handwriting for my birthday. It seems to me fascinatingly "like" in many ways—but . . . I must ask her whether she fondly piped down about my several terrible weaknesses, or whether they just happen not to appear:

A very emotional writer, who has deliberately cultivated his will. This may account for some odd juxtapositions of qualities:

impulsiveness and caution;
rashness in practical matters, with prudence and circumspection; love of argument and opposition, and tact and diplomacy.

The writing shows consistently strong emotions, combined with sensitiveness and great delicacy of feeling. There is a capacity for devotion and for sacrifice (to a person or an idea?) and constancy, faithfulness, steadfastness, which ties up with perseverance and reliability on the intellectual side. Once launched in error there is a tendency to persist in it. The writing also shows "inflammability," passion, and a desire for strong emotional stimuli. At the same time great goodness, goodwill, kindness, sympathy, altruism, humaneness.

The writer is not very punctual.

---

* Elly Ney (1882–1968). A German pianist who gave successful recitals in Europe and the U.S.

He tends to be stubborn.

He is neat and orderly.

He has considerable self-control.

But above all, this writing shows *Geist* (the dictionary is not very helpful here, with "intellect, spirit, soul"). An essentially contemplative spirit, serious and idealistic, proud and a little melancholy, appears in combination with an objective, very observing mind. It is not at all a scientific mind. Everything, taste, sense of form, "architectural" way of thinking, point toward art; the printed capitals directly to literature. The writing shows great immediacy of ideas and conceits, a ready wit, quick repartee, and intellectual initiative. Also a good memory of impressions. Grasp of essentials. Critical faculty, though not of a sharp or belittling sort. Capacity for abstraction.

Concentration, industry, application.

Keen sense of reality.

Cleverness, adroitness, versatility, knowledge of the world.

Brevity.

Reserve.

Culture, many-sided interests.

Creative push.

Sureness and independence of judgment.

Love of attacking in the field of ideas.

Activity, mobility, aspiration, impatience.

Originality, imagination.

The handwriting shows that the writer has a very just estimate of his own worth, colored by neither false modesty nor conceit.

April 26

It is warm and bright, not sunny; there are shifting translucent clouds and, through them, a soft glare "like that of British friendship," as I told George, who thought it "special." Last week no rain muddied the crocuses, and they look like orchids; and there are four patches of the little violent blue of the scillas. Dalrymple's willow is well tinted.

My new bedroom, which for the obvious reason we now refer to as the Bombay Suite, is half built. The woodshed was to have been just a toolshed with opening outdoors as before, but when I saw what a pretty little room that was, with two windows toward Dalrymple's and the stone house, I made an uproar and claimed it for an office or author's cubbyhole. It will require a little doing over by the carpenter and plumber, and extra expense, but very little.

This week was very sociable. Pavlik's vernissage was crowded with all our set, looking, I felt, especially freakish; and the choice of drawings disappointed me—wash drawings which looked as if they might fade, chiefly of two-faced women and three-legged boys and two-headed calves, in pretentious old frames; painter's work rather than draftsman's, not much of it new, and "sketchy" in the pejorative sense. Only three silverpoints.

Now, an hour of my *Hawk*, though I'm sleepy. It did get a bit out of hand in my head during the "Audubon" interlude; but it will be all right, because it pleases me so much. However I do wonder who else is going to take an interest in such upper-class trouble, bits of drama so delicate, and symbolism so extensive. Compared with the newspapers . . .

June 13

The Pilgrim Hawk is almost all on paper, all but four easy pages; only half of it must still be pounded, pared, pruned, and speeded up. Whatever I do I am afraid it will remain a miniature novel; not a story for anybody's money. If the *Southern Review* can't take it I don't know who will. No matter; it is something; and for myself in general I feel a great turning point within it. Maybe that's why I can't even write Katherine Anne a proper letter praising her to the skies for her Hardy paper: to the skies . . . I love belles lettres, God help me; *plus belles il n'y en a pas eu.* Weight for weight, emotion for emotion, shape for shape, I rate it above all but let us say four of her stories.

When the *Hawk* is in order, I don't know how I'm going to be able to bear her relative proximity without summoning her to town or coming up to her with it in my mouth like a bird dog. (A bird dog with a hawk in its mouth?) I shall be in a kind of mood to call a special meeting of the PEN Club or the like.

June 18–20

Lonely morning.

I sit stubbornly refusing to go downstairs and across the street to see the newspapers. The questions next in order, I suppose, are (a) can the French civilize them, and how long will that take? And (b) shall we have to fight them, when, and how? A practical matter, as I see it. My pacifism has not reversed itself or changed much, I think; though I suppose it must seem so. Or have I never been a pacifist? In any case,

I find I am not afraid of armament, preparedness, or even military service; relatively not afraid . . . It seems to me that a France well armed with the latest gadgets in profusion would have been no more inclined to war than a France poorly armed, as it was. It was pacific because it was well educated and prosperous, as a nation should be.

We spent last evening with a manner of hero: Cecil Beaton. He is here on a month's leave of absence from the Ministry of Information, a month's immensely remunerative contract with an advertising agency; and now he is going back as fast as he can—frightened to death of course, also frightened of not getting there before "it" happens. His imagination about the happening is no greater than you would expect; that is touching too in a way. By the way, he thinks that Auden *et al.* won't ever be able to live down their absence; I wonder . . .

The Pilgrim Hawk is a remarkable thing, if I do say so myself. For aesthetic as well as economic reasons I am trying to shorten it as much as possible. If it were short I might almost be able to sell it to the *Ladies' Home Journal* or what not. But it's the damnedest thing; I can't seem to get it under fifty pages. Harper's might like to make a bit of a book of it, who knows? Everyone would be glad of that except George and me—we want cash, for my new suite at St.-bl.

Olivet College
July 18

A breakdown, so we didn't arrive until 11½, and I preached at 2 for 1¼ hours. I was facile, not elegant; not inspiring, witty; popular. The audience is female, by and large, middle-aged, and dote upon me for my beauty. However I have a victim of male sex, age twenty-one, appearance sixteen, complexion incredible . . . After my speech we went to a pretty lake of warm water and sunned and dipped amid lovely youngsters until dinnertime. After dinner Sherwood Anderson, after that a trip twelve miles in an open car to drink beer. "We" means Porter, the Warrens, John Bishop, and young Donald Elder, very nice Doubleday Doran representative. Dead sleepy now—my big job tomorrow—I'm not scared.

July 21

Friday was a bad day. First, I happened to read two reports of the battle of London which really discouraged me. Then Klaus Mann, that tragic twerp, telephoned me to ask me for an affidavit to get "poor dear old Gide" out of France. I wanted to procure page proofs of *The Pilgrim Hawk* to read in the train, but I couldn't. And I had to bear other little crosses.

Then, last night, for the first time, I noticed the autumn. The over-all odor of it reminded me of Fabergé's Aphrodisia. I sunned myself and read the greatest of the English lyric poets. It blew and rained at twilight.

The awful dependence of middle-aged men upon young men whom they have no respect for, and vice versa. As time goes on, I may not be in a position to speak so proudly; I am now. For the present it is a sort of thing I must not discuss much. Nothing except true and equal love takes the curse off of desire.

Our happiness together is extraordinarily tense, soaring, romantic. It sometimes snaps before it lets down. If we go on past the perfect moment, Nelson's sadness of body, my skepticism and coldness of mind, suddenly develop. Whereupon Nelson drinks some more and we both lose our tempers.

August 20

While George Davis was still arguing with Mrs. Cold Caramel,* the rumor of my *Hawk* got round to the other Harper's, my Harper's, the Brothers not the magazine, namely Eugene Saxton, who began writing me clever little letters: he's a Quaker educated in a Jesuit college. So as soon as the ms. got back I let him have a look—and yesterday he offered to make a book of it alone, immediately, that is for late October or November issue. And in the circumstances—including that fine old circumstance of my having owed them $5,000 for more than ten years— the offer is practically a command. Also—in spite of my embarrassment at treating the *Southern Review* with what must now appear to be cyni- cism, in spite of my momentary desire for a bit of Huey Long's money (I won't get a penny this way)—it suits me to have a book, even a booklet, a manifesto and sample, a curtain-raiser (we hope); it will do me good.

At *Harper's Bazaar*, Mrs. Cold Caramel permitted George Davis to offer me $300, on condition that I would cut one-quarter of it. I'm not awfully conceited about my past perfection as a writer, but I think I may boast that I have never written a story which could be cut as much

* Carmel Snow. A *Harper's Bazaar* editor who, that same year, also wanted to edit a Katherine Anne Porter long story to half its length. Porter withdrew "The Leaning Tower."

as a quarter and still live. Anyway, past perfection be damned; my present aesthetic is, for one thing, never to cut, to spin and spin and yarn and yarn like an old woman, etc., or something of that sort.

I am a beehive, a hornets' nest, almost a mare's nest. John Martin says "Audubon" is not an American subject; and I have had to correct two separate sets of proof; and also Harper's make me write and rewrite and dewrite my own advertisements; but my new photographs are positively transubstantiational. Etc. Meanwhile my room is such a muddle that I make notes on my underwear and send my mss. to the laundry.

September 17

John Peale Bishop* on A. E. Housman: this type of personal, psychological study of an elder poet very much needs doing, I think—if only so that one can dismiss his humanity and go on to discuss his versification and his philosophy, with the air cleared. The impersonal kind of criticism—while style in a mystification about the poet's biography, or irritated by his personality—is likely to limp and muddle a bit. I wish everyone could forgive Housman for what he was, and study him with a new enthusiasm; for, as it seems to me, he was almost sublime as a versifier; and a good many of our best poets versify poorly a good deal of the time—Stephen [Spender] for one. It doesn't matter about Wystan [Auden], perhaps. I think he cannot learn; he can only practice. And he need not learn, as he has so fantastic a natural aptitude. We can sort it out as severely as we like, and there will still be plenty, if his health holds out.

Open letter to the editor of the *New York* Herald Tribune

October 17

Dear Sir,

I am a newsstand newspaper reader, and one of a type of New Yorker most interested in a true report of the arts and entertainments in town; and as such, I warmly congratulate you upon the engagement of Virgil Thomson.† We all agree that he is a first-rate composer and that he writes good prose. Perhaps just that combination of gifts might

---

* John Peale Bishop (1899–1944). American writer who lived chiefly in France from the thirties on.

† Virgil Thomson (1896–1989). Composer of *Four Saints in Three Acts*, with a libretto by Gertrude Stein; also a music critic and one of the original postwar Americans in Paris.

not inevitably make him a successful journalist. But because of his particular character, good-natured and fearless—and because a very bad habit of music criticism has been gradually established in New York in recent years—I believe that his work for you will be successful in due course, and of excellent effect upon everything and everybody.

Most of our critics have fallen into a dispirited undertone, or a kind of too regular, dogged, uninteresting eloquence. It is no wonder but it is a pity. It has not been a mere matter of poor style, but rather of point of view; that is, pointlessness of view. For example, evidently the rule has been that our great institutions of music, the opera, the orchestras, are to be regarded as philanthropies; therefore it must be unfair to find fault with them. But there is a practical as well as a cultural disadvantage in this respectful approach. Well-meaning wealthy people may pay the increasing deficits of music in a charitable spirit. But the ordinary New Yorker is not much prompted to go to concerts by the sense of duty. Dutiful criticism amounts to a kind of damnation with faint praise, I think. Certainly it does not make good reading.

Judging by his first week's work, Virgil Thomson is different. He loves to hear music; he hates to be disappointed; he explains what has happened and expresses what he has felt; and I feel that he is right as a rule, and in any case, he wakes us up out of our boredom. I for one shall not miss an issue of the *Herald Tribune* while he is employed on it; and there is very little periodical writing of which I could say such a thing.

Perhaps to begin with you may receive a good many vexed or shocked letters from readers who merely want the old critical etiquette preserved, or who have a special philanthropic or profitable connection with music. I can honestly assure you that I believe I am writing for a number of people like myself; and I beg you to give us the benefit of the doubt, if there is any—we may be the majority.

December 11

Since *The Pilgrim Hawk* was put on sale I have been anxious, half expecting a real practitioner of the ancient sport to turn up and point out in it some bad nonsense or misstatement. In fact, the source of my little information was as follows: One afternoon long ago I did meet a lady with a falcon; and she was even more charmingly talkative and instructive than the Mrs. Cullen of the story. I never forgot it; and over and over, as the years passed, in my own thought about my own affairs, I kept using the hawk in the way of a metaphor—likening art or death or love to it—for my amusement, consolation, or moral self-education.

Gradually it meant to me personally all the things that I have attributed to my fictitious Cullens.

None of the weaknesses of character in question, the jealousy, the alcoholism, the melodrama, were in the least true of the lady falconer I knew, nor of the amiable husband she had in fact. All the plot really is fiction, compositely derived from half a dozen other people and my poor self again, bits of all and sundry put together.

Novel reading is a pastime; and ordinarily you need a new one every few days, as if it were a clean pack of cards for solitaire. Naturally the proud and hardworking writer—and I have rather more ambition than talent, so I have to work hard—is not content to have his work played with like a pack of cards, and then scrapped.

In order to last, a novel must be functional. It must be adaptable to, and somehow serviceable in, people's private lives. Benjamin Constant was reading his simple harsh love story *Adolphe* aloud to the Queen of Holland when the news of the Battle of Waterloo came, which interrupted them. Now great awful Hitler has taken little Napoleon's place. But still today, Maugham—whenever anyone has fallen in love with him—offers the victim or beneficiary of love a copy of *Adolphe*, as you might give quinine to a friend going on a journey.

Thus, I think, novels last; and that is the kind of thing they are good for.

My father is a real dirt farmer, but I have plowed only with a noiseless typewriter. I wrote the chronicle of my pioneer grandparents in a Mediterranean village, where one of my neighbors was an opium smoker, and another who disliked me made a wax image of me and tormented it with needles, and another was a descendant of Joan of Arc's brother. All that, as it seemed, aroused my patriotism and reanimated my filial sentiment. Literature often makes use of things that are a superfluity in nature; and literary men may not amount to much or accomplish much in fact or in action.

I am an inexperienced and perhaps even a hysterical speaker in public. The last time I attempted a formal address was at the Sorbonne in Paris; in one of its glamorous, tub-shaped, ill-ventilated little amphitheaters. My brain was unable to keep up with my voice. Instead of thinking what to say next, I heard what I was saying, sentence by sentence, second by second, and it was foolish stuff; and a great shame came over me. The backs as well as the palms of my hands began to sweat; and the air of French scholarship and of French youth in the room seemed suffocating. After about ten minutes of it, I grew faint, and fell on my knees, and had to be helped into the anteroom. They gave me a drink called Cordial Médoc and let me go; and they never asked me to come back and try again.

From an autobiographical note, for Messrs. Kunitz & Haycraft's Twentieth Century Authors

I was born April 11, 1901, on a poor farm in Wisconsin. My branch of Wescotts were always farmers, and many still are: true pioneers, removing further west and making a new start every generation, avid for self-improvement and in search of fortune in vain. My ambitious, astute mother saw that this mere westward course and agricultural habit had grown hopeless, and set us retracing our steps back east, and in my case back over the sea, and living by our wits instead of the sweat of our brows. The faith of the pioneer is not very different in kind from the adventurer's scheme, the social climber's hope, the artist's vision. Frontier is where one thinks it is.

I sought education at the University of Chicago, but left it halfway through my sophomore year, in ill health and melancholia. There I began to write, but only to gain admission into the Poetry Club, ambitiously, otherwise uninspired. You might say that I pretended to be a genius in order to get on in the world; and it was as if some god heard me and somewhat condemned me to the uneasy fulfillment of my juvenile bluff and boast. As a literary man I have had good luck in every respect but one: my mere talent has never seemed equal to my opportunity or proportionate to my ideas and ideals.

My real education was in the baroque way, by the grand tour of the continent of Europe. Ford Madox Ford and Elly Ney and Jean Cocteau and Isadora Duncan taught me. Meanwhile I matured by fits and starts and, as long as I felt young, wrote with facility: four volumes. I resided in Europe all during the twenties. That was a great fool's paradise, and the perfect time and place to study human nature; nothing else seemed really important or urgent—human nature at peace and on the loose, in shiftings of morality and aesthetic innovations, significantly hopeful, instructively despairing. Europe in the thirties began to be obviously a rat trap; so I came back. Now half the time I live on the family farm, situated for this generation in the pretty part of New Jersey; and half the time in New York City with a couple of lifelong friends who kindly constitute for me a home of my own.

Early or late, certainly I should not have had any sort of literary career had it not been for the faith of those two, and certain other friends and relatives. And faith in me has always entailed tolerance and patience, and now and then a great monetary generosity as well. My semi-fictitious book, *The Grandmothers*, was a remunerative publication. But on the whole I have not made a living; in recent years I have not tried to.

Still I have not really succeeded artistically either. For a number of years it seemed to me that my ability had vanished into thin air; nothing that I could do was satisfactory. It must have seemed to others that there was something wrong with my character. Among other disabilities very grave for a novelist, I ceased to be able to take a real interest in anything fictitious. On mankind's account I believe in nothing but the truth, the naked truth; no other remedy or religion or dialectic. But can a novelist tell it? I myself have no exact knowledge of much of anything except sexual love and family relationships, and practically all in the first person singular. Is that worth telling? I now believe that it must be, if only to exercise the reader's sense of exactitude.

I cannot briefly indicate my literary taste or orientation except by giving a few samples of my critical opinion: E. M. Forster is the greatest living English author. Yeats was the greatest poet since Pope. The finest recent novel, strange to say, is Maugham's *Christmas Holiday*. Younger writers whom I especially admire and love are Katherine Anne Porter and W. H. Auden.

My convictions as a citizen, and a citizen of the world, seem simpler than my problems as a man of letters. I am scarcely a Christian, for I ardently desire revolutionary change in matters of education and private morality, according to science, away from Christianity. I also believe in continuous evolution leftward in the spheres of economics and politics; but I am not a Marxist. What is called revolution today, as with reference to Germany and Russia, I regard as an evil racket and a collective sickness. I do not believe in falsification of facts for any purpose whatsoever; nor in the least infringement upon freedom of speech, however ideal the pretext; nor in any aggressive warfare, not even a crusade.

1 9 4 1

The great and grave questions for the novelist
are: What persons can you get to pose for your
portraits? Can you paint them as you see them,
or do they look over your shoulder, and protest
and lament, and flee away? To what extent does
your anxiety about portraying people reflect and
disguise a fear of self-portraiture, self-betrayal?
Do you feel free to use the human material that
appeals most strongly to your imagination? Or
have you had to give a lien or mortgage on it to
those who provided it in the first place? Must you
work only with your second-string experience,
second-hand knowledge of the world?
—"Talks with Thornton Wilder"

January

"The Dream of Audubon" turns out to be in the public domain because Mrs. Ekstrom allowed Lincoln Kirstein to make a free gift of it to *Dance* magazine, which does not copyright its contents.

Klaus Mann is not speaking to me—and goes around speaking of my agent in tones of frightful Fafnir—because he fancies that he "commissioned" my Scott Fitzgerald funeral oration, which meanwhile I serenely sold to Edmund Wilson for *The New Republic*, where it belongs. John Peale Bishop has written an elegy, longer, he says, than *Ash Wednesday*; and it will appear beside my prose; a swell funeral, as they say . . .

Even the waging of modern war is poetic in some respects. For example, the German invaders forbade pigeons in France; no doubt French pigeons carried rebellious messages; no wonder! The British government ordered the extermination of peregrine hawks because they prey upon pigeons, and pigeons in the British Isles must carry military messages. The United States Army brought its pigeons into New York City for maneuvers, to accustom them—in case of a breach of metropolitan communications by some enemy exploit—to the peculiar landscape of skyscraping cliffs and the thundering of nervous traffic. A friend of mine sent me a newspaper clipping in which this was reported in detail . . . The birds were encamped near the skating rink in Rockefeller Plaza; their field aviary was in a trailer. After a few weeks they were taken separately and released at various points in Hoboken, Queens, the Bronx, and Brooklyn, for a clocked flight back to headquarters in the presence of a general and a major of the Signal Corps. Then they were returned to the main military dovecot in New Jersey, minus two. Two had been devoured by a hawk which nests on Madison Avenue. In the age of aviation and radio!

April 11

Good Friday and my fortieth birthday. "Forty is the old age of youth; fifty is the youth of old age." Vicissitudes to look forward to.

I have attributed this to Balzac, but Enid says, "No, it's an old French proverb."

Frederick, Maryland
April 13

I could not sleep and moved into the drawing room with an eiderdown and a book. Nelson could not sleep either and came after me; and lest we be heard by his parents, he followed me into our bathroom at the back of the house, where it was as if we were soldiers, on the hard floor and cold linoleum. I said as much. He expects to be drafted in six weeks; and I felt sorry to have reminded him of it. Furthermore, his character is very soft to suggestion; I ought not to implant any such imprudence in his mind. Months from now, it might result in his getting into trouble for some careless offense against Army morals.

In this sense, I remember, Paul once acknowledged his responsibility for our last year's trouble. He merely mentioned what is called Bitches' Walk in Central Park. N. had never heard of it, and hastened to it the next night, and there encountered his great love.

April 14

The Baltimore Museum has two masterpieces: one commonplace, a strong portrait by Hals, the black-and-white kind; and the other very rare, a good Greuze, the Marquise de Besons strumming a musical instrument. The drawing is that of many of his contemporaries and compatriots, but the color is his own at its best: one of the loveliest little schemes in the history of art. Her dress is pink, grayish, and there are slight gleaming gray touches throughout the canvas. The chair in which she is seated appears even with her shoulder, as a little gilt and a little blue; and her guitar (or lute) is of fruitwood, in exact dark yellows.

April 15

Today, with the wish that I were dead vaguely in the back of my mind, I happened to open Simon & Schuster's volume of color reproductions of masterpieces; and I imagine that I might be, throughout all eternity, certain square feet of wall of S. Francesco, Arezzo—a figure in the *Victory of the Milvian Bridge*—which makes my heart beat and my breath come fast almost in ecstasy. There is one victorious figure in silver armor on a black horse, whose face has been obliterated by the damp of the centuries. The absence of face makes a vacancy for me. And it occurs to me that I should be glad to go through eternity as a warrior like him, in impervious silver, armed with a lance; how many I would kill! Expecting no peace save in myself . . .

April 16

A week ago Nelson got very drunk at a party of artists and brought one back to his apartment; therefore, the next night he could only beg my pardon and send me home, his sexual energy all spent. I endured it affectionately, made no great fuss. In the hangover of that morning, furthermore, Nelson had received his questionnaire from the Army; so that his contrition was a minor matter mixed with dismay and self-pity and dread; and my role naturally was to cheer him up.

Tonight he told me a little more about this episode. It was not simply drink and sex; the real point of it was to spite his roommate, whose darling the young artist in question had been. I indicated my disapproval, but I scarcely expressed my aversion and distress. It spoiled the night's pleasure for me.

The worst of this kind of life is the repetition. About a year ago he got drunk at a literary party and slept with this oaf who is now his roommate; and the next night I came in from Stone-blossom for a rendezvous with him, and he begged my pardon and sent me home. But in those days I had hope of his developing a better self-respect and more tenderness and kindness toward me. Furthermore, perhaps, it may be that the pornography which is a part of jealousy stimulated my desire a little. Each time the reconciliation intensified my pleasure. Now it often occurs to me that my desire for him is as base and insignificant as his desire for others.

I am tired enough to die. God, how I have worked at this relationship as at nothing else all my life; and worked at the love letters more than at any book!

Night after night like that, like a threshing floor; and whether or not we winnow out what we need, there is always straw and chaff.

Passing a leather-goods shop on Fifth Avenue last night, we discovered a mouse in the show window. Too frightened to hide, it clung to the drapery just inside the plate glass, its little eyes terrible in the glaring light. It really had an expression of guilt.

The Leaning Tower is not only all right but (it seems to me) rather godlike. Not art-god, plaster-cast Greek on pedestal, not at all—but manikin-god, god in little man. Not sybilline as I may be at my best; never for an instant spellbound, bemused, mannered, Alexandrine as I am at my worst. Indeed, comparing us, it appears that what I can do may be good reading if the reader has lived a good deal and somewhat in my way, rightly or wrongly; and as good reading it may help quite a lot. Whereas what Porter writes is lifelike; it is an equivalent of living; right or wrong doesn't matter; it is life.

What babble! And in any case, that is not where the comparison pinches; the pinch is envy. I envy her having written this; and I also wish I were the author of her novel and her letters and her journal; I feel practically dead with fine rivalry. The fact is that, after a great, perhaps deceptive spurt in February, my work has been more or less stalled for weeks, and I am not sure that I understand why. I haven't felt as well as usual, but of course there can't be anything the matter with my health, can there? I have been having a few troubles: money trouble both in conscience and in pocket; love trouble, not too much this time, I guess . . .

April 19

Today the spring had come in like high tide, and for various reasons—forced sociability of the week in town, indulgence in the anguish

of the war, a little halfhearted sexual excess, and worry late at night—
I was tired. I puttered indoors all morning. I lay naked in the sun all
afternoon, but with my attention on one of Maugham's Malay novels,
The Narrow Corner, an absorbing but neither gripping nor very significant
story, which I finished. Meanwhile the new landscape veiled in tawny
and pearly shades was almost wasted on me. I planned to walk across
the farm before dinner, but instead I sat listening to the radio and playing
a new solitaire which George taught me.

April 20

Back to town in the train, Sunday noon.

Perhaps no one clever enough to write good fiction could invent or
easily recall the real conversation of the lower classes. I certainly cannot.
I might note down bits of it. For example: the café-car steward inquires,
"And how's the grandmother these days? I don't see her anymore these
days." The young woman answers with gusto, "Oh, she's had a few
operations but she feels fine."

A white magnolia, solid with blossoms, stands at a juncture of this
railroad and the Lehigh, as clear as though hatched from an egg, against
a background of masonry and iron trestle, coal-blackened . . .

Having entered these trivialities in my notebook, sipping my black
coffee and ice water, I then read the Sunday papers in my systematic
way: Virgil Thomson good on brass bands, Dorothy Parker good, de-
ploring Remarque's new novel, the war news bad but really nil. Just as
I finished, my eye caught the news of Norvil's* death in a motor accident
in Tucson, at which I trembled and keep trembling.

A sort of sigh of relief, along with every other sort of sigh—poor
little boy, well out of it! So sinister the romance of which he was born;
so awful his dependence on his sadistic, dipsomaniacal mother, whom
he hated and/or feared! But in fact my impression of him last year does
not correspond to this logical, consoling thought. He had an admirable
little character; and (who knows?) out of the trampling of his childhood
might have come extraordinary intellect or passion.

It is overwhelming to know as much as I know, and not to know
more. It is my trouble with respect to the war too, and my work, and
love, and domestic duty. In the general darkness full of my particular

---

* Norvil Wrentmore, who died in an automobile accident while at school, was a distant
relation of the Wescott-Harrison families. Barbara's father, Francis B. Harrison, who had been
Governor General of the Philippines under President Woodrow Wilson, was married six times.
Norvil was his son by a later marriage.

little lightning, heat lightning, my mind and senses grow increasingly passionate.

Advice to a beginning writer: Concentrate on the little things that cause feeling. What is it that Gide said?—Make a shapely, open, un-leaking dish, and the dew and the rain will fill it—something like that.

Last evening I discovered upon my poor person a fine lively spec-imen of hair louse alias *Pediculus ingurnalis* alias *morpion* alias *crab*, seated amid a fine little plantation of her eggs. So naturally I guess that my dear Nelson has slipped from his vow of forsaking all others for me. I am proud to say that I did *not* lie awake tossing in vexation and tragi-pornographic imagination all last night; and I do promise myself not to yield, upon this abominable petty provocation, to my old temptation of regarding life as contemptible and not worth writing about.

April 21

One of the hardest aspects of love, or perhaps just one of my misconceptions of it: Knowing that Nelson genuinely loves me, I cannot help looking to him for comfort when I am despondent or in trouble. Comfort and sentiment and sensuality . . . It is expecting more than he can give, evidently. Ego makes his plans; in altruism he has practically no imagination. His habit of life is upon impulse, always in a present tense. What he does (as distinct from what he thinks and feels) is of himself and for himself. Evidently he cannot help it.

The week's little episodes, minor matters of jealousy and impotency and money and bad manners, seem to me too petty and difficult to write down. Perhaps the life of love is all in its abstract issues, its obstinate ideals. As soon as I begin telling it in story form it will be dead.

April 30

Last night, I came out here, alone, to welcome the young W.'s back from Arizona and to sympathize with their tale. Old Mrs. Wrentmore was there, with the late Mr. W.'s ashes in her Vuitton suitcase—she always travels with them—and drunken Margaret would not let her have little Norvil's. So Barbara and Lloyd brought them and emptied them out in the grass of the paddock at the foot of the great swamp oak.

I said that I wanted the same disposition made of mine. Barbara replied, "You'll have to wait until you have done it for the rest of us. For I am sure you will outlive everyone." And I said, "I hope so." What a surprising, embarrassing thing to hear myself say! Barbara and Lloyd seemed not to mind. All evening I wondered what I must have meant by it, what prompted it. I must have made a savage resolve, signed with myself a new lease of life, over the weekend. I have not been working this afternoon. I have been lying face down on the lawn behind the stone house, amid the beating of the brook down from level to level, in the company of one of those great grosgrain beetles with gold buttons, thinking of K.A.P. and her work chiefly. Now I know: all three of her books are perfectly all right; she has nothing to worry about except to give them enough of her time and mere brute force. All her subject matter is perfectly timely at this moment; all her artistry mature; it's like a tide full of fish. Whatever she dips up will be what she wants, or what we want.

Later I made a tour of Stone-blossom with Barbara and Lloyd. The heifers play like schoolchildren; the stallions perspire in their box stalls. Our great parasol-shaped crab-apple tree is falling fast, and the perfume is almost dried out of the petals. Les, the head farmer, says that since he has been farming, never before has he got all his oats in before May 1.

George told me that until he seduced G., the latter's only love life had been with suburban maidens in parked cars, necking, nothing more. The effect of this was one of the delights which made their relationship so stubborn, in spite of unhappiness: the extraordinary physical and emotional force and variability of his kisses.

May 17

Maugham somehow stimulates me to talk at length, although I am not sure he enjoys it. There are so many themes upon which we seem to disagree and he is sometimes so reticent, sometimes so categorical, positive or negative, that our general discussions have not gone very well. Therefore I keep telling him my longest stories: the life of F. B. Harrison, the life of Virginia de Zayas, the romance of Katie Stewart and Walker Ellis, which seem to astonish but not altogether to please him. I have a sense of compulsion in all this; very odd. Perhaps it is partly inclination to reveal more of myself to him, to tell more of my own recent story; but surely I should not enjoy that nor profit by anything that he might say.

May 27

I hope that the amount I have taken for Beulah's wedding—$50— has not surprised or shocked Barbara. It shocked me, and it was hard to figure out finally. And my little florist having outwitted me about the orchids, I must pay for them this week. And George and I, in our harmless way, will bicker about which of us decided to have the (unplayed) piano tuned . . .

Americana, reported to me by Paul: There is a radio program entitled *The Hobby-Lobby*, on which a few nights ago there appeared a woman from Texas whose hobby is painting pictures on cobwebs. In her youth she read in some magazine that it is possible to do so; the idea kept appealing to her for fifteen or twenty years; at last she began to experiment. It took two years before her touch grew expert enough not to break every web she attempted. Now she is able to produce flower pieces, landscapes, and family portraits. She uses a miniature-painter's brush and oil pigment much diluted, and builds up her insubstantial image speck by speck, hint by hint. Whenever her friends discover any shapely and substantial spiderwork, they telephone. She brings a fine little frame or stretcher and presses it against the filaments. The stickiness which ordinarily keeps the spider's little victims until it gets there makes the web adhere to her frame. Thereupon she carefully cuts it loose and triumphantly bears it home, her mind no doubt all a-flutter with ghostly composition and feeble color scheme.

The end of *A Fortune in Jewels* is not in sight yet. I have had a bad time with it and perhaps only the fact that I know what it is to abandon half-finished novels—it is very bad for the novelist—has kept me from abandoning it. It is a long fat book now, too much of a good thing. I had a talk about it the other night with my dear maestro, old Maugham, who once forbade me to write any more about Europe; who furthermore admires me rather as a potentially great essayist than as a novelist. But as I explained my European theme he waxed enthusiastic and ordered me to finish it at all costs. I'll try.

June 12

In retrospect and self-reckoning:

I have been saying goodbye to Nelson in one way or another for more than a month, and I now declare my poor independence again. I have resolved not to resume our intimacy in any circumstances that I can foresee. It is a kind of breakdown very different from our quarrel of 1939 and very different from the trial of his passion for T. last November. My willpower may be weaker than his at a given moment, as we have often seen; but I have known exactly what I wanted and needed from first to last; and I have come to this decision not in a passion or a temper but slowly, in fatigue, and wear and tear, and little successive matters of fact. Now either I can or I cannot live without him; we shall see.

I shall try not to shrink from meeting him in the customary rounds of our similar metropolitan activities, but for a while our meetings will be hard for me, physically hard. Because I love him; I make no pretense about that, to myself or others. I am in love with him; and who knows how long I shall take to get over it, or what trifling remedies will take effect?

Just as true love is the only thing that ever does an imaginative nature like mine any good, so only time can remedy the harm that it does when it has failed. For the time being I must simply forget half the things Nelson has been, and be rid of half of myself along with him. It is nightmarish to look back; I often find myself regretting all my delight as well as this resultant misery. My imagination, like a fish dragging along on the line, drowning in its own element, cannot help blaming the bait . . . Love is a bad thing when its noble mainsprings, hope and belief and plan, have snapped. I am ashamed of wanting him, now that my spirit is so bankrupt that I cannot even offer to pay the price; which is nonsense too. No one can help it. I have forbidden everyone to be sorry for me; only to leave me to my own devices, to revive and reform and be more intelligent, to love again if I have the luck to, and work again as best I can.

None of this—pathetic or ugly nonsense, and remainder of passion, and the dull tolling note of finalty in every phrase—would come as a surprise if I were to think a little of our year's story as a whole. Last spring, bent upon his supposedly casual, harmless pleasure, Nelson found T. in the park. And finally he was able to choose between us, and on October 28 he dismissed me for T.'s sake. But that somehow failed to make either of them happy, and Nelson asked to come back to me on any terms, as he put it. Then life for us together began again.

I wonder what would have happened if I had been cocksure enough to make explicit uncompromising "terms" with him then, and tough enough afterward to enforce them. It is an immense and almost silly if. I have puzzled over it a great deal, but I cannot think that it would have made much difference . . . He knew as well as I did what had caused the past year's troubles; what the simple conditions of happiness are, for me, and always have been; what price love according to my nature. I knew that the winter and spring ahead would be a trial of my strength to change him, and of my appeal to him, particularly sex appeal, and of my cleverness and persuasiveness—against the opposite traits in him.

By the end of April all that had gone against me, play by play. Perhaps if I had loved him rather less and respected him less, I might have managed more cleverly; but it is not in my nature to love looking down.

We made a fine start. December was the noblest fool's paradise of all. This world could not have a graver, nobler aspect than I saw then: dear past in Europe falling back in ruins, and war for this country coming, coming; and there were matters of tragic uneasiness in my family; I was in serious need of more money; it seemed desperately necessary for me to work harder than ever or my career would slip out of my fingers again; and there were other anxieties . . . Yet in December I was able to take an unfaltering cheerful ambitious view of everything, because I personally was all right in love. Every bad shadow seemed cleared a little for me by Nelson's devotion, so that I could see my way. Sexual intercourse relieved every tension. I expected to be able to do my best at everything; and for a talented grown-up man perhaps there can be no greater satisfaction than that. There was no contempt for me or for us among those who had invested in my talent year after year, those who know me best. No corruption came near enough to touch me; no rivalry. And with Fitzgerald's ghost on one side and old W.S.M. on the other, my literary pregnancy started again. For the first time since we met I dreamed of a long (why not lifelong) connection of our two lives and careers. Nelson was good and it was good. His "prowess" was for me, his intoxication was with me. There had been no petty promising but I had a constant impression of proofs that he loved me. I was content and he seemed to take pride in that fact.

Then, little by little, the old boredom and vanity and disorder set in. T. came back into our lives, in a somewhat different role: Nelson's problem child, whose problems no doubt were more interesting than mine. Presently away Nelson went at the bidding of my old friend A., to take up the little slack in his married life; flaunting my priority in his affections at A., and A.'s greater glamour at me . . . After that my illusions of a change of heart in Nelson, and of a new prospect of peace of mind and dignity and sensuality for me, rapidly failed.

Drinking never impressed me as a very great evil. Nor has it, in Nelson's case, ever made him seem to me at all inferior or unattractive. Alcohol is a god, I wrote; and I remember how often I have let myself regard Nelson as, so to speak, godlike under its influence. But all spring it had a hopeless effect on our personal relationship, particularly because it is all connected and confused in Nelson's life with the difficulty of his sexual morals.

One day I wrote in my scribble book: "When love has gone wrong it is like a kind of brothel, in which the payment of spirit is mysterious, exorbitant, infinite. I can never tell how great it will be, nor understand how it is being added up. I pay more than anyone and indeed I get more than anyone. But the other clients are also entitled to what they get. I must wait my turn." As I sat staring at that beastly witty scrawl I realized how low my mind had fallen, in Nelson's honor, so to speak; in the disorder he has insisted on. How badly my heart had broken: a suppurating and crooked break . . . I knew then that it was time to give up.

November 24

If our government breaks with the Vichy government none of France will be left unoccupied, and Willie will lose the Villa Mauresque and other property. No matter, he says, for he will never care to live there again, and now he feels that the rest of his life can be spent contentedly in South Carolina. But, I protested, who knows what the French will be like after the war? His reply was in his hardest, narrowest voice with his stammer: "By that time, I'm afraid, they will have eaten so much shit that they will stink of it."

The battle now in progress in Libya is a matter of great personal concern to him. He does not mind so much about his son-in-law, although he is a charming boy; but his nephew, Robin,* is there, too, and the possibility of losing him makes his heart ache. Very fondly and gravely, but in his shy way assuming that it might all seem to me foolishness, he explained the hopes that would be wasted in the event of his death. A wonderfully amiable and talented young man, and handsome, except for his profile. And because of Willie's slight laugh at the mention of that, I guessed that it must be like his own profile, with the upper lip not well supported and the jaw too strong . . . What makes his peril especially hard to bear is that he is the last male Maugham. "It will be the end of our name," Willie said. "Except for your collected works," I retorted. It was an obvious answer but he appeared to appreciate it.

Like his illustrious father, young M. is a lawyer, but only, in the way he has planned his life, as a step into politics. He has intended to stand for Parliament and in due course, when Lord M. dies, to make a career in the House of Lords, where there is always a scarcity of young and able men. Lord M. is a good bit older than Willie and not likely to survive the loss of his son and heir. Their peerage is not one of those to which females can succeed . . . Now I wonder whether Willie might

* Robin Cecil Romer Maugham (1916–81). Novelist (*The Servant*) and short-story writer.

succeed to it himself, a charming although incongruous prospect. But
that would be certain to arouse both his sense of humor and his timidity,
so that it would have occurred to me as he spoke if it had been in his
mind.

Time magazine in its energetic vulgar style once called Lady Diana
Cooper "the daughter of eight dukes." The Duchess of Rutland having
had a reputation of gallantry, I was amused by the indecent little picture
of the Gay Nineties which this phrase suggested. It amused Willie, too,
because in fact Lady Diana is the daughter of not even one duke but of
Mr. Cust.

He told me that the man of his acquaintance who had the bluest
blood was the manager of Lord (Naps) Allington's estate. It was a kind
of aristocracy as you might say doubly distilled, for he was the offspring
of incest in two successive generations of Russells, dukes of Bedford.
Oddly enough, for an instant Willie had difficulty recalling Lord Allington's name. He said "Allingham," then corrected himself and
snapped his fingers impatiently, and I prompted him. He did not stammer
but his memory stammered. "He is dead now, poor dear, so there can
be no harm in my telling you that the very last time I saw him, I went
to bed with him. He was a delicious creature."

In this connection—I can't think just how it came up—I said that
for my part I am never as eager to have intercourse with a new lover as
with one I have already enjoyed, again and again and again. Somewhat
to my surprise Willie said that oh, indeed, it was so for him as well.
And we spoke for a moment of that great number of men who must have
what they call adventure, novelty, and a constant changing or mixing of
affairs. We spoke as if they were, in this respect, a race foreign to us
or perhaps a lower class.

Upon our last previous meeting I had brought Nelson to see him,
to be seen by him; and until almost the end of the evening neither of
us referred to it. Then without preamble Willie said, "Dear, your boy-
friend disappointed me. I do not think he is worthy of you." I replied
somehow, in all honesty and unembarrassed but perhaps a little con-
strained, not apologizing but rather explaining the nature of my love;
and he hastened to assure me gently that he meant to refer only to
Nelson's lack of good looks.

All my family has been disappointed and even vexed by this romance of mine, I told him; and I suppose that my poor darling's home-
liness may be one cause of their feeling, for they are physical snobs.
This last phrase delighted Willie, who added that his daughter Lisa is
one. He did not say that he is one himself, but presently stated that he

never ceased to delight in those of his acquaintance who are good-looking, and on the other hand can never accustom himself to anyone who is not. Which perhaps was to warn me not to expect him to like Nelson . . . I mentioned N.'s eyes and Willie admitted that they are fine and romantic. I did not mention his hands or other beauties—how unconvincing that kind of mention is in any case!—but I did say that physically, in one way and another, he extraordinarily suits me. To which Willie warmly answered, "That is the main thing."

Then he told me a story. When he was a boy, living with his parents in Paris, they were great friends with the Angleseys. The Lady Anglesey of that time, an American, was a pretty and agreeable woman, in spite of which Lord Anglesey ran away with a Frenchwoman. Mrs. Maugham, calling upon the disconsolate deserted marchioness, tried to console her by saying that he surely would regret it and come back to her before long. "For I have met this Mme X and she is, I can assure you, as ugly as sin."

"Oh, oh dear," said Lady Anglesey, "if she really is as ugly as that he will never come back." And in fact he did not, but persisted in his love of Mme X until the day of his death.

Willie asked me to call upon his old friend Edward Sheldon,* who in his fine apartment just around the corner from us lies paralyzed and blind, as he has done for more than fifteen years. I have often heard of this man's saintliness and martyrdom and his great charm and intelligence, yet neither curiosity nor expectation of pleasure would take me to see him. Willie's request will, and naturally I also feel obligation of good fortune and goodwill toward anyone so afflicted. I avoid things of that kind but I cannot refuse them. Twenty-five years ago in Waukesha I used to read aloud to a young lawyer who was twisted and knotted from head to foot by rheumatic fever . . .

I asked Willie what his friend's infirmity is. He rose and carefully closed the door of his sitting room and with an air of almost scandal, insisting on the entire lack of evidence but with romantic emotion and conviction, explained it as he sees it. Twenty years ago Edward Sheldon was the white hope of our theater, an extraordinarily gifted and successful young man. After *Salvation Nell* and *Romance* and one or two other successes, he undertook an important poetical drama based on Hans Christian Andersen's tale of the mermaid in love; and it was a miserable flop. Whereupon he fell mysteriously ill and it has gone from bad to

* Edward Sheldon (1886–1945). Playwright who, blind and an invalid, held court in his hotel suite for the cream of New York intelligentsia in the thirties and forties. Thornton Wilder's *Ides of March* is dedicated to him.

worse ever since, until now he can do nothing but think and speak.
Fortunately he has an ample income. Secretaries, and nurses day and
night, and a good many devoted visitors make a life for him; and he
never complains.

Willie believes that all this started as a nervous attack, as an excuse
for never trying to write another play; a kind of inner suicide. In despair
of himself as an artist it must have seemed easier to be a saint and a
martyr. Now certainly his paralysis is helpless, physiological. His body
has entirely assumed the role in which his spirit cast it. But at times,
Willie says, he is startled by a little sudden irrational feeling of doubt
of his old friend's blindness. There are people who fancy that it is all
a fraud; some say that in the dead of night Edward Sheldon gets up and
goes about town, heaven knows what for.

In his youth he had great beauty, and various men and women were
in love with him. He certainly was in love with John Barrymore, Willie
says, but perhaps never admitted it even to himself. Willie wanted him,
but although their friendship was intimate and when he came to New
York he often stayed with him for weeks at a time, there was never the
least frankness between them upon the subject of sex. He supposes that
his old friend never had sexual intercourse with anyone. I cannot help
thinking that this may have drawn him to that drama of the immortal
cold-blooded mermaid. He had a strange experience two or three years
ago. In the middle of the night as he lay alone in his fine apartment a
man somehow got in, intending to rob it. The cripple cried out, "Who's
there? What do you want?"—until he guessed what manner of man it
was and upon what errand. Then he explained his helplessness, and
somehow he was able to persuade the burglar to go away empty-handed.
As Willie remarked, it must have been as frightening an adventure for
the wicked man as for the saint.

I look forward with a certain timorousness to visiting this strange
famous man. Perceptive as always, Willie said I must not be afraid, but
he did not explain what was in his mind in introducing us. He wonders
how Mr. Sheldon can enjoy making new friends with—if he really is
blind—no notion of their appearance. No doubt it would be kind of us
to let him examine our faces with his fingertips. I shall sense his imagination doing just that . . . Willie must think it good for me to meet a
man whose anguished realization of an inadequacy of talent has had a
more harmful effect than in my own case. All he said was, as it were
casually, that Mr. Sheldon was a good man to talk to about the difficulties
of one's work.

1 9 4 2

He was a primitive; that is, an artist who has to
invent his tools as well as work with them.

—Fear and Trembling

Parker's Ferry
Yemassee, South Carolina
February
Last night in the train a soldier, a farmboy from Bangor, asked me
to play rummy, not gin rummy and not for money, but to keep him awake
until we reached Richmond because he wanted to mail a last postcard
to his wife. They had spent every night together for the last ten months,
he informed me. At every important station he stepped out and found
someone on the platform willing to mail another postcard to her, so that
she could follow his trip. A very common boy with a big behind and
bandy legs, pasty-faced but with a sweet smile.

South Carolina's subtle prettiness as usual: the soft stripes of dawn
in the pines; glimmering water on the poor ground; leek-shaped tree
trunks standing in the water.

William [Maugham] is in lovely temper. Evidently he has really
suffered from loneliness this winter, and just now, in N.Y., he found
some calamity and quarrel. So he is glad of my company, I gather.

All language is shrinking. For example, *genial*, in its secondary
meanings: *pertaining to generation or procreation; presiding over mar-*
riage; exhibiting genius. "We have our genial nights," wrote Dryden.

My own vocabulary has grown a little narrow and dry, and too
rational, and too much of a piece. Dryden is a good refresher:

A phrase of Sir P. Sidney's: "The Ending End . . ." the windup
of a story or a life.

vainglory: "Over *gloria dell' umane posse* . . ."—Dante

thalassic: born of the sea.

pythogenic: implying generation or production by means of filth.

lank, jaded: "The gas burns lank and jaded in its glass."—Henley

Tennyson: a dead body "dinted into the ground." Lying awake half the night, listening to the wind over the house.

This is Monroe's birthday, which is for me a great holiday, holy day. For, as I understand my story, had he not been born, and joined his heart and strength to mine, I had been born only once, and to little purpose.

Tonight, we've been warned, all our camellias will be frosted. Nelson Sr. and Nelson Jr.* picked 879 blossoms this afternoon, and brought us a lot on trays, looking like an eighteenth-century rustic wedding.

Most of my letters have been written not to tell the truth exactly, nor to reveal myself, but to advocate something, or to induce something, or to prevent something. They are little, living, momentary instruments of my policy, or heart's desire. They do honestly represent a purpose that was heartfelt, often even passionate, and never (I think) ill-intended. But naturally there is in them all the exaggeration of courtship, the wiles of diplomacy or pedagogy, the devices of persuasion. They are, in the strict sense of the word, rhetoric; not testimony or self-expression.

Upon our ride yesterday, half remembering a shortcut through an adjoining estate, we took advice of four black children whom we found cracking nuts on a log, and it was bad advice and we got lost. It was lightly wooded upland, burned here and there, with more moss than foliage; and the various tracks we followed petered out in thicket. Then we heard the ringing sound of an ax, and sought that out. It was an immense youth, of a certain beauty, very black, cutting firewood; and he had a little red bullock and a poor old car with which to bring his load back. He began to talk as soon as we came in sight, and, when we asked him the way, began an eager, almost frantic harangue. He had a resoundingly loud voice, he stammered and never paused, singsong, as a child might recite verses by rote, with the same great gesture of general direction at the end of each stanza. Not one word was comprehensible; doubtless it was that African language called Gullah, but it was also, I thought, insanity. He bared his beautifully white teeth in

---

* Nelson Doubleday Sr. and Jr., Maugham's American publishers and his hosts during World War II. They also published Edna Ferber and Joseph Conrad.

a rapturous smile, and his eyes were shining, and his ax was as bright as silver. It was a little like listening to a turkey gobbler; I could scarcely keep a straight face, and yet a little fear also crossed my mind, and William's too (he told me afterward). As he would not cease his harangue we interrupted him with our thanks, and turned our horses and rode away; and then he shouted after us his only comprehensible word: "Goodbye!"

Today after tea we took our longest ride, all the way to Clay Hall. It is the only house in the vicinity that I should be attracted to live in; not the genuine colonial but of the mere twenties; a wide stone pavilion with large windows, very low on the ground under the shawled live oaks. Its situation is the best, too: very near the sea as the crow flies, only the river is backed up all around it, coiled like a serpent in a nest of banks and islets. When one has been riding some miles through the swamp, where everything is a little broken or rotten, posting through mud and water, ducking one's head down under the loose branches, unable to see where one is headed—and then comes out there on the causeway, in the wonderful flatness and openness, pale blue and silver and grass-gold, it is like being ten years old. I enjoy the swamps, too, but the only sense they make is in yielding to their melancholy.

It is the chilly glassy twilight. William is still out somewhere playing bridge with publishers and such. I walked by myself all by my lonesome on the levee; the river seeming to have no life except a great quivering dimple here and there, shining with reflected dead grasses. I met only one bird, minute and green. This kind of place keeps putting me in mind of bad fevers; because the shapes of so many things are serpentine; because in the vast quiet even the flutter of the timidest bird seems startling, loud and peremptory.

What I have chiefly worked at is a stock-taking of all my little stories, trying to schedule and budget them up ahead. Most of them seem to me alive and pleasing. I am half afraid to touch them lest they fade, wilt, change, perish—but now it is time: "The Death of Isadora," "The Swamp Garden," "The Doughboy Penitante," "The Refugee," "The Wander-Bird." After that my three dearest dream children: "The Farmer in the Dell," "A Naked Man," and "The Wastebasket." It sounds too simple. I wish I knew how long my lifetime is to be . . .

* * *

At lunch while good cumbersome black Mary passed the shad roe, then the cucumber salad, I could see by William's face that he had something confidential to tell . . .

"Last night in a dream—you may scarcely believe it, but it is true—I dreamed that I went down on Shelley. I remember saying to myself that I mustn't try to bugger him; he wouldn't have liked that."

It gave me just a little tremor to hear this, wondering what lay in his subconsciousness, what object of his appetite the great inappropriate name masked. Not indeed likening myself to Shelley; only finding myself less unlike than anyone else here on the Combahee . . .

It is notable that in fact, though frequently complimenting me upon my youthfulness, etc., he has never felt, at least never let me feel, the least strain in this way. His discretion never fails; his good manners never fail except in anger.

Cold, but still shining bright. The white crane swoops adagio over the dark blue canals and the tawny reeds. Every morning while I breakfast I read a canto of the *Purgatorio* aloud to myself, in Italian; that is, my notion of Italian: my morning prayers!

From a letter to Barbara Wescott

March 9

Bless you, and bless it, that is, her. One always has to use the same words, which are not much. You know that I love you: more sameness. But I think you know how particular all this feeling is, how deeply inculcated in me by life itself for so many years; so you can imagine what I have had in mind and in my heart all morning, as well as I can write it . . .

Just this morning, Tuesday, our maids heard a rumor across the rice marsh that Mrs. Doubleday's butler at the big house had heard upon the telephone that Mr. Maugham's brother had had a baby. Which rumor Mr. Maugham relayed to my fireside where, with my breakfast, as it happened, I had just begun a little newsletter to you. I then telephoned both Lloyd and George.

As for Yemassee, S.C., I have never been in so solitary a place. Even the colored people live miles away. Nothing is in sight. The landscape around us is beautiful, a kind of nullity; blessed be nothing, but beautiful and especially immense. Before my window lies one immense fallow rice marsh; it looks like a white, headless wheat field inlaid with large dark sapphires, a thousand acres without a tree. Yesterday afternoon we went for a walk around it, for miles upon a sinuous narrow hummock made by slave labor. Not knowing how far it was, we kept on until we reached Bonny Hall (Doubleday's), eight miles in all. Mr. Doubleday was not pleased, for there was a great slapping wind and it might have been bad for his famous author's heart. But greatness led the way, and I could not tell him that he was too old for it, nor could I pretend that I felt feeble. Our hands and ankles are all injured by the cat briar . . . Mrs. Doubleday asked us if we had met the old alligator. Happily, we had not.

March 13

I had to spend the better part of two days drafting a broadcast about books for the soldiers and sailors. William was shocked; he couldn't see how it could have taken me more than half an hour. And yet, when I confess that I have not the ordinary talent of writers, everyone says it is a false morbid manner of speaking.

Yesterday we went riding for two hours, a long swampy way on a bank amid a kind of sacred grove of thin gray trees growing in water; then over a plain the name of which is Big State, with savage Negro dwellings scattered on it, solemn Negroes and awful small red cattle.

After dinner we went up to Bonny Hall to hear singing. This was a great barony (hence, as a matter of etymology, bonny); Sherman burned the old mansion, but the live oaks were not harmed. They are gigantic and in perfect health, with their peculiar, rather horizontal boughs, almost as thick halfway out as where they come from the trunk, so that one wonders why the weight has not dismembered them; an open kind of tree, visible all the way through even in full foliage, as pale as olive, veiled with the silvery moss. There is a semicircular grove at the back of the house, with large hedges and extravagant camellias in between. We sat out there on a terrace, and the vast cloudy branches, crowned here and there with some stars, made a background for the singers. It was illuminated by a fire on a tall cement block, as if it were a pagan altar; it was almost too flaming, so that it suggested a very serious sacrifice. There was fire enough for it to be human sacrifice.

It was a choir of four baritones, two basses, and two altos, led by one named Isaiah. Very soft and sensitive together, well rehearsed, I should think; with almost that refined musicality which was the fashion in Vienna and bad for Bach, I used to think. I have never heard more velvety voices; somehow virginal; perhaps they have never sung as loud as they could. One of the altos was the finest, an androgynous note, verging upon countertenor; and she was also the cleverest musically, in a melancholy play with the rhythm, and certain harmonies not in our mode at all.

They began with "Good evening, Mr. Doubleday, how do you do. Good evening, Mrs. Doubleday. Good evening, all the guest-es, how do you do." Then for an hour and a half, spirituals and local variants upon Moody and Sankey hymns: "A home beyond the city, Where the sun don' go down" and "Nobody knows the trouble I've seen, Nobody knows but Mr. Doubleday," and "The devil is a man You cain't under-stan." Now and then they began "How dry I am," no less piously and sorrowfully than the rest. Whereupon the houseman, one named Ephraim, brought a trayful of gin and grape juice. It amused me that, even with the tumblers in their hands, they went right on with the sorrow of the song to the last verse, for art's sake.

The Negroes here have a quiet and melancholy which is a surprise to me; none of the good spirits and bird chatter and jolly fidgets which we know in the North. I have no idea whether that is voodoo, or malaria, or their memory of injustices.

March 14

This is a fine place to work, except that the days are too short. William gets all his work done in the morning, and after lunch, he has his nap before I can say knife. And so far, I have been too sleepy to work at night; the lovely weather for one thing, I suppose. I arrived in an exhaustion, and no fooling. A poor blown shadow of myself. As my body reminds me of a kind of reddened canned mushroom, I have wanted to take sunbaths, but I have renounced them conscientiously.

March 17

Now it is turning to summer heat fast, interspersed with rough sweet rains. There is fantastic fragrance of tea olive and daphne (which is like lemon peel and honey) around the houses. Before dinner last night we got the black Isaiah to take us upon the canals in a paddleboat. The perfectly still water is all spotted with last year's lily pads, in a fine variety of rotten colors. Now and then a flock of ducks would whir up ahead of us, splashing the water white; and there were coot and bitterns and one solemnly flying great heron, Herodias. Isaiah says the alligators are still in their winter sleep. We sat close, side by side, in the prow of the narrow damp old craft, with only the faint sound of the paddling behind us, as in a gondola, sliding as if there were a magnet drawing us along. I have been reading A. Huxley's biography of Father Joseph, *L'éminence grise*: a kind of mysticism beautifully written and rather thrilling but, I think, untrue and even deleterious. So as we slid amid the pale reeds we discussed that.

Later we had a gala meal of terrapin at the big house, more interesting than appetizing, to my taste; and then we played tandem gin rummy, four on each side . . . The long Doubleday *séjours* here are not really in the way of pleasure-residence but rather a part of his publishing technique. The sub-publishers and their little wives keep coming and going; a full house of them all the time. They are a bit deadly though not dislikable. Mrs. Doubleday is sweet.

From a letter to Elizabeth Wescott Hotchkiss

Parker's Ferry
March 18

Dear Elizabeth,

Last evening I had a lovely letter from Barbara, and half of it was a gentle rejoicing upon the fortunate turn of the great event of Deborah's birth; and the other half was the news of you,* to which she referred with a note of pity and bitterness greater, I think, than she would have allowed herself if it had been her own case.

Dearest, I will not, not now or from now on, try to tell you what compassion I feel. You can take that for granted; indeed, after half a lifetime of our mutual devotion, you should be able to imagine it better than I can express it. I am going to be tough with you, and this, to start with, is chiefly to remind you what great stakes there are, for yourself and the rest of us, in your good serene endurance of this misfortune.

You have always had a tough time physically, all your life: from your childhood, when you seemed predestined to be sickly, all through the early hardship of your marriage, the poverty and laboriousness and especially the penalties of motherhood, the pounds of flesh literally which Bruce cost you, and right down to the recentest backache and bellyache. Yet, I think what a good life it has been, and it still will be. And don't forget that, in terms of your dependence upon each other in a ring-around-a-rosy as we live now (with Barbara as the rose), you have been the very invaluable one, to all and sundry. You have made a good man of your husband, who when you married him was an unhappy, unlucky, and seemingly incorrigible boy who couldn't make much of anything of life, whom no one except you could make much of. With practically nothing in your favor but love and intelligence, you have mothered a

---

* G.W.'s sister was recovering from a mastectomy.

sturdy, virtuous, wonderfully lovable son; but there are several more
critical years ahead for him, and you must not let him and Tom down
by losing heart . . . Beulah is indebted to you for the fact that she has
a good well-bred daughter instead of just a kind of Williams girl with
complexes. Lloyd, I think, could not have managed his great audacious
venture of Mulhocaway, especially with respect to his reassembly of all
the family, without your help. Especially Mother and Father would have
had a very depressing and exasperating effect both in Barbara's life and
mine if it had not been for your intermediacy; a shock absorber between
us and their lonely aging emotions more effective, I suppose, than any
of us have realized. And all that is going to be harder than ever, not
less hard, in the next few years.

Life is so bad all the time—and now there is an especially bad
time ahead for everyone, when death will be as you might say in fashion,
with half the world in uniform and the other half in mourning—that we
can find good excuses and certain compensations for not living. Which,
I believe, is the only really great immortality . . . So, dear, keep
reminding yourself that you are going through this misery and indignity
for the sake of some more years at least as good and certainly no worse
than the past; and I think that will make it seem easier. For you have
a happy resilient nature.

Be careful not to fret about your beauty. A little more or less, who
cares? Those who love us, as a rule, by and large, most of them most
of the time, do not care. We have come to the middle time of life when,
more or less, our bodies are going downhill. It is all relative. In any
event, compared with what we were in the flower of youth, we are ruined.
But as the flesh fades or fritters away, the spirit seems to develop
somehow . . . I, the most sensual and in a way the vainest of men, have
had to begin to face all that. While in the great long final prospect it
seems enraging, insufferable, day in and day out it is not so bad. I begin
to take a little pride in my peacefulness and decent sense of humor.

Now you see, dear Elizabeth, with all my tough doctrine, as tough
as I can make it, I am not pessimistic. I think it will work out all right.
The real difficulty of any ordeal of this kind lies not in the facts nor
even in our own minds; in our posture of spirit; in the way our willpower
takes hold in us, for good or ill. I know a woman who, after about ten
years of ideal marriage and the birth of one child, had a terrible stillbirth
followed by the removal of her ovaries and all that abomination as you
know it. But she allowed herself to feel so mutilated, so marred in her
womanhood, that for a long time she could not bring herself to resume
sexual relationship with her husband. Some shame of nerve, grievance

of body, made her indifferent and cold. Naturally enough, presently he took mistresses and then fell in love with one and married her; and my poor friend has never been able to forgive him, or her successor, or herself, or even providence itself. I tell you this because no one could know better than you how foolish and fateful her shame and grievance were in the first place. For many years you had happiness, which she forfeited by mistake. Now probably the same temptation or pride and coldness will arise for you again; but I dare say you'll manage.

When I commenced this letter I meant to tell you all about the Southland and William and my career and whatnot; but now it is time to motor to Charleston for our broadcast. Barbara will give you all the news of my holiday. I'll be seeing you next week.

March 18

My sitting room adjoins William's bedroom, and after breakfast I can hear him in a strong voice saying some prayer or reciting something; but as he is a shy man and in a way forbidding, I doubtless shall never discover what it is.

New York
April 7

I shall have to change my way of life or my point of view. Certainly my social life has never been so stagnant: a couple of septuagenarians and a couple of the trashiest young men. And the life in the country more and more numerous and intertangled in a knot, Gordian by the looks of it. I must try to discover and develop some sort of new interest; or try to revamp my life so as to bypass all these vain passions altogether, and live more like William in Yemassee.

That same old William, in his irritation with me for threatening to give up *A Fortune*, told me that I was as bad as Leonardo! He went on, I may say—naturally enough, as we do not agree about anything except our mutual regard and enjoyment—to one or two worse insults in detail.

April 9

I do not like spring this year. Although I am a tough and complex fellow of forty-one, my life now happens to be as simple and enclosed as if I were in a school. The parrot in me can only fidget and squawk.

Men often go mad for the act of love, and women not often; I dare say that the act itself is a more concentrated kind of experience for the man, individual, independent, performable, lonely, and thus maddening. On the other hand, as a somewhat Tiresian man myself, I must say that it is that part of the whole which I call "feminine" in nature—adorational and empathetic and irrespective of my own immediate pleasure—which seems to me the greater part. If the experience could be cut in two, and I were to choose one half, it would be that. Perhaps because it seems remoter from all the other actions and satisfactions of our life; and perhaps it partakes more closely of the character of love itself, that love which is over and above pleasure.

The only way one can produce a great deal of report easily and quickly is to bypass life to some extent; to be "old," out-of-date, innocent of a large part of what is going on; and to base the report on good old tenets of humanity tried and true. That is the professional way; it is William's way, for example, for the most part. But it cannot very well be our way just now because those tenets are appearing to us as rather tried and *un*true.

Doubtless I shall never produce much but it will be discovery rather than restatement; truer.

Roughly speaking, summarily speaking, my trouble is always just too much literary material, raw indeed and hot and in the present tense, and never enough finished literary product.

Stone-blossom
April 24

I love my life; every moment of it, whether productive or unproductive, pleasant or unpleasant, I have no desire to die. But once in a while, I suffer from a furious inclination to put myself to death, as a punishment for not living well; capital punishment.

Rereading *The Grandmothers* today, I found this odd thing, zodiacally speaking: Given the date of the marriage of Marianne Duff and Ralph Tower, Alwyn Tower must have been born under Cancer, the Crab, which is the sign of the heart, which walks backward. Not a bad sign for that sort of storyteller, telling with backward glances, in retrospect and reconsideration and, indeed, revision . . . And I suppose that on the whole my work of literature so far has in fact been done rather by my heart than by my head; and perhaps it has been less helped and less hindered by my sex than it has seemed.

1 9 4 3

She loved him; love and repugnance were one.
She thought, I am a wicked and lost woman.
—The Grandmothers

New York
January 1—early morning

At the Greyhound Bus Terminal an old farmer itching to be sociable came up and informed me that it felt like snow; that he had gone up Broadway at midnight; that everybody in the town had come there, all crazy. "Didja ever see a thing like that, aye golly?" Here and there went a Greyhound employee with delicate swaybacked step; he had the profile of a paper doll and silky lashes, and on his cap was stitched in bright good-sized letters: *Pillow Service.* My ears and eyes were beginning to wake up.

While we waited in the bus for it to start, the driver, one with a hangover complexion and a great paunch tightly belted, appealed to a dressy gray-haired woman for sympathy and got it, along with her jolly old sexual smiles. There had been five sections last night, he told her, all revelers, drunks, girls. How dismal he felt, how stoic! The sort of physiognomy and physique that a clever film director would select for the part of a bus driver; the masterful type for a terrible storm, the dead type for a crash in a ditch. These suburban buses always seem and perhaps are dangerous. All those who were bidding farewell to all those who were departing looked anxious. There were scowls of weariness like mine; there were short kisses, and love to this and that relative at journey's end, and fretful talk of changes to be made from this bus to other buses, tickets to be exchanged, dollars and cents to be refunded.

Two sailors arrived at the last minute, very chilly-looking in their pea jackets and yawning; and bent their long and tight and neat persons down into the narrow places across the aisle from mine. Loudly they asked each other what was to be done with their knees and, grunting, did it. Upon learning how long their trip was to take, one jested, "Say, we shoulda hadda horse, we'd've got there quicker," which the other appreciated. They were at least as bowlegged as horsemen: riders of dolphins bareback, blowers of conch shell with loose mouth, like Mantegna's, like Dürer's, homely and sallow as ocean itself.

I found my seat uncomfortable. Where my feet should have rested there was a hump in the floor over a wheel; nothing to brace against, nor any elbow rest nor headrest; jiggle and heave and no rest at all. This no doubt stimulated my view of everything out the window. For instance, miles away, beyond the Newark airport, across the salt flats, there was a train going backward but in our direction, and failing to keep up with us. It reminded me of a herd of elephants on the veldt, the trunk of one on the rump of the other ahead; it reminded me of a herd of black beef cattle eating their way across their pasture. Up in the air between our highway and Newark I mistook a gull for a little airplane; then I mistook a great airplane for a kite. So all seemed topsy-turvy in this part of the world: city and countryside mixed, exotic and homely mixed, heaven and hell confused. Then we turned off the road I know and went past an amusement park, abandoned for the winter or perhaps forever, shabby, silvery, shivery. KEEP KOOL IN DREAMLAND POOL, the sign said.

Because the two sailors beside me in the bus were not very handsome, at first I did not even wonder what kind they might be, sexually. Now I considered it and thought that there could not be much doubt about it. They constituted a couple: the one big and vain and amused, the other little and loving and amusing. Now the big one also took note of my perversity, how unlike his, and perhaps prosperous-looking. It pleased me to be so noted, and in turn, I regarded the couple with a certain increase of good humor. The big and particularly homely one had charm: broken nose, heavy eyes of washed-out blue, coarse eyelashes which reminded me of a pair of miniature Fuller brushes. There was something lovable about the little one, gazing up at his mate in entire admiration, chattering to please him, smiling at his own chatter with superfluity of teeth.

When the bus stopped ten minutes at the Somerville Diner, we three drank coffee and ate doughnuts side by side at the counter; and perhaps I glanced at them too appreciatively. What happened next took me by surprise. The big one followed me into the restroom and, lowering that strange apron which distinguishes sailor pants from all other pants, formally but good-naturedly showed me his large sex, sheathed in coarse-grained skin like morocco of the Levant, palely blond. I managed to give no further sign of appreciation. It was the sort of episode that perhaps one cannot tell at all without seeming to have felt very keenly about it, or to be leaving a lot untold. I did not feel keenly; I am telling it all. It was my last chance, so far as he was concerned, if chance it could be called. Back in the bus all the rest of the trip he ignored me; he fell asleep, with homely aspect, his little one still smiling and still admiring him.

On the steps of the diner after this infinitesimal adventure I paused a moment to take deep breaths of the New Year's air of the true country. It must have penetrated my mind in a way as well as my lungs, with its chill and banality and normality, dispersing the hot shabby images of the night, quieting my too keen curiosity and too intellectual reminiscence, counteracting even my amusement at the shapelessness of the sailor. For a while I forgot all that sort of thing, gladly. I sat gazing, not backward or inward, it seemed—extrovertly, out through the shatterproof glass of the bus at the brief conclusion of the winter afternoon in the sky, the vacant scope of agricultural valley; objectively, but with as much fervor as if landscape were a possible lover, or as if skyscape were what happens to be my particular problem now, an absolute lack of possible lover.

Just beyond Somerville, where Somerset County and Hunterdon County adjoin, is the end of the flat Jersey, the commencement of those hills in which, according to meteorologists, all of New York City's thunderstorms are secreted; hills hirsute with sumac and dogwood, virile with hundreds of little springs of good water. The change is abrupt; it is what I had sampled on the steps of the diner: no more acridity of suburban central heating and filling stations and greasy grills—from now on acidity of cow, ammonia of horse, sachet of harvest shiftlessly left to rot, oil of stubble, essence of hedgerow, attar of clod. You inhale it even inside the bus; then, after three or four more thrusts of the accelerator, you see it descending away before you, vast flatnesses which are not really vast or flat at all; little ups and downs in fact displayed all at an angle so that the eye can make the most of them, and softly battlemented afar: Round Valley and the Cushatunks, Vuskanetcong and the Kittatinnys, and such places denominated by the Indians with their coughing consonant, clanging vowel. It is like an Indian happy hunting ground; not quite. We have emasculated it, shorn it, pacified it; it is like a watercolor by Dürer as well.

Over all, all-important, the sky, with the sun cloaked in it. In truth sky is not important. It is nothing, nothingness, just darkened and dampened by whatever kind of land or sea lies beneath it; color-filtered by the traditional or the individual imagining. The nature lover is a perverse one, a fetishist, a maker of fuss about nothing, like any other lover. The first afternoon sky of 1943 lay above the highway ahead, more like a nude body than anything else, with a healthy sallowness like a sailor's, due to dampness of the ocean fifty miles away, with fine muscular highlights all over it, with one small but impressive coarse-grained cloud in the middle of it. And up high, away from the cloaked sunset, it gave a little sidelong blue glance, a glance of infinite offering, good nature, provocation: the awful manliness with which infinite air invariably seems to face and challenge lonely man. And the wintry land seemed to respond to that glance as well as man, as well as I.

From a letter to Barbara and Lloyd Wescott

February 26

This is a milestone date in our lives: this afternoon Monroe received a letter from George to say that he is leaving us. He has offered to move out of Eighty-ninth Street before next Monday the 7th, and he wishes us not even to meet for some time. We shall sublet that apartment as soon as possible, and I will help Monroe find another and get settled in it, and then I will live at Stone-blossom, the dear home you gave me for this half of my life.

When George said farewell to Jonathan Tichnor,* he no doubt realized that it was not a true farewell; he could not care for anything but the hope of the end of the war. It would have been unbearable for him to live unhappy in the setting and circumstances of so many happy hearts, unloving with Monroe, whom he has loved so greatly; and he has been ashamed of all the deceptions and self-deceptions of the last six months, which have made him seem, to himself above all, a weak character; and he wants to learn to live by himself in some new way.

I am glad it is settled, for George's sake. For four years, he has been spellbound, discontented with his life, dissatisfied with himself: afraid of the future, sick of the past, changing his mind all the time, in one way or another not sober, breaking his promises to himself, unable to promise anyone else anything, bored and sad—and he could not help it.

His absolute final decision may suggest emotional violence, quarreling, etc.; but there has been none, except that one thing in his heart. Monroe would never require him to choose, one thing or the other, or present the least ultimatum in that way. The plan was all patience and

---

* Jonathan Tichnor. George Platt Lynes's friendship with his assistants Jonathan and George Tichnor marked a partial break from Monroe and the Wescott clan.

kindness and going on as always, with their relationship cut down to a kind of parallel of that between Monroe and me, with terrible misgivings all round but no bitterness.

I am anxious for you to know that we have tried hard to keep our household together; and also to understand why I feel that George has decided rightly, as the truth of the matter has been. Of course I have been able to foresee and estimate the gravity of what was happening better than he or Monroe could. I have done my best. Monroe knows as well as I how fond you both are of George, and twice this evening he has talked of that, thinking how you may miss him, because he is younger and gayer than we; wishing that his intimate misfortune did not have to keep George away from Mulhocaway, etc. But it cannot be helped now. We will try to make it up to you somehow.

Knowing all about our lives, you need not be told that Monroe is heartbroken, and knowing him, you can imagine more or less how it affects him, how he takes it: with that sort of starry-eyed and shy or stiff way he has always had in sorrow or pain, a kind of brilliance mixed with humility, and no anger at all. But I don't think you need worry about him. He is spoiled in the way in question—the one way I have not been spoiled—but he loves to work, and he has me, perhaps at my best now: we shall see. Unless his health plays tricks he will be happy again, when the time comes.

From a letter to George Platt Lynes

March 3—evening

The first page of your new letter, the emotional page, worries me badly. My poor George! At first reading I thought it a little selfish or irresponsible, but now I feel that it cannot be as simple as that. It has your truthfulness of feeling, which is always extraordinary; and I think it shows a lack of what I call imagination, which you have often lacked. By which I mean a kind of ability to put yourself in another's place.

Or perhaps I have just misunderstood it somehow. I do understand you yourself, I believe; and I understand about loving Monroe: the fact that you have not ceased loving him, and the fact that you cannot love him in the old way. Your love of Jonathan is stronger, though perhaps lesser; which is perfectly simple, and could not be helped. But I do hope, dear, that there is not a page just like this in your letter to him which I shall take to him tomorrow. Because I think it must be bad for him to have his feeling complicated by remote hopes; by seeming changes in you the exact significance of which is uncertain. He must have simplicity now, and a distinct path ahead of him; peace of some sort. He has had almost more trouble than he can bear.

In spite of his hurt and bitterness, he seemed quite willing to go on, all spring, all summer—who knows how long it might have been?—without expecting anything of you that could not be had for the asking. And I was prepared to play my sad but well-meaning, loving part. He had not done what I would have done in the first place. He could not have done it, given his natural nobility, gentleness, and scorn of extreme emotions, even his own. He overestimated your appreciation of all that, he underestimated your new love. It seemed to me that, as he had begun in that way of his, he must go on in it; and perhaps time would have worked in his favor.

It might have, for it is a kind of god; and Stone-blossom has been a good place for you. One of two miracles might have happened: either you might have cared for him again in the old way, or he might have ceased to care in that way . . . And then you yourself decided that this was hopeless; and you said that it was the best thing for you, the thing that you had to do to make peace with yourself.

And Monroe let you go without any argument, or compromise, or counterproposal, and without a whimper—because he was convinced at last that it was best for you. I think that I am justified in speaking for him on that point. Your letter seemed to me, too, absolutely convincing; it was an absolute farewell, and I did not see, I do not see, how Monroe could have asked or expected or hoped for anything after that.

At first, I must say, I could not think or feel anything much except a great fear of Monroe's dying of a broken heart. I have taken care in all my letters not to dwell on his shock and extreme sadness, and I do not want to now. He loves me, and that will serve for the present; and he will be happy again in due time. But it may be a long time, and you must use your imagination about his position. Trust me.

And you must be brave. I am anxious about you, but you know, I cannot feel altogether sorry for you. Not only because this is all your action and decision. For a far simpler reason than that—because you are in love with someone who loves you. Monroe is envious of you; he said as much one morning. I would have been envious of you not very long ago . . . Listen, George: As I look back upon your life as a whole, I see how it has always suited you to dream of the future of what you want; to be uncertain of it; to work toward it. This makes perfect sense. You will be all right. But you must be patient. You must not be pitiful; above all you must not do or say anything to make Monroe pity you.

You have begun a new life, of your own free will, in your own passion; and so these days or weeks do not matter; the main thing is all far ahead. Monroe has lost an old life, that is all; and so these days and weeks are all-important, perilous, a little chaos, until he can get his sense of direction and start anew. You are the lucky one, because you have done something, chosen something, decided something—whereas Monroe has only had something done to him—which is a far less healthy condition of soul to be in; don't you see?

March 5

Sometimes I feel as if I had been living for a long time with a couple of blind men.

March 7

An image that often grips my mind when I have seen disaster in the lives of those close around me and there is nothing I can do against it is one of Bosch's *Temptations of St. Anthony*, the simplest of the series, in the Prado.

The saint is all alone, sits staring with dislocated eyes, the gaze of one eye shooting up, the gaze of the other eye intent on something or nothing there in front of him; with folded hands, in a normal, noncommittal landscape, attended by only small but strong devils, as it were, vermin.

Haven't the interpreters of Bosch's art (Tolnay, for one) missed the point of this picture to some extent? Isn't it an image of that mental illness, *acedia*, which afflicted monks in the Middle Ages, perhaps precisely because they had withdrawn from worse evils in the world at large: a malignant boredom, a form of laziness.

One has to be lazy about others' troubles.

March 11

The intense need of pleasure of the senses may correspond to a state of ill health; as you might say, diabetes. Many men may go on leading useful, able, amiable lives if they have their insulin . . .

Monroe and I were very poor when we first came to New York in 1922—the pay for the critical work assigned to me by *The New Republic* was pin money—until I engaged myself as a sort of secretary and reader-aloud to an old financier, philanthropist, and art collector, Henry Goldman, who was going blind; and after a few months I accompanied him and his family abroad.

Mr. Goldman was romantically pro-German, like most German Jews in those days; and his favorite philanthropy was assisting the German universities to re-equip their laboratories and to bring their libraries back up-to-date. Heinrich Spies, one of the great men in organic chemistry, had had a lion's share in this expenditure; and one evening he invited us to his plain bachelor apartment in a suburb of Berlin, to express his gratitude and his hope of further assistance. His hobby all his life was the falsification of precious stones; and after dinner he brought out a large tray of his flashing little masterpieces, any one of which, he maintained, would fool any jeweler. Strictly speaking they were not false, only man-made—secrets of nature found out and repeated in the mortar and crucible and furnace; the long loose processes of mineralogy narrowed down to a few carats at a time, and accelerated; an artificiality suggestive of art, in a way.

The proud artificer admitted to us that when he had a brilliant student without funds for his education, he would assist him to fabricate a sparkling handful, which a certain dealer who admired his work, and who was impatient for Germany to re-establish its supremacy in science at least, would put fraudulently on the market in India. This delighted Mr. Goldman, a naturally wily although honorable old fellow. Meanwhile my thesaurophilic eyes had been shining in contemplation of the trayful, which the Herr Professor observed; and as a compliment and token of recompense to his benefactor he presented me (his benefactor's employee) with a fine sapphire, remarking that sapphires were symbolic of truth.

I took it to a young silversmith away out on the Kurfürstendamm and had him set it in a ring as well as he could contrive and I could afford, and sent it back home to Monroe—still unemployed, still living where I had lived with him, in a room below street level under the deafening Third Avenue El. He has worn it to this day: a becoming thing on his smooth, autocratic hand. Meantime, five or six years ago, Heinrich Spies discovered how to fabricate, and did in fact fabricate, gold—the first alchemist in a millennium or two to solve the problem. He was awarded the great Prix Curie for it, and his picture appeared in all the Sunday supplements: a frail dressed-up old gentleman looking less like Faust than like Nietzsche.

The moon is important to me. Like many men in whose lives imagination has been much employed and developed, I have a passion for bright light, even a folly about it, be it sunshine or firelight or electricity, no matter what, even a drop of dew or a piece of glass. But from smoking to excess, and too much of the written word one way and another, and conjunctivitis and insomnia, I am light-shy. Unless I frown and squint and look sideways I get wretched greenish-reddish spots before my eyes. Hence the night is the best time for me to enjoy brightness; I can look at the moon to my heart's content, and therefore I love it.

July 3

Last night along the river there was an unfamiliar species of firefly. If I have ever seen any of this kind I have forgotten them. They give a greenish light and they do not sparkle; they float, they glide, they blow softly, for two or three feet at a time. Down the stream amid the loose dark drapery of the sycamores and willows went their uncanny reflections. They do not seem to have any energy except light, floating along in the air, then relaxing and resting in the dark.

Speaking of prayer: This morning, when I thought my pearls were lost and after frantic searching discovered them, it came very naturally to me to kneel by the bed, in contrition of my carelessness, in jubilation of my good luck. It was wonderfully pleasant, with sense of humor entering into it somewhat. I think it would be good for me to practice some such formality regularly, if only for a sort of autosuggestive effect.

Metropolis:

New Yorkers who live in houses envy New Yorkers who live in apartments; New Yorkers who live in apartments envy New Yorkers who live in hotels; New Yorkers who live in hotels envy New Yorkers who live in hospitals, and vice versa, and ring-around-rosy, and pot and kettle, black, black.

From a letter to Katherine Anne Porter

Early September

The lawn-mower and the autumn-leaf rake still lie outside the window where you and Monroe respectively left off wielding them . . . Just before you left I had an annoyed feeling that our fine plan was going to slow up and seem to balk—for all the world as if it, itself, were the conclusion of a novel—but not at all, it has speeded up; and by the time this reaches you I think there will be nothing to it except your choosing one of two places: Lake Mohonk Mountain House or Harbor Hill Inn, Cold Harbor, New York.

It was dear grand sterling Janet [Flanner] who found out about the latter (you see, one always has to forgive her liking for crullers and other faults of taste) I wrote her a postcard just after you left, and yesterday she spent one hour upon the telephone hither and thither, calling me here and at 410 to report: with barks like a good dog, in her old fondness for me and great admiration for you. I also got my sister Beulah to interview all and sundry at Harper & Bros., and I visited a very businesslike and seemingly imaginative agency, and I saw George twice, and tried and failed to reach some other people—but Harbor Hill Inn, which was one of Janet's three places, which Monroe telephoned to this morning, seems the best. Either that or Lake Mohonk Mountain House . . .

They aren't much alike. Lake Mohonk is a huge summer hotel (as you saw by the photograph) with a boys' school eating in it, and figure skaters out the window—Monroe has a notion it might not be simple enough, or not solitary enough, or not European enough, to suit you. My sister Elizabeth is, as you know, all for it.

Harbor Hill also has, I understand, a lovely view: not so Swiss, no figure skaters, it looks over the Hudson. It is small, and personally run by an American lady once married to an Italian, name of Montefiore; and the cooking, they say, is famous. It asserts in its little printed folder (which I believe Monroe has instructed them to send you) that it is especially conducive to literary composition; and some friends of Janet's who have stayed there say this is no vain boast; it makes sense. What Mrs. Montefiore offers you is a small cottage a bit away in a small woods: which is heated by an open fireplace and by a coal stove—but, she says, there are three men to keep that going for you. She will send breakfast to you there on a tray, and luncheon as well, if you wish. Or you can lunch, and in any case you will dine, in the main house. Disadvantage, the only obvious one: no bathroom in your cottage: you will have to bathe just before or just after dinner in the main house.

There isn't much to choose in the matter of price: $40 a week or something like that at Harbor Hill . . . It is not indeed $21 a week but we knew better than that, didn't we? I can't add or subtract or multiply or divide, or even remember. I shall trot down to the Gate after lunch and see how rich or poor Barbara feels. I hope she can cope with it all. If she can't I shall get after your other adorers, George for one. I hope Barbara will feel rich enough; I know she feels very exclusive and possessive, which you certainly encouraged by your dedication. She is *ancien régime* anyway.

A letter from Nelson Lansdale in Rio, boasting of glamour—a round of hotels and restaurants and bars, and money to burn, with a sailor with topaz eyes disguised in his (Nelson's) sack suit, which is what he calls "discretion" . . .

No one was ever less capable of seeing himself as others see him, but what pleasure he takes in seeing himself as others would, he thinks, envy him.

A point about modern art: In the beginning, when what is called office surgery was done in barbershops, a barber's pole was intended to represent an injured leg or arm wrapped round with bandages. Thus, function to abstraction; abstraction to decoration . . .

As I crossed Fifty-ninth Street, someone thrust a cane walking stick between my legs, which nearly upset me and my armful of packages. It was a blind young Negro, not tapping the sidewalk but waving it before him like a wand. Later that afternoon, in front of Bloomingdale's, waiting for the traffic light, I stood close to two Negresses of refined type, perhaps lady's maids, and I heard these words: "So I said to her, very solemn, I said: Why should I be the one to take your eye to get it fixed?"

While I have been shrinking indoors with a little influenza, the parching radiators and drafts here and there, cold feet and clogged breath and steaming inhalations of benzoin, have been all my weather.

Outdoors they have had salubrious cold, bare sunshine, severe sunsets, and the darkness at night gray, and the stars yellow. Now for months I shall not have the loud breathing of my brook to sleep with; there is a great silencer of ice on the dam.

1 9 4 4

---

*For my part, I like works of fiction to have
meaning, the deeper and more consequential the
better; and unless I find this to my satisfaction,
fiction reading amuses me very little and leaves
me discontented. Story form can convey a greater
and more accurate truth—as to human nature in
its various manifestations and inhibitions, and
general human fate of the day and age—than
any abstract or generalized literature, dogma or
dialectic or deduction of science.*

—"Somerset Maugham and Posterity"

Stone-blossom
January 5

Dora Maxwell is the niece of a gentleman Guernsey breeder in
Texas or thereabouts with whom Lloyd and Barbara made friends some
years ago; they did not know Dora then, or scarcely. Her father has an
odd profession, in which I believe he stands high: traveling around the
country planning and planting groves and golf courses and the like. I
have met him now and then when his work has brought him East; a
gentle, very silent man with old-school manners who loves music.

Dora has great charm of appearance, but not pulchritude. She is
what the French call *rondelette*, though not a bit fat; and she has sea-
blue eyes. I sometimes complain of her Southwestern accent, a sort of
invigorated form of South'n. She is thirty but she seems young, and is
not the least spinsterish either in the old-fashioned manner or in the
hard metropolitan manner.

She has been George Lynes's assistant for several years now, beginning as a technician with the films and proofs and prints; then gradually, as his studio became practically big business, taking over the
negotiation and management of it all. She is one of the ablest girls I

know. But the general respect and enthusiasm is based, certainly, on something else: tact, gentle integrity, and subtlety. Never seeming to pay much attention to what goes on around her, she has known all our secrets; and we have found her wonderfully helpful, in the oddest circumstances, with principles as innocent as a child's but no unworldliness, no ignorance of any sort of human nature; and meanwhile she has led her separate, rather severe life without severity, never clinging or even confessing any loneliness. From the start of her friendship with Kiko* we found ourselves wishing that we might have her in the family— at least Barbara and I did.

It must be a year and a half since they began to be attracted to each other. Our first reaction, that is, my first reaction, was to be fairly sorry for Dora. We could not understand what Kiko had in mind or in heart. He has a mysterious face, and I could not tell at what point he was ceasing to be a boy, beginning to be a man. Sometimes he seemed to be behaving almost badly toward her, as very young men do, thoughtlessly or heartlessly; casting a spell and just keeping her under it, careless of what it might mean to her or do to her. Off and on, whenever he was around, she was his close friend, his comrade, his playmate, and that was all; and it seemed that he might never go a step further, but neither would he withdraw a step. This autumn Dora confided to me that indeed he had made her unhappy. It had been her folly to fall in love with him, and she had concluded that he cared nothing for her except in comradeship and playtime. She pretended that she had got over her disappointment, which I pretended to believe; and she added that, having given up hope of love, she would try to draw closer to him as a friend, and to find out something, whatever it was, that made him mysterious. She too thought him lonely somehow, and perhaps unhappy.

Then suddenly it all turned to romance. We did not need to be told what had happened. It shone in Kiko's face as if he were out of breath from dancing; or as if he had caught some sort of fever that turned out to be delightful. One thing in the changed expression of his face has fascinated me—it struck me the other day when Dora showed me an assortment of photographs of him, from boyhood when he first came here up to date . . . His eyes used to seem small, sad or listless, while his mouth had a look of pretending that everything was all right, with his lips turned up or held up; not complacent, but something like that. Lately his eyes have been sometimes steely, sometimes starry, but often he shuts his lips tight or they droop a little. It is as if, with happiness

---

* "Frederico" or "Kiko" (Francis) Harrison was a son of Barbara's father by a later marriage.

of mind (in his gaze), there were no further necessity of pretending about his emotion (the expression of his mouth).

That was the month of December; it was all they had. One weekend they went to Mont Tremblant to ski, and they reported that, at 40 degrees below zero, it had been heavenly. They wanted to return there the next weekend but they could not get any place in the train or room in the hotel. Meanwhile there was boom business at George's studio, and all the week Kiko worked in the darkroom with Dora. He spoke of marriage but without really proposing it, and Dora was far too happy to ask anything of him or, for that matter, to deny him anything. I think it did not occur to anyone, certainly not to Kiko, how much she wanted the formality of marriage, ring and bell and book. On Sunday night, January 2, they dined with Monroe and me and some other people, including Maugham, during which Dora whispered to me that Kiko had expressed regret about their not being married, and this made her almost as happy as the fact of marriage would have done. But then it was too late. Kiko's plane was to leave at one-thirty the next day, on Monday, January 3. At about eleven-thirty that day I went to the studio to say goodbye to him, and then he told me that he regretted their not being married. I promised that we would all care for her as if she were his wife, which pleased him. I told him to take as good care of himself as he could without losing the war, which made him laugh. By that time a great blizzard had begun, and the one-thirty plane was grounded.

George had engaged Dora for dinner that night, in order to distract her from her first loneliness; and Kiko's departure having been postponed until one-thirty the next day, he came along. After dinner, while George was in another room telephoning, they decided to try to have some sort of ceremony after all, that night, or the next morning, in the time the blizzard had given them. Dora remembered that the *Daily News* Information Bureau advertised that it knew everything of that kind. It recommended their going to Baltimore, where there is latitude in the law for sudden romances. They tried to telephone Barbara in Florida, and Mr. Maxwell in Oklahoma, but of course that was the hour when the armed forces telephone and their calls did not go through. They telephoned me at Monroe's apartment, but I had gone to the theater and Monroe had forgotten what theater. So, with Monroe and George, they took a ten o'clock train.

After the theater I found a message from Monroe. Their plan was to return immediately after the ceremony, which would be perhaps 4 a.m. or 5; but they promised to telephone me in the meantime. At 2:15 a.m. they telephoned: the *Daily News* Information Bureau had somewhat exaggerated the simplicity of the laws of the state of Maryland. Would I, please, meet them at 8 a.m. but not in Baltimore: in the courthouse of Elkton, which is just over the state line from Wilmington, Delaware, and an hour nearer New York. They would need that extra hour in the morning in order to get back to La Guardia Field in time for Kiko's plane . . . I was very sleepy, and for a moment the uncertainty, discomfort, and loneliness of that trip seemed more than I could abide; but they seemed so eager and tender that I was ashamed to say so. Then I found that I did not have money enough, and I could not think of a soul in New York that I should have been willing to wake up and borrow from. But I remembered that Monroe's father had given him ten dollars for Christmas, and finally I found it tucked into a briefcase with a bundle of Christmas cards.

To keep awake, I went on down to the Pennsylvania Station ahead of time. It was a fine sight: the waiting room, which is an imitation of the vastest and most beautiful imperial baths in Rome, full of the armed forces even at that hour. A great many of them were asleep, flat on the floor, or in Roman or Renaissance attitudes on those broad gradual balustrades leading up to the street, with tousled hair, pale cheeks, sour breath. I was hungry but I could not find a lunchroom open, so I bought all sorts of patented candies. I was too tired to think, so I bought four detective stories. My train to Elkton left at 3:50 a.m.

I made an unexpectedly good connection in Wilmington, and arrived at about 6:30. There was a train from Baltimore due at 7:15, and I waited there in the little bleak station because I thought my wedding party might be on it. The town itself was some distance away, and it was pitch-dark and rainy and windy. Presently across the fields and vacant lots came a crowd of very young girls, in mackinaws and galoshes, with colored handkerchiefs tied under their chins and cigarettes in the corners of their mouths and hoarse, sleepy, friendly voices: defense workers on their way to Wilmington. My wedding party was not on that train; so I set off across the muddy vacant lots, with a cur dog keeping me company, very friendly; and I strayed into the Negro quarter, where there were no sidewalks; but presently I came to a somewhat main street and followed it until I came to a small crooked building with a good deal of electricity spelling out its name: the Ritz Hotel. Just inside the revolving doors Monroe was waiting, with his slight shoulders hunched up in his heaviest overcoat, his chin up, and his eyes laughing. Beside him George sat sprawling on a modernistic love seat with the kapok issuing out of the torn rubberette; and with fierce emphasis but in a whisper, lest he give offense to the hotelkeeper, Monroe forbade me to sit, lest I pick up some vermin or something out of it; but I sat anyway. It was in fact the dirtiest hotel I ever saw. Kiko and Dora were in a telephone booth announcing their engagement to Mr. Maxwell, who was sleepy but happy.

They had had a bad hour in Baltimore, from two to three, with their misinformation and lack of information, and a sense of having made fools of themselves. They sent Kiko into the USO to inquire, in his too courteous, too low tone of voice; but the USO did not give him any answer, only a couple of cookies. He also inquired of a Navy MP, who denied everything. They telephoned to a Baltimore newspaper, but it was even less informative than the *Daily News*. Finally Monroe scraped acquaintance with a person there in the railroad station awaiting a train to Florida, and he told them to go to Elkton; and they telephoned a parson in Elkton who was sleepy but encouraging. Then they treated themselves to an all-night Boris Karloff film for an hour, where Dora and George were able to fall asleep; and then they started to Elkton. By that time they knew everything, except that while the courthouse opened at 8 a.m. the license bureau did not open till 9; and the last train back to New York and La Guardia Field was at 9:32. It was a fine courthouse, the only ornament of Elkton, paid for by marriage licenses, no doubt . . .

The secret of the laws of Maryland is that, although they require forty-eight hours' notice of intention of matrimony, there is a waver for men in uniform whose papers show that they are in transit somewhere. But a mayor or a justice cannot marry you; it has to be a parson. And up the street from the Ritz Hotel, there they were, the marrying parsons, side by side, with bright signs like a red-light district. We decided not to employ the one to whom they had telephoned, because he was the farthest from the courthouse. Instead, Kiko and Dora chose one who had neon lights, and went in and consulted him. He was still in pajamas but he assured them that he would don his Sunday-best while they were getting the license, and have all ready, lest we miss the 9:32 train.

So we waited in the courthouse corridor for an hour. There was a bench which seemed preferable to the Ritz Hotel's love seat. Opposite us sat two other couples: a country-bumpkin infantryman with a pale chunky bride who did not seem old enough, and a high-yellow pair dressed in the height of fashion. The ladies' room was not open so we guarded the door of the men's room while Dora did her wedding primping. Monroe whistled the Wedding March from *Figaro*, which he does sweetly; and I, remembering how in the opera while it is being played Susanna pricks her finger and draws blood with a needle, did likewise with a pin. At last the license bureau opened, but the clerk did not have all his wits—he could not spell either Philippines or Oklahoma, and made other difficulties—so that it was 9:16 before Kiko and Dora reappeared with the blessed document.

But the parson was wide-awake and ready, in his little sitting room with too much furniture and too many homely ornaments. I was Kiko's best man, perhaps because I happened to be standing nearest him; perhaps because I wanted to be, and was pushing about it; perhaps because Kiko chose me. For a wedding ring they borrowed George's great square gold seal ring with two fleurs-de-lis and the moon and the arrows and the Stone-blossom horse on it; and afterward Kiko wanted a ring, too, so he borrowed Monroe's sapphire. The service seemed long, with our remaining sixteen minutes ticking away; the great ancient usual phrases, but not exactly as usual: it was an abridgment and combination acceptable to all religions. Dora started to say, "I take thee, Kiko," instead of "I take thee, Frederico Harrison." I shook in my knees as I always do. I also cast down my head, because the parson had halitosis, and I was amused by his shoes, which had no heels at all on the outside; but he was a kindly man, and not cynical.

He took us to the railroad station himself. The train was late, so we need not have hurried. We had not stopped to sign the wedding certificate, so we did that there on the platform, with each other's back by way of desk. There was a bright cold small rainbow, and it lasted until the train came. A cloud of small dark birds appeared, and danced and cried merrily in a tree nearby. A great freight plane flew down heavily, probably full of gunpowder, which is Elkton's other specialty.

All the way back to New York Kiko wrote telegrams in my scribble book, erasing and recommencing a great deal, and consulted Monroe about savings accounts and life-insurance policies. The United States pays him a good wage, with eighty dollars a month more as a married man. George napped, Dora wrote addresses of people to whom announcements were to be sent, then she and Kiko held hands. Monroe tried to nap but he was too excited, and I was as happy as I have ever been in my life.

We need not have hurried because, when Kiko got to La Guardia Field, he found that someone had taken his priority away from him. In fact he did not depart until the following night, so that he even had a little honeymoon after all.

March 7

Strange day: because unexpectedly the love of my childhood came to visit me—who first kissed me in a bower of mock-orange in blossom twenty-eight years ago, whom I last saw thirteen years ago. Fortunately a distinguished and amiable creature, and not undistinguished in the simple way of places like Milwaukee; unfortunately not at all attractive physically.

Now I am alone again, in that loneliness which, more and more, is becoming a habit, almost a pleasure: beside the radio, with Albanese singing Lehár and Victor Herbert.

I dreamed of John Yeon* which was all simple happy eroticism at first, then anxiety, in which he turned into an unknown or composite figure surrounded by little blond young men. They kept breaking engagements with me while they had rendezvous with each other; and finally I had to go and dine with his mother, while he was off somewhere with his playmates. As I woke up I heard myself complaining of this bitterly. "I am not Falstaff," I said, "nor is this the dirty-clothes basket. But I do not want to be shut up in a clean linen closet either . . ."

In case two people are in love, and it is a good love, of all-round advantage to them both, then I believe that while they are living together, they should be faithful to each other; but I do not believe in chastity. I believe that in the prime of life everyone should make love two or three times a week, doing as best one can; and generally speaking anything, any sexual relationship, is better than none. After all, sexual intercourse is good in itself, because it is a healthy physical function, and a part of the way we are made to function.

The fat white sow running with the hindquarters of a rabbit in her mouth, her tiny blue eyes shining fiercely like a cat's.

March 16

It is wintry still, and tonight I am having to take cold preventatives; but it has seemed to me beautiful weather. Presumably because I am a man from the middle of the U.S. I like dramatic changes, and in one hundred hours we have had two nights of moonlight, a noble snowstorm, and now rain half-frozen and blowing about.

Dora Harrison has been here, a little worn out but well. Her romance all serene; their intentions on both sides now, I understand, "honorable." I liked W.H. very well when I met him at Monroe's. But he has fallen from Lloyd's good graces at least for the moment, for having calmly put

---

* John Yeon. An intimate friend of G.W. and an aspiring architect.

his feet up (with holes in his sock furthermore) and gone to sleep after dinner, when Mr. Merriman, the famous Guernsey auctioneer, came to dine.

April 4

There died today our dear John Peale Bishop, whom immoderation of love and alcohol and talk wasted and wore out.

April 7

The three sets of dikes which protect one-third of Holland from the sea—which the Germans now threaten to demolish—are called, respectively, the Watchman, the Sleeper, and the Dreamer.

May 15

A drunk in the dining car, trying to engage me in conversation while I was trying to work. "I see you are a busy man. I am a seaman, I sail the seven seas. You have to concentrate and calculate, it's a pleasure, isn't it? I am so happy . . ."

These were his exact words.

I was so charmed that I held my scribble book up between us and wrote it down word for word as he said it.

Then to my surprise he and the dining-car steward spoke in French. I questioned the latter about it a little afterward. He had learned French in the other war, the world war. The drunk, he said, was Belgian, a merchant mariner discharged for some psychoneurosis; he used the world-war term for it, shell shock.

Debo* is passionately learning the language, and one of the exercises she likes best is "Where is Kiko?" to which she replies gleefully, "Navy." It is odd that, just when her passion is to learn the meaning of words, some that are mysterious to her should charm her so.

June 6

The invasion: the sixth hour of the sixth day of the sixth month of 1944. What have our astrologists and numerologists to say about this?

June 19

All night, fireflies in the rain. All morning wrens in the rain, undiscourageable, with their song, which is like boring a little melodious hole in the air or driving in a thin golden tack.

---

* Debo (Deborah) Wescott (1942–   ). Daughter of Lloyd and Barbara, niece of G.W.

July 23

Chapelbrook, Ashfield, Mass., the week after finishing *Apartment in Athens*: In the most comfortable chair in Mina's* sitting room; her English sheepdog, Muffin, looks like a prodigious amount of combings of some old giantess's hair, blond intermingled with ashen; matted and dandruffy.

Woods Hole
August 8

At daybreak, a school of fish having come in too close to our beach, the small black-masked gulls, perhaps a hundred of them, gathered to feed on them, in a pandemonium of cheeping and yelling, dropping to the surface and instantly rebounding from it, up and down on the water. It looked like winged popcorn in a popper of sunbeams over a highly polished stove.

Stone-blossom
August 25

I have kept hoping to get to Washington the first part of next week, to see Katherine Anne. I have only got started at my *N.Y. Times* review of *The Leaning Tower*. I am as stupid as a stone on the one hand; as inspired and complicatedly inbrainy as the Cumaean sibyl or something. They have allotted me only 1,200 words, and I have about 1,200 distinct ideas which I haven't yet given up incorporating in it; and at the same time I propose to do a shrewd bit of advertising of the merchandise in question. Until this morning I proposed to fix a date for Washington, and then take that for a deadline and whip myself through; but this morning that seems imprudent.

August 26

News here? Infinite or nothing. The weather is heavenly but the lawn, etc., are as burned as old newspaper. As Monroe and I took our *tour de propriétaire* barefoot along the brook, we encountered a fat young copperhead. We ran for great rocks to break his back with, but he slid away under the mint and we did not dare follow him. Life is like that . . .

August 29

Forgetfulness is the devil, I have decided. It keeps rising around our feet, whiffing around our heads, imbuing us through our pores. God

---

* Mina Curtiss. Sister of Lincoln Kirstein, biographer of Georges Bizet, and lover of Alexis Saint-Léger (St.-John Perse).

knows we have imagination about life and about each other, but it is opaque, like the exudation of a squid, sepia. It is all abstraction, principle, prejudice, inhibition—and we never know the story, or if we do we never tell it and therefore we forget it.

An image of Mozart: Into my ear this melody fits like a golden key and unlocks my mind.

An image of the misery of existence: In my bedroom early in the morning the idiot fly, loving me with his itching foot; waking me and escaping me, buzzing and coming back. I had had a desperate jealous dream. I felt a sickliness in the pit of my stomach, as I often do until I have had my coffee. There on the floor lay my clothes, slovenly, where I had dropped them the night before. Somewhere a cow bellowed and bellowed.

One of the cleverest and least kind criticisms ever made of my way of writing was made by Rebecca West, whom I greatly admire; for whom I also feel a real personal affection; and who, I believe, is friendly disposed toward me. But she is a wit, and even her close friends are not quite safe from her intelligence.

What she said was that I had devised a peculiar form of fiction about life in my native state of Wisconsin, and this was the formula: There was a small boy who loved his grandmother so much that when he grew up he wrote a book about a small boy who loved his grandmother so much that when he grew up he wrote a book, and so on, *ad infinitum*. She did not say *ad nauseam*, but I am afraid that was the idea. She pointed out that all my work up to date had been in the manner of an introduction or presentation of myself, elaborate and over and over. "Dear Reader, I want you to meet Me. Reading public, Glenway Wescott . . ." And that was that, Miss West thought, and what of it, she wondered. Her advice was for me to hurry up and get on with it and give some good reason why I was worth meeting.

Of course this made me wince, and of course it made me laugh, but I took it seriously and I have never forgotten it, and I think that, little by little, it has had a good influence and helped wean me from that subjectivity which, in one form or another, handicaps a good many writers today.

1 9 4 5

Read this as fiction if you prefer to. A part fiction
is error, and another part is forgetfulness; and
when a great many years have passed, the same
is apt to be true of truth.
—"The Odor of Rosemary"

Stone-blossom
March 23

If I am still to have lovers I must bestir myself with some regular exercise: softer and softer belly, unmanly arms, etc. Naturally I have lost confidence in myself about this: I am too weary or busy, too preoccupied or absentminded. But it shocks and alarms me when I reflect that I have begun to allow these same weaknesses to come up, as to the care of my teeth, hair, fingernails, etc.

Having money to spend, and more in prospect, has not given me as much pleasure as I hoped; for which I am partly to blame. It has gone in confusion, and in more ways than one I am left with a bad conscience. I must take my checkbook and paper and pencil, and see what becomes of it. I must also list my plans for Stone-blossom in some order of priority, and expedite them as fast as possible, and postpone other temptations.

As to the budget of my heart and senses: First and foremost, there is my new enigmatic lover, in him I find beauty and compatibility more than in anyone this long while; who may return soon and take care of me. If he does, how much simpler my life will be than I have expected! I think it is too good to be true.

Meantime it is spring here—bright but chilly—I am sitting on my new fine soft sofa in front of a lonely fire. I am not really in residence, no servants, all cluttered and dusty, no hot water, etc.; and so it will have to continue for a fortnight or so, while I play wet nurse to *Apartment in Athens*: interviews and little orations and broadcasts, and various negotiations. The part of this that is definitely hard work is rather fun;

but what one is supposed to enjoy is not enjoyable, although one has to pretend . . .

A letter from Nelson Lansdale, whom I have not seen at all this winter, announcing his departure to Germany under UNRRA, for the rehabilitation of slave laborers and general handing out of our presumed bounty. He says that his life has gone badly and this is a kind of escapism. I am to dine with him on Tuesday. I am curious to know whether this is misjudgment on UNRRA's part or merely someone's amiability or corruptibility. He is not the kind of American whom Germans respect; I am not happy about it, it arouses my particular sort of pro-German sentiment.

Which, in a way, brings me to *Apartment in Athens*. It started off with very large sales, first in Chicago, etc., but now, as I must say I foresaw, it has begun to strike a bottom. It will not be a real best-seller. Unfortunately, from that point of view, it has been reviewed both pro and con as a war book, with nothing much about the middle-aged love story or the children or the philosophy. A playwright named Paul Green is working on a draft of a play, but as he seems inspired to soften it up in every way, I plan to reject it.

I cannot say how tired of it I am. People all ask me the same questions; and now that I have worked out the answers I hear myself over and over like a phonograph. I am tempted to change things just to make it more amusing for myself . . .

From an address to the Book and Author luncheon at the Astor Hotel in New York on April 10

. . . Let me conclude with a little statement of my belief and disbelief about the Germans: personal and categorical.

I do *not* hate them. Hatred in my opinion is a silly emotion except as it may be a concomitant of physical fight, actual combat, or real revolution. It is not very useful in the mind of the noncombatant citizen. For one thing, we can't keep it up. It leaves us with a hangover; a kind of remorse and a correspondingly silly fit of forgiveness, as it was after the other war . . .

Do you hate a tiger? Do you hate a malarial marsh? I don't. Only when there is a danger to myself and to those I love, an immediate menace and specific enmity, a specific menace to all I believe in, I do not feel called upon to look at it from the tiger's point of view or the mosquito's point of view.

I admire the Germans, taking them almost at their own estimation; allowing for the fact that their moral sense especially in international relationships differs from our moral sense. They are a supremely well-educated, gifted, hardworking, law-abiding, and patriotic people. But by their own candid account and great repeated demonstration, they feel a decided hostility toward us and envy of us and scorn of us. I am afraid of them. They grow stronger against us each time we defeat them in a war and let them have the peace as they want it. It is not hatred to say no. It is not even disrespect to say no.

I do not despair of them either. I have no tragic-feeling sense, or bitter resignation to another world war; not yet. The problem of the century seems to me simple; it is up to us. The Germans are a serious people, and intelligent, according to that idealism of theirs which is deadly to our idealism. They are entirely honest in their belief that the world would be improved if it were governed by them; not to mention the glory and the profit to themselves. Indeed, *if* you accept their premise—if you have no self-interest in the matter, if you do not care what the cost may be, in individual agony, in waste of civilization, years of nightmare—their concept of themselves in history makes a kind of sense.

Generally speaking, they are not foolish or psychopathic or suicidal or anything of that sort. Sometimes it is a part of their craftiness to pretend to be. They simply expect to be able to conquer the world sooner or later. They came so close to winning this war that actually they have every right to think that they may win next time. Even now—in the excessive zeal and pride of the statesmen of France, and in that disapproval of Great Britain in which our liberals indulge and that fear of Russia which haunts our conservatives, and the sentimentality and frivolity into which we Americans may be expected to relapse as soon as peace is declared—even now they have hope. All we have to do is take that hope away. If, for a generation or so, we keep united, indicating to them that we have resolved not to be conquered, that we have learned our lesson, that their dream of world rule is in vain—they will give it up! They will turn to some more practicable ambition and less destructive historic role.

Now that the war is almost over there is talk about our re-educating them; and a good deal of this seems to me ingenuous and vain. Although the modern techniques of propaganda, even the Nazi techniques, derive principally from our journalism and advertisement, we have made a muddle of it ourselves. Our wonderful free press has been a thing we have been fighting *for*, not fighting *with*. Certainly we have achieved a great unification of mind, in our far-flung variegated land, melting and blending the foreigners who have come here—and Germans make the very best Americans in the shortest order—but it is our way of life, on the spot, which does it; not a conscious educative method. As a matter of fact, even in its effect upon ourselves our great system of education has disappointed us, so far. I think we should let the Germans re-educate themselves. For better or worse they are good at it.

Stone-blossom
May 15

It is over now, the salesmanship, the acting like a success in order to be successful. I did things I had never done before, little speeches, broadcasts, etc., things I might never have been willing to do—but I had a good excuse this time, as this book was among other things my war assignment. I wonder about next time. "Career" is a strange problem. *The Pilgrim Hawk*, most favorably received by the critics, sold only 2,300 copies. One Friday afternoon five men, especially one man, decided that *Apartment in Athens* was to be a so-called best-seller. Some 380,000 copies were called for before publication; but only another 12,000 or 15,000 have been sold since. Wild horses couldn't make the three hundred and ninety thousandth book buyer buy. The objection has appeared to be the same as to my previous writing: "cold, brilliant, remote." I may add that, as this jackpot is being expended, it has not given me a great respect for money as such . . .

It is a fateful, although pleasant hour anyway. My house has been closed for months, heatless, servantless—then there was a floor to put down, and some other disorder, while I sprang into town and back, back and forth, as an organ grinder's monkey. This is the first day with no "necessity" of doing anything "unimportant"; the first writing day; alone at last, alone with a manservant.

It is early morning, beautiful, and in the uncurtained window which I sit facing there is an obtuse angle of old crabapple boughs, so that a fiery red squirrel leaping from one to the other appears to fly like a bird, across a lonely, pallid-bluish sky.

May 31

Lloyd and Barbara have just left me. Over their heads, as they sat on the sofa, there shone a glass jar full of sexy-pink peonies, under Soutine's *Blue Boy*. It was an eyeful, luxurious: Barbara very pale and Lloyd farm-color.

They were both tired out: Barbara by having been to town to see

Dr. Burchell, Lloyd by having made hay. Nevertheless I began what is now up to me in the way of reforming their way of life; and they took to it well enough. Burchell quoted medieval Latin and Sainte-Beuve to her today for a change, and praised my literary art to the skies. Lloyd was bothered by fawns, the size of puppy dogs, hiding themselves down in the alfalfa in front of the mowers.

June 1

Two little letters have gone to David;* not important, but as it were warbling, woodnotes wild, of fox sparrow, or perhaps a screech owl.

There is a red squirrel on the lawn outside my window; up and down with hot flashes, like electricity, like neuralgia, like love.

I have done a good deal of work on my Cain and Abel book but I have not actually begun it—that is, not with a sharpened pencil in a new scribble book on a page marked 1—having some infantile sense (good sense in a way) of finding or making an occasion of it, dramatizing it a bit, so as to bring myself luck.

It is a life, although not easy: heaven is often more complicated than hell . . .

June 4

I have refilled my leather triptych for photographs: Monroe, David, and W.S.M., i.e., Life, Love, and Letters. Life is all things, for better or worse, so there can be no quarrel with it, it keeps one going; Love, for the time being I am against it, I presume it's for other people; and Letters, that's always all right, though just now I hate it.

My peonies in the glass bottle still hold—I care not to touch them, to change the water; they would tumble. Their pink has turned a little bluish, more improper than ever.

The weather is not good for much, except in bed or at a desk. I have been fairly diligent at the latter—interspersing my own creation, at its most problematical just now, wild and cloudy, with *Seven Pillars* [T. E. Lawrence]. This always fascinates me but I don't like it much. Under the great quilted or buckrammed style, an ugly form of man; ugliness and fleas. Certainly I am doing more than $100 worth of work on it.

A news item: In spite of good conservative principle, having purchased my unjustifiable Tanguy, etc., I have fallen a bit behind with my reserve fund for possible 1946 taxation . . . Pleasant excitement,

* David Posner. An intimate of Monroe Wheeler.

therefore, when I heard that I am having success in England: £250 on the advance sale, that is, circa $1,000. But, as I figure, subtracting what is due Harper's and their agents *and* Sir John Anderson *and* Mr. Morgenthau, I personally am left with $84.48!

By nature I am mercurial, I have a scatter brain, and my talent is the merest heat lightning loosely bright anywhere and everywhere—it is Anti-Self. When I get a chance to concentrate, see how I turn to it wildly, almost desperately, as if it were a godsend—a form, a pattern, a pole, an abode, though it be make-believe.

Now to work.

June 5

All day long the black cattle have bellowed, in a kind of undulant adagio. It was the castration of the bull calves—only it was their mothers who did the complaining, not they.

Tonight I have some small logs in my fireplace; their flames are the ruddy color of a tangerine, and they snap their fingers.

June 18

I have drunk up the remaining cold coffee and warm orange juice. I have walked all around the lawn and all along the brook, and found that in a sense all that has gone away too.

I did notice that the pink roses by the sun bath are large and relaxed and almost colorless, like a lover contented.

I found myself disgraceful in my comfortable nakedness; I got dressed properly, warmly.

Childlike, youthful: the delight in dates, and little ceremonial actions.

June 22

When I am on the ground I am terrified of the air, even morbidly; therefore I put off flying for years, until last December. And then I found it so astonishing a sensation, so beautiful, that I never noticed my fright.

I like to tell myself that perhaps death may be like that; so astonishing that in the final moment we shall cease to care . . .

Almost the full moon; one month having come round, only one. But although when the month began it seemed a great upset, having to dance to a sudden new tune, it really was not so. We have kept much the same thought of one another from the start; it was never less than friendship, or in other words, perhaps, it was always more . . .

This morning I work not with memory of delight, nor expectation, nor even hope—but with anxiety neurosis, that sore point in the psyche which is like a lost splinter when one has something too hard to do—my book, my damned book—with sense of doom, tendency to failure, loneliness.

How odd courage is! and perhaps the same for poor petty civilians as for soldiers. The essential is to act it, to go toward it unhesitatingly, all absorbed in one's pride of bearing and posture and pace. And of course, in reality, when the time does come, the payoff, the showdown, it's very different, it's pretty bad; but then it's too late, one can't give up or turn back.

June 23

There were Monroe and myself and guests, a husband and wife and a youngster; and out of my pocket I produced a comic little bottle of cantharides which David had brought from Egypt—"To become strong put a small piece from (*sic*) Spanish (*sic*) Fly in a cup of tea or coffee"—which set us joking; especially teasing the youngster, to whom evidently it made some little pornographic suggestion. Lloyd's joke was, "Americans don't need Spanish Fly!"

"Ha, that's what you think!" the wife exclaimed, with a not ill-natured but intense glance at the husband.

It made me shiver. For I could imagine, if there were any truth in what was certainly implied by her exclamation, if he ever chose to retort to it, what he might have to say for himself: for example, that in the process of the gestation and the bearing of their baby, the odor of her sexual organs had altered and hadn't been quite the same since; for example, that the flesh of her thighs had aged, dimpling and puckering, with here and there a certain dark varicose vein or dark varicosity; and for example, other decadences, in nature's way.

Is it so? Is that what husband and wife finally have to say to each other, goading each other to it? Is it, in the case of this particular husband and wife, true?

Sometimes I feel so sorry for the human race (men are such fools, women are such bitches!) that I could kill them; to save them from suffering, as it were, euthanasia.

Mrs. Arshile Gorky said that her husband had always enjoyed painting portraits until one morning when a beautiful woman sprang down from the model stand, took the brush out of his hand, and exclaimed: "Let me do my mouth myself. I do it every morning and I know how!"

June 24

Bill Miller,* in his somewhat flamboyant nudity, joyous almost to the point of seeming oppressive to me. Then he asked to see my famous boxful of Neapolitan photographs, which belonged to Jacques Guérin, which had a grand visible effect on him in which he took pride and joy, with boyish joking.

June 28

Tomorrow I will go to town and I will get Barbara a room at the St. Regis, air-cooled, for ten days or two weeks. So far, so good. The only thing she expressed a desire for was music; so I am lending her my phonograph and records and even Tovey.

Later I went across the brook and beheaded a great patch of Canada thistles, sweating too hot—too lonely for a mere sunbath—and I also made three beauteous bouquets (new hobby): one of thistles and small white asters; one of honeysuckle and *wild* roses out of the hedgerow; and one of mint, hemlock, and a multiple brassy-yellow flower that I do not know by name.

July 3

There is an entire great category of love which is hell, which artists especially must beware of: deathward—to waste oneself (whether all of a piece, in the grand manner, liebestod, or little by little in multiplicity, promiscuity, frivol and fritter); to immolate oneself, in the feminine way; to alibi oneself for not working, etc. I have a good peaceful certainty that this is not so, in the case of David and myself.

Big talk; big and bold, conceited, fatuous.

I know: Whom the gods will destroy they first make mad. I know: When merchants of Canton wish to dine on live monkeys' brains, they give them alcohol until they dance on the dinner table . . .

July 4

To be not even extraordinary, worth telling the story of; but only a worker and a lovemaker.

* William Miller. An intimate of Monroe Wheeler, he modeled for G.P.L.

July 5

Sleepy last night, moody and almost lamentable, I forgot to note the principal event of yesterday: Every year on the Fourth a softball team of the kids of Mulhocaway play against a team of the girls of the jail:* at sunset, Tchelitchew-pink, on the institutional greensward in front of its toy church against its languid flag—the spectator girls, Cadmus-faced, all around sitting squat or lolling but at the high points of the game bursting up onto their feet, jitterbuggy and ear-splitting.

Ethel Sahl, the Marijuana murderess, pitching to my young nephew, for example. A tall young Negress of the purest Lake Chad type, for example, famous for her bad temper; dangerous with a baseball bat.

My brother arriving late from the hayfield, across the field walking in his way like a limber crowbar; weary and melancholy—(especially melancholy toward me, in the present great little family deadlock) . . . He played an inning just before dark, towering over farm children and slum women; not just for fun—after all, he is no longer that young—but as a kind of gesture of Americanism, as he is a more and more authoritative trustee of the place, almighty there.

Dear America, poetical Fourth—for years I have been waiting for some little workable plot, to make a story of this scene.

July 7

It seems to be fate to have to bother like hell about allergic alcoholism in strange forms: my peculiar fate or man's fate in general nowadays? Sometimes I seem a little extravagant or idée-fixed about it.

This certainly is the strangest form, in my servant John's case: In the nine years we have known him, none of us has ever seen him in the slightest degree "under the influence"; but whenever he kicked up one of his rows with Lloyd he made a speech about it. We have not taken it very seriously; he is psychoneurotic in so many ways.

A while ago, upon my return from New York, I found that he had put a lock on my liquor cupboard; and he made one the speech. He said that in any case he would never take more than a nip, but he didn't want to; and at Lloyd's he used to control himself heroically, but now he has grown too old to be a hero. I replied that it didn't worry me at all, neither did I begrudge him his nip, but that every man has his sense of weakness, etc., and knows best about it . . .

Thursday I did my most concentrated day's work so far. I no-

* Lloyd Wescott gave his assistance to the local women's reformatory and sometimes provided jobs for former inmates, among them, Edna at Stone-blossom and Dorothy at Haymeadows.

ticed that John seemed a bit gloomy, but as I was too, I let it pass. In the middle of the afternoon I was called out of my study by a long-distance phone call, and on the sitting-room table found this note: "Mr. G. Wescott. You did not lock your whiskey closet, therefore I left the job for good. Good night. Time 3:10 p.m. John Csere. P.S. There are two steaks in the icebox."

I trembled with anger, and in self-pity almost wept.

July 8

Lloyd is so angry at John that he wants to take away the cow Rosemary, from whom his wife makes my (and their) butter. My father worries about my living alone with such a wild man lest his psychosis develop into a homicidal fury! In spite of which I, resolutely although insincerely (in a way), wrote John an appeal to come back; calculated to rend his heart in more ways than one.

Even before receiving this, he called me on the telephone, to convince me that his leaving me was a noble gesture, for my sake even more than his own. It wasn't the amount of drink, he said—and in fact as I remembered my bottles I could not see that he had taken even a nip—and it wasn't that he ever actually got drunk: it was the principle of the thing, it was thievery, and it made him too ashamed.

I do expect that he will come back in a few days. But plainly enough, although it is easier for me than it was for Lloyd, and this is a dream of a job for him, I am not really going to be able to control him, to tame him, to cure him. He will keep raising the ante: higher wages and less work, etc.

How odd! For perhaps he really is an allergic alcoholic; one of those for whom, after the first eyedropperful, it is all automatic, without a moral issue, no question of self-control—and he knows it and is panic-stricken by it. It is according to the latest medical opinion. How awful . . .

July 9

Pauline Potter* never comes until after the Fourth because of some pollen which makes her sneeze. But this year the weather has been odd and she sneezes. So for the most part we sat indoors and gossiped: Harry Hopkins† on Russia; the new illiteracy (her prospective husband, a

---

* Pauline Potter. Socialite who later married Philippe de Rothschild. Maintained a long friendship with G.W. and M.W.

† Harry L. Hopkins (1890–1946). Political administrator who served in a number of positions in the federal government, including as President F. D. Roosevelt's director of the Federal Emergency Relief Administration.

diplomat, only reads memos, *précis* of summaries of digests); the failure of de Gaulle; the life of Rebecca West . . .

July 10—midnight

It is one of those nights ringed round with thunderstorms, but we're in the almost dry, almost empty center.

Everything is morals for my brother, somewhat, somehow. Even when he draws a bad hand at poker he says, "I guess I don't live right." So for an hour tonight he tried to persuade himself that it was going to rain on everyone else's hay, not on his. It only takes a few spatters.

John wants to come back after all, and I took him back, oh, not wanting him; but in hardiness of mind and sense of duty, to keep from wasting my working time the rest of this week and next week house-keeping. I am a little afraid of him. There is an uncomfortable insincerity about it, too.

This is lemon-lily time; sprinkled like light around the back lawn. Their seed-catalogue name is Hyperion—which must refer to Keats, not to the moon—and each blossom lives but a day. One ought to go alone every morning and harvest away the dewy gummy dead petals, yesterday's.

July 14

I wonder if it may not help me to write a little diagnosis of Barbara's unhappiness from her most recent confidences, as to her plight of mind and heart, for her sake; and what of it, and what next . . .

Lloyd, with his puritan imagination and male ego, has changed the farm from what she expected it to be, and made of it the scene and the means of his becoming a model farmer; which is not the same thing as just farming. It is a non-profit-making idealized lifework; and while Barbara has been occupied with Debo, she has been left out of it. It is all now according to his concept, and as it were, chiefly to impress his fellow farmers, democratically minded if not politically minded—and in this he has not only somewhat neglected her but overruled her, for she feels a deep scorn and dread of everything in the way of public life.

Accordingly, she believes, he has wanted her above all to become a model farmer's wife, like other farmers' wives, and in a way like our mother, whom he strikingly resembles—in the common farmhouse, with the more local hired girls, with no housekeeper or chauffeur or gardener, with family instead of society, with endless duty and no self-indulgence—and Debo to be brought up not by a governess but by her personally, not as the little heiress, but as the model farmer's daughter.

And in the folly of love, assuming that he loves her less than she loves him, therefore taking the burden of the proof of love all upon herself, she has fallen into a desperate conviction that unless she succeeds in becoming the kind of wife that his type of man requires, he will grow cold to her. She has been making a despairing and foolish and obstinate effort.

Now, having failed with Debo in the one matter of getting her to eat, and having been ordered by Burchell to engage a governess, the sense of her failure in general has overcome her, and the knowledge of inevitable failure in other ways up ahead, and the expectation of losing his love: hopelessness and weariness and of course rebelliousness. She loves him so that she cannot or will not run away; she cannot even imagine ceasing to love him. The very thought of taking the responsibility for Debo again—the present governess is only for the summer, so that is the immediate issue—makes her cry. "Of course," she said, "when the time comes to engage another, if I can find another, of course he will give his consent. But I honestly believe that in his secret heart he will never forgive me."

Stop and think how this same conviction applies to the other changes in their way of life and standard of living which are necessary for her happiness: the new house and the requisite staff of servants, etc. How it would apply to anything that she might undertake, in pursuit of happiness by her own endeavor; anything she might fancy, to pass the time while he is absent, in a way of her own. For it would have to be an undemocratic and unagrarian and unpublic-spirited way . . .

Obviously there are morbidities in all this: the fear of not being loved, the excessive need of love, the reticence, the exaggeration, and the darkest possible view. She is aware of them, indeed miserably self-conscious about them. Half the time she is afraid that he is right and she is dead wrong; that he is healthy-minded and she is losing her mind.

But as to her main complaint: I myself (as well as Monroe, and my sisters, and even W.S.M.) have for a long time felt Lloyd's idealism and fanaticism: the dream of agriculture, the farmer in the dell. We have noticed his disapproval of everything that reminded him of her former pleasure-seeking European habit of life; his penny-pinching in household matters; his lack of enthusiasm about the new house . . . Like a lot of very virile, very lovable men, he does not know his own strength. He is not perverse, as she is, but in a sense he is more neurotic; he shuts his eyes.

It is what, in cases of law, is called a *folie à deux*, in which neither party can be blamed very much by himself or herself. But we can all honestly testify to the little steps, heedless, obtuse, by which she has been brought to her present unhappiness. It is not a mere imagined or invented thing.

July 15

A tepid, scented night, with the westward moon clouded away, milky; and the fireflies down close to the thickets, perhaps too humid to have much energy.

I am half ashamed of yesterday's discourse upon Lloyd and Barbara: the embarrassment and quibbled nakedness of two such good proud spirits—and even if worst should come to worst, they would behave better than I ever behave; they would dress up even failure and bitterness for their friends' sake; there would be no disgrace except perhaps my telling or writing . . .

July 16

Today I made a bouquet of wild carrot: which was the thing to wear in your hair at an Elizabethan party; which the Pilgrims brought over for their gardens but which ran wild. I made it beautiful but there was something wrong with it: it was like a lot of idealism gone wrong, it was too white, too pale green, it was like some unwarranted, pity-worthy passion . . .

Evelyn Waugh's latest, *Brideshead Revisited*, has fascinated me; it is very strong. He really has got his religion alive and tragic in it this time.

From a letter to W. H. Auden

July 17

This is simply a fan letter. All week I have been reading your *Collected Poems*, with such enjoyment and emotion and various uses. Thank you.

The most familiar poems are the ones which surprise me the most by their newness; which is a good sign in art, isn't it? It means that, having accustomed myself to the way they read, having got rid of the seven veils of originality, I find the real mystery still dancing.

A new impression as I read this time, very strong: your tragic sense, in spite of the smiling style. It is the manner that is the grand manner for us now: no stamping or hollering as in the classic past, but trying to behave if possible, speaking as kindly as we can.

Your verse has been highly praised always, has it not? and yet, I

keep feeling, never entirely *described*—as it is so many things to so
many men. To me this time, chiefly, it is a teaching; a teaching to music,
and with the little pleasures of imagery by the way, to warm up and
soften up the mind as it comes to the point.

Oh, it works. The other evening I dined with one very near and
dear to me who is in trouble, who has been unable to tell it without
wronging herself, exaggerating or unhealthily criticizing herself, weeping
or making bad jokes. Well, after dinner she asked me to read my favorite
poems by you; which I did, half a dozen not quite at random. And how
good and how obvious it was! She then promptly told the story straight,
so that something could be done about it, for the first time.

We are all grateful to you.

July 18

The sunset was like great wreaths of arbutus, in a pale west. I love
this place more and more, and tonight I loved it enough to be grateful
for Monroe's case of the absurd great lawn. It is like a vast French
carpet. The young rabbits were as unafraid as kittens. I played Flores-
tan's aria, which gives me gooseflesh. And then the honey-colored moon
rose into the dreaming hickories.

July 23

News item:
Katherine Anne has had her hair turned somewhat brown by her
penicillin cure, and sent a lock to prove it.

The black cows have lately been divided, assigned to the two bulls,
Hamlet across the road and Claudius in my meadow. And today one of
them, a she-devil, escaped and got upon my lawn. I telephoned, and
was instructed to hold her there until a posse could be sent, lest she
chase herself down the road for miles; and like a dope I obeyed. Back
and forth I ran, back and forth, trying to keep her on the far side of the
brook, and every time she got across she punched holes four to six inches
deep in my poor dear sod, weakened by the flood.

The trouble with farming is the sentimentality, I said to myself.
For surely the daffy creature is not worth what, in man-hours at the
present wage scale, it will cost to restore the lawn. The obvious thing
to do with her was murder—perhaps Bethea could have done it—and
no more bother about points for a while! Why can't my brother have
small pets, let us say Pekingese, or Nubian goats? I must try to keep
from making these remarks to him, just now . . .

In the midst of all this, to my amazement, magnificently in upon same lawn rode Barbara on Arabelle, blithely apologizing for doing even more damage than the cow; alas, true. I replied that it was worth it to see her on horseback, which I did mean sincerely. Unless I misinterpret, this is the best sign since all the trouble began to break. She is the most beautiful rider on earth, and gave it up.

This was Bethea's first day—on the whole a good day, although scarcely literary. I shall be able to make a Cordon Bleu cook of him, to my taste, and he's gentle and picturesque: he's so fat, and smokes cigars.

Schubert, Opus 163, the quintet with the pizzicati like tears— Monroe says it is grief, but I say it is only pain, with consent, with a chance . . .

July 26

At nine o'clock the west was still light gray with a tinge of violet across it, there were folds of mist close in the field, and the evening star was rosy. Then I heard an owl crying, the smallest owl—to think that that sweet flute is cruel hunger! I have wanted an owl all summer and I said to myself then, "I live in heaven."

July 29

Penance for an uprising of my out-of-date temper and, generally speaking, the debt to nature: I spent most of the day outdoors working hard, lawn-mowing, raking, etc., weeding and tidying. On account of the flood and incessant wet ever since, the lawn has run wild for sixteen days: the power motor couldn't take it until it had been cut once by hand. I am lame from head to foot, and stupid to match.

These are the tedious days with my new manservant. He breaks my dishes, he buys tomatoes from far away, boxed with cellophane, and Kraft cheese; and he seems a bit melancholy and indolent. Up socks, Wescott!

There is a bomber captain with whom I have exchanged a couple of letters. He admires *Apartment in Athens*, but what he is really grateful to me for is my Scott Fitzgerald memorial essay; he worships the memory of Fitzgerald. Now he is on leave and I may lunch with him. But I have a theory—I wish I didn't—that those who indite the best letters on literary themes let one down in person with something of a thud: it seems to be a compensatory talent.

Louise Crane telephoned from the Cape in an emotion to say that Ellabelle Davis, her Negress lieder singer, on some slight hemispheric tour, is stuck in Miami, Jim Crow trouble of some sort—can Monroe muster up some good neighborliness? Perhaps. Then her mother took the phone to inform us that William is staying on in Hollywood—they are spending three million, they need him, and they must be giving him a good time (that knowing George Cukor!) or he'd bolt—will we come up by ourselves? Yes, we will. I think I want to, and furthermore, Monroe will not take a holiday at all unless I join in it.

August 2

This afternoon I found an acre of thistles, the heavy Scottish kind, such beautiful flowers with large dark butterflies over them everywhere. I also found blackberries that hang down the bank of the Mulhocaway above the old swimming hole: juicy with the exhalation of the water splashing just there over stones, ripened by the refracted sunlight, dead ripe so that whenever I touched a bush some fruit went plop and downstream. I stood in the water to pick them. I had to break great spiderwebs between me and the best clusters; it was enchanting.

August 3

I have tried to make up my mind that Serkin plays the E flat major concerto as it should be—having bought it, my money's worth, please!— but I can't, he doesn't. That is, the Emperor Concerto. Monroe once asked to be buried to its slow movement.

August 4

Today is my father's birthday. I had asked them to dine, and Mother suggested my having a birthday cake—which reminded me that formalities must be good for ailing old souls—so I gave him a considerable present. (I can't think when I last did anything like that . . .) Also we exchanged honey and peaches and tomatoes, which made it like some olden time.

August 5

The amusing life of Monroe Wheeler: W.S.M. wouldn't take any pay for this summer's advisory work, in order to be free to walk out if bored. Now they wish to make him a present of an oil painting, fifteen grand's worth, and he fancies a Renoir—and Monroe is to do the preliminary shopping. The money's worth is probably not in Renoir but in Pissarro or Sisley. This, W.S.M. requests, is to be kept secret.

"... my sweet-sour expression, spoiled but virtuous, voluptuous but tough, heartbroken but happy. In only two photographs have I ever recognized this mood, to me most natural: one taken by the little Englewood professional who gave George lessons, the other by George himself, at my ease, propped up on pillows on the daybed in the rue de Vaugirard, flattering to my profile, with my forefinger touching my upper lip"

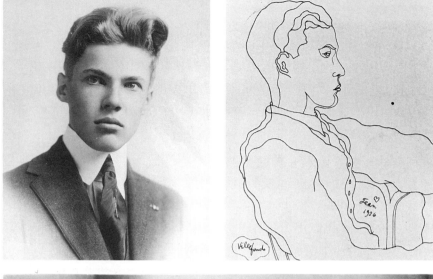

(*Opposite, top to bottom*) Wescott as a boy; a tracing of Wescott by Jean Cocteau; with Cocteau in Villefranche, 1926; with Thornton Wilder in Villefranche, 1928. (*Above*) Wescott and Monroe Wheeler. (*Below*) Wescott taken by George Platt Lynes in Paris, summer 1932

(Opposite, top) Two trips to Coney Island: *(left, clockwise from bottom left)* Cecil Beaton, Jean Cocteau, Wescott, Marcel Khill, and George Platt Lynes in 1936; *(right, clockwise from bottom left)* Wescott, Lynes, Wheeler, Katherine Anne Porter in 1937. *(Opposite, bottom)* With Fred Danieli, one of Balanchine's dancers, in the mid-thirties. *(Top left)* Portrait of George Platt Lynes by George Hoyningen-Huene. *(Right)* Wescott and Wheeler. *(Below)* With E. M. Forster at Stone-blossom, May 1949

(Left) Barbara Harrison Wescott in 1932. *(Below)* Glenway and Lloyd Wescott

(Above, top) With Bill Miller and Somerset Maugham. *(Below, left)* With Miller. *(Right)* Wescott posed under Tchelitchew's *The Lion Boy*

Mulhocaway Creek, 1942. *"Can this be the nude snapshot of me shown to Tennessee Williams in Mexico City by someone whom he disliked, as told in his autobiography? Much ado about nothing. My ado especially"*

August 6

Henry Moseley was a young British physicist or spectroscopist (if there is such a word) killed at Gallipoli in 1914, aged twenty; and it was said that he was probably the greatest loss in that war because it seemed he was on the verge of finding out atomic energy. This was most urgently called to my attention in 1918 by a learned old friend who wanted me to stop trying to be a poet *et seq.*—and this, as it signified one thing and another, I have incorporated in my book, with a figure shadowy offstage like Moseley. Therefore last week I procured a couple of books of popularized science, not quite popular enough for poor me at that, and I have been trying to decipher them, for the sake of one page.

Then I tuned into the middle of a news broadcast, and it was the middle of a sentence about the nature of the new bomb; it was spooky for me.

The pretentious thought I might almost have is that I have been suffering from intuitional fidgets or something of that sort. The broadcaster says that when it was first tried out in New Mexico three weeks ago a blind girl miles away saw the flash!?

Lovely even this morning when it has begun to rain again: as if it were an invisible swarm of bees in a huge hive of emerald.

One thing I did yesterday was to weed and cut back all the little Gloria Mundi rosebushes, which were sick . . . When I was young in Chicago there was a good-looking well-off exceedingly amorous woman (I wish I had got to know more about her, I'd put her in my book) who at a given time of her life developed some kind of religiosity and went to London and became a charwoman, as you might say for the fun of it—that sort of thing. Injurious things, Gloria Mundis: my arms look as though I had got into an intimacy with a sadist.

Debo now calls her parents Mr. Wescott and Mrs. Wescott, and takes delight in it.

August 9

Last night, the night of Russia's declaration, I wanted to wait to hear Janet [Flanner]'s broadcast from Paris, and I sat there scribbling for almost two hours; not even bothering to be accompanied by Schubert at the last.

Janet talked about minuscular Pétain as well as the huge atom; but as to the latter she quoted the great solemn Duc de Broglie, one of the chief smashers, whom I was pleased to hear from.

August 10

The hundreds of starlings seated on the two telephone wires, all taking flight at once, all giving a push, with their weight shifting from their feet to their wings; so that the fine black lines parallel on the dark cloud oscillate awhile after they have flown—it was like a little geometry lesson in a dream.

The first Frenchman I ever met was a small young vicomte with a small damp mustache, in New Mexico when I was eighteen or nineteen; and he told me a terrible story of life in the French trenches in the other war: He was about to go to Paris on leave when he heard from his superior officers that they were coming to make an inspection; so what do you suppose he was inspired to do? He ordered his men over the top, which started enough artillery fire to turn the officers back to headquarters; and not very many of his men got killed; and off he went to Paris only a little late for his various rendezvous.

Woods Hole, Mass.
August 14

It was a luxurious little journey. The air bumped and Westchester resembled a great bed of white phlox with blue foliage below. It took only two hours to Providence including the bus trips at each end.

There we called on the extremely handsome museum director, Gordon Washburn. He lets his eyes go this way and that, as a butterfly its wings at the end of the day when the day has been warm. He almost passionately admires *Apartment in Athens*. He almost passionately desires to buy one of Barbara's remaining Soutines.

He has just bought Renoir's big portrait of the Thurneysaen boy as a Greek shepherd: mystical bisexuality of Renoir's old age. (Cf. one of Yeats's letters to that lovely souse the Duchess of Wellington . . .) After showing us his other pictures, a mixed and somewhat shiftless but fine collection, he took us driving in his station wagon, to see the old mansions of Providence up on the hill.

Then we met the great Anne O'Hare McCormick* and her somewhat doddering husband, and motored the rest of the way in a cozy Cadillac, seventy-five miles. Leaving the heat behind us; coming into the slightly gray oceanic sunlight, which always reminds me of the Waterford glass, and the fragrance of salt, over the narrow inlets fringed with tidal mud— and then this house: like a palatial bathhouse, unpainted, with a great

---

* Anne O'Hare McCormick. Popular political journalist for *The New York Times*.

lolling deck; you dress in your bedroom and take your choice of ocean or bay.

Just outside my window, just offshore, is a furled sailboat full of golden small boys all standing, all in a row; as crowded as in that piece of symbolism which you find in medieval woodcuts entitled *A Ship of Fools*. A ship of innocents, or perhaps I should say, ignorants . . . Allowing for a change of tone from darkness to sunshine, they sound much like the gulls.

After dinner Mrs. McCormick made international gossip, of great interest but (to me) dismal general effect. She is not a reactionary, she is a proper liberal, but the darkness of the view she takes—her knowledge of our American power and blundering, her dread of Russia, with Stalin more and more czar-like, her exasperated pity of the rest of Europe amounts to almost reaction; at least stupefaction. I don't like the great newspaper mind, right or left: too much experience and not enough introspective psychology. A sort of promiscuity: maximum excitement about all sorts of things, but inability to go all out for anything, inability to love.

The night was rather as if I had died and gone to what was presumably heaven, cool and vacant, with the muttering of gulls making no sense in the dark; I did not sleep well.

August 15

Yesterday Jacques and Marianna Barzun* and Bobsie Goodspeed came to lunch, and we all entertained each other well enough. Then blessed old Padraic Colum came and read aloud a new bit of philosophy by Grode, upon which I helped comment. As I may have mentioned, Josephine is losing her eyesight, and she supports the poor poet to read to her, especially when she has no talkative guests.

I had one little thrill, very little and in a way sardonic: Mrs. McCormick telephoned her office and I overheard this sentence: "Yes, there on my desk; it's my end-of-the-war piece, but of course if the war has not ended, you can't run it." To think that the *Times* is the greatest newspaper on earth, that's all there is, there isn't anything better!

Then we went for a stroll, around the promontory where bankers live in vast unobtrusive buildings, chicken-coop-style—and by good fortune, or if you like by that intuition which entitles Mrs. McC. to her very large salary, got back just two minutes ahead of the news.

I am always interested in the circumstances in which great news

---

* Jacques Barzun (1907–   ). Author, scholar, and teacher.

is brought to one, scarcely less than in the news itself. Sometimes they are more suggestive of the future: the asides of fate, under its breath. I wonder how it was on Guam; doubtless more moving, perhaps, alas, not more significant.

I was glad to be, not out anywhere amid the excitement, but in a mere sitting room with little old individuals whom I know well enough to situate in the history lesson. Of course the radio brought us nationwide hubbub, *ad nauseam.*

The chief event on the radio (for some reason the cat got the President's tongue) was a long rhapsody by the famous Corwin elocuted by the famous Welles, with great wheezes and sobbing notes, with music by Wagner and others. We happened to dial into it after it had started— for a moment we thought it might be some new senator, resurrected Huey Long or overeducated Bilbo; for a moment it seemed intended to be funny, perhaps a comedian, surrealistic and bathetic. But then we began to get the rhythm, the collectivity and the chant of Whitman gone rotten; Whitmanism and Bandburger, and what Monroe calls McClichés. It made me ashamed of our victorious civilization as such.

We also sat up to hear the first translation of the Mikado's rescript as telephoned in by the translator from San Francisco to the typists in New York, a word at a time as slow as their respective wits and fingers, often misspoken, repeated, and interrupted: the commentators breaking in, thwarted of their optimism, sputtering and blustering against the antique or perhaps eternal insolent mumbo-jumbo. It seemed an image of the historic plight now: the extreme stupidity as to public morality and government, balanced against the extreme intelligence of inventors and manufacturers . . .

For several hours this morning I talked with Monroe about our world ahead, wonderingly, wearily; especially as to the situation of thinkers and artists now that the U.S. has the power, the question will come up, no getting around it: as epoch-makers with regard to civilization-as-such, are we worth it? I believe it will make me severe with myself, and perhaps scarcely indulgent toward others who appear to me to have brains and talent . . .

August 19

The lively combination of wind, sand, brilliance, and mixed temperature is more drugging than any Roman bath by the brook at St.-bl.

The scientists are scared to death of the atomized world (they are mostly biologists, of course). We'll have to trust to what ideas and ethics and ideals we have accumulated, it will move so swiftly now, we won't have time to bother with a reform of education, all we'll have time for will be a few individual masterpieces to dignify our era with—so the scientists seem to think . . .

Yesterday we lunched at Hyannisport at Hansi Lambert's; which I was especially pleased to do out of curiosity about the seventeen-year-old baron. Beautiful, with a columnar neck like Bill's; tip-tilted nose; and scarcely any look of Rothschild, except in his desert-bright eyes. He gravitated straight to Monroe as they do at that age; the way he listens is honey to them. What he had to listen to in this case was a very wise complaint of the education they give at Yale—he's departed to Oxford.

News item: The Fifth Flotilla of the British fleet has had a modern new prayer for their daily use, in which among other things asked for is "a keen sense of honor, that we may never give ourselves the benefit of the doubt." A good definition . . .

Stone-blossom
August 22

The full moon minus one night. I read aloud to Barbara from a heavily written essay on Donne, and listened to Janet's broadcast from Paris; then walked home. The summer dust on the lower leaves of the roadside makes them silvery. The night insects are going so that if one stops to listen it seems unendurable. The freight of war still passing through High Bridge reverberates—rain tomorrow?

CBS specifies the right to print our *Invitations to Learning**—now and then they appear in a volume—and we get Ediphone transcripts to correct. They horrify me and I work over my part in a fury; it takes hours. Today for example, *South Wind*—and as my "guests" were like molasses that morning, there are pages of messy me, that is, there were. The other two scarcely touched their transcript, and they will hate me for the contrast when they see it: the cheeks of my style scrubbed pink, bald spots combed over, and teeth sharpened . . . It is the sort of thing my dear Helen Strauss, my agent, loves me for—but I think it is vice as much as virtue.

August 27

Saturday night George appeared with a wretched story and problem. Jonathan Tichnor has been behaving badly, by which I mean not only

---

* CBS's *Invitation to Learning* was a radio symposium devoted to the discussion of landmark works, chaired by Columbia University professor Lyman Bryson.

unfaithfully (at least disloyally) but obscurely, mendaciously, and damned recklessly.

My role is simply to keep George from behaving badly, for his and the general advantage, whether in the end it turns out to be heads or tails. I couldn't like it less, having a role of any kind, with precedent for further bother about it in due course, Lord, how long . . .

But, whoof!—he was good to me in the years gone by; and I suppose that I am in fact, as he feels, the only one who knows all and understands him, and sometimes can make him behave reasonably. My trouble with him always has been that, whether in frivolity or anger, he stops and commits some folly just before asking me to advise him.

This time, just before telephoning me and taking the train, he composed, and left for Jonathan to discover next day, a two-page single-spaced letter; and brought a carbon of it for me to see. A terrible letter, written in fourteen-year-old anger with forty-year-old fine points; calling a spade a spade, calling the mendaciousness "lying," and referring to money matters, etc. All would have been lost . . .

But this time, I was not too late. I sat up with him until 2 a.m. persuading him and helping him to write and rewrite another letter, only three-quarters of a page double-spaced; and I made him take it to town by the morning train and substitute it for the terribleness.

Then, while George returned to town, I put on my gloves and took my pruning scissors and wandered up along the river, in a wild meadow amid inquisitive but sleepy cattle, somewhat nervously watching out for copperheads, for this is their season—to get bouquets of the giant Scottish thistle, which is a flower I love. It is the color of the temptation of St. Anthony, I say . . . The sun was voluptuous, the wind autumnal, the sky very large and broken with large clouds, like a purified and electrified Constable. On the far side of the meadow stood a great crop of corn crawling with light like a swarm of greenish and yellowish bees.

August 28

I resolved not to write David [Posner] last night, too gloomy, but to read *Virgin Soil* until I grew sleepy, instead. But it seemed lonesome not to write, so there I sat until all hours, thinking the inexpressible, scribbling the unwritable or almost unwritable . . .

George telephoned. Jonathan had left a letter to say that he had come in late Sunday night for the express purpose of breaking the news that he was leaving; and then had found George's letter (fortunately the second letter).

So one half of my weary discourse over the weekend was in vain, but not the other half; for naturally I figured it both ways. Jonathan has resolved to change his way of life entirely at once, poor youngster; and to change his sex, which will be easier, at least in the beginning.

August 30

This morning I happened to find this, in an essay on Benjamin Constant by my distinguished old friend Alyse Gregory; and it made me laugh out loud. It refers to his love letters to Mme Récamier, which are generally ridiculed; which she praises nevertheless, for all that they reveal of "this dolorous enchantment": "When a person of such exceptional gifts does not hesitate to expose his innocent follies, surely it is a matter for praise." !?!?! I wonder . . .

September 5

We dined at our neighbor Jane Loeb's, uncomfortable de luxe—wondrous Montrachet, French maid flirting with me, perfect Austrian pudding with *Schlagobers*, super-phonograph which kept stalling. Her diabolic pretty infants named Jigs and Penny came down and zoomed around our dinner like hornets; and the former threatened to spank her mother for forgetting to send them back up to their nurse on time. Around her shapely waist Jane had wound the merely tanned, buckleless skin of an important boa constrictor, *souvenir de voyage*, which wouldn't stay put; I had to keep helping her rewind it.

After dinner she took us to the county fair: uncrowded—which I liked, as it gave opportunity for me to examine all at my ease: the yokels and yokelesses, the year in and year out professionals, mysterious riffraff in family groups (there was a fantastic couple of anguished alcoholics), how they live in their trailers and trucks, etc., all in a glaring electricity, a howling amplification of the Andrews Sisters and "Lilli Marlene."

Bertha Bert, the "ha-morpha-dite" (as the barker said it), "worthwhile" all right, though as you might say on the realistic side; not poetic. Honest, though my characterful Monroe, who fastidiously would not push up close with the crowd, denies it . . . The one comic detail was *her* maltreating *him* to prove that *it* had no nerves; the mysterious detail was his-her-its having had a dearly beloved husband in the Marines, killed on Saipan.

A number of years ago Elizabeth and I saw a hermaphrodite, but the police were not pleased and forbade him-her-it to expose the interesting dual part—he kept a bit of purple bathrobe folded over it. If one really cared one could have a special showing at a doctor's in the village, by appointment—we didn't. But he told his life story, which was pitiful and at the same time burlesque; and I have always regretted not having written it down.

September 9

Thursday night we had our newest New Yorkers to dine: the Hopkinses, who have settled in our midst under contract to the International Garment Workers and to Harper & Brothers, as I may have mentioned— with Pauline Potter and (by one of my subtleties more effective than usual) Barbara. It was absurd, it was such a love feast. I have not, upon previous less intimate occasions, experienced Hopkins's famous charm; it is something. He answered all our questions about Russia and all that, which as a rule he refuses to do. With me he insisted on discussing contracts and literary taxation—his lawyer is better than mine, he tells me—very funny. Monroe is his favorite, and they are already laying fierce joint stratagems against bigwigs I could name, to make N.Y. a better place for the arts. The century of the uncommon man, as I sometimes point out . . .

September 10

I had a letter from a young man from South Dakota inspired by my early novels; desirous of coming to see me in N.Y. for advice about his novel-in-progress; enclosing sample pages, precious and sweet, and, yes, inspired by but modernized and talented; inquiring whether the well-known Guernsey breeder is related to me; which interests him because his livelihood is advanced-registry cow testing for the University of Connecticut! Curious . . .

September 14

As we came out of the St. Regis there were the millions awaiting [General Jonathan] Wainwright; and motorcycles streaking and screaming up the avenue. I was sorry not to stay to see it; now there is only MacArthur left for me to observe the welcome of.

September 15

Yesterday was strange, bath-hot (culminating in a cloudburst at dusk); and in the recording studio the air conditioning was on the blink; and we had to do one quarter-hour over because of a faulty wax plate; I came near to weeping at the bottom of page 258 [of *Apartment in Athens*] but kept my voice steady and did not muff that record; however on another record I blew forth the *p* in "put her in the water closet" so that the needle jumped, and there went another quarter-hour, etc.; but we did get done.

September 19

The following is (to my mind) one of the sublime small facts of the war: The great salt mine containing 22,000 objects of art was mined for destruction—the entire mountain would have caved in—but this was prevented by the removal of the explosive through little ancient disused exits which the Nazis had no knowledge of. This is the great detail: the local salt miners, caring not a damn for anything except their own livelihood for centuries past and for years to come . . .

Last night one of Monroe's really entrancing dinner parties for Pavlik. Monroe has wanted me to swallow my grievance against him, to overcome my fear of him, on the theory (to simplify it a little) that one must not hate the man whose genius one loves . . . Pavlik was at his best, with his horridest shortcoming now and then. Also Bill Miller, whose thatch of blondness is gilded by the summer seaside sunshine; and he is a little shy about it and has bought the first hat of his life to hide it in the street.

September 21

I have the most beautiful Mozart of all (Tovey agrees): the C minor concerto; Casadesus's Paris recording. Also, having begged and begged the shops for Beethoven's B flat major quartet, Opus 130, in vain—haunted by a half-memory of the cavatina—I find it at Baba's, uncovered somewhere in the course of the housecleaning. A memory of my dear Frances Robbins,* the summer before her death, in Maine. She had kept the Curtis Quartet during their rehearsal period, and therefore every year they came to see her and play for her. She had a great fairy-tale log cabin up steep over Frenchman Bay; the logs on the inside skinned and waxed and golden, like a violin and acoustically perfect. That last summer they played Opus 130—I lay on the floor at Frances's feet—we made them play it twice. Then I went down the coast for a couple of days or, to be more precise, for a couple of nights, a ridiculous excursion; and while I was away she had the first embolism.

September 28

The young man, not as young as he appears, who asked to see me for advice upon his novel, is homely but with something that I call beauty: a great bird-nose, delicate eyes of very dark topaz with blond eyelashes, crooked teeth, a becoming scar down his chin, tall and slender, with a giant's hands—half ethereal Shelley, half animal-peasant.

* Frances Robbins. One of G.W.'s earliest patrons—she helped support the writing of *The Grandmothers*—and a devoted friend.

Oversexed but less loose than anyone, with a fanatical love of women, especially of his wife, whom he has left because she hindered his writing. I have never known an odder story than his life; certainly never more hardship endured for education's sake, then literature's sake. He brought his book; it is very good. For him I am the chief writer in the world.

Last week came a cablegram from Jacques [Guérin] announcing his arrival Sunday or Monday. I have scarcely any curiosity now, but with my old understanding of him and the strangeness of the fall of France, nothing could be curiouser.

Sometimes I wish I could be shut up, immured, for the rest of my life.

October 3

My house is chilly but I won't light a fire when I'm alone (a sign of my amorous nature?) and I have a new Casadesus Mozart: B flat major, not the difficult one in that key but the very last, with its quietness of approaching death, almost sleepiness.

October 4

Jacques has been looking in vain for a Russian sable coat for his mother, and Barbara wants me to sell him hers, a bargain at forty or fifty grand. If I can arrange it, it really will be the funniest thing that ever happened. At first Barbara didn't want to see him at all, but I thought she should, as an exercise in pride; also for his stories, the death of Soutine, Picasso's old age, the purchase of Stendhal's library, etc. After all, she once fell in love with him; and I, not only in misery but on principle (for one may not fight a woman), came back to this country until it was over; then Monroe forced me to resume my friendship with her, and I wrote *The Babe's Bed* in her house, for her, and in proud return she gave me the Courbet of the children.

Incidentally, while I was reading my cow tester's ms. I gave him *The Babe's Bed* to read, and it happened to be copy no. 1, Monroe's copy with uncut pages; which he very courteously did not cut but read at a bias, with his predatory nose thrust between the snowy Pannekoek paper. And he found it overwhelmingly exemplary in some way, so he wrote me; so that the novel to be (I hope) financed by me may also be influenced by me.

I made good politics for him last week, to get him money from the Saxton Fund;* with Mac, very warm and trustful but at the same time

---

* The Eugene F. Saxton Fund for promising writers was named for the late Harper & Brothers editor. "Mac" refers to Frank S. MacGregor. He and Edward C. Aswell were G.W.'s editors at Harper's.

shrewdly managing me a bit (which I so admire in him); and with Aswell, troublesome, afraid of me (I am beginning to get a reputation for my publishing-house fighting), but always eager to push in close and breathe hot down his authors' necks while they write, hot and cold. An editor whose training was the cult of Thomas Wolfe, faugh!

Monroe telephones to say that George asked to come for the week-end, and that he refused. A fortnight ago he formally warned me (using that very word) that as soon as he grew indifferent to Jonathan he intended to woo his way back here; irrespective of my feeling in the matter. With equal formality I recognized his right to do so, and even gave him some of my disinterested advice about it. Poor wretch.

What a band we are! But life won't be long enough for all the writing, and certainly my heart is not great enough for all the living I get myself into.

Stone-blossom is especially haunted tonight: soft thuds, little low tones, even latch liftings. Long ago, a crime of passion was committed here: an Italian farmhand killed the girl he loved and her disapproving father . . .

October 8

Should I have refused to let Jacques come to Stone-blossom at all? (This was the only free weekend; Katherine Anne and W.S.M. lined up for the next two.) I hoped to have a young Italian but someone must have outbid me, he never turned up; so there I was, cooking, etc., while playacting in the role of international lifelong friend, glamorous typically American country gentleman, harder work in a way than the domestic service.

The funniest (and in a way, bitterest) moment was when he seriously and with *politesse française* bawled me out for hanging up my pornography for all the world to see—that is, the *Lion-Boy.*, etc.—especially as it may in due course affect my young niece. "Vice" a matter of no importance, no interest; *but* the old morality (family and infancy, femininity and finance, law and order) universal, eternal! With certain lively and indeed witty implications as to what this pornographic interest must mean as to the way I live, now in my middle age . . . This, after the prudish housekeeper; it never rains but it pours!

October 25

The saga of Barbara's old father is evidently entering now upon one of its culminating cantos: fifth wife, eighth child, no money, offensive Fascism, etc. Euthanasia would be good; but that of course is a Fascist kind of thought. In this kind of muddle of humanity, my intellect almost always is impatient of what may be called democratic process; so damned slow.

A more cheerful thing: I did get a year's grant of money from the Saxton Trust for my cowherd genius. His original request was for $1,200; I told him to raise it to $2,500 when he reapplied, but he didn't, he raised it only to $1,800—and oddly enough, Aswell the chief trustee agrees with me; we're going to have to plead with him to take the full amount. He's a ticket.

A lovely two days in a way . . . I go down by the phonograph to eat soup and stewed prunes, to drink hot lemon juice; and I was deeply touched, pleased, almost moved, somewhat moved, by Strauss's *Symphonia Domestica*. Is this corruption of taste, or what?

Outside, it is wet and penetratingly cold. My sugar maple perhaps intended to turn scarlet, then decided on yellow, the strangest yellow, as if it were strawberry gilded over . . . I have an almost theological belief in gardens and I think that trees should be cared for as if they stood in flower pots . . .

I have read a most beautiful novel. Fancy my never having read it before! Namely, *A House of Gentlefolk*, Turgenev . . . It made my flesh creep with aesthetic sensation and with human tenderness, from start to finish.

I have also read Robert Graves's story of the Argonauts: Sir Walter Scott or even Dumas plus the very latest anthropology; gay and instructive, but heavy going before you get to the end, 500 pages.

October 30

It is true that as I have settled down again, oh, not unhappily, to work, I have been wonderfully aware of one of the functions or utilities of love—I mean, the real thing: it gives one an advantageous indifference to a great many people; without exactly fencing one in, it fences them off.

As for money, I once heard an old woman say, "Everything about money is unpleasant except having it."

November 1

On Columbus Avenue Barbara got walloped on the behind by Halloween boys with a sockful of sand; which hurt her so that before dinner she lay on the floor bottom up.

Evidently she sensed my uneasiness about her conquest of Jeff

Keller—she says he is not really sane, at any rate not human—a "machine" in all he does, a cow-testing machine, a horseback-riding machine, a fucking machine, but (she thinks) probably also a writing machine. Lloyd did not like him but seemed not uneasy, unless it was about me as a Saxton Trust recommender—he thinks him capable of anything, except writing.

We all dined then, with Sylvia Spriggs* and Pauline [Potter], at the Coffee House; and so to Teyte's recital: perfection. I have had a box, which of course costs a lot, and now is the time when I must reprove and discipline myself as to all that, gosh; and yet it was worth it, worth it; we were so at ease, as if we were lying in each other's arms under a tree—Barbara, Lloyd, Pauline, Pavlik, Monroe, and I—we were so comfortable and beautiful.

Teyte sang like an old angel—Mozart and Gluck, Golaud's letter to Pelléas, Verlaine and Baudelaire and Corneille. It was a boisterous triumph with an audience of personages, flashing with news cameras—and she was so happy that she sang certain songs a little too broadly; and at the very end seemed to be feeling all the way back to her notorious girlhood, tempted perhaps to lift her sable-edged blush-satin and show her famous legs. But when she sang, *"Là, tout n'est qu'ordre et beauté, Luxe, calme, et volupté,"* it was (my) religion as well as art.

November 2

Last Friday when John Yeon and I came out here together I was in a kind of panic, using that word almost in its original sense: dread of Pan. Then Saturday morning, all day Saturday, and Sunday morning, I really came to life. It was as though I were wearing a close undergarment of the finest woven little fire; it was an angelic sensation . . .

November 6

A charming hour with wonderful William [W.S.M.]. A little tired out, burning his candle at both ends: writing every day, frivoling every evening. He has delivered his historical novel to the printer; now he is writing a set of six stories upon commission; with other plans ahead. On the whole, I have never observed so happy an old age.

There is a maniacal way of writing into which I fall sometimes, when, although mistrustful or disapproving of my subject matter, a stub-

---

* Sylvia Spriggs. British early biographer of Gertrude Stein. She was Barbara Harrison's roommate at Oxford.

bornness comes over me and I can't or won't give it up until I have tried it every which way; a perfectionism which really aims at the wastebasket.

Worship of Mozart: it is a madness but it helps. I now possess nine concerti! (Schnabel does not please me; his many admirable ways notwithstanding. In the slow movement of the twenty-first in C major, with the great sacerdotal plucked strings, he gives a sort of initial grunting emphasis to every measure . . .)

Now, just now: there is a skunk, so close, so strong! I got up to make sure that the doors are all closed. Perhaps he is in the cellar. No, I can hear him in the dead leaves along the front foundations of the house. The fact is, there has been a devil in and around this entire day—well, he can have it now; I shall inter myself in sleep; good riddance!

November 14

In former years I could honestly have said that the types who wrote me fan letters were somehow inferior human beings: vain, soft in the head, parasitic, pathetic (with, especially for *The Pilgrim Hawk*, a few vitally psychopathic, nuts). But now, for *Apartment in Athens*, I heard from a good many who are evidently worthwhile, interesting, even handsome—why? what has changed? Is it a particular merit of *Apartment in Athens*, and if so, what? Is it America changing? Is it perhaps that, among Americans, mere "success" interests a better class of men and women; those potentially successful themselves? Or is it the war?

November 15

A cocktail party at George's: models and (so to speak) young men. The elder of the latter as they age are getting homely, like gingerbread men. Optimistic note: Lauri Douglas is marrying a huge handsome boy who wrestles, and by staying elderly in a corner with him I managed to find the party gay.

November 17

Last night the incomplete moon had a somewhat wicked look, pinched, dull, like a sorceress in Hans Christian Andersen. This morning the emerald grass is coated with sticky-looking frost. It's time, of course.

Prater Violet [Christopher Isherwood]: Monroe and George are enchanted by it: Willie and I on the other hand quibble about it a good deal in the grandest manner.

The famous, somewhat arbitrarily inserted page about love toward the end, for example: it is wonderfully well written but (to me) shocking—so heartless, so cut-and-dried in unhopefulness, so disdainful of every sort of beloved past or future.

I know that when I was a youth, if I had been engaged in any intimacy with anyone who then in impeccable prose had discounted it and sold it short like this, there would have been hell to pay.

November 18

Monroe and William have departed; I have paid a call on my parents and come back home to my precious loneliness. I have the Ballades of Chopin played by Casadesus when he was younger; a wonderful recording, clean and warm, a little brutal once in a while like a boy in love (I like the one in F minor best, the long one, the gentle one).

I think that William said, tonight, the funniest thing that I have ever heard anyone say. George has telephoned Monroe very pleasantly every morning for three weeks, and at last Monroe has accepted an invitation to dine tête-à-tête tomorrow. Tonight he mentioned these facts, with Lloyd and Barbara present, in a way which made it a kind of family council, though of course we did not counsel much. Apparently William, who has always seen the worst happen (it happened to him, lifelong), took it more seriously than the rest of us. Suddenly he said, "This reminds me of something I once said to my sister-in-law. It was thirty years ago, and, I may add, she has never been able to forget it. I said, 'My dear, you are a sort of woman whose idea of happiness is to eat cold mutton in a howling gale.' " We all shouted with laughter.

He said a pathetic thing, too, in this connection: that he has come to the conclusion that one ought to interfere in others' lives more; he wishes that his friends had been more forceful in their opinions of his life, interferingly.

A funny thing: We found him gazing at Pavlik's *Gemini*, and he informed us that, having been struck by the beauty of it when he was here last, he had tried it and, alas, found it not perfectly feasible. Whereupon I tranquilly explained what he ought to have done; and then we went walking up the mountain.

December 4

I know a youngster who let himself be classified 4F—he was a ballet dancer, and it happened that he had just then his first chance to dance, in the road company of some show. But he grew unhappy about it, noblesse obliged him somehow—so he returned to his draft board in N.Y.; they would not reclassify him; so he enrolled in an ambulance corps and he did good hard work in Burma. This fall in some remote long-named town in India he encountered an English ballet company on tour, which promptly engaged him to dance important parts; and now he is on his way to Egypt and Europe, with a year's dancing scheduled.

Tonight Stone-blossom is as noisy as a ship, especially my bedroom, where there is the scratching of the young plane trees added to the looseness of shutters and eaves troughs.

There are pleasures of solitude which I must not underestimate.

December 12

Two days in town that seemed a week long:

I had to take Barbara's pocket Renoir on loan to Harry Hopkins— he hasn't been able to see anyone, but he sent his nurse out to bring me in, and it was very pleasant. He is in Memorial Hospital, therefore naturally the talk has been of cancer. Not that, I think; certainly he doesn't think it is that. Then, all afternoon, the annual meeting of the Authors' Guild, which was a great noisy row—but we were elected with a good plurality. It's going to be as bad as your forestry and road legislation. Then a pleasant and elegant evening at Josephine's* with old Horace Kallen and Lecomte de Nouilly, the biologist, and the usual. Today a couple of hours with my agent—we've got to negotiate my new book contract sooner than I expected—for one thing the book boom is subsiding steadily. I went down to Trinacria's and spent twenty-two dollars on olive oil, prosciutto, provolone, mortadella, sardines, etc. It is the pleasantest store in N.Y.—the handsome youngsters fed me wonderful jawbreaking sandwiches while I shopped . . .

I returned to find my cook white and trembling as a worm. Last night, fallen asleep with whatever dope it is that he takes, he caught fire and burned his bed up. I am lucky to have my dear house and belongings.

A young soldier has written from Okinawa asking what I look like. Can I answer him fairly, convincingly?

I am forty-four, and I am youthful-looking, for one thing; a family characteristic. I like my looks all right (when dressed); others do too, although I don't think I have been loved for my appearance. I should say that I haven't got sex appeal in the immediate, suggestive, or arresting way. My face in repose (I am told) is gloomy and seemingly arrogant, but I smile and smile, talk and talk . . . The kind of complexion which

---

* Josephine Crane, New York literary hostess at 820 Fifth Avenue, where the lectures she sponsored were called "Monday Classes." She was also G.W.'s late-summer Cape Cod hostess.

gets flushed or else turns pale; eyes gray-blue; hair of no particular shade, not dark, with lately some silver threads amid the not-gold. Height five foot eleven; weight one hundred sixty—as you might say, the general design of what should have been a fine figure, spoiled a bit, by indolence for one thing. Also I have a hollow or declivity in my chest, a family inheritance, which gives me very wide shoulders and a slightly effeminate, though not portly belly (hence my interest in being dressed) . . .

December 20

No news. I have been happy—although troubled or (I should say) problematical, and not, here at my desk with *Children of This World*, as efficacious as I should like. Monroe has not been exactly happy; certain of his old friends and familiars have been getting him down and taking little revenges on him—and when that happens, naturally I take stock, I turn a little bitter, I observe how much of human nature is mere deviltry.

But it takes more than this to faze me and nothing ever really fazes Monroe. I believe in bitterness, at any rate in the combination of bitterness and happiness.

December 24

Anna Karenina seems real, and there is a hallucinating sense of reality in Balzac; whereas all Turgenev is a dream. Nothing gives me more pleasure as I read; nothing touches a greater number of heartstrings. His weakness (for me) appears to be that I forget. His plots are too vagarious drifting, his characters interchangeable . . .

December 25

Fantastic weather here: great whips of rain snapping every which way. I have been miserable all day, though not *unhappy*—I went out on the early train, sat through the Hotchkisses' tree; took the parents, the Millers, and the children to a roadhouse for a midday meal, talked of Father's health, and sang hymns with them all, and helped with supper and dishwashing; then came back to town on a grim train, crowded. Nothing for me or of me personally, except one letter from David and except my sisters' singing "My true love hath my heart, and I have his," Marzials's duet to P. Sidney's poem—they do it for me every year.

December 28

On Christmas eve I sent Pauline some red roses with a note explaining that they are the most powerful emblem I know: the species of rose that Monroe used to bring me when I lay in the hospital ward in Chicago half-crazed and half-dead, aged nineteen. I meant it to bring her good luck; but it frightened her and finally today, in a quavering voice, with a lump in her throat, she phoned and asked for a clarification.

An old punchy prizefighter, inspired to tell the story of his life to one of John Huston's wives, began with this sentence: "You see how it was, I was a change-of-life baby . . ."

1 9 4 6

. . . the novelist's lonely, uncertain, haunted desk.

—Images of Truth

In many ways 1945 was the most gratifying year of my life, certainly the most enjoyable; but I have not been able to give myself much credit for it. The work which brought success, etc., was 1944's work; and my pride in it did not last out the to-do. Then there began again my peculiar shrinking from the next work, mistrust of myself, habit of disappointing myself, strange, stranger than ever. As it were evilly prophetic; as though the natural sequence and sequel to good luck were bad luck . . .

We spent the New Year's weekend without a guest, with Lloyd and Barbara just back from Southern Pines. On New Year's Eve Monroe and Lloyd went off to the bowling alley in Washington, leaving Barbara and me at Stone-blossom; whereupon she rose and went home at 8:30, to write a poem or something. So I watched the great year out, lonesomely, yes, but serenely. I didn't dare play my all-powerful Mozart concerti; I played Strauss instead. I didn't dare write to anyone, lest I fall into false philosophy or some other inappropriate or untimely self-expression. I read a trashy novel, and when the bells rang and whistles blew finally, they startled me. I wanted nothing except to make love. But very certainly my late strange happinesses have taught me just one simple lesson: I must not be willful or self-seeking about that, therefore I kept serene.

I (by the way) have a new picture. It is by young Hyman Bloom; and in tones of jewel and enamel it represents nothing more or less than an amputated leg. Barbara gave it to me.

As it turns out, my last dentist victimized me; so now, so to speak, I am having a couple of false teeth pulled out and a couple of real ones put in. Also, I am to dine with that pathetic creature, Edna Ferber. Having sold 700,000 copies of her latest, least good novel, she has left Doubleday and she wants to be published by a "more literary" house!

Parker's Ferry
Yemassee, South Carolina
January 13

It is astonishing how Monroe has bewitched William [Maugham]. He couldn't be fonder of me, but he knows what I am going to say— and his force of mind is such that I am inclined to say just that, nothing new—he has heard my stories. Whereas Monroe has fascinated him. He mentions him every other minute: he is keeping a plum pudding for the night he will arrive, there is a new version of gin rummy which he will like better than the old, etc.

There is a certain tyranny about all this. He never forgets for an instant that this is the culmination and windup of his American life, and we are to play our great parts to the end. I am very melancholy and pleasantly false, playing my part. Extremely sensible of the fact that I came out of sense of duty, pseudo-filial . . .

January 15

I have proceeded to write, about my boy and girl in Eileen, Illinois,* stark naked and interlocked in a Chevrolet coupe, having closed the windows tight and kept the motor racing through their intercourse. And about a fateful young woman, Anna, known as "The Lark," whose pretty face turned ugly if anyone gazed at it, whose fine soprano flatted whenever she sang in public. Today, I must take up a blackmailer named Niemann whom I never laid eyes on; and some bedbugs; and a bad dream; and a memory of my brother as a boy learning to walk.

For a windup of Wm.'s career Doubleday wants to publish a great omnibus containing *The Painted Veil, Christmas Holiday, The Summing Up*, two plays, a lot of stories, and the El Greco study. And now Wm. has asked me to write the prefatory essay, and I have accepted. A tough assignment, and fun.†

The dreary cold water has ceased to douche down upon us, but instead we have a wind and finger-stiffening, scrotum-squeezing cold. What a fraud, these climatey parts of the world! There is no fireplace in my study, so I stay in the sitting room, sweet with pitch pine, with Gerald Kelly R.A.'s bad portrait of William in his youth and beauty in a velvet smoking jacket gaping at me.

* A story entitled "The Stallions," one of a number of works abandoned by G.W. after serious effort.
† The essay which later appeared as "Somerset Maugham and Posterity" in G.W.'s 1962 book of essays and remembrances, *Images of Truth*.

January 16

This is Alan's* thirty-sixth birthday. Wm. was grief-stricken at the loss of his looks; nevertheless all is settled for his companioning and secretaryship from now on to the end: the Villa Mauresque in May, to order the burned garden replanted, the bombed windowpanes replaced, the pillaged cellar restocked, etc.; then England for the summer, India in the autumn.

Alan is such a funny creature: a lovely cockney cameo face filled out now so that it is more than a bit woodchucky. Kindness personified; very capable; dapper through and through; antique-loving.

There is something nightmarish for me in the repetition of my coming back here; my terrible memory brings back every word, every torn dead shrub, every tethered pig or cow, every whiff of marsh fragrance, and every mouthful of rich food from the other years . . . For William there is no repetition because his only reality is out there at his desk: the four or five books he has written the while.

January 17

One of the odd things about being here is that I am drinking too much. I want my usual cocktail before dinner, but then every night William brings out one of his bottles of wine, in the selection of which he has taken a good deal of trouble, and bullies us into drinking every drop of it; and it is too much. It is partly not wanting to waste anything and partly an old-fashioned merrie-old-England anti-puritanical principle; and so far I haven't rebelled. But the result is that, while he and Alan play cards after dinner, I sit dozing by the fire with a newspaper or trashy book like some old colonel. I am not even competent to write my letters; and then I go to bed and fail to sleep or sleep badly.

The very cold night cleared away the clouds, and by evening the sunshine had warmed us up a little; so we went for a long walk. There was an incomparable sunset, and as it happened we saw it through the Negroes' cemetery, the voodoo cemetery, which is a grove of the oldest, most twisted, moss-wound oaks: lumpy molten gold, and a stream of pale bright green running away to the south, and a bank of pale bright purple which finally caught fire, Then suddenly it died away, leaving smoke, soot, silt.

Then the full moon rose, just between the swamp and the marsh,

* Alan Searle (1905–85). The man who was to become Maugham's personal secretary, final companion, and heir.

and I went down on the levee alone to watch it. The tide was rushing out with a noise, and it shook the golden reflection as if it were a flag whipping in a wind. All around me there were water birds ill at ease, and I heard what William says may have been turtles, growling or barking.

January 19

Alan asked the cook Nora if she enjoyed reading. Oh, yessir, she answered, but I only like exciting books, so I only read detective stories and the Bible. William was charmed by this; it is so close to his own habit and principle.

Alan is a strange man, sweet cockney, so comical to my ear, and indeed to look at—but with wonderful awful tales of his many years' work of penology, and (I think) as right as rain for William.

I made rarebit last night—good enough, except that the cheese wasn't ripe. William says that after his seventy-fifth birthday he is going to eat and drink everything he likes, as much as he pleases! and take Nembutal every night . . . So to speak, to hell with it!

Gossip: When Edward James was a little boy he happened to arouse the amorousness of Sir William Harcourt, the statesman. He complained to his mother, and she made a hue and cry, and in consequence Sir William committed suicide. (By drowning in the bathtub, if I remember rightly.) Therefore I think we should not be astonished at any of Edward's little-boy naughtinesses now.

January 20

A novel is an odd thing. I remember, in my ragbag ms., coming upon a page where I had ordered myself not to think about a certain problem until I came to it: the crime, blackmail, etc., which gave my villain an opportunity for revenge on his brother.

Well, yesterday perhaps I solved it; very oddly. I woke up with a vague dream or daydream of eroticism, and that prompted me to try to formulate that brother's sexual morality, in a conversation on the café terrace outside the gaming rooms at Aix-les-Bains—and out of this missing piece of plot suddenly sprang, as of its own accord, as if it were little fireworks, one bit igniting another. Can I make it work? The catch is that I cannot or will not attempt a full-length courtroom scene. Complex enough anyway. This brother is to be a kind of model male; an absolute of virility, goodness without morals.

The formulation of morality itself, the conversation in Aix, as I sketched it on six crazy pages, was a failure; too intellectual, etc. A worrisome and strange day's work.

No letters; no notion of anything at home since Monday. Strange, how being here affects me this year: some form of anxiety neurosis; partly because of my misfortune and misbehavior toward David. Perhaps also because William is so old and foreign to me, or I to him—that is without the least knowledge of my real private life and particular nature. Therefore in grand conversations that we have about life and letters, psychology and philosophy, etc., I am not I exactly; it is as if my life were all over, I have to speak as an abstract intellect, inoperative, without willpower.

Stone-blossom
January 27

Here I am up North again.

Upon SOS from my sister, taking only a day to decide and arrange and depart, home I came, to fire Philip, my servant, Little Horrible; and to lock up the house; and to soothe and cheer up my somewhat exasperated family. He had set fire to his bedroom and did not even successfully extinguish same—the mattress still lay smoldering when Eddie the painter arrived next morning. He also had let some chance nocturnal friend go off with the car, which was found in a ditch; and gave an explanation of this which did not satisfy the state troopers—it was like a detective story, with footprints in new-fallen snow. Etc.

I am greatly to blame, knowing so much of his devices, for having gone away and left him to them. It was my distracted and lazy dependence on him, having failed to keep any other servant all year; it was trusting too much to my luck. Well, as it appears, my luck still holds, or very nearly.

He had been making unsuccessful attempts to get into intimacy with Lloyd's employees, two in particular, tough middle-aged men—with yarns about me, etc., by way of buildup—and while I suppose it amused them for a time, after I went South they began to complain like hell; and meanwhile, pub crawling up and down Route 30, he had been making all sorts of scandal. As all this started to come out and blow up, he unburdened himself to both Elizabeth and Monroe. In the unpleasant pathetic vein; and then, in what perhaps we may call despair, went out and collided with a truck at 3 a.m., smashing the car to scrap iron, injuring himself a little more in his psyche, not otherwise.

To town tonight, and out again for a day with a locksmith, if I can get one; then back to Yemassee at the end of the week.

Presumably I shall recover my zest and my sense of domestic management.

Parker's Ferry
Yemassee, South Carolina
February 5

Another day—a sunbath upon the fragrant rye grass; the proofs of Wm.'s little historical novel, which has all sorts of merit but (I'm afraid) no glory; a walk across the spongy heath, burned over, so that it is like charcoal rubbed into gold; a dinner party at Bonny Hall, characterized by amiability, not by wit . . .

What a time it was, the ten days in the North! So many sides of my life coming to a climax all at once that I could not really live it; I just went through the motions; it was a bad dream; even the good things were a bit bad for me, because I could not think what they signified. Now in this vacuity I begin to make sense of some of it.

Harry Hopkins's death troubled me very deeply, surprisingly—not just the pride and interest of having known him, but in the brief months a certain reality of friendship. I suppose that was a part of his power.

Early in the morning [his wife] Louise telephoned Monroe to say that he had "ceased to suffer," so that the end was to be expected presently; and it worried her to be responsible for Barbara's Renoir in the confusion of the last minute, or the minute after the last. So he toddled up to the hospital after; and she reported that in a moment of lucidity Harry had looked around the room and murmured, "The flowers fade but the pictures last." It is a kind of story that one scarcely cares to tell; it won't sound like the truth.

At the funeral, to my surprise, there was Marianne Moore's brother, whom I hadn't seen for years, to make the invocation, as chief chaplain of the Navy; and it was surprisingly fine, with something of her gift of strange phrase, and a glorious wonderful very deep, dark voice with a crack in it, something rather like the voice of Albert Lambert *fils*, of the Comédie-Française.

February 9

Our weather is fine, but not dependable and not absolutely warm. It beams, it warbles in every bush, drawing me outdoors; and then breathes icy down the back of my neck. I certainly have been overeating and perhaps have put on a few pounds; but I am not brown. We don't live right; elderly. We mix our nature with so many reminiscences of cities, and our human nature with shoptalk of literature and (in my case) bad conscience about literature. It is nothing like Stone-blossom in May, nothing. Anyway I have been absurd all week—Byronic, Manfredish, in a vain gloom with a senseless secret—though amiably reasoning and yarning like any Somerset Maugham character the while . . .

Poor William: his malaria got him down. Perhaps, too, as he is correcting the proofs of *Then and Now*, he finds it dull, with dwindled power. One aspect of his having Alan is not a success from *his* point of view—spoiled! You'd think he was fifty-two instead of seventy-two. He lost his temper today, getting after Sunday, the chauffeur, like an old red colonel.

February 10

I must begin to plan my return home, when and upon what pretext. I haven't been clever about it with William and I am weak about it, in the oddest way. He is so touching, as he never has been before. I really am his son, part of his family; all the more so now that Alan has come, the companion of the rest of his life.

At sunset, there was a great fire on our marsh, frightening at first—William and I resolved to sleep with our arms around our manuscripts. Half a mile of tall flames, torn up by the wind; fading down, then arising again . . . I went down alone between the canals, close to it; but when I could hear it panting, its perhaps morbid fascination turned to ordinary fear, which brought me home. It has put itself out now.

February 12

One of Philip's tricks was to rummage in my desk and read my journal, etc.—he made Elizabeth a scene about certain references to himself which he came upon in this way—and one thing my imaginative family is afraid of is that he might steal a packet of letters and try to blackmail me.

(I hasten to add that he did no such thing; he wasn't very brainy. I took a most minute, fanatical inventory, and missed nothing of any consequence except the set of photographs George made of Paul Cadmus's improper drawings. As they weren't signed, I don't suppose I need to alarm Paul about it.)

One might think that, after all of that, I should write no more letters. But after some grim thoughts I decided that any inhibition in this way would gradually work through and through me; unwholesome, enfeebling, especially to a literary man. How deep-seated a habit it is: a lifetime of self-revelation, self-anatomization. If I broke it, something else would break too, or at least change. I fancy that I am too old to change much without a great waste; and perhaps I am too respectable to bother about anyone's incidental or accidental disrespect. Two hundred dollars' worth of locks and keys, and a new application of that vigilance and mild misanthropy which are in my nature anyway, ought to suffice . . .

It is a sort of thing that a man like myself may go through life without ever thinking of; a man like William's sort never forgets. It has amused me to observe how, every afternoon when he has done his little stint of correspondence, he tears everything into small scraps with a kind of spiteful haste and energy; and now and then he calls our attention to the fact, and says that he trusts we all do likewise with whatever he may write us. And yet I feel sure that he has never indited a line of any intimacy; not in the last fifty years at all events.

I may confess here that I fell into Philip's trick myself one afternoon. It was very funny. That last weekend he was in such a state that he packed only possessions of some value and left all the rest. At the railway station he informed me of this, and insisted that he wanted nothing sent after him, and asked me to make a bonfire. A day or two later, when I returned with my locksmiths, I wandered up to his rooms and found a really disgusting muddle: the floor littered and the closets packed with beer bottles, ballet programs, chicken bones, sheet music for the violin, medicine bottles, rags and papers.

Out of which I picked up a letter from his old mother which had her address in Maine printed on it, to verify same; and then idly, in mere human interest, I read a page (dated October 30) and happened upon this: "I am glad you are so happy and they"—(that is, the Wescott family)—"like you so well; and who knows but the old fellow"—(that is, myself)—"may adopt you and you will have a nice home all your life. I think you are quite lucky." I shouted with laughter, and as that was one of the more doleful days I was grateful for it . . .

Stone-blossom
April 11

It is midnight, the end of a good strange thoughtful day. After dinner and indeed birthday cake, I took some of my family to the movies—it isn't easy to differentiate one evening from another out here, or even as a rule desirable. There is a ring around the moon, and a faint spectrum veiling it. On the way home our headlight fell on a little barn owl, confusing him. A bird I love, the one whose cry is like a flute shivering down the scale; the one with a monkey-like mask and ears out of proportion. We stopped, and I tiptoed very near his branch, but he drew one wing across his face to abate the light glare, and fluttered off.

April 15

My fan, the major from Okinawa, came over from Fort Dix the other day. A very nice major: almost in awe of me; culture-loving and indeed somewhat cultivated though not educated; and handsome, in rather the style of Lawrence Tibbett young. He is having mysterious aches and pains, and the Army is not releasing him until they find out what causes them or until he is satisfied with the explanation they can give. He thinks it is neurological, something that runs in his family. But it almost embarrassed me, I could detect so much in the way of psychiatric background for it . . .

Washington, D.C.
April 19

When I called on Alexis Léger* in his little apartment across the street from Dumbarton Oaks, I told him that the prose of Valéry meant more to me than the verse, which he agreed with, and perhaps was selfishly glad to hear . . . Then he told me about the pact that he and Valéry had entered into with one another when they were very young men—never to stoop to making a profession of literature. Therefore, thereafter, Valéry in the Ministry of Finance, Léger in the diplomatic service. And then, when Léger was about to be sent to China, Valéry asked for a private talk—and confessed with profound humility, simply, mysteriously, that he was going to break that vow, though (Léger understood) with no real change of opinion . . . Valéry was going to make a career, with the glorious consequences that one knows, including a drudgery of journalism, an incessant frequentation of the greatest ladies' salons, etc., and the conventional campaign of self-promotion to become an academician, and the *éloge de Pétain*, etc. . . . And the explanation that he gave was that Mme Valéry was pregnant, and they hoped it would be a son, and the thought of fatherhood unnerved him, reconciled him with the world, because he was ashamed to think that when his son went to school, and his schoolmates asked him, What does your father do in life? his son would have to answer, The Ministry of Finance.

Stone-blossom
April 22

Out the window I see our Monroe with his shoulders up like an owl's wings—it's coldish—planting something that came in the mail. He has become almost as addicted to nurserymen's catalogues as George;

* Alexis Saint-Léger (pseudonym, St.-John Perse) (1887–1975). French diplomat and poet

the results of course more modest. When I get rich I shall have to provide him with a gardener.

April 28

Wonderful old Ernest Jones* is here, lecturing on Freud for the centenary, and he has enumerated the attributes of genius as generally understood and accepted, as follows:

inspiration
periodicity, or cycles of production
absolute honesty
originality
a sense of the really significant
power of concentration.

To which he has added two, of his own observation: skepticism and credulity.

It seems to me that I qualify pretty well in Dr. Jones's two traits, especially the second . . .

My honesty is fanatical, but not absolute. I am too Machiavellian . . .

May 15

Speaking of Bernard Perlin's† silverpoint, William said, "It is the only portrait ever made of me which shows how handsome I was in my youth." When a man of seventy-two, proud and hypersensitive, is prompted to say that of a drawing so exact and severe, I do think it a great occasion.

The profile of myself moves me deeply. It shows me something of myself, or of my sad self-opinion—a look not of frustration but of passion wasted; an expression of a kind of vain foreknowledge, scarcely expecting to be believed; a sadness which looks opinionated and malicious. It reminds me a little of my observation of, my notion about (of all people) Ehrenburg.‡ How strange, and of course in a way flattering.

As I walked back home from dinner with Barbara, the lights of Stone-blossom shining down the road to meet me might have been a song of Schubert's. The black cattle were grazing just beyond the fence;

* Ernest Jones (1879–1958). Colleague and biographer of Sigmund Freud.
† Bernard Perlin (1918–   ). American graphic artist. Created silverpoint portraits of G.W. and M.W.
‡ Ilya Ehrenburg (1891–1967). Russian writer and political journalist, author of *The Fall of Paris*.

and the chains around the necks of the aristocrats among them tinkled in the darkness.

May 19

I found the *Henry IV* plays so enthralling that Barbara and I have been seriously considering going to a scalper for a pair of seats to resee Part 2; fifty bucks a pair! Of course they are not of a well-constructed dramaturgy; and the best of Shakespeare's poetry is not in them—but on the other hand his greatest prose is; and Falstaff is the greatest comic character in all literature. The Old Vic actors are good; the direction superlative . . . Unfortunately, in that damned deaf barn of a theater, the way they act—light and fast and (as you might say) eighteenth-century—some of the time you can't hear them. But I have never seen better pantomime: now like ballet dancers, now like comic acrobats in a vaudeville show, in all the fooling at the inn, and the bits of eroticism, and the fighting.

They were brought over with some excess of ballyhoo, and now naturally a good many people have gone into a corresponding tailspin against them: manic-depressive New York.

While certainly very little of Shakespeare's good poetry is in *Henry IV*, some of his best prose is; and that is my passion and my hobbyhorse. All our big howwow style derives from blank verse, right down to Henry James and, let us say, Thomas Wolfe; but his prose led to practically nothing, but (I think) the greatness of the language lies somehow where it points.

And I delight in Falstaff, as others do in Don Quixote; as a characterization surpassing the text, a creature with a life of its own in one's mind, like mythology . . .

June 22

It was a good circus. The new giants were really handsome, and the dwarfs polite, and the fat woman young, with a sweet luxurious voice. To my amusement I recognized the snake charmer, having had an afternoon's talk with her at Bernadine Szold's years ago. She exhibited not only her trained python but a large new boa constrictor, still virginal, shiny and jungle-colored.

There was a huge hot crowd, and all through the sideshow and the menagerie I had to carry Debo on my shoulders; her hands tensely and moistly clasped across my forehead and the strength of a snake in her legs. All afternoon a thunderstorm threatened, a purplish cloud came down close, reflecting on everyone's face and hair and sweaty colorful sport shirt.

What a beautiful thing a tent is—the color of rawhide, with a wondrous light coming through great stains, seemingly of oil and rust; and a navy-blue or blood-red star reinforcing it wherever the thrust of a tent pole held it up.

There was a white horse with translucent nostrils; the blood appeared in them as it ran. I admired a clown in loose garments which he dilated immensely (by means of an umbrella inside), who danced like a bubble, then wilted down from head to foot in a melancholy way; and another, lean and painted and gorgeous in sequins, handsomer than the corresponding Fratellini—this makeup and getup, whitewashed face and glittering garb, is one of the traditions which descend to us from the Greek theater.

The most talented performer is still Colleano, dancing on his wire, reminiscent of Nijinsky, with silly, fluttering, fluid body and the feet of a bird.

July 3

André de Vilmorin's dining with Pauline and I asked him, "Do you know Alexis Léger?"

And he answered, "By God, I do indeed! He was my mother's lover all during the years when I was a little boy."

His account of his errant mission and job in the United States: The great firm of Vilmorin, producers and suppliers of seeds of flowers and fruit and vegetables and grain for entire Europe—one of those ancient, obstinate, glorious, almost academic, almost governmental, but almost international establishments like Rolls-Royce, Vuitton, Reuters, Deberny-Peignot, etc.—has to look ahead because it takes many years to produce and develop a new species of plant.

They have now concluded that the time will come, alas, when even Frenchmen will not insist on, will not be able to afford, bread made by hand. For mechanized bakery requires a different type of wheat, with a harder grain . . . No such hard-grained wheat grows well in France. Therefore they have begun the long fascinating expensive mysterious process of developing a cross between the wheat of la Beauce and the wheat of Montana. This is a simplification of what he told me . . . I would like to talk with him by the hour, for days, for weeks . . .

From a letter to Deborah Wescott, aged four

Bastille Day

Dearest Debo,

I miss you, I love you, so this is (in a manner of speaking) a love letter.

Last night we picnicked under the old maple tree by the ford. It was Edna Gebhardt's birthday, and also Tom and Beth's wedding anniversary. We had a coconut cake (by Mrs. Curtis) with a candle apiece on it; and each of us bet that his candle would burn the longest; Edna won. Bruce made a fire of dead sticks which the old tree had shed. Elizabeth sang, and so did your father: silly songs of his boyhood, and also, in remembrance of you, "The Man Who Broke the Bank at Monte Carlo," which he learned from you. The full moon rose and shone on us . . . We missed you, but there was no sense in that; for even if you had been in the state of New Jersey instead of the state of Maine, anyway, by that time, you would have been in the land of Nod.

I have another bit of news for you: Do you remember my Muscovy duck, sitting on her eggs in the lying-in hospital inside the hulk of the willow? Well, when I returned from New York this week, she had hatched her brood and already had them in the brook, teaching them to swim. The two youngest kept doing it backwards, letting themselves slide on the current down toward the waterfall, which worried and irritated Mrs. Muscovy. Most of them are butter-yellow; some are brown.

I may tell you, furthermore, that I found one of my milk snakes watching them from the levee, with his mouth watering—he evidently has an appetite for sun-roasted duck. But he is not really very big or very strong; and judging by the look in their mother's eye and the way she drew her bill down at the corners, I think he may have to go hungry. She will flap him in the face and tweak him by the backbone.

Last night I dreamed of you. The dream was that we were in France, and when it came time for me to return to Stone-blossom all by myself, and I was saying goodbye to you, you gave me one of your looks and I cried. It was loud crying, and it woke me up, and then it took me a minute to stop it. But I am pretty good at stopping, just as you are, when there is really nothing to cry about.

Now, dearest Debo, be good; eat a good breakfast at breakfast time, and a good lunch at lunchtime, and a good supper at suppertime; and have fun—and keep out of the poison ivy, and be careful of the knock-about waves—until we meet again.

July 22

A morning very dim and of a double temperature, clammy-warm, as if it were a vacated bathhouse. Stone-blossom silence far from silence: the voice of the wren fiercely normal, deterred by nothing (how I wish I could work as it sings!), and a pulsing tractor motor; and also a kind of silken petticoaty sound, perhaps the corn growing—Lloyd says it will do six inches this week.

July 26

A strange day and a half in town: A party given by Mac[Gregor]'s young friend [Robert] Brundage for Sylvia and Eugenia and Helen and the Hollidays and myself; oddly infelicitous, Mac is an odd man. A drink with Bernard Perlin: the silly creature has let one of his girlfriends talk him into illustrating a child's book; and with that conventionality-by-timorousness which seems to characterize American artists generally, and with increasing disapproval and spite against himself for doing it, he is not doing it well. I should have raised hell but the timing didn't seem right, either as to the stage of the work or the terms we are on.

I got my holiday plans straightened out. Having a great deal to discuss with dear Samuel, especially his poetry, which is misguided, and his love life, which is unlucky, having also a lively curiosity about Harvard, I had invited myself to spend the weekend with him before joining Monroe at Josephine's. But then he couldn't or wouldn't have me; and suggested our meeting somewhere on the coast instead. An innocent tyranny—he must not have had any notion of the congestion everywhere. Anyway, wonderful Mesdames Collins and Ashmun solved it for me; I have a fine double room and bath at the Chatham Bars, which is not only the bit of this continent thrust out the farthest into the Atlantic but the swankiest. It will cost me a pretty penny, but I shan't begrudge it. The poor young man is having ex-G.I. nerves badly, with his doctor's thesis to get through before he has to face his first class-roomful; postgraduates at that . . .

Chatham is the part of the Cape that I wish I owned a stretch of. There is a plane to Hyannis this year; only an hour and a bit over Long Island Sound . . . Then on Friday Samuel returns to his thesis, and I to Josephine's. Monroe meanwhile will have visited Paul Cadmus and Jared French, on Nantucket; and I shall be back here circa the 16th or 17th. I have suggested that Bernard Perlin come here the weekend of the 9th–11th to draw the parents.

Woods Hole, Mass.
August 12

This *is* an earthly paradise, with all that the phrase connotes, boresome and delightful both; with our dear old-lady-angel; Josephine is a sort of grandmother to me—and servants so good that you can't tell them apart, and the weather that people sell their souls for. I sit alone on our boardwalk porch or on the beach. Alone?—in fact, several houses overlook it, but everyone is asleep in them, almost always asleep, and they too have their own beaches. Almost at my feet are a sandpiper and two terns taking their exercise, andante. Also, not far out, two Greek gods in a sailboat: they talk, I can't hear them, but judging by their appearance, if I know types of humanity, it is comic-strip talk; I imagine a line looped around it against the purplish and pale green water. Only their sail as they bring it down gives a great dramatic whisper, which I understand better . . .

August 17

I failed to read to the bitter end of poor Eleanor's* novel but I did give her a fairly severe talking-to. No one praised it—that is, *personne de connaissance*—except Katherine Anne. What a devil she is! She sets up the ideal of the anti-best-seller or the best-non-seller for these cross youngsters; and actually it is not what she practices: the only way she keeps out of the Literary Guild is by never finishing her novel. Hollywood seems to be a crazy place; George reports to us pretty regularly, always something shocking. He invited Katherine Anne and Christopher I.† to dine, they had never met, and on their long return to wherever they reside, they got into a literary quarrel and scratched and boxed one another, so fiercely that one of them had to get out by the side of the road and wait for another taxi!

I have another extracurricular job coming up, for the Dial Press this time, with whom I made my debut years ago: an omnibus of "great" French nouvelles, corresponding to the American one recently published in which my *Pilgrim Hawk* is included. Thomas Mann is doing the Germans for the same series. They expect a sale of 20,000; perhaps as much as $8,000 for baby! Not quite settled: they want me and I want the job, but my agent and I are sulking to get good terms, especially

---

* Eleanor Clark (1913–   ). Novelist and essayist; wife of poet and novelist Robert Penn Warren.

† Christopher Isherwood (1904–86). British-born American novelist, author of *Goodbye to Berlin*, who became a resident of California and a lifelong friend of G.W.

a proper royalty for the several authors not in the public domain.

I am a little tempted to start off with the *Lettres Portugaises* as an example of the semifictitious self-revelation out of which (I think) the art form in certain of its aspects developed. Then perhaps *La Princesse de Clèves*, if I can afford it, as to length. The eighteenth century is a problem, as I feel that fairy tales (Hamilton *et al.*) and allegories or cautionary tales in fancy dress are quite another kettle of fish and breed of cat. *Manon Lescaut* is novel-length. I vaguely recall with pleasure a rather bawdy, Tom-Jonesy thing called *Thermidor* by one Godard-d'Harcourt . . . Then *L'Ingénu*, or even *Candide*, as the public we are working for has scarcely read anything French. Then *Adolphe*: the model, as I conceive the matter. Then any one of half a dozen Balzacs—*La Femme Abandonnée?*—and *Un Coeur Simple*. I want to reread Gautier's *La Morte Amoureuse*. Then perhaps *Carmen*, for our illiterates, though I might prefer *Colomba* or *Arsène Guillot*.

I intend to put in a couple of oddities, for the critics to chew on—many of them will fancy themselves authoritative in the French field, and unless I surprise them just a little, they will only pick on my translations, etc. I have read a volume of Barbey d'Aurevilly with pleasure: there is the show-off style, and vulgarity in other ways as well, but I found it amusing and, at intervals, rather thrilling. Then comes another emptyish period. In my unregenerate, modernistic days I used to like LaForgue's *Moralités Légendaires*—? Someone has recommended something by Renan entitled *Patrice*, and something by Courteline entitled *Ah Jeunesse*; and of course I must review Anatole France: *L'Étui de Nacre? Le Mannequin d'Osier?* And to conclude, Gide's *Symphonie Pastorale*—*Le Diable au Corps* and/or *Les Clefs de la Mort*—and of course Colette. I haven't really gone to work; indeed it will scarcely be work, with a limitation of 300,000 words, except to write the introductory essay, next spring.

August 18

Foolish ideas about sex as about illness, perhaps because these are the experiences one is least able to control. For there is a great connection between the reason and the will. When a thing cannot be helped, one is inclined not to think any more about it, becoming thus in a measure primitive and superstitious, uncritical and egocentric. A very civilized, self-sacrificial temperament may find this to his advantage upon occasion. It releases his strong feelings, it helps him to act.

Long ago an English acquaintance informed me that a good many British soldiers, when they have a venereal disease, will try to give it to others, in the belief that this will rid themselves of it; as in a game of tag.

I wonder what became of Teresa Neumann, the modest and evidently genuine Czechoslovakian woman who, I was told twenty years ago, would catch the diseases of those who came to her; who then immediately recovered. In their stead she would be left with a mild case of whatever it was—somewhat the reverse of a typhoid carrier—and recover presently, then hold herself in readiness for the next contagion. The stigmata were vouchsafed her every Friday; she ate and drank nothing but the wafer and wine of the sacrament, and seemed on the way to canonization.

August 19

I took Benzedrine yesterday morning to counteract the sleepiness I have suffered from in trains lately. It was efficacious. All day long I wrote and wrote, with pleasant fickle inspiration, three or four small themes at the same time, now and then word-perfect. Only it was hard to get anything entirely inscribed before something else arose to charm and distract me.

However, this sort of flightiness, faster than words can follow, is characteristic of my mind in any case—small-scale minute and overkeen; (not at all stoic toward itself); mercurial, multiple, and (so to speak) peripheral.

Benzedrine?—The train on the adjacent track moved slowly but seemed immobile, whereas I could feel the motion of the train I was in, and I could see the platform sliding away. Though a commonplace illusion, I found it nightmarish for a few moments because I couldn't stop it or snap out of it or blink it away; and the effect of the stimulant, I think, was only an intensification of my self-consciousness, a susceptibility to auto-suggestion. Which must be a part of the mystery of drug addiction in general; also of alcoholism. A part of drunkenness is the thinking that oneself is not sober.

The Pullman porter was tidying up the smoking compartment—the good and (as you might say) bourgeois type of Negro, fairly black, stout, middle-aged—when the conductor came in and began pleasantly teasing him about his impatience to get back to his mistress, a cook, upon our arrival in New York. As I gathered, they had been parted quite a while, for whatever reason, and he must need her by this time, etc.

To which, with a wise happy chuckle, the Negro replied that it was not a need; it was a habit.

I joined their conversation for a little, to ask whether he had ever tried to break the habit.

He said no; and, chuckling some more, added that, once one of his girlfriends had tried to break him of it, but he hadn't stood it very long.

Then he told us how he had suffered in this particular when he was a young fellow, a doughboy in France in the other war. It would get so bad that he couldn't eat. "Sometimes," he said, "when I'd lie on the ground, the rain beatin' on me, that comforted me some."

After a consummation of love exceedingly forceful, ravishing, and profound, I murmured, "It is all right because it is you." An idea so spontaneous and secret that I should not have realized that I was uttering it aloud if my dear one had not asked me the meaning of it . . .

This is what it meant: If anyone whom I did not truly care for and understand and trust had done it—exercised all that power over me, and so overwhelmed my mind, with that conscious and various and prolonged animality of which evidently no animal except *Homo sapiens* is capable—my reaction would have been to want to kill him.

For there is a kind of paranoia in maximum pleasure. And I have led too proud a life, on the whole; and my capacity for grief and grievous indolence is excessive; and my great imagination is not stable enough, etc.

It is all right because this dear one has no love of trouble, no lust for power, no particular need to have his vanity gratified; and in one way and another, as regards pleasure, he is not foreign to me, not even unlike me. He is what I call good. I do trust him.

Perhaps it would be all right in any case, for the very simple reason that in ignoble arms I should never respond like this, yieldingly and wide open. Perhaps in the event of these arms letting me go, in the event of my not finding anyone else good, there would be no wild temptation or shameful vulnerability—only loneliness, with my sensuality self-isolated and defensive, circumscribed and (before long) closed.

One of my attacks of pre-auroral insomnia: so here I sit, a couple of hours ahead of my household, sipping my thermosful of inky Yuban, lonely, wanting something salubrious to turn my mind to . . .

I suppose I am a type like Coleridge, only without opium; and, I must admit, without an Ancient Mariner, so far.

But let's not give me up as a bad job. I love Monroe like religion and I will fight—I will fight even myself—to prove it.

Every evening a letter worth copying, a page worth keeping, and a memorandum for the morrow.

A day's work every day now, now, now, now.

1 9 4 7

. . . what interests one in a novel, in the last

analysis, is the quantity of glimpsed detail, the

asides and the incidents along the way; not the

over-all turn of events or the holocaust at the

close or the happy ending.

—"Talks with Thornton Wilder"

Winter

All these years I have wanted to have, in my maturity, in terms of maturity, a satisfying, full, and appropriate love life as such, as one might say, a year of happiness, and, as it were, just to discover what it would be like, what all the unhappiness implied and pointed to.

Well, now I had it, not a year—but eight or nine months: between me and Nick Anton; for most of the past year, there was the sweetest, best behaved, and most passionate romance of my life since I was a youngster. When the end came, the payoff, all in one bill, some months ago, it threw me into a sort of bankruptcy of emotion and morality for a while.

Rough, as it happened—upon three days' notice and in extreme psychoneurotic, seemingly desperate regret—Nick dismissed me from his intimacy. He would not tell me the story, but I know a good deal. Certain of those he is most dependent on have thoroughly wicked natures and principles. No one in the category of rival romancer; nothing of that sort . . .

The moral of it very strange, if any—the moral of happiness, of having had what one wanted. It is as if I had become addicted to a drug—I am pretty sick, for the present; but self-respecting, and not making any row, not taking it out on other people.

My thoughts are like bees swarming out of that hive where they have been living constantly with Nick, working for him—all up in the air, uncontrolled except by instinct, collecting all on one narrow insufficient unstable windy branch, crawling all over one another, over and over, stinging one another. Now they must be quieted down, smoked down, cut down, and lured into some new hive.

I don't want to go to Silver Hill [for therapy] because I believe it would diminish my gift to write. I believe that I need all my mystery, my fierceness, my extravagance—let me risk my crack-up, for my work's sake; and I think there may be some salvation in work still . . .

It always is the same kind of thing. First there is the deep defect, injury, fissure—with good luck it may never matter too much. Then there is one's wickedness, spoiledness, idleness, and others' strength, hardness, misunderstanding.

But what a fuss I make! My neurosis is not very deep, my present pressure not altogether irremediable or incorrigible.

Only Monroe knows what a grievous nature I have—and he must now remember what he said to me when I was a boy, on the grass of Northwestern campus: "If you become a great writer, no one will mind . . ." The really grave fact of my life is that I have not been able to fulfill those expectations of me which he invented, partly for himself, so long ago. And the really dread emotion lies in the probability of my outliving him and in the simple fact that I have not the slightest idea how I shall manage in that event . . .

Aloner than usual—meals alone, out of cans today, snowbound . . . Lloyd does not get back from South America until Sunday night. Elizabeth has taken Mother to town for various shopping and doctoring. But Monroe will arrive tomorrow, and I may tag along back to town when he goes. Anyway Mr. Van Wyck Brooks* is giving me a dinner party Monday—fancy that!

Yesterday I went down to spend an hour with Debo, and after a good bit of roughhouse, she said, "I don't *like* to have such a silly uncle, but, oh, I *love* him being so silly!" then laughed along with my laughter, then repeated it with the strangest gentle self-mystified expression.

Out of the window: In spite of the storm a downy woodpecker is working up and down the difficult thin twigs of the old apple tree. It must be decaying or infested with parasites, or it would not be worth his while. With a fierce vivacity—how rarely one sees this energy in a human being!—perhaps in certain young businessmen out to make

* Van Wyck Brooks (1886–1963). Essayist, critic, and scholar, and closest friend of editor Maxwell Perkins.

money, when it is a matter of their vanity as well as covetousness; or
in someone at a party, some witty talker full of Benzedrine. Whereas (I
suppose) what animates the bird is just starvation.

With an aching, overburdened heart I find it hard to listen to
music—great music puts one to shame, and popular or semipopular
songs are sentimental, lachrymose, ignoble. Reading, on the other hand,
even the light current matter that one takes up by chance, almost always
catches the mind here and there, throws out a spark, kindles some
thought . . .

This, for example, I found in Nancy Ross's novel: Sheep which are
fed to the ticking of a metronome at a beat of 120, and *not* fed at a beat
of 50, soon learn the difference between the two tempos. In a few days
they entirely ignore the sound that promises them nothing. But if you
reduce the high rate to 100 and raise the low rate to 80, so that they
have difficulty differentiating, they make mistakes in going to the feed-
box; then presently they develop states of hypertension, irritability,
nerves, illness (especially eczema!).

No wonder, then, that so many of us, who are creatures of a far
more complex nervous structure—in our modernized world in which it
is harder than ever to distinguish positive from negative conditionings,
the right from the wrong, the helpful from the harmful, the true from
the insincere and tricky—show increasing characteristics of indecision
and strain, cynicism and exhaustion.

The cure of my soul: Every night, I will clear the top of my desk
of everything except the manuscript I am supposed to be working on.
Nothing else to catch my eye in the morning: no memoranda, no letters,
not even manuscript unless it is *the* manuscript.

Am I envious of Monroe's having taken the fine subject matter of
our burglary? Not exactly, but I wish that he had shown me his report
to the police. There were various details in which his wonderful peculiar
character appeared dramatized, which delighted me: for instance, his
silly fearlessness, like a wirehaired terrier, when life is mastiff or wolf.
When Norman with his gun ordered us into the closet, he got stubborn,
he wouldn't get out of bed, he wanted to argue—it was a fine moment,
with my old bullying "Come on! Shut up! Hurry up!" added to the voice
of hell and the argument of metal.

In the closet I still had difficulty keeping him still, and when he
whispered to know what I had left exposed by my bed and I replied by
a gesture outlining my chain on my bare body, he gave a little shout,

"Diamonds!" which I thought would draw Norman to us in a minute; and he called through the keyhole, "Kid! Kid!" still hoping to dissuade him.

When we had broken through the door, the first thing he said was, "Now I am going to take jujitsu lessons." Little aging man against that MacArthur-trained trigger-happy bruiser; mongoose against cobra.

The next couple of days I suffered from a kind of fear—cobra fear—always in the same way and the same connection, whenever in telling the story or in reconsidering it I came to the two visual images, just where he stood and just how he looked—then my flesh would creep, up and down, like arpeggio on a harp, like a strong tickling hand, right up under my chin sometimes, and then suddenly in a few minutes it nauseated me.

Not Monroe—he has not admitted one moment's fear or fearful imagination. On the other hand, he suffered more than I from anxiety neurosis, *Schamfurcht*: the newspapers, what line the gossips might take, etc. But even as to that, he was brave and fierce. The elevator men reported that now and then we have lent our keys to various friends; and Detective K. spent two hours at the museum trying to get the names and addresses of those friends. "Detective K.," said the wirehaired one, "I see your point, and in fact I have *hundreds* of friends, but as it happens, they are *all* of my own kind and class"; and that was that. Afterwards he gave the whole 17th squad hell for having tried to shift the onus of their inefficiency onto everyone's presumably private life. Actually they were quite efficient and lucky. But we can't have our trinkets back for another month.

Meantime, the elevator men, fighting off suspicions of themselves, gave descriptions of our all too numerous friends and acquaintances; and now that it is over, some of them feel that we owe them big tips, a feeling to which we have not sufficiently responded . . . All fairly comic in a way. In fact a good many people must have been disappointed in us, in our disillusioning virtuousness as it turned out—our being jointly compromised with a pulchritudinous purple-hearted cat burglar would have pepped up a number of cocktail parties, at this lassitudinous time of the year, as one more monotonous New York winter peters out.

Before calling on Janet Gaynor and Adrian* on my way to the National Institute [of Arts and Letters] dinner, at which I am to be formally instituted: I got into all this kind of thing simply because of

---

* Adrian (1903–59). Costume designer for numerous films, including those of Greta Garbo.

the declaration I made about not returning to Europe; the reason I gave: cultural patriotism . . . and then I do care about the Institute grants—money is sacred, that is to say, money for young literary people is sacred.

As for Katherine Anne's candidate, Eleanor Clark, the only problem is that I have not met a single soul—excepting K.A. herself—who can testify to any sort of enjoyment in reading *The Bitter Box*. We all feel and finely proclaim her every other meritoriousness. Nothing wrong (I think) except just a misconception that she starts with—the joke that is not funny; tragic strip derived from comic strip; Kafka, and other influences of the mode just now. Oddly enough, she lets herself be influenced by things that, with her strong and cross crystalline intelligence, she rejects: existentialists and such. Why?—because they come from the right side of the railroad tracks?—One word from her, as to what she plans to do next, would fix me up for her wholeheartedly.

Bernard [Perlin] and Robert Drew* came to dine, reveling in that fancy little dinner of leftovers which I brought in from Stone-blossom, and taking it as a celebration of the first public hanging of a picture by him: *The Sleepers*, in the Whitney annual.

From a letter to Katherine Anne Porter

Barbara: It wasn't bronchitis—that has been our line for the friends and neighbors, etc., and for future reference, a way for her to bypass people when they ask about it after it is all over—it was the wish to commit suicide. I had observed it developing for some months; which was tough, as for the first time in our life I had no influence over her. It would have been bad for her if we had proposed shutting her up or curtailing her independence in any way, even that way—and in fact I did not expect her to do it, only I thought that in digging in her heels against doing it, she might let her mind go over the brink. So we stood by. After all, there is just one thing to be said for us, and for her destiny in general: we have given her a good deal to live for: Debo, sex, literature, landscape. So finally, with my sister Elizabeth's wonderful fast recovery in mind, she herself chose to go to Silver Hill. So far, they haven't accomplished anything much—except that she delights in the place; recites the credo of it quite starry-eyed; speaks of "my doctor" as she used to speak of "my husband"—and she's not fooling him much, apparently. I have the highest hopes—there's no hurry.

* Robert Drew. An artist and designer.

* * *

George is rather like the Communist Party; that is, with utter sincerity, he always has two or three objectives in mind, whatever he does or plans. Now he has sent to me a great rosy jovial amiable young man, ex-captain of the Irish Guards but half French, rich by birth but squeezed by his family and job hunting like crazy. After three days of him, I should say he's insupportable and delightful. I have tried to warn him of the realities of myself and of my life on both counts, but I doubt if he has paid attention. He lives just up the street, and he simply inquires what I have to do, and comes and calls on me allegro in whatever spare time we have—three separate visits the first day. He questions me about everyone, and I tell him the great yarns and he doesn't stop at that, but also immediately propounds the great questions: family, career, love, sex, religion—in the first two of these categories I have already exercised some decisive influence—though on the more intimate matters, all the carts have got before all the horses. Unseductive on my part, I should think; perhaps already decidedly avuncular. He is handsome and dear, and surely my senses must be troubled; but as he is so unprecedented a type of young man, I am not afraid of him at this point. In my wretched circumstances as they are now, it must be good for me. To sum up: diversion and counterirritant, mustard plaster and songbird.

At our second meeting yesterday afternoon, Messrs. Van Wyck Brooks, [Louis] Untermeyer, [William Rose] Benét, and myself, with Mme [Lillian] Hellman coming late and just concurring, granted Eleanor the blessed thousand bucks. It was a blessing that Katherine Anne mentioned "Call Me Comrade," for I procured copies of that and of "The Ball" and sent them with a warm letter to Mr. B., and he liked them best. He opened the deliberations by saying that we might as well start with those upon whom we would surely agree, for example, Eleanor Clark; and by golly, we did agree immediately.

Sentimental addenda: While naturally we can't help remarking that So-and-so lives properly in a garret whereas So-and-so has just had a Book-of-the-Month, etc., we have been making it a point of elegance not to harp on that argument. The day before, apropos of I can't think what, I had called Eleanor on the telephone and she had confessed that she was in a jam: no more Doubleday French-readering, bits of sickening reviewing, and some job in prospect which would interfere with whatever it is that she is writing. It was a real luxury of spirit not to have to bring that up.

And when I telephoned her this morning she was so happy, she made sounds like Mélisande at the impassioned points in that opera. It really seemed that she had had no expectation of it! Then she berated me for not having proposed Cummings and, when I remarked that her heart is as soft as her tongue is sharp, expressed amazement. "But, Glenway, I haven't a sharp tongue, have I? You don't think I have, do you?"

Upon the eve of his departure for Europe, Monroe assured me that I have not disappointed him; that in his opinion I am a great man, whether or not I produce any more books; that my letters and notebooks will suffice for my fame and reputation, beyond death, in the time to come.

Night before last, without my urging him particularly, Patrick* told me what makes him so romantic and yet so detached, so skittish, like a dangerous though well-meaning unbroken colt. The second time in his life that he had sexual intercourse, aged eighteen, he got syphilis and had to make his cure while soldiering, with old-fashioned British brass-hat doctors. Except for this, never having overcome either the fear or the disgust, he is almost a virgin; and he thinks it will prove incorrigible unless he finds a great true lasting love, of which he dreams all the time. Of course, as I warned him, the danger is that the dream will perpetuate itself as such, idle and atrophied. His being a Roman Catholic doesn't help. Also he has put off deciding whether or not to try to be normal—his family and family friends don't help.

But what a fine, touching spirit! He was a real war hero—no one else has given so overpowering an impression of the cruelty of England's war: the field hospitals, the amputations, the gangrene, the almost crazy stoicism and cheery sentimentality to keep up one another's courage, etc. What fantastic health, fundamentally—to have come through all the battles, all the bone surgery, all the Salvarsan with those bright eyes of a baby and that skin of a freestone peach.

He is a dear boy, but really his behavior is not good. I don't suppose that anyone in the prime of life, or in the flower of youth, who tries to avoid sex—afraid of it, disgusted by it—can be really virtuous. One of the oddest things about him is the way he rummages—picking up my scribble book and trying to decipher it, opening doors of clothes closets and complaining of the rundown heels of my evening shoes, the ancientness of my ties. He'll be like a puppy dog on the scent, if he ever comes to St.-bl. Effect of Army life.

I keep expecting him to trouble my notorious old senses sooner or

* Patrick O'Higgins. Portrait photographer and Helena Rubinstein's publicist.

later, more than I can tolerate, and I worry about hurting his feelings.

I feel that there must be a lesson in it for me, God knows what; another step in my endless, practically useless education.

Great conversations with Ll. and Eliz. yesterday. Dr. Hiden seems to have had some difficulty getting Baba [Barbara] to turn her mind from the past to the present, the status quo here—therefore he is letting her come home for a fortnight or so, the first week in April. She won't consent to the removal of the office from the sitting room. Peacock's bedroom is going to be fixed up as a sitting room for her, as a compromise. Furthermore, as her self-assigned ambition (corresponding to Eliz.'s guitar, etc.) she chooses to work for the farm, milk records, etc; which Hiden seems to regard not discontentedly so far. But Eliz. and I are bristling and stiffening from head to foot . . . Perhaps the time has come for me to write him a snorter.

Hanochevski quit last week but Tom and I brought her around. It was just sex, really—femaleness, wanting to be wooed, in that unspeakable language of hers. Yesterday she brought me two wonderful jars of infant green tomatoes and miniature green peppers pickled with great sprays of dill; which I think I shall take into town for my party.

One of the melancholier St.-bl. mornings . . . At daybreak, the hour of concentrate-of-coffee, after a night of Nembutal, it was snowing fast and soft, with all the twigs in cotton wool as though they were expensive antique enamel, and even the backs of the black cattle whited in places. Now it has begun to its melting. This winter has been so aesthetic, winter for winter's sake, unfunctional; we're tired of it.

Spring

I believe that I shall have to discard most of the pages I have done and begin all over again, with a new outline and new style. I considered it last weekend and I was afraid to try it—now if I do, it will be in desperation. There appears to be no more life in my old ideas, I have labored over them so, to make them fit.

Ll. came home with me and talked for almost an hour about Baba. We do not see any change in her except her improved physical condition and cheerfulness due to sleeping, exercise, etc. Only folly in her planning for the other two Silver Hill requirements, work and play, so far.

Now I will take my roughest mss. up to bed, looking for easy parts.

* * *

Do I want the new Jean Genet?* I'm inclined to prefer ordinary common-or-garden pornography in inartistic English; which makes me laugh at myself, perhaps also at them. Not to mention Boris Kochno† bawling me out for writing just best-sellers, when I have the genius and experience to be the American Genet!

A joke on me: "Give him an inch of sex, he'll take an ell of love."

A pleasant old word, *ell*. Just now, for the first time, I have looked in the dictionary to find out its exact length. It varies from country to country, from twenty-seven to forty-eight inches.

Someone gave B.K. the address of a homosexual dive in an apartment on Second Avenue; not exactly a brothel but a place of orgy, of the utmost squalor and pathos. Hour after hour, half the afternoon, half the night, the clientele sat at a round table, most of them too drunk to have intercourse. Two of them withdrew into the corridor and had a fight, and returned and sat down again. Like a play by Eugene O'Neill.

And the host or brothel-keeper, who was the drunkest of the lot, said to B., "I like you, I want to give you something"; then fumbled in his pockets and brought out a dime. "It's all right, I can spare it. Here, take it."

B. may be a liar, but probably not in such detail as this.

Last night in the dining car, I sat facing a little forty-year-old aquiline old-maidish woman whom I often see; I think she works in Plainfield and commutes. Perhaps she was drunk, it was not apparent—except that she played an entire scene of great emotion to herself, making great soundless speeches, denouncing, imploring, despising, flirting, sublimating (and there really was something sublime about it), with grimaces to match, like a very good old-fashioned actress.

How I love words, even some German words!—

Aberglaube, that is to say, a but-belief, something you subscribe to in spite of some consideration, a conviction *quand-même*; that is to say, a superstition.

Tätigkeit (which Goethe makes such great use of), the equivalent of which in current colloquial American is "know-how."

---

* Jean Genet. G.W. is referring to a revised edition of Genet's novel *Funeral Rites*.

† Boris Kochno (1904–). Advisor to and occasional scenarist for Sergei Diaghilev. Later the regisseur of his own company.

* * *

How strange it was at the ballet last night: the dream crowd. I did not see Nick, which was just as well for my sickish gastroenteric nerves.

But the numbers, scores, hundreds, with whom I have been friendly enough to know what to say to them! (It appalled Patrick; suddenly not at all Irish or French, just British—drawing away in the crowd, his rosiness and goldness somehow a little extinguished . . .)

A pretty moment, comedy: Down a corridor rolling or sliding at a great rate like a wound-up toy came Truman Capote; there at my feet, looking straight up. "Aren't you Glenway Wescott? I recognized you!"

"I recognize you too."

"I like your story about the hawk."

"And I like *your* story about the hawk."* Then with absolute absurdity, seeing the concern in his little gangster face, the terrible sweetness, I added, "It's the second-best story about a hawk ever written; naturally I think mine is the best." Taking the advantage of my stature and my age—and it seemed to enchant him.

One thing I came to town for was to dine with Rebecca West at Emanie's— She's still a great charmer, though heavy, heavy now, avoirdupois and exhaustion and that steam-rollering temperament which in fact she has always had— Alas, sixteen dinner guests semi-self-serving; pleasant at my table, though, with Edna Ferber and Jane Grant (H. Ross's† first wife).

But how anti-Willie [Maugham] she is!—hurt by a bit of his savagery just lately, for one thing. The trouble is that he never will listen to one's story—one sentence of it and he has got his little plot, and he's off.

The point of real interest in R.'s remarks was that it simply doesn't occur to her not to despise all his recent literary career. I don't suppose a great writer ever has so entirely put off the really consequential public.

My poor sister Beulah has lost that unlovable husband she is so in love with. Strange: at any given moment, I suppose, there is as much anguish of that kind going on in the world as there is of war or anything.

Yesterday I worked ten hours, a bit more than five hours today— with time out to dry Beulah's tears and to start a negotiation with Doubleday to get a fair payment to Bernard for using his W.S.M. silverpoint as our frontispiece. I'm still awake, so I ought to be able to add on a little more tonight.

---

* Capote's "The Headless Hawk" appeared in the November 1946 issue of *Harper's Bazaar*.
† Harold Ross (1892–1951). Original and longtime editor of *The New Yorker*.

It did me so much good to confess and bewail to Barbara on the telephone Saturday morning. That is a part of the devil in me—always determined to try to help others or to seem helpful, though with misgivings in my mind as to the effect on others in reality, and with a constant feeling in my heart that she and Monroe would like me to mind my own business, for my work's sake; and at the same time always requiring more help from others than is legitimate, notably from Barbara.

Off now to New York to go to the Bach cantata concert with Nick. I gave him a pair of tickets for the series for Christmas, and he invited me for this, *quand-même*—I thought he had forgotten it or changed his mind, but then he telephoned. An incongruity, but he would have misinterpreted my refusing and his feelings would have been hurt, and the eventual gradual consequences of his feeling hurt would have made me angry, etc.—and I may as well keep my fences in repair. But I do believe—it does seem—I don't mind about him anymore, except for the bitter shame of my not having done what I should to deserve that happiness while I had it.

Later: The Bach concert was lovely, though very lonely. I committed a blasphemy, I soundlessly sang one of the chorales along with the chorus, putting M.'s name in it: *"Ob gleich Sund' und Hölle schrecken, Monroe will mich decken."* But it wasn't morbid, it was a dear game.

Last night I worked until after one, forcing myself, not to very good effect; then slept four hours and a bit, and went to work again, and presently had one of my fits of inability, dizzy gaping effect, as of some injury.

So I went for a walk. The very early day, Godlike. There had been hoarfrost, the shadows white not black. The season of buds, which I love—the hedgerows seemingly dark, then empty—until you look closely, and every tip of twig is like a miniature unheard-of flower.

Two days at St.-bl. with Bernard and his Robert. When the weather is so fine, the company so approved and attractive and kindly, there is induced a kind of belief in heaven; which is sad and momentarily almost death-wishful, because of course at the back of one's mind I disbelieve.

Then two days of various activity in New York, meaningful but futile: an evening with William S.M. and Alan; a session with MacGregor to expound my new plan of writing; and the old-fashioned, almost childish ceremonials of the Institute, receiving the new members and awarding the annual grants to young writers and artists.

Grotesque and heartbreaking address by Helen Keller on "The

Power of Speech." During the processional music she stretched her hand out before her and down toward the floor and made sweeping gestures not in time with the music, like some insane orchestra leader; which was to intercept the sound waves, I was told. When she made her speech, her companion stood just beside her behind in a close embrace, and occasionally she prompted her or communicated with her by fingering up and down her back. Her voice is the most terrible sound on earth: a great soft gurgling and croaking, with a note of anguish, only comprehensible here and there. Nerve-racking. Marianne Moore and Anne McCormick shed tears, but Mr. Damrosch,* aged almost ninety, lost his temper, muttering aloud, "It's too long, too long," and stamping his foot. Miss Keller's exalted and vague gestures reminded me of old Pueblo Indians during the Pueblo dances, when they invoke their animal deities or when they recall their ancient traditions.

My niece Eugenia was married on St.-bl. lawn Wednesday. It couldn't have been prettier. Eliz. persuaded Bernard and his good Robert to come the day before to set up a bower of snowballs, viburnum, and wild phlox on that old Burgundian osier-work which has been in the attic for years—over which Baba decreed the erection of a great green-and-white-striped marquee. We lunched from two white tables outdoors, with French champagne provided by little brother, etc.

That night we motored in to dine with Monroe, Diana and Reed Vreeland,† and Pavlik. The latter began by teasing me about my amorousness upon some gossip he had lapped up, which he followed with one of his preachments, egoism plus theosophy; and I found myself declaring that, with all my admiration for his painting, I wanted no more personal relationship with him, no more of his talk. We got through the evening fairly well, though he rather spoiled Mon's stories with arguments in his own behalf. He waited until the others went home, then tried to make peace with me on his terms, but I couldn't or wouldn't yield. It maddened him and distressed Monroe, but I think I shall be pleased to stick to it.

Now I have been out to see the full moon as gleaming golden as something in imagined antiquity; and I have listened to Kreisler's Beethoven Opus 12, especially the Adagio of the E flat major; and I have written one more self-indulging, self-healing letter—and my feeling is

---

* Walter J. Damrosch (1862–1950). German-born American composer.
† Diana Vreeland (1903[?]–89). Fashion editor at *Vogue* for twenty-five years. Her husband, T. Reed Vreeland, was a banker.

almost like that great page of Goethe, when Faust dies. *"Zum Augenblicke dürft'ich sagen: Verweile doch, du bist so schön."*

Remember that love is not a good-thing-in-itself—it is an even more dubious matter than pleasure—it is to be constantly appraised in terms of the happiness it brings, the virtue it inspires, the work it is conducive to . . . The instant one ceases to get good results by it, one ought to begin being ashamed of feeling it . . . Take care not to pride yourself on quantity of love, persistence in unrequitedness, degree of grieving.

Dog Days

Anglophobia: Carlota Joaquina, Queen of Portugal, so hated England that when she heard of a British general getting kicked by a mule, she bought it and cherished it as a pet.

I was about to fire my present idiot servant and not hire another, but Eliz. outsmarted me by giving me her wonderful Anna, complete with peasant brother and eighty-three-year-old mother, who has to be hung on to for a while, for the general family needs. A treasure . . . I think I've mentioned my economic situation, not pretty—I am living at the rate of about $600 a month, upon an allowance from Baba of $200 (to be repaid again upon successful publication of a book)—in addition to which I have in hand $1,200, the last return from *Apartment*, with not another cent in prospect. I shall have to refinance myself somehow, rebudget myself. If it were not for Baba—the doctor wants everything to go on as usual—I'd close up St.-bl. and take a room in the Ghetto.

At the age of five, Debo's love of vocabulary, which she picks up anywhere and everywhere and, with or without understanding, employs wonderfully well by ear, in plausible sentence constructions . . .

For example, this morning she stood looking down from her mother's window, informing her mother, who was still in bed, of what she saw: the farmers unloading a cow from a truck. "Are they making her back out, down the tailgate?" her mother inquired, to make conversation.

"Yes, she is backing down now, with a slow, impudent step."

From a letter to Marianne Moore,
upon the death of her mother

In the final time, for her there cannot have been any dismay or inconvenience (even of body). For she had a far-reaching, planning intellect, had she not? Also it must have been far easier than any number of daily undertakings the year round in recent years, easier than eating whatever spoonful, than shifting the least distance from bed to chair, pillow to other pillow. Whenever it may have been that she took her last little walk, from shadowy indoors out to fresher air or brighter light, I dare say she regarded it as rehearsal, and she may have been pleased especially with her confidence in your literary genius to communicate all that she still had in mind to say to us . . .

Forster said to Don Windham:* "One thing that troubles me about American young people is, if my observation is correct, their lack of sentiment."

"Oh, I don't think it *is* correct," our friend replied. "In a way they are too sentimental, of which they are well aware. Therefore they fight against it."

"Oh, certainly," said Forster. "Yes, one fights against it, but one should always lose."

Strange saying of Baba's: "No very old person is genuinely good. This distress of the conclusion of life, the unemployment and the dis-illusionment, the loneliness, to say nothing of the decay of the body, are too terrible, too hard—it takes every sort of selfishness, belligerency, egoism, just to keep on living."

Perhaps Nick and I are too pleasant with one another for our own good; so enjoying one another and all sorts of things together. For example, last night he might have had something important to tell me about—and sometimes any pretext will serve for his being tongue-tied, anyway—or I might have had some complexity to resolve or shadow to illumine. What chance had we? with ideal steak and ritual ice cream and black cat and white wool, with tarantellesque Beethoven, with early pseudo-sleepiness and the dream of the senses, and then real sleep and dreams of nonsense, and the mere cheerfulness and worldliness at break-fast . . .

---

* Donald Windham (1920–   ). Novelist and playwright who collaborated with Tennessee Williams on the play *You Touched Me.*

* * *

Sometimes I fancy that I am like an ox, even a couple of oxen, a dark one as well as a pure white one: I feel all heavy and strong and patient, all too well broken to harness. Whereas I fancy that Nick is like a young stag with wild limbs either tremblingly immobilized or stampeding timorously; with glances accumulating in his too-wide-open eyes as little storm clouds accumulate; with nostrils dilated sometimes by entrancement, sometimes by disappointment.

The Pursuit of Happiness

Happiness is a method, a process, an endeavor—not a goal. (Unless you mean by happiness the mere absence of anguish—not being put in a concentration camp, not having cancer of the lung—and other disasters so far beyond our control as not to engage one's morality as an individual except in the way of patience, endurance, stoicism . . .) As a goal, happiness is a snare and a delusion.

If you ask yourself at a given moment, "Am I happy?" the answer is almost invariably "No." If you love someone so that you are deeply concerned for his or her happiness, turned away from yourself—if you have some great work to do and keep hard at it—sometimes if you are a fool absorbed in folly, or a criminal absorbed in vengeance or in dishonest devices . . . you don't ask . . .

Unhappiness is not being able to make up one's mind, one's conduct, one's life. Dividedness of mind . . .

This was my conclusion to an *Invitation to Learning* broadcast on *The Moon and Sixpence*, but, as it seems to me now, it hasn't much to do either with Strickland Gauguin or with W.S.M. It is my own morality.

I'd rather grow crooked than wither; I'd rather burn than freeze. But for me, me personally and me auctorially, there will be no salvation whatever unless I can work it out between myself and myself, hour by hour, dollar by dollar, little job after job, in desperate willpower and lonely comfortless pleasureless regime. There can be no vision in the midst of fate; no answer to fate (I suppose) except mere discipline.

My strange family all getting on, in one way or another. Baba is tired out but still improving. At the moment she and Lloyd are in Iowa somewhere, viewing cattle. Bernard thrilled by the prospect of his show at Knoedler's and perfectly peaceful with [Robert] Drew. Monroe and I have bought one of his small pictures. Nick seems to have fallen in love, with one of those beloveds who turn up more or less regularly in my bewitched life. I am glad of it, though with some concern.

Meanwhile I haven't been writing to any purpose and my financial setup is hopeless. With the burden of Baba's illness, and I think also influenced by the therapy she has been submitting to and by her better thinking, Lloyd has developed extraordinarily; and he and I have drawn closer than before.

Finally he and she put their heads together about me; Eliz., who really "knows" me best, also entered into the great maneuver; and they smoked me out and gave me choices. At first Ll. proposed that I close up Stone-blossom—the old neurosis, and sexual deprivation, and the melancholy of family affairs, etc.—and re-establish myself in N.Y. This I refused to do, not only for others' sake. Eliz. backed me up in this, denouncing the compulsive unrewarded way I have frequented that metropolis: always egoistically hoping, always in fact just altruistically helping others, always in my endless triangles.

The upshot of all this is to be a better Stone-blossom, with my good Anna and perhaps even some secretarial assistance when I get my work under way—discipline and luxury. But on the other hand a real financial limitation upon my trips to town, no pleasure, no fond hopes, no pursuit.

This has induced in me an almost mystic exaltation. It is hard to express, for on the one hand I am sad, sad, but on the other hand I am not protesting or even discontented. For I know the life I am able to live in imagination; and I know how I have changed, my sentiments all clarified and pacified, only sensuality burning, and it can burn in imagination, if one doesn't insist on being happy—and all this may well lead to literature.

Good morning—morning gray and chilly, and silent except for a hardworking plaintive train beyond the hills and except for neighbor Dalrymple's small rooster with an *idée fixe*.

Howard Sturges, in the elevator as we left Lady Ribblesdale's tea party, remarked or rather exclaimed, "Glenway, Glenway, you are looking so well, you're in such good looks, fresh as a daisy!" then added with who knows what degree of malice, not much seemingly, just for fun, "I believe you've had your face lifted!"

He is twenty years older than I; handsome, only somewhat whittled away by his life of pleasure, calloused, blear-eyed, wattle-necked.

Therefore, for fun, I replied, "Yes, wasn't it a good idea. When you need it, call me up, I'll give you the address of my face-lifter."

Talk with a taxi driver: It began with his asking me to wait while he went into a bar to piss, then proceeded more or less casually to surprising themes: *pissoirs* in Paris; the conditioned reflex as a factor in modesty; recent evening dresses with extended skirts and wide-open bosoms; and what bad bridge players women are, too talkative, even his own wife!

"I tell you, you can live with 'em all your life, you never understand 'em."

He was young or youngish, good-looking in an unappealing way, somewhat stout, with two or three days' beard.

I had ceased to listen attentively, and opened my newspaper. Whereupon, impromptu, without a transition, he told me about a wonderful stag party he and some other G.I.'s had been taken to in Paris during the war.

"Hell, I've been to several stags here in the U.S., I never experienced anything like that, I'll never forget it.

"The principal act was a Shetland pony. I suppose they had it trained, Shetlands are pretty intelligent. The girl in the act—she musta had something on her hand, cold cream or something—took out his pecker and worked it up for him. Then she got herself in position bending over a table, and then he jumped up with his two feet on the table and slid it in her. I couldn't believe it hardly, a Shetland's got a hell of a big pecker; but you could see she enjoyed it.

"It's one of the most wonderful memories I ever experienced," he concluded with a soft earnest intonation.

Then he added, "At the end a man came out with a hard-on, and he slid it in the pony."

I inquired how it ended: in uncontrolled excitement, with everyone going for one another, and having a party? Or were they mostly shocked, shocked and depressed?

"Something certainly shoulda happened, but nothing did. I guess they felt embarrassed. I guess they were all ashamed to let the others know how they felt."

He went on to complain of the deprivation of the troops in France, with the great prevailing dread of women because they were so dirty and diseased. His tone of voice grew small and strange, recalling and perhaps refeeling the sexual starvation.

At the door of the St. Regis, it embarrassed me a little to give him an extragenerous tip, but it would have embarrassed me even more not to. He looked sorry to take leave of me.

Moss Hart, when he first took residence in Bucks County, chose a modest stone farmhouse; but as his dramaturgy came to be crowned with success after success, he added two or three little wings named after the plays which defrayed them, and then finally, as the proximity of the road worried him, he planted a profusion of young trees all around. Called upon to admire this latest final venture, Dorothy Parker said, "It just goes to show what God could do if He wanted to, *and* if He had money."

Ditto, in a conversation about the self-assurance of Dorothy Thompson: "Well, of course, she realizes that she doesn't know as much as God; but I suppose she does feel that she knows as much as God knew when He was her *age.*"

1 9 4 8

. . . The world is never *well lost for love.*

—Journals

Sans Date

One night when I was talking at Pauline [Potter]'s, she noticed that Monroe was making little notes on the back of an envelope. The envelope slipped down in an upholstered chair; next morning her servant brought it to her and she deciphered what was on it: certain thoughts by or about Santayana and one sentence of mine, so marked: "Glen." M.'s wish to preserve it, emphasizing its meaning to him, seemed to her so romantic, so dramatic, that she wished never to admit her indiscretion in reading it. Therefore she kept it to this day. The sentence of mine was: "I am famous for my fidelity to those I no longer love."

Midnight conversation with Bruce*—about Princeton, about his sexual appetite and frustration. I lent him the *Kinsey Report*, and his father forced him to return it to me, unread.

Luncheon with Eunice Jessup†—to inquire about psychoanalysts. Heard her account of Karen Horney's expulsion from the association of psychoanalysts, for going to bed with an impotent patient and reading a paper on the case . . .

I often think Ravel superior to Debussy; notwithstanding faultless tedious *Pelléas et Mélisande* and certain songs. Does this betray that I am middle-aged, with a downward trend of taste, a general inclination toward easy forms and popular feelings?

* * *

---

* Bruce Hotchkiss (1930–   ). G.W.'s nephew, Elizabeth's son, he was the inspiration for the fictional hero in G.W.'s 1930 work, *The Babe's Bed*.

† Eunice Jessup. Sister of novelist Eleanor Clark and wife of *Life* editor and writer Jack Jessup.

Howard Barnes, the *Herald Tribune* film critic, says there is a ruling in the code of the Motion Picture Association that the word *nurse* cannot be used on the screen because it suggests the female breast.

Last night I picked up *The Pilgrim Hawk* (Cyril Connolly* in *The New Yorker* and Mark Schorer† in *The Hudson Review* have referred to it flatteringly; Robert Drew is currently reading it) and read a few pages, and experienced one of my rare moments of pride.

Characteristic Stone-blossom news item: A great blue heron ventured onto the lawn and seized a twelve-inch trout from the brook; and my little Slovakian Anna, scarcely his size, chased him with a Fuller brush, a bathroom brush, and made him drop it; and now it is about to be eaten, but not by me.

Remember back to the evening when Lloyd (apropos of G.P.L. *et al.*) spoke of homosexuality as a way of life under a curse; a set of traits of character ill-fated—and I protested, pointing out the unsatisfactoriness of heterosexual lives, the failure of heterosexual marriages, etc. But then I ventured to state what in general is the trouble of homosexuals: that they are stupid. And the cause of their stupidity? Male and female the great pattern of the human race; He created them so . . . Homosexuals either do not know women—or they know psychoneurotic women in false relationships. *Notre Dame de Sodome*, etc. "If I am better than the average, it is thanks to Elizabeth, to Frances, to Baba . . ." And Baba sat there with a complacently happy look.

This weekend we had fair cool weather, with uncertain sunshine and vacillating cloud—the puberty of the year—and we walked and walked, across the pastures and along the rivers and through the thickets and up and down the little hills, with cherry trees in blossom in the hedgerows, with a carpet of violets here, a bed of rare plantation of Dutchman's-breeches there, and the mandrake not male any longer but female, shaking out its little shining skirts, and columbine like a sprinkle of blood on the outcroppings of limestone . . .

In my relationship with Bernard now, every now and then—when Robert for some reason has relaxed his extreme control of his life or he has circumvented it somehow—I have an opportunity and privilege; a night or a witching hour, once in a great while . . . This afternoon, for

* Cyril Connolly (1903–74). British essayist and critic; wartime editor of *Horizon*.
† Mark Schorer (1908–77). American novelist, critic, and biographer.

instance, sprawled for an hour on the hill under the tower, talked of Robert indefatigably for perhaps an hour: catharsis for him, tactics of their future relationship suggested by me . . .

And then when it was time for him to get ready to go back to town, with less than half an hour before Ll. and Baba's coming to dine with us—unpredictably, in a rebound from his sadness, in characteristic simplicity and spontaneity of his lust—he threw his arms around me and kissed me, and then drew me up the stairs to my bed and took me and retook me.

Miss T., the singer, is getting a divorce in hopes of marrying S. He has encouraged this by going to bed with her every five or six months in recent years. By his account of the matter, she is desperately resolved to have him, and the reason is the grandeur of his penis and his slow, stubborn, difficult fornication. He has resolved *not* to marry her, but will not tell her so categorically or cease to frequent her, for the occasional intercourse gratifies him. It is not that it is very pleasurable. He complains that he finds it difficult to incite and maintain his erection with her; indeed also complains of the disproportionate tightness and force pressure of her vagina. I take it that she must be a very perverse young woman.

S. seems to have little or no sense of the immorality and unkindness of keeping her enthralled by his sex, nor any dread of the bitterness of her disappointment in due course. When I reproach him, he somewhat jokingly says that it is good for his reputation as a professor to have a known mistress; and somewhat seriously, that his psychiatrist has found indications of his having a deep and neglected appetite for heterosexual experience!

Indeed I think that with the dimensions and the neurological nervous system of his organ, he might well find intercourse with a woman more satisfactory than with a man. But this would require an entire and successful psychoanalysis, and even so, he will never commit himself to any sort of monogamy or undertake the emotional or economic responsibility of a marriage.

All this illustrates on the one hand that childish and sickly irresponsibility which is so frequent in men of preponderantly homosexual habit; and also that ruthless self-concern which Freudian psychotherapy seems to have encouraged in them.

In my opinion, *The Ides of March* is the finest novel in our language in the past decade. I read it with a tingling of my skin, a catch in my throat. Now I have reread it and studied it, with increasing satisfaction.

I would give five years of my life to have written it myself. I cannot see how anyone with an aptitude for reading or a predilection for literature can fail to enjoy it.

Most of the substance of it—naturally, as it is a novel—is simply human nature, timeless and universal; a dozen unforgettable people, meaningful, with psychology and morals overlapping in their life stories as in real life. The epitome of friendship, between Caesar and Lucius; the pathos and hatefulness of immorality in the case of Clodia; the personification of disastrous passion in Catullus, and of ideal love in the actress Cytheris . . .

The beauty of it is not only Wilder's famous fine style and uncanny characterization—every character with his own way of thinking and exact tone of voice—but, this time, an entirely original novel form. An originality that works, furthermore, and does not make hard reading.

I went to Chicago this month, making an address at a writers' conference for my airfare. I saw certain old friends, and found out some things about my boyhood that I didn't know at the time. On the whole, it was fascinating but melancholy; and as it happened, the new "friends" I made did not please me, nor I them, though they pretended. Very odd, for the first time in my life I found people's sexual morality vexing, shocking. And then the extortion and blackmail about homosexuality in the Middle Western cities. No danger if you are poor. But X had to pay $100,000 in St. Louis!

A handsome tough shopkeeper devoted to truck drivers pretends to be a plainclothes morals-squad policeman in order to have his way with them. To me: "The first time I've ever groped a best-seller."

A visit to the Field Museum—

The bower of the bowerbird.

Little Roman bronzes, a sow, a recumbent goat, to be used on weighing machines. How did the artist manage his two undertakings—representation and exact ponderosity—at one and the same time . . .

Vaginal and rectal speculum.

A bronze vase with hand-shaped handles.

All sorts of insects in amber.

Fool's gold, that is, iron pyrites?

The skull portraits from the New Hebrides, and the great vast immense wooden snake from the Cameroon.

From a letter to a young writer

You must excuse me for not writing you a detailed, definitive criticism of *Roman Holiday*, with credits and discredits carefully balanced, with my own aesthetic of fiction to back it up and make it inspiring.

While I have a more explicit and expeditious mind than the average fiction writer in this country nowadays, I find it most uneasy to write criticism. To be worth anything it has to be as precise as science, but with jargon; and it has to be impersonal, which in my case, as I am a creative man with work in progress, it scarcely can be. Furthermore I do not believe it would help you in the slightest.

The fact is that I do not like *Roman Holiday* at all, and my objections are the same as those I voiced when you first sent me a manuscript seven or eight years ago.

To be sure, I have the sincerest respect for your long, steady, courageous, unencouraged endeavor. And very evidently you have learned a lot in the seven or eight years. I especially appreciate your greater naturalness, brevity, and clarity; although on almost every page I could cite sentences that no born writer would pass, and faults of disproportion and implausibility and tediousness in the whole.

But all that really is beside the point, as I see it. For you did not have a proper and viable concept of a book in the first place. Synopsize it, and you have no plot; sum up its morality or philosophy, and you have no theme. The overall impression it makes is of yourself writing, not of anything in particular to be written. It is a fantasy, not a recollected experience; a daydream, not a vision. More than anything else I find in it your cultural aspiration and worldly ambitiousness; wanderlust away from where you are in fact, discontentment with what you are, disdain of what you know. Perhaps if you had the talent for poetry, you could handle this kind of subjective matter, dividedness of mind. But prose fiction above all has to be truthful.

Given the tragic circumstances of ten years ago, the shock and fright and loss which must have got embedded deep in your spirit in that connection, you have been a wonderfully healthy-minded man. You have a certain realism, and fortitude and patience, and power to work, and warmth of feeling, and sense of responsibility. All things considered, your employment, your marriage, your relations with your parents and your brother, amount to practically perfect behavior; adjustment to environment and to fact; what psychiatrists call "successful neurosis."

Evidently you took the main impact and bias and bewitchment of the past in the strange way of imagination. As I suggested the last time we met, sometimes one can effect a kind of self-therapy by means of writing; confession without analysis. Probably not, at this point, that great story of your youth—you would need a good deal of preliminary practice at small native middle-class subjects, genre sketches. And that, I gather, does not appeal to you. Perhaps the time will come . . .

Psychoanalysts, it seems, have now divided the amorous excitements and passions into three categories:

The anal (corresponding in the term of life to the senile period), characterized in the nonsexual side of one's life by constipation, inhibition, stinginess, selfishness.

The oral (corresponding in the term of life to the infantile period), characterized by sensationalism, gluttony, dependency.

The genital (corresponding to the prime of life), characterized by sympathy and empathy, by mutuality indeed in all things; and by a sense of the consequences, and of responsibility. A coordinated responsiveness, and flexibility and adaptability and control of one's senses . . .

These psychoanalysts seem intolerant or disdainful of the first two categories; and they call the latter "creative." What they really mean is "procreative"—a state of resoluteness of mind and warmth of heart, and sense of responsibility and of consequences comparable to that which, in the married state, is most conducive to the begetting of children and to bringing them up properly, in security and tranquillity.

To hear them talk, you would think that all married couples with large broods of children were happy creatures, well adjusted to the culture and of their time, gentle and scholarly, good citizens, etc.

I'm afraid I haven't as great, as warm, as kind a heart as X so fondly suggests. It's just that I find that only my *un*selfishness really works. Advice or counsel I can give; for that in the nature of things is disinterested, a matter of alter ego; choosing between others' claims, others' offering and advantage. Whereas power, even power for good, is balance-of-power. Even love is a balance . . .

Wednesday I dined with C. and his clever boring friend V.; then went to a party of B. and W., not a happy party. A new photographer with an assistant as pretty as a picture, on both of whom R. concentrated. B. at his wittiest and indiscreetest, remarkable, like some top-bracket Parisian; Truman Capote trying to be likewise, and failing dismally. L. scandalized to find me there, cutting me, taking flight. Poor G.P.L. flying into one of his tempers, pitiful and ugly: a matter of $10, someone's share of a fortune-teller's fee, for which I disciplined him hard and (I think) successfully.

Terrible days for Baba—the Streetcar Called Anger—and for Lloyd and me with her, walking her desperately disturbed mind up and down, up and down, as it were a racehorse with a colic, not to be allowed to lie down in any of the extreme positions that it postulates, for it might never get up. (Lloyd's opinion of Silver Hill: "They gave Baba a set of false teeth to hang on with.")

Chuck picked up Cheiro's *Palmistry for All* with the liveliest interest; so I examined his palm and found a line I have never encountered before, the Via Lasciva, which is indicative of unbridled sensuality and extreme passion; which indeed, as it crosses his Line of Life, prophesies death in some such connection. I would have held my tongue about this, but as I sought the pages of Cheiro, to make sure, he read it over my shoulder; and it seemed to worry him in Earnest. I referred him to the age chart; the crossing appears somewhat after seventy; this entirely relieved and cheered him. Unbridledness itself no great worry . . .

The last thing Lloyd said to Eliz. was, "Don't come back married to a cowboy," and she promised. And in yesterday's letter she reiterated that promise, but with the admission that it was going to be difficult. What a girl!

Taking leave of me, she was more dead than alive, with her heart acting up, giving her splitting headaches, in addition to the two kinds of gut-ache. So I reminded her that it was all just something like a surgical operation; certainly she would be better off after it, stronger anyway—though of course there is never any guarantee of happiness in life, and so on, especially not in later life. To which she answered instantly, "Oh, no matter about happiness. I am happy; I always am, in a way; I always have been."

And as I stood there, watching her car out of sight, I thought that in the always possible event of never seeing her again—airplanes, Rocky Mountain fever, etc.—what an overwhelming memory those words would be.

As I was playing a new recording of Monteverdi's *Orfeo*, Anna was reminded of the Negroes singing in the gutter, in Baltimore, where she worked years ago.

"Oh boy! it was beauti-ful. You'd leave yourself right there with them.

"But the poor Negroes! they don't get much respect."

Reading Edith Sitwell's* *The Song of the Cold*, with the prospect of Monroe's dinner party for her. I find fine lines that I am afraid of not remembering exactly, and very subtle ways with metaphor, all her own.

> *When through the darkness Orpheus came with*
> *his Sun-like singing*

or

> *Where the women walk like mourners, like*
> *the Afternoon ripened, with*
> *their bent heads . . .*

The point of both these comparisons depends on the sentence as a whole. *Darkness*, coming first, gives meaning to *Sun-like*, though the combination of the visual and the auditory is extreme. Can an afternoon *walk*? No matter. A sense of inexpressible emotion is indicated by her simply not trying to express a part of what she has in mind; from the funereal way of walking and from the words *ripened* and *bent*, there arises in the reader's mind a thought of autumn, of harvest field, of Adonis.

Other ways of making her readers' minds do a large part of the work: offbeat phrases by which we are mystified at first, then prompted to solve the mystery ourselves. For example:

"And summer grows from a *long-shadowed* kiss."

"Emeralds are *awake*, up on the branches."

"That worm, the small *corroding* hour."

The damnedest feature of life from my point of view—in a life in which nothing actually happens, nothing—nevertheless there is a deadline for every bit of it—late always.

My mechanized melomania, with the recorder—a vice indeed, as Edgar Wind fiercely remarked, mindful of all sorts of Germans—is a help; a sedative; even, in the expensive grand-bourgeois way, an exercise and discipline. At $5 a spool, from the New Friends of Music FM station, etc., I can take, in a fortnight, more Mozart quintets and quartets and trios, more Buxtehude and more Bartók, than Baba will listen to in a year.

---

* Dame Edith Sitwell (1887–1964) and her brother Sir Osbert (1892–1969), poets and critics, were friends of G.W. and M.W. since the early twenties.

Baba is in a mood of sweetness; only troublesome in theories and in arguments: anti-department-store, anti-Freud of course, anti-UN. I now incline to think that the neurosis is not really the trouble, that at any rate it may not yield to treatment as such, because it is anchored to something else; and the something else is that little psychosis which has been in the cards a long while, a couple of generations in fact. But perhaps time is on our side; and Eliz. with her simple wisdom, and I in my assiduity and willingness, and Lloyd with his extraordinary maleness and good heart and extreme strength of character, perhaps can take care of her.

Tonight as I sat alone with the toy—rather like a bee packing its honey away neatly—he walked in and sat down for ten or fifteen minutes, with nothing to say, making an awful face. He wouldn't take off his coat or even his cap; he said that Baba would be missing him, he must not linger. "I am just so restless, so restless." I had nothing to say either, I merely kissed him.

The Brandenburg Concertos are my bible. For example, no. 6 in B flat major, for the strings grosso.

Tired of reading Dante—no, not tired, but full of him to the brim of my mind. I must let some time pass to digest, to freshen my palate, to grow hungry again . . . Therefore I have begun to read Racine instead. He strikes me as being half Dante and half Freud. It is a cheap sort of joke, but it makes sense. I wonder if it can be phrased as to express the sense and avoid the glibness . . .

My solitude, extra days here, etc., is all right in itself; so long as nothing arises to suggest to my mind any particular possibility of desire or hope. I am like an egg-stealing dog that has been given eggshells full of red pepper . . . All right, unless I get into any kind of position in which I may seem to be asking a favor of anyone, or indeed to be offering or promising anything. Suddenly I get embarrassment-stricken; as it might be, panic-stricken.

That was what had to be overcome when I realized that Nick wanted to be invited to St.-bl. last weekend, too proud to invite himself; and as soon as I observed that process of my mind, it was fine.

It was a happy weekend: happiness weighing on both our hearts a little, but both bore up strongly. No inkling of a job as yet; and he inquires about the Museum of Modern Art, Harper's, etc., not really expectantly.

And upon his return to town, poor dear, he took to his bed with what the doctor has called near-pneumonia. And I am afraid that it is the joblessness, and even a certain bitter regret or (rather) angry impatience at not being able to love me: with all that this house must suggest to him: security in son-ship, youthfulness with impunity . . .

Monroe's first dinner party for the Sitwells. One little round of the conversation was led by them onto the subject of the bores and boredom: "Who would you say is the most boring person in this country?" It had a sound of their having often practiced it together; a kind of duet.

Osbert's conclusion: "But, Edith, one must admit, everyone is someone's bore."

An anecdote of the late Lord Desborough in his old age: Spying at his club someone he had made a practice of avoiding, he confided to someone else, "I don't like that chap. I keep meeting him. He's a terrible fellow. Now I think I'll go over and give him twenty minutes of my huntin' and fishin' stories."

Upon my declaring my enjoyment and admiration of the Tietjens novels of [Ford Madox] Ford, Edith answered amicably, but with finality, "No, it's flabby work." And Osbert chimed in, "Freud Madox Fraud, we used to call him . . ."

English malice well exemplified by Osbert especially; with all the right mild and self-assured manner.

Edith then asked my opinion of *A Passage to India*, with an excited note in her voice which seemed to me to bode no good; if I were to take up the cudgels for Forster, or speak too warmly . . .

In a review she had picked up, someone had pronounced *A Passage to India* "great."

"He is a dear good clever man, and we are devoted to him, but it tries one's patience to have him called *great*. Don't you agree?"

"Maugham also feels that, very strongly," I said; and to render the subject less controversial, I remarked on the fact that Forster has not published any fiction for twenty-five years; which is the most mysterious case in contemporary literature.

"Oh. I should not say it was a mystery. Have you ever met him? If you had, you would understand very well. I can tell you what it is: physical debility . . ."

As for my letter writing, perhaps only passion (and not just love) is necessary for me to be in writing trim after dinner and later; avid-awake and painful-alert. At any rate I have a folderful of fragmentary scribbling and false starts—"Dear B." and preamble and a paragraph of half-something, broken off—and this and that bit of image or incident or idea, without the plot or point or chronology. In other words my writing to him has fallen into something of that morbidity which governs my literature; that inoperability of mechanism as between life and letters: the differential.

But the fact is—let's face it—both Bernard and I have been in love, unluckily in love; with its consequence a kind of heavy tax upon our goodness of character, depreciation, amortization, and all that. Alike and unlike: he, not admitting it—naturally, with a mind so sore from the failure of Robert—and I, unable to do anything about it, under more little weird restraints than ever, not even putting my charmlessness, my impotency, my eunuchism to the test this time; only I myself actually slapping myself down. Bernard surely underestimating the power of sex, from somewhat too frequent easy opportunity; I (as I am accustomed to being told) overestimating it, in dull domesticity and sickening celibacy . . . Well, we'll survive it; and, friendship being what it is, somewhat at each other's expense, boring each other about it.

The only odd thing about me, I guess: how anyone can love life so much and so fail to enjoy living.

Years ago I knew a wretched boy who was planning to take monastic orders on account of six persons that he hated inexpressibly—he thought that at earliest Mass, when all six would be relaxed in sleep, not putting up any resistance, he could take advantage of the ecclesiastical white magic and transpose it to black, and exert and aim it at them, to make them suffer . . .

I have a damned bad cold. This is the stage of acute face-ache. A comical nice Italian of my acquaintance years ago said: "Americans, only the same three bad healths: *the* sinus (see-nuss), *the* nair-voss brekdown, *the* remove-everything."

Which reminds me of my pneumonia, in 1942 or so—but in my case then, it was one of my tricks, suicidal. I had four or five reasons to be disgusted with living—a thing of G. Lynes, a thing of K. A. Porter, a thing of Eliz., and so on; not to mention my final emancipation from Nelson Lansdale, by his departure to Brazil, which was more acceptable than the rest, in my mind—but perhaps my lungs didn't like it: body so obstinate . . . It was my sophistication that damn near killed me—feeling like hell but thinking it was only the hell of anger, despair, disgust, I went around one whole week with a congesting, darkening lung without going to the doctor . . . As it turned out it did me good—

the brush of death, or at least consideration of death, roused up my love of life again.

It was the practice of Cato the Censor to have intercourse with his wife during thunderstorms, thus to make sure of his human happiness in spite of Zeus' threatening.

From two letters

1. To the Guggenheim Foundation

I recommend Djuna Barnes to the generosity of the Foundation very warmly, and with a particular sense of right and principle, as it were insistently.

Only perhaps a half dozen writers living now have shown any real originality in the use of the language in narrative, full strength as in poetry or poetic drama, or made any innovation in the form of the novel. As Miss Barnes is one of these, with international reputation, and at first- and second-hand a decided and continuing influence on the younger generation of our novelists, it is a shocking fact that she should be living in poverty, and given no recognition or honor. And certainly so much hardship, and the seeming indifference of those who generally appreciate fine quality of writing, have made it more and more difficult to go on with her lifework, indeed have discouraged her from thinking it worthwhile; and it will be lamentable in the history of American literature, a reproach to us.

She lived abroad in the twenties and the thirties, and her coming back here upon the outbreak of the war was ill-fated. It coincided with a serious illness, and her way of life grew too solitary, proud, and disillusioned. But at this point I and various friends can assure the Foundation all is well enough now; she has turned her unhappiness to a philosophy, better indeed than that underlying her writing to date; a real revival of career and reputation is to be expected of her—only she must have some help until she has completed and published some new work.

The quantity of her work to date is not great—two important novels, one brilliant but somewhat too artificial satiric work, and a collection of short stories—but the quality is extraordinary: all of a piece, in strange thought and otherworldly, almost eerie style, all constantly controlled and polished and definitive; nothing loose, nothing inadvertent.

Her more recent novel, *Nightwood*, might be described as a kind of lesser *Wuthering Heights*; citified and cosmopolitan and therefore more sophisticated, less elemental, as of its day and age. I make this comparison not invidiously but to classify it and to suggest that something about it which may at first reading seem irrational, immoral—psychological melodrama, in somewhat forced but never insignificant expression—has a great tradition in the past, and has given pleasure when the effect of oddity has worn off.

With due respect let me carry this reference a step further. Suppose there had been a cultural agency a hundred years ago corresponding to the Foundation, and in the apportionment of aid it had had to choose between Emily Brontë and other gifted novelists of the time, including Charlotte Brontë. It would have seemed entirely correct and conscientious to decide against the author of *Wuthering Heights* as no longer promising, not professional, perhaps not altogether healthy-minded; but in after years all concerned would have felt sorry.

So much for Miss Barnes's reputation in general, and already demonstrated power of writing . . . Now I will say a word of her specific purpose of writing a poetic drama; though, as it will occur to you, I have no experience of the stage. In my judgment of Miss Barnes's talent, this is a most appropriate, promising undertaking for her now. The notable characteristic of her fiction has been the great element of poetry in it (perhaps more than suits the form of the novel). Also the various protagonists in her books have characterized themselves and one another mainly by conversation.

The manuscript of her play in its present state is not readable but a look at it impressed me greatly: sketches and sketches of every part, every utterance studied and revised again and again, every word adjusted, to have the right overtone and pace and sound-of-voice, which must be the way to do it.

2. To T. S. Eliot

I realize that this communication may reach you at an inconvenient, perhaps impossible time for you to take any trouble about it. If it so happens, I promise never to give it a reproachful thought, and not to mention it to anyone.

Djuna Barnes is an old acquaintance of mine but not an especially close friend, and in all the troubled past decade I did not meet her or hear news of her. Last spring someone suggested that she be given a small sum of money from a fund which the National Institute administers; but I found that this had been done some years ago, and by the rule she is not eligible a second time. Then a noted lady playwright sent her a little present, and afterwards asked to be introduced to her, which I arranged; and in this connection I spent two or three evenings with her.

She spoke frankly of her sad wasted years, her present distressed circumstances, and her plans of writing again, extraordinarily definite and encouraging. She said that it was a visit from you, and severe inspiring talk, which seemed to have turned the tide in her life; which of course I was deeply touched to hear.

I urged her to apply for one of the Guggenheim Foundation's fellowships; and now in spite of bitter pride, dread of rejection, and surely some of her old perversity of bringing herself bad luck, she has done so. I have just written to Mr. Moe and his committee men as one of her sponsors.

But I feel the gravest anxiety lest they reject her application. So far as I know, they have never taken my word for anything; and I am afraid that in the recommendations of her other sponsors, the note of pessimism or at least bafflement may creep in; and poor Djuna is not likely to take a setback very well. Perhaps no one could assure the Foundation upon any very strict word of honor of her still being able to produce great work. On the other hand, in such a case of brilliant intellect and profound though tragic temperament—with what we can recall of the productivity of various artists under even worse curses than this— I think it blasphemous against the great unknowable creative spirit not to give her the benefit of the doubt. But I have scarcely known how to put this to the Guggenheim administrators.

You know how it is in this country: It is not the dissipation or even daffiness which prejudices people against such a one as Djuna; it is the unsociability and the sorrowfulness and the proud passive attitude. She speaks of herself with such terrible honesty and irony and indeed malice; and somehow this gets into the atmosphere . . .

This is what I wish you would do, what I think would impress Mr. Moe and his advisers more than anything: If you have time, if your good opinion of her has not entirely altered, write just one sentence on a piece of notepaper or even on a postcard: "I think . . . I wish . . . I recommend," anything of that sort; and address it to Henry Allen Moe, 551 Fifth Avenue, New York 17, N.Y. Not bothering with their form papers, or with any particular explanation or argument; your name will serve.

Please believe that there is not any cynicism or disrespect of the eminent administrator in this suggestion. In my own admiration of you, and remembrance of your right critical judgments all these years, certainly I would react just as I hope he will.

Incidentally, I asked Djuna whether she had given your name as one of her sponsors; and she replied in her proudest and fondest tone that, if her life depended on it, she would not trouble you now with any such pettiness. It was like a page in one of her books. And needless to say, I will not tell her that I have taken this liberty of writing to you.

I brought [Katherine Anne] Porter out here for the weekend—in wonderful form, in wonderful genius indeed, though so uncoordinated, though so egotistical, and in a sense baby-talking. We philosophized mostly, in wonderful dark temper, with her old Roman Catholic intellect and new inspirational paganism; about the assassination of Bernadotte most interestingly. Terrible, how everyone has practically kept silent on the moral issue and consequences. Only the usual depraved ideas of our time: that the victim is "also" to blame, that the blood is on all our hands, etc.

One of my best weekends in a way, one of my worst in another way. Felicity, yes, but how strange: for a man so selfish to grow so unselfish at last, for a man so indolent to labor so at others' enjoyment; and with incessant interruptions of every purpose. Geordie [G. P. Lynes] came out on Saturday, just for the day, and we held him steady amid manifestations of B. and W.'s restored happiness (for instance, a new tattoo identical on their respective biceps, a mysterious "24"). They now blame L. for almost everything—indeed I had to propagandize a bit on his side, for the future general welfare. They love me dearly.

I remember saying perhaps outrageously some years ago—in sudden consciousness for some reason of how overactive my life had become, run ever-ready, running hither and thither, serving all sorts of causes public and private including lost causes—that surely I would get on with my career better if a bit incapacitated, for example perhaps in a wheelchair.

Did the gods hear me? It was time they paid some sort of attention . . . They did, once before, in my teens, when I pretended to be so wondrous talented, practically a genius, not in any real sincere conceit or self-assurance but in emergency of straitened youthful circumstances as a kind of expedient, to get on in the world, or at least to keep my head above water, to justify my too evident homosexuality, etc.—and as to that, talent or genius or whatever, certainly I was taken at my word, stuck with it, with thereafter practically no excuse for not making my bluff good.

The other evening I dined alone with Alan Searle, Maugham's secretary-chum—and by way of inquiry into my love life, he quoted

W.S.M. as saying that I am cruel to my lovers, rebuffing them from my bed upon various fine points of sentiment or idealism. Disinclined to criticism as such, something of a cockteaser—yes, he used the word, he applied it to me! For instance, "your charming friend P., so devoted to you, so brusquely rejected by you . . ."

Dinner with Edith and Osbert [Sitwell], so lovable, and with Osbert's friend David, who is like a lean aging swan, and with poor Patrick, who has just had another irruption of shrapnel out of his thigh, anguish. He now enthusiastically frequents the Melcarth household, augmented now by a second wild beauty. None of them seduce him, to be sure, but they furnish his imagination for the uses of solitude.

I think the recorder has paid for itself a couple of times over, already—in surcease for Baba, indeed all relief between her and me. Tonight she was wild-tired (and Ll. too had a look I didn't like)—so I marched her up here, and she lay on the tapestry bed, while I tried Act I of the Glyndebourne *Figaro*—with no fault—except a difficulty of where and how to cut the finale, non-stop for five records.

Too tired, and small wonder. I went to town Sunday evening, to attend Laura Hobson's* party for the new senator from Minnesota,† the civil rights man—worthwhile. I worked yesterday morning, took B. and W. to lunch, ran some errands, then put in five hours at the Institute: the Nominations dinner. Mr. Hopper solemnly rejected Georgia O'Keeffe: Saroyan and I debated Isherwood vs. O'Hara, etc. This morning I got up early and came home with Baba because she is cookless and husbandless. And on the way she tried my patience beyond endurance—making me talk about Freud, and lecturing and heckling me, trying to get me to say what she knows I don't believe, etc. She now blames F. for "the entire despair of the modern world," and of course I can't fight back, and sometimes I could kill Dr. Horney.

All my other events small, small or abstract: of the flickering fire of mind, solemn and serene coldness of heart.

Carl's‡ visit most agreeable—though a little tiring, in the conclusion of my nasty cold. He did not "carnally endear himself" to me (Barzun's

---

* Laura Z. Hobson (1900–86). Novelist, author of *Gentleman's Agreement*.
† U.S. Senator Hubert H. Humphrey.
‡ Carl Malouf (1917–   ). Artist and sculptor, and a G.W. intimate who hosted many parties at his Manhattan apartment.

quaint phrase), nor for that matter, I to him; but there were other enjoyments. He is a born instinctive storyteller. Reminding me of Panait
Istrati; also born in the Arabian Nights Belt. (I wish I had been, instead
of the Bible Belt!) For instance, the starved impassive little Austrian
boy whom he fed night after night, then seduced in a thicket of pine
trees; and who, next night, brought along another little boy, even littler,
whether chaperon or substitute Carl did not ascertain. And a fascinating
story of a young pickup so tough and ambiguous that Carl was terrified
all night—in clothes of a bum, but his pocket full of money—low-class
speech but speaking of books and music. At one point Carl asked, "Who
are your favorite writers?" And the answer: "Scott Fitzgerald. Glenway
Wescott." No harm in him, as it turned out, even unselfishness, femi-
nineness, etc. No name and address, no future.

My fans; what a strange band!

Pitiful news: Denham Fouts [p. 59] is dead; Thursday evening
December the 16th inst.

Bernard has been staying in the same *pensione*; went away to the
mountains to make some sketches for *Fortune* and, returning Friday
night or Saturday morning, found Denham's friend Tony overwhelmed
with all the nightmarish duties: autopsy that day, kindly but bothering
police, funeral on the Monday or Tuesday, etc.—and as of that date,
he had not notified anyone, Denham having left no proper address book,
no line of communication to the parents.

Note that it was not the worst death: He went to the bathroom and
did not return; ten or fifteen minutes passed—he had fallen to the floor,
apparently a simple and instant heart failure.

I was one of the first of the elders-edifiers-influencers in his accursed
life. When he was really young and quite incomparably good-looking
. . . To employ two too wonderful words of Joyce's: "Foible-minded and
fable-bodied." Gallowhur was ahead of me, I must admit. Anyway, his
life may be taken as an illustration of my practically never really influ-
encing anyone. Christopher I., by the way, who loved him dearly, once
said that the whole trouble is his minding not having a sufficient prick;
even as himself, and as myself, so differently . . . Denham in his turn
has had a good deal of most deplorable influence; on both the B.'s, big
and little, on M., *et al.*

And now *Life* magazine wants me to arrange a meeting of Cocteau
and Marianne [Moore], to take close-ups of their faces while they con-
verse.

Ice in the country again, Eliz. telephones. She returned the 22nd; wonderful spirits. Her cowboy, though a delighter, and (she still believes) good for her in those crucial weeks, inspired very hard considerations at the last. The very pattern of T.: a hero, eighteen months of paratrooping; ripped apart, only one lung left; no notion of anything to live for except to keep living—he discouraged her from singing because he was jealous of her listeners, etc. She wants never to see him again. He had a pair of rings made for her, of a cross-cut agate—she forgot them in the ladies' room of the airport in Chicago.

The strangest Christmas . . . On the Eve, after dining with all the family, there I was alone with Bernard's letter about the death of Denham: pint-sized good-for-nothing Keats, or undersexed pseudo-Byron. So I spent Christmas morning writing Christopher.

1 9 4 9

One does not, for example, feel the least benevo-
lent toward humanity, if one loves it. Perhaps
love is always sexual. And it is usually hopeless,
sooner or later; ignorant, from first to last;
thankless, too soon.
—A Calendar of Saints for Unbelievers

Jean Genet, a kleptomaniac assassinophilic pornographic writer, is the great celebrity in Paris now . . . A high-ranking policeman came to Cocteau and said, "He's so difficult, your protégé! To keep him happy, we not only have to put him in jail; that doesn't suffice. What he'd like would be for us to establish a bookshop in the prison court, so he could steal a few volumes every week or so."

I've got to get it through my head, I guess, that whenever I plan for a given day, something will always interrupt, some high wind will blow— and learn to work accordingly—to stop waiting and praying for suitable normal working conditions. After all, H. B. Stowe wrote *Uncle Tom's Cabin* in her kitchen amid some half-dozen children, with three meals a day in the oven, bread rising, jelly jelling, laundry soaking . . .

A report of our Institute grants committee meeting; though anything can still happen. The short-story writer Peter Taylor ("A Long Fourth") seems settled—Delmore Schwartz not well supported by his nominator Van Doren. Joseph Campbell also almost surely chosen. I got page proofs of *The Hero with a Thousand Faces* from his publisher and am delighting in it.

Somewhat to my surprise my last-minute candidate James Agee also met with general approbation. His *Let Us Now Praise Famous Men* is an oddity indeed: a great volume of poetical prose about sharecroppers, illustrated by Walker Evans, shapeless or so arbitrarily put together as to make no matter, but important in theme, movingly humane, and comprising some of the best prose for prose's sake in our American language. Out of print; my own copy had disappeared, so I borrowed one from Eleanor Clark— His verse, with an introduction by Archibald MacLeish, who joins me in nominating him, also good . . . With a family to support, he has been on *Time* magazine for several years, doing little or no other writing; but just now has resigned, hopes to make a living as a freelance with time for literature in between, and has commenced a novel.

I also proposed Louise Bogan as a critic, precisely because she is so lucid and brave—great commotion among the committee poets: how she seems to have insulted them!—but on the other hand what compassion they feel for her! I should not be surprised if they turned to her in the end.

Then just at the last minute I got page proofs of John Horne Burns's forthcoming novel, *Lucifer with a Book*, to be published early in March. Mark Van Doren thinks *The Gallery* a no-count thing that anyone might have written; and my blessed dear Marianne has just read it and she hates it, hates; a real tirade, but upon grounds of its coarseness, which I dislike yielding to. The new book is very different, just as shocking, but remarkably different from *The Gallery* in thought and style and construction. Miserable private lives of the faculty and terrible youngsters in a preparatory school—less like Thomas Wolfe, more like Dreiser—real satire, with moral indignation. It is not at all my kind of fiction; I have met him twice and not liked him; etc.—but I do believe that he is the most talented, the most promising of the youngsters since the war.

Little charms of newspaper reading: the appropriate committee of the UN is raising hell with five nations for a disquieting rise in their consumption of heroin and the worst offender is (three guesses!) Finland.

And Yves Tanguy was born in Courbet's bed!

For so long a time, almost everything I have written—letters, journal, documents of the more or less public life, even my letters to Bernard—has been, first and foremost, expression of my feeling, and, second, clarification of my thought—the process, the process! But not the actuality, not the little picture or the dramatic happening or the words uttered. And probably this is one thing that has been going wrong with my novel: a constant stimulation of the critical analytical faculty at the expense of the creative or the inventive or the recollective.

* * *

We had a singing party last night, with Elizabeth's man, Lee, who knows four hundred songs: all the dirty songs of the war in the Pacific, evocative but dismal; Tudor love lyrics; endless horseback ballads.

Just now, dusting in the library, Anna said that she had been shocked to hear, from her end of the house, how much less well he sang than Elizabeth. I had taken it all down on the wire recorder and the spool was still on the machine. I turned to what, as I recalled it, would be a good song for her.

Then someone called me on the telephone, and suddenly I realized what she was hearing and dashed to the rescue: "The Joys of Copulation!" "The cats with syphilis, The cats with piles, The cats with their arseholes wreathed in smiles."

There she stood, listening, with her head on one side, unfazed. "Beau-tee-f'l songs! Not bad voice—but no oomph, no oomph!"

My father's brother was a parson, with a rich wife. They have just died, a day and a half apart—the end of the strangest love relationship ever, certainly the strangest homosexual's marriage. My father knocked on the head by it, the likelier to die soon—I had to spend most of the afternoon with him.

I am as nervous as a cat just now, letting Monroe go for months; on the same day letting Ll. depart with Edna and Eliz. and George, leaving Baba and me alone for weeks. Her state of mind now stranger than ever, proclaiming a sort of ecstatic celebration—she has discovered the secret of the universe; it is no longer a matter of Horney thrilling her. She thrills Horney (she says), and day and night she writes some great treatise or manifesto. So far the secret, etc., has not been revealed to me; but I'm in for it next week.

X told me a comical little tale of Noël Coward at a luncheon. Out of a clear sky, the celebrated man asked him to come to his room at 3:30 p.m. to go to bed with him and his current lover. "A roll in the hay," he called it, and X accepted, in sense of humor and snobbery— as he himself admitted—more than any lubricity.

He found Coward and his youngish consort already in bed, in happy anticipation and hot excitement; and Coward himself remarkable and admirable for a man of his age. He spent almost at once and then, invigorated and cheered, sprang out of bed, did an exercise or two, and whistled while he dressed, occasionally glancing over at X and his lover out of the corner of his eye.

* * *

I came to town by bus Tuesday morning, to make arrangements with Edith Sitwell (she got only nine negative votes out of one hundred and twenty-five) and to hold my final grants committee meeting, and returned by bus that same night.

Back this morning by motor with Baba (at last we did talk "philosophy"—I had energy enough, matutinal) and lunched with Osbert alone, pleasant. Then I shopped for my party. Daffodils were only 33⅓ cents a dozen, so I had a lot. Two bottles of gin and one of Scotch—but my crowd only drank one of gin and one-half of Scotch, plus almost a bottle of sherry (isn't that odd?). The list: Edith and Osbert, Marianne and Wystan [Auden] and Cummings and Marion in ravishing looks. Douglas Moore and wife, Bill Benét, Mark Van Doren (whom I like much better than Carl) and wife, Maude Parker and husband, Mr. and Mrs. Delana, Felicia G., Patrick and his girlfriend Robina Tennant, Lillian Hellman. Too many, I thought (literally only one absentee, Mrs. Benét)—I had to work like hell—but O. and E. basked, from the stroke of five until the stroke of seven, and everyone had the time of his or her life. Really, as successful as one of Monroe's parties, but as different as could be—livelier talk and easier circulation around the room because of the homogeneity of literature.

A little yarn of O.'s: A few years ago Julian Huxley fell in love, announced to his wife that he was going away with the beloved—he had arranged to meet her at the Café Royale—and at the close of the afternoon, preparatory to the rendezvous, lay down for a nap, removing his false teeth. His wife tiptoed in and took them and buried them in the garden. And that was the end, not of the marriage, but of the romance!

In the way of malice, what Osbert likes best is in two or three parts or movements—a catch in his first remark, to which his victim can reply in character, then his rebuttal all planned. A feint, a seeming retreat, then a counterattack, surprising. This gives him the added humorous exercise of calculating how his victim will fall into the trap . . . For example: There are dreary highbrow critics in Cambridge, lately admired by our young university group, a certain Dr. Leavis and his wife, Queenie. Criticizing something they had written, Osbert pretended to think that they were sisters or, more probably, sisters-in-law. Upon which Dr. Leavis wrote to say that he was a man. Osbert's answer: "Dr. Leavis should have made this clear in the book itself."

When I congratulated Edith upon her amiability and fortitude in submitting herself to whatever has been expected of her in America—crowded and boresome sociabilities, worrying interviews, sieges of unflattering photography—this was her remark: "Walt Whitman is my patron saint," adding, "I took a vow not to lose my temper in this country . . ."

Her discourse at the annual meeting of the National Institute was grand. Canby* wriggled across my lap and bought it for *Saturday Review* before the applause died down. At the eleventh hour she had been inspired by a subject: the similarities between Whitman and Blake; got up at 4:30 a.m. Friday and worked all day. A surprisingly cogent and plausible comparison. More pointed and less meandering and Ph.D.ish than her usual critical piece. I suppose her success with the scarcely well-educated old fellows mostly derived from her beauty and her voice— and (if I may say so) from my court chamberlain work before we went in to dinner.

A big turnout: that old Petroushka, John Marin,† for instance, whom I have never seen before, tried to sabotage Edith by little cackling remarks during her last pages. Cummings behaved like an angel; O'Keeffe, in great looks, behaved as usual like O'Keeffe: kept making the sort of snaky face that one would make if one wished to appear very wise and thought that snakes symbolized wisdom.

As for Edith's own good behavior, I think she consciously somewhat modeled herself upon the Queen . . . In her Institute speech she confided to us that in her sitting room at Renishaw she has only two photographs: one of Walt Whitman and one of Queen Elizabeth.

In 1923 I was taken to Edith's flat in—could it have been Bayswater? and left behind a walking stick of cherrywood that I was fond of. When I returned for it, E., haughtily apologizing, told me that she had presented it to a friend to get it out of the way.

The other evening when I arrived at the Gate for dinner, I found Barbara all a-tremble and wan. For days and nights, all the preceding night without going to bed at all, she had been writing Dr. Hiden, the Silver Hill man, an account of her recovery of health and of the secret of everything, the philosophyschological theory (Horney plus her own ratiocination) which has brought about the miracle. And she had not succeeded in getting it typed that afternoon; and she had her heart set on showing it to Horney the next afternoon.

So of course I undertook to type it, which she consented to without

---

* Henry Seidel Canby (1878–1961). Critic and *Saturday Review of Literature* editor.
† John Cheri Marin (1870–1953). American painter.

any fuss (that much certain healthy-mindedness), and I sent her to bed, and I did type it: two and a half hours' work, nine pages. In passing let me emphasize the fact that in all sorts of ways in everyday life she certainly is healthier-minded, stronger, and happier-behaving than she has been for a long time. For my part, in my way of mere worldly wisdom, I ascribe a good deal of that to the fact that her way of life is less idle, less boring. Just as an amusement, even therapy is better than nothing. Only now and then one minds the fact that she has less sweetness, less charm—she has been made a little bigoted, hypercritical, a little tyrannous upon fine points of morality; especially with reference to me, in hopes of inducing me to get psychoanalyzed by Horney too, and with the Horneyan non-acceptance of homosexuality . . .

I am getting to be the most called-upon character on earth—with some politicking (UNESCO and anti-censorship) lately added to my usual amateur psychiatry and parish-priestliness and vocational advisement and public relations counsel specializing in foreign celebrities, and so on—and I have a month's stack of unanswered letters.

From a letter to a young writer

I don't suppose I could help you place any such articles, even if I found them literarily to my satisfaction. I don't believe there is any favoritism in the magazine business; certainly I am no one's favorite . . . And it is hard to get a trustworthy agent unless one has a lot of work in hand. Simpler to wait until you get back and can offer it in person.

Now shall I say a word about the problem of the writing, this kind of writing? The common weakness of the amateur or the novice is his preconception; his trying to conform to some impression he has formed of what kind of finished product someone else would make of the kind of raw material he has to work with—he goes about it in a too professional spirit, pseudo-professional. Especially pitfallish if he thinks of market first, as you are doing . . .

The last thing the true professional learns is to write effectively in any manner, to fake his form or style—some never can learn it—and if they do it is at the expense of vivacity and veracity, of air and pulse and texture. One reads that sort of thing only if one very much wants to know—or if one already knows and very much wants to be reminded of—what it describes or relates.

So for a rule of thumb, just pretend to begin with that you are not

going to be able to write it well; that success or failure depends entirely
on the contents. Search in your memory for the foolproof incidents, the
amazing little scenes, the unheard-of characters—list them, and write
them, as it were, one at a time. Avoid every sort of preamble and every
sort of transition as though your life depended on it—that is where the
above-mentioned faking, making believe that you are a professional, is
most likely to appear . . . Whatever is necessary in that way, to hold
your piece together, can be put in at the last—and for magazine publication, the briefer the better.

And don't compare your incidents or scenes or characters with any
you have read; don't try to please particularly, not even your imaginary
elite reader, not even yourself. Just remember, and try to make the
paragraph match the memory—just as you turn the focusing mechanism
of a camera—then reread what you have written, and refocus . . .

How strange it all is, about Baba! Last night upon her return from
town she telephoned that she had been happier all day long than she
had been at any time in the last twenty-five years or more—not worried
about any turn of the tide the other way, any trough beyond this crest,
because (she said) twenty-four such hours are worth however many years
of futility and grief and irritation.

And happy about what, if you please? Just that damned tract that
I had to type (Horney was "thrilled" by it!). The style was so bad that
I should say it was positively symptomatic. Melodramatized abstractions,
juvenility and religiosity; not one phrase of formula truthfully applicable
to her life story or present circumstances, at least not specific in application; and all exclusively self-concerned (not egocentric exactly, but
with ego diffused through everything), as though life were a vacuum to
be filled by her new thought, as though there were not other persons of
any consequence to her, as though she were never going to have to come
up against anything in matter of fact.

Being so happy (she says) makes her sorry for everyone else. And,
I may note, she has not spoken of her husband at all, except once, when
she asked me when I expected him to get home.

All this makes me wish, once more, that I could consult someone
knowledgeable, authoritative; partly in curiosity, partly in anxiety, almost fear. The fact is that I know only something about neurosis; nothing
about the psychotic states, the manic-depressive, etc.

Now it has rained a lot; once more the tawny and somewhat verdant
earth looks ready for spring, but probably it is not ready. The crocuses
and fritillaries have started up.

From a letter to Christopher Isherwood

I now have a plan of coming to Hollywood in about ten days' time, to stay somewhat less than a week—from about the 11th or 12th to the 17th.

In good sense and courtesy—wanting not to seem to suggest that I wish to be "entertained," not to make you feel in any way responsible for my having a good time—I meant not to give you notice of my arrival, just to turn up.

But suddenly it occurs to me how disappointed I should be if you happened not to be in residence. Or perhaps you will be extraordinarily busy just then, with extra work, or with sociability enough (or more than enough) already proposed by others resident or transient.

If so, and if you will kindly tell me so—perhaps just telegraph me (410 Park Avenue, N.Y.C.), without specification of the circumstances or other bother—I easily could and gladly would postpone the little excursion until later on in the spring.

Not that my designs on you are very great or very willful—only they appear important to me. I want to read your journal. Monroe said that, as he knows me, and as he esteems your writing, there could not be any better reason for flying across continent.

And I want to spend an evening or two with you, an evening or two with Bill,* jointly or separately. No matter what sort of evening or evenings; just let me take you somewhere where you'd be amused to go, or let me tag after you somewhere where you may happen to be going, if and if . . .

I was touched by your thinking of asking me to stay with you. Even with all feasibility a hotel will be better for me. Co-residing with friends, I fall into a kind of shyness, or perhaps I should say that I get overstimulated, or perhaps I should say, self-conscious. You will be working, and furthermore I mean to go on working a bit myself, and I am as delicate about that as a cat, I must have a little sandbox in a corner . . .

Oh, I have had it—life, etc.—all of it; but with what fantastic troublesome coincidences! Perfect bliss with terrible incompatibility; greatest passion with zero coldness; luxury without freedom, and lust restrained by ambition; entire affection with merciless incorrigible self-

---

* William Caskey. A photographer and a close friend of Isherwood, with whom he lived and traveled from 1945 to 1950.

ishness—and at last, as it begins to appear, when all this can be added up, it will have amounted to happiness . . . Certainly I am happy enough just now, though without many indulgences, almost without enjoyments.

Item of Institute news: E. M. Forster is coming over to make the little Blashfield address at the May ceremonials. I killed Cock Robin (I am boastful)—though I want my proud friend MacLeish to go on thinking that it was he. The problem was to get enough money so that he shall not have to do other lecturing or anything he shrinks from—all set. Perhaps he will travel back with Monroe (mid-April)—and in Paul and George and Jared's absence he can have St. Luke's Place all to himself.

X must remember, in the way he is living—with all the enviable simplification of morals, the love of beauty predominant, and the privilege of foreignness and of foreign exchange—there are elements of disorder, of coarseness, which may well go to the heads of young persons. If he wished Y to continue as a kind of romantic son, responsive to and respectful of his elder considerations and desires, then probably he should not have taken him along to baths, etc. Youth has more sensibility than sensitivity, almost always.

Beautiful: The Sung bronze, Lao-tse on the water buffalo, in the Worcester Museum. The Mayan war goddess with a dead warrior in her lap, in the Peabody Museum.

An English friend of mine (or friendly acquaintance) was married to a famous beauteous courtesan, and when she wearied of him, she directed her lawyer to threaten to accuse him of abnormal immoralities, unless he hastened to make a satisfactory settlement. This angered him, so he directed his lawyer to have her watched by detectives; and in the end indeed they caught her in intimacies with someone, and he divorced her and gave her no settlement at all: not, you see, what they call a gentleman . . . Then some years passed, until she had opportunity for revenge. He was in this country during the war, and got into trouble with the Exchequer, and suffered relative impoverishment. But it was not for long, as he happened to be the favorite nephew of a millionaire uncle who was dying. Only, when the will was opened, it bore a codicil, cutting him off with one dollar; furthermore specifying that this had been decided upon information furnished by the courtesan, the ex-wife . . . Whereupon my friend said to me a thing which has always made me laugh: "Did you ever hear of such a silly woman? Of course I wouldn't have given her a penny—but still, I would have spent it in the circles in which she moves; and some of it would have trickled back to her!"

Blessed Nembutal, doubling not the duration but the efficacy of my sleep—removing from my subconscious its hair shirt; consoling my libido for its predicament of loneliness; somehow salving all my little incidental resentments, chafings, and the bumps, bathing away feelings of disgust and incongruity, hypocrisy and boringness.

Luncheon at the Askews'*—brilliant, especially Marianne, in her finest mood. I do think that she is now the best talker I have ever heard, in the non-dialectic or coloratura way—changed and improved in the last couple of years.

Then my farewell dinner party for Osbert and Edith and David, with Pauline and Joe Campbell—and the Louis Kronenbergers† after dinner.

We had a go at the critics. Edith especially fine against Desmond McCarthy—"Our worst pest! Now who, would you say, is your worst pest? Must it not be, perhaps, Orville Prescott? Edmund Wilson is also, oh, certainly, abominable" but—and away we went. Desmond McC., she said, is "like a housemaid or charwoman marching along with a parade. If only he would not interest himself in poetry; he is deaf to it, he can only hear, as he marches, Sousa's band."

She also gave a great little example of Shaw's humor. At the famous birthday banquet for Wells, his lifetime's mistresses were all present, and any number of offspring—and when Shaw's turn came, he began, "Ladies and gentlemen," etc. "When I think of my dear old friend Wells, it is often not as a writer but as a family man . . ." Marianne delighted by this!

At Pauline's request I told the death of Isadora [Duncan]. Of all my stories somehow the favorite; it never fails. And I believe I could write it exactly as told, pathetic *presto* or *vivace*.

From a letter to Raymond Mortimer‡

Before daybreak, having had a bit of writer's nightmare: with my double-strength Nescafé I turn to the Sunday *Times*: Nothing by you in either of them; and I feel cheated. Your peculiar gift is saying so much

---

* Kirk Askew. New York art dealer.
† Louis Kronenberger (1904–80). Writer and *Fortune* magazine editor.
‡ Raymond Mortimer (1895–1980). Critic for *The* (London) *Times*.

in the little form; almost every time, you stir conversation in me; if I were a rich man I would call you on the telephone after each piece.

Your recent review of Elizabeth Bowen* humiliated me, as I had done one myself. I shrink from reviewing, but in her case, tit for tat . . . And as I am no expert in the little form—they assigned me just six hundred words—I persuaded myself that I should not or could not quibble over her faults. The thriller pattern does please me, I am always waiting for someone to do something with it—as Balzac after Paul de Cock—and also, I must admit, with a near deadline, I skipped a good number of her big dense four-square lyric paragraphs, which improved it for me in a way. It would make a good scenario for an opera, but not so good as [Maugham's] *Up at the Villa.*

You ask for a report on the Sitwells, with punches not pulled. Edith was elected to the honorary membership of the Institute—with Virgil Thomson against it, in sharp little politics—and I gave a short *éloge* at the dinner, and she responded with a comparison of Whitman and Blake; fun. But I haven't exactly enjoyed her, personally; except that I think her one of the most beautiful women in the world; I go around to the St. Regis for two modest words when telephoning would do as well. Beauty an important factor in the over-all success, I think; we are all *physical* snobs. Her lectures and readings *per se* not exactly the stuff to give the troops . . .

And, while extravagantly thanking me for my politics in the Institute in her honor, she has not said a word of approval of my *éloge.* Could this be because in it I included a quiet compliment to Marianne?— though finally she has learned to be fond of her: our little pomegranate or persimmon of genius . . . I must add that I have not had a word from Marianne either. Poets!

Osbert has been a disappointment, because I believe I would enjoy him and I haven't really been given a chance. We make like *chers confrères.* The entire trip has been a little hard for him, I think: Edith's glory and his rheumatic knee . . .

The gravediggers are on strike, bodies are accumulating, and Cardinal Spellman has led a contingent of one hundred scab seminarians across the picket lines.

Lunch with Patrick [O'Higgins]—it was his birthday, E. had arranged a rendezvous for him: someone of one-hundred-percent pulchritude,

* Elizabeth Bowen (1899–1973). Irish novelist.

detachable from a small party last night, ready and willing . . . This, I presume, somewhat upon my prompting; or to be exact, upon my revealing to him the nullity of P.'s nocturnal meanderings (P. having somewhat pretended otherwise). P., of course, at the prospect, miserably anxious, mulishly stubborn, pure as the driven snow. How I bawl him out!—especially pathetic for him today, as birthday discourse. I have never known anything like it: such an extreme of self-knowledge and self-helplessness, fever and dry ice. If one were to seek a certain definitive example of neurosis—none better . . .

At Pauline's opening, Mrs. Anthony Eden moved across the room to be with Mary Warburg, which permitted the worried saleswoman to seat in front of me a trio of Frenchwomen who had arrived with no places reserved and were making an issue of themselves: one handsome and coarse and sleepy and another long-legged and very nervous, fawning upon a third—the most ruined tiny woman you ever saw, like a lightning-struck monkey, with infirm uncertain little motions, with a wild dark stare; even her hair sick, the line of her jaw somehow decayed away (or scarred), the line of her lips set so far down and so hard that it might have been a paralysis, or possibly a madness, or probably an anguish. Suddenly I knew who it was—fancy my never having seen her before!— Mlle Chanel.

Pauline's work seemed to me better than ever, somehow abstract; less modish, less temporary-looking, and in that sense more creative. I kept wishing that it could be in a good medium, to be preserved and exhibited; not just on impermanent and even unmemorable (however lovely) human beings. Some things reminded me of Cherubino in the scene of Figaro's piping him away to the wars; and some of figurines of Tanagra, and indeed of Nadelman; and some of Isadora dancing.

Strange, the unlasting arts—like the boy buried in Antibes, do you remember? the boy from the North (or perhaps just named "Northern"), aged twelve, *saltavit et placuit* . . .

Carl's party, as per my expectation, monosexual but rather undersexed; a waste of time, but not regrettable because so good-hearted. I so to speak scintillated—"especially charming young writer, handsome but not appealing"—with my cold-hearted judgments; something like a combination of Cocteau and Coleridge. (An odd point: the only thing those two have in common, intoxication . . .) I did not drink at all last night, yet when I get to talking well there is a drunkenness: wastage of my mind getting into my bloodstream. The way chemical by-products of manufactures sometimes seep into adjacent springs or brooks . . .

I ought to have taken a pill, I didn't, and I only got three and three-quarters hours of sleep, with dreams of literature and morals. Then this morning for two hours, in Penn Station, I talked to my sister Kate, still going strong. And when I got back to 410 Park I had a sudden almost worrying dizzy spell; something like *le petit mal*. Comical.

A lesson to be learned from this (what a pity Katherine Anne has never learned it): The grave ill effect of my tremendous talk upon my poor writing, and of my involvements in life and others' lives generally, is not the waste of time but the waste of energy (I can always find time enough or make time enough)—not the distraction but the exhaustion. On the other hand I don't think that merely renouncing these excitements, puritanism, and sense of duty, and sense of shortening lifetime, solves the problem for me. When I spend a few good days in the metropolis, in good company or in circumstances of some significance or oddity, I discover in all my mind a better brilliance than in the country, in routine domesticity. What little writing I have occasion to do comes easier, with more self-assurance. I need a certain stimulus: warmth of others' psychology (if not their physiology), focus of their attention to me, perhaps even sense of superiority to them. I am healthier-minded as an extrovert than as an introvert. The sunflower, if it turns its back on the sun, just withers.

I remember observing this in Katherine Anne's case: how in the city overstimulation would kill her, like some plant with a dose of 24 D; how in the country she bored herself to death. We need both ways of life in fairly frequent alternation . . . Only, in my case lately I have allowed the two ways to overlap too closely, and worse still, I have overdone my sociability, my talking, indeed my thinking for others—so that when I get back to my solitude I am tired out, my introversion is more depressive than ever, it makes a vicious circle. Also I have not taken sufficient account of the fact that I have been growing older, I tire more easily.

In a sense I am hijacking Christopher—having in fact only seen him four or five times in my life (never, I think, alone), meanwhile making so much friendship in my own mind, imaginary, now I've got to make it stick; but I dare say I can. As to John [Yeon], the more or less exactly opposite setup—surely no one who loved him could help being demoralized. And very possibly what I shall have to do about him will be to beat a strategic retreat, with more dignity and esprit than two years ago—then I was taken so by surprise, it was only tactical.

I remember what he did the first night, two years ago. He had sent Jim, his lover, to stay with friends: I had not yet heard mention of his existence. I was in the bathroom brushing my teeth, with the door open, and saw John come into my bedroom and toss something on my bed. It was a great envelopeful of strength-and-health photographs, and suddenly I realized that that was all the good night there was to be; he had closed his bedroom door across the hall. I lay sleepless for a couple of hours, in a veritable cramp of mixed emotions. I may add that the photographs were not nearly improper enough to serve the purpose for which they must have been intended.

But if he is more kindly disposed this time, less perversely inspired, or, it might be, just lonelier, fine, fine! I shall not insist on retreating. In our post-Freudian morality, never entirely giving anyone up as a bad job, always understanding and consequently more or less having to forgive, indeed we waste half our life . . . But we can forgive both ways—we should, if we forgive at all—relaxing when the tide runs out, away from us, remembering to take advantage of it when it turns back.

The reason violets are thought to have an evanescent perfume is that one of the little volatile gases constituting it is narcotic—the first whiff benumbs the nostril, so that the effect of the second whiff is weakened.

Night flight, west: midnight, in the plane at LaGuardia . . .

I have a most undesirable seat, right between the motors, and on the aisle; and a portly elderly gentleman by the window, with his newspaper spread out, not only deprives me of view but, now and then, of reading light. This is a DC-6 named *The Mercury*. Next time I'll go back to my slow, smaller, but roomier DC-3.

No view—just the map of N.Y. in jewels, and the rivers in naked darkness; then suddenly we struck cloud. I happened to be peering out between the gentleman's newspaper and his chin just then—a great wink, as one might die, with the best of luck.

Chicago at 3 a.m.

I have slept thus far. A cold night, with patchy iridescent clouds, and the three-quarters moon.

6 a.m.

To think that I have already slept more of this trip away than I do many a night in my own good bed. Back-wearying and neck-cricking. I awoke saying to myself: Death, the great wink; Life, the great nap.

Across the aisle a youngish man with a handsome face, with an unusual, unbecoming configuration of baldness. When he wakes up he shakes himself a few times, somewhat as a dog coming out of water will scatter the drops out of his pelt.

Nick also does the same at the end of lovemaking—but strange, come to think of it, after my orgasm, not his. Strange in every way, our good agreeable relations now, so spaced out, with no tensions for better or worse. We speak of it unembarrassedly, with a sort of emphatic happiness, or at least contentedness. For me, of course, it depends on my having vacuity in my life; nothing at all would happen were it not for the fond forced repose of the flesh between times, accumulated warmth, readiness. Just as I might go to a brothel once in a while, if there could be one not beneath the dignity of your consort . . . But for N.'s part, I do believe that the present suits him almost perfectly. Mystery! Is my mere affectionateness really better than my strong true passion; my unselfishness with quite a little insincerity and playacting for others' sake really more suited to others' natures than my entire desire and real need? Cf. Bernard also. I don't complain . . .

Day is breaking behind us, but the cloud beneath us is full of midnight still. The oceanic-looking cloud . . .

Now, praise God—my everlasting luck (luck is a god)—we have left the cloud behind, and the adjacent kind gentleman has given me the window seat. It is washed away and desiccated country; an immensity of contemptible futile flatness; Noah's world, post-deluge.

Whatever possessed the few people to settle here—nothing at all around their minimum dwellings, not even scrub brush; only the earth somehow strangely stained, rusty or sulphury. Here and there a peculiar great dark round spot; a dried-up lake?

Up ahead, the rough-and-tumble tablelands, in this light of dawn looking like song and story: battlements, castles, temples, Angkor Wat and Maxfield Parrish. Black-and-white mountain ranges north of us (my view is south).

Now the shiniest sunshine.

Not, I suppose, like the Sahara—flatter? harder-surfaced? an immeasurable crust. Is this what nature made, before ruthless mankind came and plowed? At intervals it has been broken through, only a flat patch or scab of the original surface left here and there—modeled, as with insane sculptor's fingers, down and down into the flesh of the earth, into the entrails—multitudinous close-packed form that makes one's flesh creep to look at: like plumage but in high relief, with the slanting rising sunlight; like seashells but all grown together.

What a strange impression of human nature it gives, to see houses perhaps twenty-five miles apart! If any one man were to choose such a place of residence and way of life, one would with certainty pronounce him psychopathic. Thousands, all abnormal in the same way, have made history; sublime.

The loveliest color on earth, a certain old rose of soil, with almost imperceptible tinge of the spring; spring even here, in the sterility. Also a lovely braiding together of Negro-brown and white-flesh-pink in the great dry watercourses.

For fifteen or twenty minutes, while I was shaving, snowfields.

Then, like twisted pewter set with white enamel, the noble sharp mountains above Palm Springs, and the San Bernardinos across the valley. Then on the Pacific slope, cloud again.

Santa Monica

In the filling-station lunchroom just across the cement and asphalt from the beach, just a few steps down the street from my motel . . . Here in extraordinary immaculateness I am given the best possible pancakes. The jukebox renders "Pretty Baby," but how heavily! not at all in the manner of our youth. I have kept forgetting to buy a thermos bottle. Two hours' wait for coffee—my habit is such that it is like being in slightly bad health.

My room in the motel is also too immaculate, and as comfortable as in any Ritz or Carlton. But as in all famous winter climates, I have been chilly most of the time. Just warm enough not to dress warmly, etc.

Christopher's house is lovely, under a little green-wreathed precipice, with a brook in a sort of cement moat. Noteworthy how well off he is: thirty-five grand last year, twenty this year.

Way of life—I suppose it is general here—all rather *vague à l'âme*, with an unpunctuality and indeed inconvenience which turns every prosaic detail of everyday living into a kind of peculiar poetry; often, I should think, melancholy and demoralizing poetry. Straying around, waiting for others to stray around, talking just half-intimately . . .

There is a young architect named Johnny M. who is most intimate with Christopher and Billy—homely-faced but with a quite ravishing smile, quizzical, ambiguously fond, beautiful of body, 1906 (?) Picasso on a large scale, giant stripling—whom C. has been somewhat pressing toward me, with a surely very sound view of pleasure for both of us. I talked with him on the beach almost all afternoon—and last night, after a sort of party at Christopher's with some other neighboring young men, he brought me home to my motel, and I asked him to come in.

"No," he answered. "I'm tired. I'd better not."

Then, almost coldly, that is, purely, we held hands for a minute or so. Then I got out of the car. Whereupon he asked, with the above-mentioned smile, "Are you having a good time?"

"Yes," I answered.

"I've loved *hearing* you," he said, with emphasis on the participle. By which my experienced old heart was both touched and discouraged . . .

The life in Isherwood's journal is so intense and true that I wish I did not have to read it while I am here. It interferes with my experiencing meanwhile; induces an absentmindedness, an inefficiency of ear and eye. I find myself neglecting that inner wording and phrasing of my impressions round about, which more than anything guarantees my remembering.

I should like to tell him this, as compliment no. 1. But if I did, as he has been schooled to a certain modesty always, and as he wishes me to appreciate this place where so much of his life of greatest consequence has passed, he might regret letting me have it.

Quite perfect holiday. Nothing to it except two things: really incomparable, that is, unique conversations with Christopher alone, hours every day. The sweetest and saddest brief slight love affair—with the Picasso boy, the giant child.

Minimum of Hollywood—a long luncheon with Wm. Morris, Inc., who care and care about me, putting me on a pedestal; an evening and an afternoon with Bernadine. Santa Monica canyon has its quite separate life, neighborly—where I encountered Salka Viertel* and the author-son Peter, and Brecht's son Stefan, a fascinating devil, and George Hoyningen-Huene,† but none of the famous: Christopher and I too jealous of the time with one another; the distances too great; his deadline on the South American‡ book too pressing.

So natural, but fantastic, the degree of our intellectual compatibility, mutual curiosity, and admiration, with emotional inspiration or

---

* Salka Viertel (1889–1978). Viennese refugee whose Santa Monica house became a salon for expatriate intellectuals. She collaborated on several filmscripts for Greta Garbo.

† George Hoyningen-Huene (1900–68). Russian-born photographer.

‡ Isherwood's travel book *The Condor and the Cows* (1949) is the diary of a South American journey.

challenge one to the other as to our work ahead. Subject matter all our friends, Forster, Aldous, Willie, Wystan, Stephen; religion; sex; philanthropy in all sorts of phases; and of course writing, writing, writing . . .

Now the humorousness of San Francisco, and the mystery of John [Yeon].

En route to San Francisco

Up we go—a sky of Claude Lorrain. Azure and pearl and crystal, with tawny lights—too beautiful for fear.

Into the rain and the radiance, over the great white fringes of the ocean, over the clouds, slanting into golden sunset and back through greater clouds. The sea is truly purple, the sunset comes to us through cavernways—sensational. We are going up in a great spiral to 20,000 feet; out of the clouds into the blinding eye of the sun. Now the clouds are shrinking below and they are pale blue; and the earth lies in a blackish and verdant dusk.

All incomparable in my little flying experience.

San Francisco

I scarcely had expected my luck to hold after I came away from Santa Monica, but it did: different luck. John in his way has touched me and aroused me in my ambition; even John!

These two years have been the worst for him—near to suicide, etc. (he told me all his story). But now he has three houses on paper, to be built this summer. He has put his friend Jim in an apartment in town, and half dismantled his fine sitting room and made a workroom of it. He has hired a draftsman and model-maker—an entirely unintimate relationship (the young man prefers to bring a lunch box prepared by his wife, etc.).

He had reserved a great room at the St. Francis Hotel for Friday night, then we were to have moved to Charles Porter's. But he so delighted in our luxury to be alone together—our great windows looking straight down into the pigeons and pansy beds and statuary and loose poor humanity of Union Square, our twin beds (symbolic), our meals wheeled in by sophisticated waiters—that he would not move; and of course would not let me pay any of the bill.

Oh, my strange lifelong romances, almost marriages long distance, remote-controlled; almost adulteries, non-sexual—this one, I may say, not quite non-sexual, not yet . . . I have never seen anyone happier, morning noon and night—to be loved with my bizarre constancy, and not only loved but "understood" and (disinterestedly, that is, in disregard of my selfish interest) not disapproved.

In the evening we consorted all over the place with our raffish friends—those of two years ago plus some others. Far jollier than the New York equivalent . . . A city with an almost indefinably different spirit from any other; at no matter what social or moral level.

The rough trade and street boys of San Francisco have a peculiar habit or convention. There in Union Square they do not loll on the benches or stroll about—they stand separately, stock-still and upright, like sentries. Long after midnight, one here and one there, their expressions solemn, only their eyes lively—as though they had been mesmerized and the mesmerizer had gone off and forgotten them . . .

And for all the rest, the usual California beauties and enjoyments: views, terraces, open automobiles. Once more I was driven around Marin County—the forms of its vast hills so much simpler and more peaceable-looking than those around Los Angeles (Northern California is like Sung or Tang sculpture, Southern is like Ming . . .), with the new minute grass like green gauze flung over them . . . We lunched on the island of Belvedere in the bay, on a small pier with a rose arbor over it, amid bobby-soxers in yachting caps and dungarees—one of whom, I swear, had a handkerchief or perhaps two handkerchiefs wadded up and stuffed down in the right place to make a basket—with the city across the water so delicately dispersed on its mounts, and ladder-like streets all as white as Carol's Rome, bone-white. Here and there along the roads, gusts of mingled mimosa and eucalyptus, reminding me ecstatically of us in Villefranche.

I visited my Aunt Lou and Uncle Walter, aged eighty, whom I had never seen—they came pioneering out to the mountains of eastern Oregon before I was born. They have seven great-grandchildren in San Francisco . . . When she came toward me down a long shadowy hallway it made my flesh creep, it was a ghost—so startlingly does she resemble her mother, my grandmother W.

K.A.P. and I had a fine afternoon and evening together (I gave up seeing the Winterses* for her sake). She is living poorly, not being paid well, working her head off: two lectures a week, but each one is *two* hours long! All her talk is about wanting "a permanent home" with some "security," so she can get her props out of storage—preferably in N.Y.,

---

* Yvor Winters (1900–68), poet and critic, and his wife, novelist Janet Lewis, were friends of G.W. from the late teens, when they were all members of the Poetry Club at the University of Chicago.

because she so minds being left out of the sociabilities of the great, etc. She even minded not being asked to meet W.S.M. when he was *chez* Allison. Then she wants a year in Italy. No matter about money, for "by that time" she will have finished her novel. She gave me another heart-breaking hair-raising account of the damage Charles Shannon has done to her—I well believe it, but of course at this point her constancy of love is almost as evil as his treachery. (What a fantastic wonderful letter she would write me if I told her this!) Her wits more addled than ever— no integrity (as I use that word, to mean the opposite of sincerity). In the Institute anti-censorship [effort] she pretends not to have been told what the issue was, pretends to have meant to support my side . . .

New York City

Back home last night—with a troublingly clear perception of what is good about home, and what not good. Naturally I wanted to arrive in a vacuum, to a sanatorium bed or an office desk. I wanted time to have a stop. I wanted others' lives to be in abeyance—until I had collected my rather overexalted wits, at least until I had got a good letter off to Monroe.

The telephone began to ring as I entered 410, spooky. Also, with never a nap in California, and after the night-owling in San Fr., and with some extra reaction to just one Bellandenal and/or altitude on the return flight, I was quite miserable with sleepiness the first twenty-four hours; therefore inefficient.

My father is in Harkness having his heart studied; and they appear to be finding very fantastic mic-mac of his psyche, nothing like what G. has been diagnosing. My sister Marje is in St. Luke's with pneumonia. Some writers have sprung a conspiracy to get Mrs. Ames, the poor dear directress of Yaddo, fired for harboring Communists*—K.A.P. had got me concerned with this before I left California—Eleanor Clark was waiting for me, and I did help a bit. John Dos Passos and all that lot, on the other hand, including Robert Lowell, wanted me to join them in challenging the visiting Soviet authors (particularly Faedaiev, the one who calls us "jackals and hyenas") to a debate—I sent them packing, I told them that in my opinion it was *not important*. Our private theatricals (the Yeats play with me behind a screen as the ghost of Swift) are postponed. I had forgotten to write the six little citations of the Institute

---

* Agnes Smedley, an admitted Communist Party member, had, with Elizabeth Ames's permission, lived for five years at the Yaddo artists' colony, where the rules limited a guest's visit to three months.

grantees: deadline on that, with a sense of Marianne's critical breathing down the back of my neck.

Last weekend while E. was in N.Y. her oil heater went berserk and coated the entire interior and furnishings of her house with one half an inch of shiny black, damp, malodorous soot. So she is at St.-bl, as a refugee, while the insurance company is making about $1,000 worth of replacements and restorations. Also she is having a blissful love affair with none other than R.S. Really the life of the Wescotts is like Yosemite National Park.

Since both these romantics almost desperately need a *rez-de-chaussée*, there is serious consideration of my taking one of them, to be regarded as hideaway and writing place for myself. Baba would of course warmly approve of it for E. and R.S.; and therefore wouldn't worry about my "relapsing" into active sex life. I on the other hand could pretend that it belonged to one or another of my sisters, so that I should not have to lend it to Geordie, Samuel, *et al.* Do I suppose that a little more complication might actually *simplify*? A writing place (I will *not* indulge myself in notions of it as a lovemaking place) for free . . .

Letter to the Board of Directors of Yaddo

The extraordinary maligning of Mrs. Elizabeth Ames has been brought to my attention by various friends of Yaddo, friends of mine. Also I have seen the statement in her defense which is being submitted to you by Eleanor Clark, Katherine Anne Porter, Harvey Breit, and others. As I have never been a guest of Yaddo I think it would not be proper for me to ask to sign this; but upon my own account I wish to express my entire and emphatic agreement with them.

The present charges against Mrs. Ames are as absurd as they are malevolent. I have had the honor of friendly acquaintance with her, and have been in confidential communication with her as to the ability and character of certain applicants for the hospitality of Yaddo. I am entirely convinced of her sound and high principle in every respect, including that of political orientation.

Yaddo under her administration has been a great good place for the cause of literature and the arts; and like the majority of its beneficiaries, I give her the greatest credit. Perhaps she has been overoptimistic or overtolerant—certainly so, in the case of these two young persons who have now turned on her so ungratefully and treacherously (if, as I understand, they have been guests of Yaddo)—possibly in the case of Miss Smedley.

But in the case of Miss Smedley, Mrs. Ames sent her away because her political extremism seemed troublesome at Yaddo and compromising to Yaddo. Miss Smedley has complained of this in at least one letter which you may refer to.

But let me respectfully point out that as the matter stands now, Lowell and the others are the troublemakers. I wish that they might be not only controverted and rebuffed but formally reproved by your meeting for repaying Mrs. Ames's kindness and toleration with their presumption and self-assurance and spite.

I find myself remarkable in one respect: I seem to be getting through my middle age without having to believe anything—knock on wood! I am wretched in a way but not ideological. Gide's Communism, Christopher Isherwood's Yoga, Tom, Dick, and Harry's Catholicism, seem to me therapeutic, something like a change-of-life; even Maugham tried his level best to believe as the Brahmins believe.

The case of Gide differs from the others a little. He seemed personally not unhappy just then, at least he did not admit any misfortune or distress. His arguments were intellectual, very distinguished, clear and good. Only his gullibility was contemptible.

The case of Isherwood seems to me the happiest at this point, post-credo. He has been able to relax his state of conversion, to digest his disappointment, to forgive himself for not quite qualifying, not making the grade—evidently without seeming to forfeit any of the improvement in his state of mind. His religiosity has waned, but he has kept the philosophy, and, for the most part, the peace of mind.

In my observing this, is there some personal partiality, in that conversation with him still turns mainly on themes that my mind excels at: tales of the world we live in, gossip of character and coincidence, sex life and technical problems of our writing? On the other hand, the extremest of my prejudices is that against Hinduism.

Let me not too fatuously, pharisaically, congratulate myself. Let me acknowledge certain muddled contents of my mind, customs in which a kind of religiosity may creep in: a perhaps spurious optimism.

Pauline gave me dinner but didn't want to accompany me to the Braque show—not only tired but a little ill: a slight but stubborn infection of ovaries or thereabouts for which she has had to take penicillin all week.

Therefore, alone . . . the attendance seemed to me unusually brilliant and impressed with itself; not old-style but first-nightish. Mr. Jack Kriendler, for example, gave a dinner party, and some of his men had great raffish décolleté girls. The Robert Sherwoods, the Sydney Kingsleys (new hit play), Miss Dietrich, Jack von Ripper with a fantastic heron-legged beauty. The Crossets, the Meyers, the Brennans, the Hochschilds, the Fr. Taylors, the Bouveries, Mrs. Burden, Mrs. Parkinson, Henry McIlhenny, Pavlik, alarmingly thin. Henry McB. still patched on the head. Allen P. working hard, vivaciously; Braden seeming shy; Barr seeming worried and sour. I talked mainly to Alice B. and husband and escort (J. Caffery), and to Betty P. and to the Sherwoods. Stuart Preston is on the *N.Y. Times*, replacing Sam Hunter. Incidentally, Cocteau's *Lettres Américaines* in some Paris paper are (I hear) infuriating trash, indigestible corn—Pauline, for one, infuriated. Indeed his living on so vigorously is applaudable but has disadvantages, inconveniences, incongruities—automation of himself; and movies are disclassing . . . Wm. Morris, Inc. is wooing Isherwood. Harcourt Brace, since taking in Reynal as editor-partner, seems to have gone slightly crazy with vanity and spite, especially because Helen [Straus], my agent, took R. P. Warren to Random. For which they blame Albert Erskine, and punitively, they have withdrawn *Flowering Judas* from the Modern Library while it was selling 10,000 a year—Porter would leave them if she were not in a state of advance serfdom. Fancy her having accepted an advance on her journal! Helen wants some of my unpublished *poetry* for a sort of anthology *Life* is doing! Incidentally, Eliz. Ames has been vindicated and reinstated at Yaddo, with a nice headline in the *Tribune*!

All seasons of the year please me alike; and they are a pleasure very calm and grave—darkly underlying them, the tragic conscience of lifetime passing and of my never getting enough work done: my life an immense debt, an unpaid bill . . .

I almost deplore my having refused Nelson Lansdale's invitation to celebrate my birthday—no other celebration in view, except the family repetitiousness. Perhaps, to put it very cruelly, returning to one's vomit is just the thing to do on birthdays, and to one's blood long since shed and dried, and to one's spilt milk, for wisdom's sake!

Is it not fantastic!—his undiscourageable adoration of a Me that never existed, and the absolute of obtuseness as to what I would enjoy and ever did enjoy; and I remember, once upon a time, he wanted to drive with me on a country road at night, with the lights turned off, and argued that if I really loved him I would not worry!

My Christopher: a new love affair, for this non-amorous time of my life; a new dear one, for this philosophical time . . . It makes me so happy to have him love *The Ides of March*—strange romanticism of literary men, inexplicable to almost anyone.

And that crazy Thornton has been back for weeks, avoiding me again or, I should say, still. Of course I could pursue him and pin him down, I could go to New Haven as I went to Santa Monica. Perhaps the reason I don't is a set of very little matters, prejudicial: his bitten and not perfectly clean fingernails; and Jed Harris*; and his hypocrisy about queerness . . . ?

I naughtily accepted an *Invitation to Learning* broadcast (Santayana's *Sense of Beauty*) because a new CBS man telephoned to me in Cleveland and gushed at me. I dare say Irwin Edman† chose me. I have just received the volume, and not yet read it—it looks inferior to *The Life of Reason*; juvenilia. I'll manage; I'll play *amicus curiae* and ingenu to Edman and Bryson.

Bernadine is here, and it is extraordinarily pleasant to have her. She has changed greatly. She is a very good woman, so unvain (unlike K.A.P. in this regard) . . .

"The sky is a riddle of stars," wrote Sean O'Faolain.

Alone here at home tonight, lonesome, I have been outdoors and looked up, and made this variation on O'Faolain, which I think I prefer: The sky seems a tremendous question; and a few stars here and there gave answer, prompt and cheerful but not satisfactory.

As I awoke I found myself saying to myself: "My happy birthday," with the adjective emphatic, heartfelt.

The last day of my forty-seventh year seemed, alas, in a way, typical: On Saturday night Baba had invited the head world federalists in the county to dine; so, to indulge her, I forwent the relatively comfortable train, took the late bus. An aristocratic, foolish, but not stupid young satyr (somewhat giving me the benefit of his temperament by constant glances of his heavy-lidded sparkling eyes), and his aristocratic pretty new wife about to have a nervous breakdown . . .

* Jed Harris (1900–79). Broadway producer and promoter who worked with Wilder.
† Irwin Edman (1896–1954). American philosopher and author.

After only four and a half hours sleep, I woke in uneasiness about the broadcast. Just because the book did not please me, and I felt not quite competent, I overworked at it.

Still it went better than most. Especially, I think, confirmed by Beulah, my microphone delivery has improved: a more relaxed voice, easier to listen to. Old Lyman Bryson, not having worked with me before, waxed enthusiastic, made charm, and took me to lunch; which was a little tedious, as four other CBS employees joined us. They said frankly that my presence justified them in putting their luncheons on the expense account.

Lest I forget, Lyman Bryson told a pretty story, of his grandson aged five. Playing by himself in their suburban back yard, he was observed kneeling on the sidewalk, holding and straightening out a large angleworm, sawing it in two with a straight-edged stick. The observer, his father, felt troubled by this; wondered what he should or should not say, perhaps just a word of protest or deprecation; but he said nothing. The five-year-old, inattentive to him, leaned closer over the angleworm and in a soft fond pitying (and perhaps self-pitying) voice said to it, that is, to the two separate squirming parts of it: *"Now* you have a friend!"

From a letter to Joseph Campbell

As I must have confessed to you, when I had the proofs of your *Hero* for the grants committee, I only skimmed it, disgracefully—the others wanted it, and took their time. Then you gave me the first copy, which was dear of you, but in a way a futility—for I was tired out, with one thing and another, and then I went gallivanting, out West, etc.

Now at last I am reading it as I like, as it deserves. It is an entrancing and profound experience.

Are you getting any sufficiency or satisfaction from the reviewers, *et al.*? Not much, I suspect—and that suspicion prompts this letter, as it were, to console you. The great portion of your life so devoted and spent—then a sort of silence, or only, now and then, from this and that quarter, some peep or murmur or mere formality.

A quibble about this bit, where perhaps you left some little recess or shadow; enthusiasm about that bit, where one of your gods happens to look out unequivocally, where something glitters, an ornament, a jewel-like precept—that's probably all you'll get, for a long time. Even from your peers, even from your friends, me for example. It is going to take us a long time to get it through our heads, as a book, an entirety and unity.

If you had made it a smaller thinner drier (even more egotistical) synthesis, with oversimplification or with mystification, you'd have got more credit. As it is, by its nature, it is the kind of book that does good, rather than the kind that has success. Thank God. All of us will be quietly seeking something for our own salvation in it, feeding on it and digesting little by little. As I say above, an experience . . . Let me tell you that I shall be surprised if it does not become perceptible in due course that it has made you a great man of the time, the day and age. You'll have to wait and see.

Monroe and I are going to want you and Jean to spend a weekend here this spring. My wild acre is Botticellian with daffodils.

Venus-scarred from top to toe, and married within an inch of my life—and notwithstanding all my high-falutin philosophizing, and merciless austere psychologizing when asked, I do think better of just eroticism than of love-in-idleness or love-from-loneliness or love-vanity or love-competition—as (with or without sex on the side) it appears to be among so many Americans, 1949.

Allowing for the fact that he has no creativity, no talent, and his ambiance is almost all worldly, established artists and aristocracy, I think Monroe is the most extraordinary man in the world. But can one allow any such thing, and still make any such statement? I think I can, quite sincerely. All of us creators, more or less creative, are such sickly and melodramatic types. We rather horrify me. Only in the end we get forgiven, and we forgive ourselves, when we have some good production to show for it.

Monroe scarcely got his stride in Italy, new there, with no Italian, and his bad French and the Italians' bad French. But presto, when he got up North: Brancusi and Braque and Picasso and Emilio Terry and Claudel and Miss Bowen and Forster and [Harold] Nicolson; and the wild great ladies; and all the old friends; and the good-looking youngsters whom he has crushes on, or vice versa, and whom he mixes in with the melee, one I take to be Freud's grandson, and another, Pierre Brasseur's son . . . Best in Paris, where, he says, "there is a sun so strong that it pulls you up into the air." I dare say he will be more dead than alive when he gets back—this Saturday or Sunday—but evidently it has been his happiest journey.

Forster is bringing his lifelong beloved policeman, Bob Buckingham, next month. Now I must admit that the National Institute is a dear old organization, to have underwritten that. And it was I, said the wren . . .

Monroe arrived early Saturday morning, and Ll., who had spent the night in town, drove us home to Stone-blossom by late lunchtime. It was blissful to have him to myself for two days before his satellites of the museum, etc., got at him. How beautifully he reports his grand Europe! But, alas, he forgets fast. And, indefatigable in psyche if not in physique, never really retrospective, he made me work hard for him, four and a half of those precious hours: putting on paper for Prince Gasoline his next great project, a two or three years' forecast.

On Tuesday Thornton W. and I spent our long-prepared, overprepared evening by ourselves, from 7 p.m. to 2 a.m. Not exactly enjoyable to my way of thinking, or way of feeling; not a real meeting of minds, somehow a frustration or a bafflement. He, on the other hand, seemed entranced from start to finish; and at 2, when I cried quits—whiskey on top of penicillin—he went wandering away excitedly around the town. He called me "Young'un!" Also, again and again he quotes my words of twenty years ago; also he gives me credit for a plot for a play of which I have no recollection whatever, of which I have now made him a present. What a singular great creature! Now in retrospect I am enjoying the evening intensely, deciphering his ideas, many of them wrong headed; and turning my small, slow, but strong flashlight here and there in his darkness, secretiveness.

Gordon Merrick,* an amiable, baby-faced, Priapus-bodied friend with whom I flirted unavailingly a good many years ago (after OSS, he stayed on in France) has now sent to me a peculiar young Frenchman, a country nobleman who grew up in the *maquis*, who has come here to learn agriculture by working as a farmhand if possible, if we please. His name is Henri de la Celle and I gave him an hour's interview on Wednesday; then asked him here for half the weekend. With solemn, almost anguished good manners, château-style; and a certain antique beauty: very tall with elongated face, like Henri II, that is, like a stag.

The farm has grown showier and more business-like in recent years, though still deficit-financed; my brother's dreamworld. Henri was starry-eyed, and my brother himself also pleased him. The latter took a very

* Gordon Merrick (1916–88). Novelist whose homoerotic fiction enjoyed wide—and, for the times, surprising—popular success.

friendly line; and pointed out to me that employment itself was the easy part, *if* bed and board were available . . . Stone-blossom is the roomiest house in the valley, and that, for the obvious reason, scared hell out of me. I have had no sort of beloved for a couple of years; a state of affairs which Lloyd and Baba strongly deplore . . .

So, not without a little temper or at least melancholy, I felt obliged to specify to them that this was not Henri's line or approach at all; that I had no such design, no such hope.

But meanwhile they found him likable, respectable; and yesterday my sister solved the problem of his habitation, and with some element of romantic comedy even in that solution. In this entire valley, on all the roster of my brother's employees, there has been only one boy whom I have ever regarded with concupiscence (with absolute virtue as well, I hasten to add): one B.M. of a certain strange beauty, a little dimwitted, with a kind of fond politeness—nineteen or twenty now; beauty a bit coarsened. And *voilà!* Henri is to reside with him, two or three miles away, with his widowed mother, who says: "Oh, it will be so nice for Bill to have a friend, and Bill can drive him around and show him the country, and they can learn from one another." And so out he came last night, and I got him up at six, and away he went—to the grass silo, to the manure spreader, to the artificial-insemination unit, to who knows what? and I shall scarcely see any more of him, if all goes well.

A wonderful thing: I am always more or less the same to Monroe. Whatever happens, he always seems to have foreseen it, as inherent in my pattern, of character, my fate. An odd thing: he takes only a sort of momentary objective interest in anyone's psychology, as such. He does not dismiss all that as not important; only it has no fascination or romance in his view. He thinks of it as if it were something physical: like digestion or allergy or the like. And now, as to my working harder, continuing happier, I am not sure that he believes it. Perhaps just as well; for I talk too much, and all this will indeed have been just another subjectivity, another dissipation of psyche.

One cannot write *criticism* unless it is in series, choosing one's books; so as to impose and elucidate one's terms, relative values, etc. Otherwise one cannot help being concerned with whatever is being praised to the skies in the next column, and so on—it becomes a matter of advertisement or counter-advertisement. I don't enjoy it much, as I do it. Certainly in the case of Miss Bowen's book, her mistaken notions of what wants doing interest me more than her various obvious excellences.

The four Tietjens novels of that terrible old friend of my youth F. M. Ford still mean a great deal to me. The present curriculum of Henry James and James Joyce and Gertrude Stein, and indeed Kafka, seems to me so disastrous to the art of the novel.

I remember Thornton Wilder's face the other evening when I declared that Molly Bloom was a kind of equivalent of *Manon Lescaut*, and would eventually be detached from Joyce's admirable but tedious form as Manon was from the Abbe Prévost's five-volume memoir-novel.

Little controversies like this stir in my mind just now because I have promised to give six lectures at Kinsey's* university in July; six in the same week.

As to my worldly interests, liberal politics, professional noblesse oblige, kindliness toward the very young, kindliness toward the very old, etc., so long as I live at Stone-blossom, my correspondence along those lines can only increase. This week I have had eight so-to-speak important such letters to write, as requested by or in behalf of Christopher and my parents and Lillian H. and Baba and Thornton and Louis Kronenberger and Lloyd and indeed, come to think of it, Thomas Mann; not to mention some brief formalities, not to mention long-distance telephoning . . .

I have been troubled by what Nick said about his half wishing that he could manage without having to take a job. With such sympathy— for in a way he has had peculiarly bad luck with his several employments. With, on the other hand, profound mingled feelings—for, most of my life, I have had all the leisure he might long for; it is easy for me to talk . . . But on the other hand, I feel the penalty for having become spoiled in that way, the difficulty of being one's own boss (even for an artist); I know how large a part of happiness in the long run of life depends on the circumscribing, steadying effect of regular work, and on mere financial independence: no gratefulness, no ambiguity, in that way. I suppose that in fact all that is by chance circumstance and individual; never quite the same for any persons . . .

De Chirico: I remember his strange handsomeness in the twenties:

---

* Alfred C. Kinsey (1894–1956). Zoologist and sexologist who met G.W. at a formal dinner arranged by M.W., and later sought his help in the work of the Institute for Sex Research in Bloomington, Indiana.

pale as a clown, with a nose so great that it looked false; and cold, slow, uncertain glances of a water bird, and somewhat sinister heaviness of movement, as though he had swallowed something enormous.

My novel is not dead; it just keeps rising and rising in my mind, changing shape, like a very yeasty dough here and there all over a kitchen. It won't stay in my pans; I just don't seem to have the strength to knead it hard enough; how and when shall I ever get it in the oven?

Mr. E. M. Forster is booked to arrive the morning of Friday the 20th; AOA Flight No. 159. Paul and Jared fixed up for him the ground floor of 5 St. Luke's Place, which they lately rented.

Now it is summer—today I found my brown water snakes romancing on the stone margin of the brook. She slipped out of his arms (or perhaps I should say arm, singular) and hid; and he just stared at me until I got bored and went away.

Eliz. is in lovely form, in lovely voice, and amorous hither and thither. Beulah also is singing well again, at last—duets are all the rage—and otherwise flourishing.

The so many children, on account of whom old Mother Wescott-Hubbard never knows what to do, have been in particular ebullition, variously cheerful and doleful. My poor Patrick, jobless and penniless and sexless, has been threatening a bad crack-up, and believes that I am the only one who understands him; but what is the good of just understanding? X has had syphilis, very young—but that I seem to have known how to cope with, how to talk about, etc. Henri de la Celle, who has been insisting on employment as a farmhand on my brother's farm, has finally been hired. Not to mention the commotions made by brother himself, that overwillful overenergetic tycoonish male, who is collecting a million and a quarter in the country for a model hospital; and ditto by my Monroe, of very nearly ditto temperament, who, the instant he returned from Europe, began on his new project of a model art magazine . . .

Wayside details of American life:
Halfway to New York (motoring in with Elizabeth) we came to the scene of an accident: a ragpicker's great truck smashed, overturned, and strewn on the road and the roadside. The first glimpse of it, up

ahead, gave me gooseflesh; for the old clothes in two main heaps might have been piled-up bodies. In fact the truck driver, the ragpicker, was nowhere to be seen. Had he already been taken to a hospital? Perhaps he still lay hidden under his plentiful rags . . . Though we asked ourselves these questions as we passed by, the little spectacle of misfortune and destruction inspired, on the whole, a humorous, even joyous feeling; perhaps in remembrance of this or that clown's performance, or indeed of Petroushka, or some remoter atavistic association.

When we got to Jersey City, the cops turned us away from the entrance to the Holland Tunnel. Presently we observed people on street corners pausing to read newspapers: HUDSON TUNNEL ON FIRE. A considerable disaster; the explosion of a truckload of an insecticide, one of those gases which may cause some change of red corpuscles, some loss of mental faculty.

Another headline (Hearst): PSYCHOLOGIST BEATS CHILD TO DEATH TO CURE FREUDIAN JEALOUSY. Which in due course probably Monsignor Sheen will cite in evidence . . .

What Elizabeth and I came to town for was a joint booking at Teachers College; to lend some bit of (perhaps) prestige to sister Marjorie, who is seeking employment as a teacher, not easy for a middle-aged provincial grass widow. As someone said mockingly: "Wescott & Wescott, Songs & Patter." It was a sufficient success, with an uncharming audience. Teachers College has a low standing in the academic world, anyway—there is a saying, quoted to us by Joe Campbell: "Artificial pearls before real swine."

Back home now by the early train . . . Elizabeth is staying to spend an hour or two with her great secret man. An *amoureuse* in the old grand manner . . .

By my quartet of *amoureux* jointly, I have been given the job of finding a *rez-de-chaussée*, a room and bath, hideaway or love nest. With the generally explanatory fiction that it is for my own use: not indeed to make love in—too late!—but to work in with a secretary when I come to town; and sometimes I find myself listening to and half believing my own fibs, and indeed who knows?

Monroe of course takes a very dark, scornful, indignant view: The very idea! How foolish you are! How selfish they are! The greatest writer in the country! And you let them turn you into a kind of renting agent! That line . . .

The fact being that I am not the g.w. in the c., not by a long shot; and that my near and dear ones do not really so regard me (it is only their flattering and somewhat self-flattering convention, left over from my ardent troublesome youth); and that, if I were, or if presently I get to be, they would, they will, yield the balance of power to me, easy. Like a pecking order . . .

Reason enough indeed to remove to Europe and stay there, foreign affairs and exchanges permitting—just to be out of the way of burdens such as the above. Certainly my talent was weakened by staying abroad so long, in the early thirties; and the readjustment at home was hard. But now I have regained sufficient vitality of style, realities of theme— and I would go back, probably to France, if I were alone in the world.

But would I, at this time of my life, wish to be alone in the world, or to have the transportable idle type of consort, without life or career of his own? No, no. *Et sequitur.*

Here in the bus, on my right, is a young soldier exactly like certain portraits of those Nordics, Lombards, or (?) Ostrogoths who invaded and ruined Italy in the Dark Ages: with a great coarse but shapely nose, taffy hair, and remarkable complexion like pink calfskin—energetically making friends with a dark stout less-young man, who is not innocent and whom it troubles.

On my right, a young woman presumably from Florida has in her lap a good-sized alligator handbag with a most realistic alligator in three dimensions occupying one whole side of it; and her fingertips (and fingernails with scaled-off red nail polish) keep fondling it in every detail.

Young Monsieur le Comte is a great success on the farm.

He has spent the night and day here, his day off; having a rest from his fatiguing limited English; being lectured by Monroe and me, turn and turn about. He adores us, especially Monroe; and he is very pleasing to me—pure Clouet, very tall with sloping shoulders and breast-like pectorals and narrow waist, with frizzy black hair, and beard-dark chin. But he is so antiquely polite that he seems to me unapproachable.

Besides C.M.'s flat temporarily, I now have another on apparently more permanent terms: the cheapest lodging ever heard of, in the idealest location. It is a maid's room in one of those new Loewy-designed glass-fronted buildings just west of the Plaza; on the ground floor, tucked in between the elevator shaft and a doctor's service entrance; $40 a month. I haven't seen it yet. It needs some furnishing, not much. I suppose I ought to take a lease if possible.

In the days up ahead, Mr. Forster . . . The subject of his address on Friday is "Art for Art's Sake," and I dare say it will be a lesson to me; though with the ambiguity of being taught it by him, who has appeared to be so nearly impotent as a writer this long time . . . I am meeting him tonight, at last.

Monroe really does give notable dinner parties: ourselves and the great old gentleman [E. M. Forster], and Mr. Bob Buckingham, his dear lifelong policeman, and Joe Campbell, and Dr. Kinsey! Funnily enough, Monroe is worried about it. He hasn't dared tell E.M.F. that K. is coming, and keeps nervously forbidding me to let the news item out, lest there be embarrassment about B.B. They are both coming to us for the weekend. Eliz. will drive us out right after the Institute of Arts and Letters ceremonials honoring Forster.

One thing we found out the night we dined with Kinsey, which I think is not in his published volume: his interest in the basic differences between male and female. There is evidence that men, ancient and contemporary alike, primitive and sophisticated alike, all have enjoyed some play of imagination about sex: deliberate or at least conscious indecencies, wish-fulfillments and exaggerations, and special erotic vocabulary and imagery. Whereas women respond mainly to the direct stimulation of the senses.

Kinsey's interviewing of artists, his new line of inquiry this year, has brought this out. Female artists, asked to specify the erotic factor in their reactions to works of art, scarcely differentiate between it and various other excitements: love of nature, mother-love, religiosity, no matter what. Recently, too, a number of laboratory biologists have been proving certain differences of gender in the cerebral cortex itself.

Forster summed this up with comical simplicity yesterday. Bob Buckingham had spoken of someone so womanish in affectation and gesture that, in whatever circumstance, surely he could not be expected to behave otherwise than a woman would.

"Oh no, Bob," Forster protested, "no. That is what we learned from Dr. Kinsey. Extreme as some men are in their effeminacy, still they are men. Because—they all love *smut!*"

Upon which he paused for just a second; then without emphasis, as an afterthought, softly added, "Indeed I was rather comforted to hear it." And gave his characteristic small laugh, a peculiar chuckle high-pitched and long-drawn-out—it reminded me a little of the crowing of a cock pheasant . . .

Kinsey is a strange man, with a handsome good sagacious face but with a haunted look—fatigue, concentration, and (surprising to me, if I interpret rightly) passionateness and indeed sensuality. With all his scientific conscientiousness, and pride of science, and faith in science, he has the temperament of a reformer rather than a scientist; fierily against hypocrisy and repressive law of every sort, censorship, etc., and against Judaism and Catholicism and Irishry.

B.B. enjoyed himself greatly, and toward the end contributed certain little observations of English impropriety, which was dear and funny; and promised to show Kinsey, upon his next trip abroad, Scotland Yard's five rooms of confiscated "art." K. complains that our police, helpful in every other way, will never admit finding anything like that—presumably they carry it all home for their private collections or make presents of it to their friends . . . ?

I sometimes think of keeping a *sottisier* like Flaubert's.

Vulgarity of Monsignor Sheen: In his current volume, in a passage about the Annunciation: "Nine months later the Eternal established its beachhead in Bethlehem."

Padraic Colum remembers a sermon he preached just after the other war—a sudden new celebrity of the Church, with bright Irish eyes and somewhat Savonarolan profile—in which he referred to the Virgin Mary as "the first gold-star mother in history."

From a letter to François Reischenbach* in Paris

This is to thank you for your dear thought of taking me to Salzburg. Of course I cannot accept, not this year. Until I have become a regular writer again, nothing could tempt me anywhere—not even Mozart; not even love, not even eroticism, not even that tenderness more peaceful than either, which you and I have invented uniquely between ourselves; not even the Ile-de-France or the Tyrol . . . Until I have a book to show for these several wasted visionary futile felicitous years, I shall not feel deserving of anything; *digne de rien*. Tempted indeed rather by death, once more—unless I can behave better.

But, you see, I speak even of that cheerfully. For I will behave better. Therefore, dear François, as to Salzburg or the equivalent, I want a *rain check*, please. The very thought and proposition is precious— thank you with all my heart. For it means that, at last, peace has been made in terms of some reality: when a Frenchman can invite an American to accompany him to Austria. It is important and historic.

Let me tell you something I have been thinking, a peace-making

---

* François Reischenbach and his brother Philippe were art dealers, patrons of writers, and friends of G.W. and M.W.

job for someone in France. It was first suggested to me (I think) by the Bach duet you sent me—your French singers now have a better style for the great Baroque music than any Americans or Germans. Then I happened to have one of my fits of passionate partiality for French music—for Berlioz, for Fauré, for Gluck, even for Ravel. Then I heard a pair of not-young Australian women wonderfully trained (by old Plunkett Greene) sing a cantata by Couperin; unheard of. I began suddenly longing for a great program of music that, for some reason, I missed hearing when I was young: *L'Enfance du Christ*, for example; and music that, at least in this country, no one younger than I has heard: *Le Roi Malgré Lui*, for example . . .

The point is, I want a French Salzburg. There was a notion of it, before the war. Paul Valéry wanted to use the old intact theater of Versailles, clearing out the political benches for the time being. Why not? Mlle Nadia Boulanger* would have some power to do it; and I was tempted to write her an inspiring letter.

A blissful hour in Washington, by myself at the National Gallery. It occurred to me to bypass almost everything that I know best and love best—and thus I discovered that the three big landscapes of Cuyp and the very large Jan Steen, *The Dancing Couple* (with something of Le Nain, even something of Watteau), are great (?) masterpieces.

But it was the Poussin that made me tremble with delight. *The Baptism of Christ*, with all the agitation in the center, gesticulating arms, etc., which the eye resents; with the clear reflections in pools of water on either side, and the burnt-orange cloth in a heap down in front, and the nude with his shirt half off, over his head—could he have seen the London Piero?—and the glorious youth in the capacious pink-orchid cloak?

Last night Elizabeth and I and Edna and Henri drove to Stockton, via Cherryville—the new moon promising warm weather, the fifty-mile view bluish and dim but grand—and dined under the spreading electric-lit maples; and all the way home Henri kissed Eliz. in the back of the car. Half a virgin, with a strange history of amorous mother, etc., he seems bewitched about equally by Eliz. and Monroe. It has been one of our greater tricks: the good fortune we have made for this youth, America just as he wanted it, in one way and another. He thinks of us

* Nadia Boulanger (1887–1979). French composer, conductor, and teacher whose American students included composers Aaron Copland, Virgil Thomson, and Ned Rorem.

as *"l'Amérique! que c'est merveilleux!"*—and probably will regret us always. He understands nothing, but he is a good boy, worth taking trouble with.

A strange and amusing incident, there at Stockton after dinner. When I opened the door of the men's room, it seemed full up: three huge college boys in ice-cream suits, drunk. I started to back out, but two of them protested: "Come on in. It's all right. There's room." And so there was, but none to spare. The third, the drunkest, was in a murderous rage at one of the others; dead-pale, with perspiring lips and brow, with trembling fists in position. The least drunk had him over-powered, grappling on to him from behind, from head to foot; he and the murderee-elect kept talking soothingly, rationalizingly. My presence confused the murderer a good deal; he extended his feeble fists and made extra little lunges in my direction; they had to soothe him about me as well as the original subject matter—"Don't mind him! He's a good guy!"—while I did my peeing; rather impressed by myself, to be able to. For the effect on the whole, the heavy breathing, the immobility with straining muscles, the fond but foolish nervous repetitious phrases, was more like a scene of sex than of combat; and rather more like animal sex than human—one of the slower animals, dog or pig. Drunk as they were, the angriness on the one side, the peacemaking on the other, seemed an unreality, a pretense. And so I left them . . .

Fleur Cowles,* that is, Mrs. *Look*, has got a step ahead of Monroe with her modern-art magazine; she has hired George Davis to be her editor. (A weakness of Monroe's in general: he cannot bear to bring himself to make use of very manifestly horrid persons.)

In reports of the places expatriates now favor, there is an odd curiosity and fascination for me: I try to think back twenty-five years in truthful perspective, to make sense of the differences . . . For, after all, Rome equals Montparnasse, Ischia equals Villefranche—and I (to all intents and purposes) was Truman [Capote]. Which last point I make with no intense irony, no ouch! For we have at present only half a dozen new, earnest, talented fiction writers, and he is one.

Twenty-five years ago our various connections with elder Europeans were important to us: old Ford, Cocteau, even Gertrude St., even Mina Loy; isn't that a difference? Also I think there must not have been quite

---

* Fleur Cowles. Wife of *Look* magazine publisher Jack Cowles, she created the magazine *Flair* along the lines of *Vanity Fair*.

so unabashed and homogeneous and self-conscious a homosexual society
as' such. It was still rather a sin, with something of Byronic fatalism.
One of the notable emancipations in recent years is the kind of thing
homosexuals feel free to say about one another; as I remember, we didn't
. . . And when Hemingway took a crack at my morals in the Paris *Herald
Tribune*,* it was with a decorous ambiguity; not everyone knew what he
was getting at.

I remember a conversation one night in '38 with a well-known
Montparnasse character, that old aunt of an ex-doctor whom Djuna
Barnes put in *Nightwood*. He was drunk, and gave me hell: How audacious and romantic and gifted I had been in the old days; whereas
now, alas, I had turned into a sort of "distinguished" figure, accepted
and stuffy, with my talent dried up . . . I defended myself as best I
could, humorously. Then suddenly he asked, "And what ever became
of that beautiful little Spanish boy you used to keep?" He meant
Monroe—who, I may add, scarcely sees the humor of it.

I have neglected George almost all month, but went in yesterday
to advise him about a selection of portrait-photographs to be published.
Bill has been away down South, and he has hated every minute of it.
Their relationship still seems to be beneficial to him, deleterious to G.
Youngsters digest lotus so much better than their elders. I thought that
Bill looked lovelier than ever, in that getup of dungarees, etc., which
has become all too regimental for them all; with his sex exquisitely in
evidence.

Nick is weekending with Eliz. All serene; except that he hasn't a
job and, if the truth were told, doesn't really want one, though next
week I believe he is to be employed painting fire escapes, as a helper
to a bizarre and beautiful medical student who appeared with a paint
pot on his fire escape one afternoon . . . A general joblessness is
beginning. How worrying that will be, with all our imagination-ridden
boys. I am afraid that, in a way, we Wescotts are bad for everyone;
conducive to a certain unhappiness up ahead. I don't mean just on
account of the happiness we are able to give boys like Nick and Henri
for a while—I am not so pretentious and unrealistic—but rather the

---

* Ernest Hemingway, speaking with a reporter in Sylvia Beach's Paris bookstore in 1927,
held up G.W.'s *The Grandmothers* and said, "In the first place, every sentence in it was written
with the idea of making Glenway Wescott immortal. And . . . what's the use of my telling you
what's in the second place? You work for a kind of family newspaper and you couldn't print it."

good fortune which they observe us in, which they somewhat overestimate and misunderstand. It is like the garden of Hussein . . .

There is no nastier color than gravestones, when it is a successful graveyard, planted thick like a flower bed or a field crop.

Having virtuously kept Bernard's letter unopened until the end of the day, I read it as I walked down to the Gate for dinner, and downhill toward the bridge I felt a little dizzy, and for a moment in absentmindedness took it to be the effect of walking with reading glasses. No such thing; it was the great snarl of honeysuckle just there, the first weekend in full drunkening bloom. It has been extraordinarily cool all month, too cool for the corn—cold tonight, with gleaming moonlight.

In the texture of the best-woven, best-meaning life, one comes upon disheartening sickening bad bits, almost unbearable incongruities. We do bear them, and try to forget them, succeed in forgetting them. But probably in due course certain of our shortcomings, otherwise mysterious, somewhat derive from this kind of small matter, disgust or shock of this or that. If we had less sense of proportion about it, less stoicism, we should understand ourselves better.

For example, Monroe's foolish though capable and devoted old housekeeper, Laverne, composing a chicken pie for his dinner party on Thursday, tucked away the liver and gizzard and other such fragments in a paper bag in the cupboard under the sink, to be carried home to Harlem; but let it slip her mind and left it there. Upon his return from Stone-blossom on Sunday night, the nauseating, indeed frightening odor met him as he stepped out of the elevator (the weekend had been hot); and he had to spend an entire hour, retching and angry and inefficient, tidying up, scrubbing and disinfecting and deodorizing.

Bernard's drawing of E. M. Forster will never be disappointing—it is one of his most beautiful pages, in delineation and volume and spacing and texture. Of secondary value as a likeness; doubtless his fault, as Bob B. remarked and he admitted. But he is not a really visual, envisageable, portrayable man. One wants a motion picture, for that sprightliness on energetic but hypersensitive feet, and the excited ungraceful movements of his hands; with sound track furthermore, for the laughter starting and stopping always so quickly.

Lately, all the Wescotts have been in an intense overrationalizing voluble bout of Wescottry. Something like the *Johannesnacht* fugue in

Meistersinger: *"Wonne! Wonne!"* I think it will appear in the end that not only has family life been hard on me; I have been no good at it. I seem to stimulate passions, to fortify egos, to prevent superficiality, perhaps to inspire drama, with grand effect—but I do not influence anyone one bit.

Has anyone ever tried to make a novel of any sort of dramatic passage of family life while it went on; little daily chapters, with just enough flashback for the reader to know what the devil it was all about? A new form; not all to *my* hand, I guess. Would it harm the *dramatis familiae*? Could a literature-loving family be persuaded to permit pub-lication, or perhaps not to read it themselves? For the novelist would need full license, to work in some entirely fictitious elements, to unify it and delimit it and frame it.

Days of special pathos and even melodrama in Wescottdom. Under our somewhat elegant frivolity, resolute pleasure-seeking, we are a vi-olent lot in our way—I think there must have been Renaissance families like us.

The background of it all, and the cause of a great part of it, has been Baba's psychotherapy. More than a year ago, she determined that I should be psychoanalyzed, having learned to regard my homosexuality as a tragedy and a curable psychopathology, and to disbelieve in my literary ability, or at least to despair (and perhaps disapprove) of its further development without psychoanalysis.

On the other hand she has ardently approved of my organizational and government activity, etc., indeed, at the time that I determined to resign from all that, she suggested that, instead, I should take a job on the Public Relations Staff of the State Department . . . This a minor matter; she did not bully me or scold me in the slightest—only it dis-turbed me deeply as to my pride of authorship, and on account of my feeling of economic dependency or, to be more exact, indebtedness.

I need not go into detail of the economic setup in our family, with Baba never deigning to look at her checkbook. *Les bons comptes font de bons amis*; and nothing could be less *bon* in that way than my case, with St.-bl. not my property, hanging on to it grimly for Monroe's sake, for our old age; encouraged in all those extravagances which others appear to enjoy more than I, not encouraged in some which I desire especially (a secretary, and travel, etc.); more spoiled than anyone, more grateful than anyone, yet with the proud constant thought of having committed myself to repaying it all when I have a best-seller (Eliz. inscribes every cent in her great complex ledger); expected to feel security for the rest of my life, not in fact feeling anything of the kind, with Ll.'s great gamble of the farm, the uncertainty of Baba's decisions when her analysis is over. Therefore I have gone on trying to write the best-selling sort of novel, instead of all sorts of short things that in the circumstances would have been easier . . .

> . . . *perche d'amaro*
> *sente 'l sapor della pietade acerba.*
> . . . *for bitter*
> *is the taste of stern pity.*
> —Dante, *Purgatorio*, XXX, 80–81

From a letter to Lloyd Wescott

You must realize that when a man argues as wildly as I have done this fortnight, it is because he is retreating, feeling his defeat, beaten back from position to position. During our several conversations (likewise with Monroe) I have sometimes had a sense of stating my case convincingly in my way and my terms. But each time, in the night and next day, when I have thought over the various points you have made, and recalled my own extreme, crude, and even cruel assertions and retorts, I realize my failure.

In the last thirty-six hours I have done the hardest, loneliest thinking of my life; and there seems not to be much more fight in me. You have almost entirely persuaded me of the ill effect that my changed relationship with Baba has had on me, from the moment she began to think about my psychoneurosis. We now have to decide whether it renders our way of life here together, that is, my life at Stone-blossom, impossible. I acknowledge the almost tragic aspect of homosexuality as it has turned out for me in recent years, impinging somewhat on everything else. I recognize the errors and grievances that have developed in my mind from economic dependency. I shall now seriously consider being psychoanalyzed, though I see greater objections to it than to any other course.

But whatever decisions I may have to make, we must keep to the fundamental trouble from now on. It is this: my overwhelming disappointment and guiltiness at not having written any fiction since *Apartment in Athens*: five years.

The real reason for my unproductivity has been just my weakness, foolishness, self-indulgence, pursuit of pleasure, laziness. All my life I have had to force myself to write; sitting at my desk somewhat longer than anyone else has to, in grim determination and concentration, waiting and waiting to feel my talent . . . No inadequacy of talent as such; in any case no diminishment, no change. I have only grown impatient and cowardly about it. And the rest has followed . . .

At last Eliz. has sent up by her secretary a little letter which acknowledged that relations between us were strained, due to the fact that we had not come to an understanding about her "friendship" with Nick; but with the specification that she wished me first to hear of it from him.

Dreading conversation with him more than anything, I was trying to devise some decent kindly refusal. When she telephoned in an impulsive, seemingly affectionate manner, asking me to take her to dine that night at John's restaurant. Now, I thought, as I waited for Elizabeth, I could restore my self-respect: self-forgiveness would be in order. I had a good excuse to stop seeing Nick. I felt a kind of relief. It had been so bad for me not to know the truth; to be unable to stop accusing myself, imagining it, making it up out of whole cloth, in morbid fantasy.

Eliz. and I met fondly, correctly; and on our way to dine, she discoursed to me on her theory of the eroticism of women: that it was periodic, as if it were a kind of menstruation but in cycles, but often very long cycles, often years. For example, she said, Baba had passed into the phase of not wanting intercourse; Elizabeth, herself, on the other hand, having been free of desire all that time since Silver Hill . . .

Finally, as we were dining, I broached the subject.

"But, Glenway," she protested sharply, "did you not read my letter? I told you that I would not talk about it. I want you to talk to Nick first . . ."

"But I don't want to talk to him."

Whereupon she instantly grew angry, turned pale, said she would not be able to eat her dinner unless I changed the subject. And I did change the subject, with not the least anger on my part; everything under control, very brotherly, manly.

Later in the evening, back at St.-bl., at our ease out on the lawn in the dark, I spoke to her gently, expounding my lifelong tragic feeling about relations between women and homosexuals. I spoke of my horror of any sort of competition with women; my self-respect in never having felt guilty in my sexual abnormality greatly depending on my having given precedence to the norm by instinct or on principle. And I kept from alluding to those particular sexual perversities which most likely made me more pessimistic about Nick in a relationship with women;

neither did I dwell upon his hopeless unemployment and penury, or his suggestion to me sometimes before that he might ask Ll. to employ him on the farm. Also, as of greater interest to E., I pointed out how long I had been N.'s only adviser, only philosopher, only believer and yea-sayer—therefore it was bound to be very artificial, very difficult, if not impossible, for me to speak to him without discouraging him profoundly, and he is by nature inclined to pessimism. I kept arguing that it was for her and for me to think of his character and of the present situation; for us to come to an understanding, affectionately, truthfully, loyally, and to leave him out of our councils.

At the same time I *did* point out not only my unique happiness with him in 1946, but how heartbreaking or at least nerve-racking it would be to discuss all that!

But she kept saying, "It is not for me to decide. My relationship with him is of his choosing, and as he wishes. I do not love him, nor he me—there is no question of love, it is friendship . . . Hasn't he a right to be heard?"

To which I replied, gently but firmly, "Of course he has the right to be heard. But by the same token, I have the right to refuse to hear."

She seemed to see my point, and we parted very evidently at peace, as loving brother and sister.

Party line: I happened to pick up the receiver to call Mother, and got the tag end of an interrogative sentence of Elizabeth's and the beginning of an answering sentence of Nick's—both their voices so poignant—and I hung up at once.

As I feared, she was complaining to him that I would not talk to him.

Next morning at six, I was awakened by steps in the library, and up the stairs and into my room walked Nick, having stayed up all night and taken the milk train at three. With his look of wild unhappiness, of Mediterranean wounded pride and repressed Mafia violence, he demanded to know, "Why are you so upset about my friendship with your sister?"

There followed the most painful long talk of my entire life, mostly an explanation of my excuses for not talking. And poor Nick was not quite up to it. But he was brave and stubborn; he kept asking, always upon the principle that my refusing to answer was an answer in itself, and the worst kind. Upon my using the word "happiness" in some connection, he said, "But don't you know? There is no question of happiness in my mind. I cannot allow myself even to think of happiness, because if I did, I really would blow my top."

Then he told me that all his life he has wanted the experience of intercourse with a woman. One day when Elizabeth was sunbathing with him, she slipped off the upper part of her bathing suit and revealed her beautiful chest without breasts, with only the straight firm scar from her operation like a saber stroke. To Nick, she suddenly seemed like a woman changed to a boy by a terrible, cruel accident, and at that moment, a burning sensuality came over him.

Yesterday I turned myself over to Bob Solley, who took me seriously and sent me to the psychiatrist that he has the highest opinion of. Remembering my arrogance on this point in general, this was surely an act of humility; and indeed, an act of fear (day before yesterday frightened me). They both suggest that for the time being I am not to talk to anyone about this. I did not even announce the fact to Baba last night. Certain, for good relations with her, I want to avoid discussion of whether I have found the right psychiatrist or not, whether he is a Freudian or not, etc. I don't know, I didn't ask . . .

Pioneer sayings: of my grandfather W.:
"Never get in a pissing match with a skunk."

LITERATURE NOT NECESSARILY TRUTHFUL—Dickens and Dostoevsky, for example, wrote nightmares—but one cannot write at all unless one thinks it is the truth.

It now turns out that Elizabeth has been having a love affair with Nick for four months or a little longer.

In July, when I could no longer talk to Lloyd without raging or despairing, I went to a very good psychiatrist, mainly as an act of good faith and of humility; and he helped me a great deal, he comforted me and steadied me, he sufficiently restored my self-respect, and he kept me in mind of my selfish interests: my need of Baba's financial backing awhile longer, my tenure of Stone-blossom (if possible), and my literature to be written, in which he believes strongly. I must say that Elizabeth and Nick do not call it a "love affair." My not observing their terms, in our several distressed conversations in June, angered them. First and last, a good part of the trouble has been just ghastly semantics: as Elizabeth stated it in our last conversation, some six weeks ago, Nick is just her closest friend, and if and when he wishes to have intercourse

with her, well and good. She does not think of him as a man, he is not
a man, he is a homosexual; and a relationship between a woman and a
homosexual is not like any other relationship and as a homosexual who
has never had relations with a woman, I cannot expect to understand
what it is like, etc. This has been the crux of the matter for me: the
disqualification of my judgments on account of my homosexuality; the
supposition that in the circumstances none of my feelings can be disinterested, only my own amorousness and frustration.

In their view, my sin has been "jealousy." In fact, for me, that has
amounted to very little; only a touchiness, while the matter was still
unsettled or at least altogether obscure to me.

Someday perhaps I can tell the whole story; or perhaps put all my
accumulated scribble together, and fill in the lapses, in journal form.
It scarcely is a story; it is a novel; and I am not much of a novel writer,
only a novel liver . . .

Time (for me) is not only a fatality, but as one might say, a divinity;
and love in great degree is created by it, built up through the years. I
do not cease to love, or to be more exact, it takes me a long time to
cease, even when the practice of the relationship becomes disadvantageous in some way, or when profound disagreements have developed.

I have not yet entirely ceased even to love Nick, and as for Lloyd
and Baba and Eliz., I do not expect to live long enough to cease . . .
Little actions anger me indeed, in spite of love—I overreact, angriness
is my worst sin—but on the other hand I forgive quite soon, and
wholeheartedly.

Peculiar and fateful: I've got to change my handwriting. My fine
impracticable print script . . . my love of unfinishable perfection. My
small crepuscular-gray speed-writing (semi-shorthand) which no secretary could ever transcribe—which often grows illegible even for me—
comes from the capriciousness of my thought (*touche-à-tout*) and its
extreme pell-mell rapidity; and more disgraceful, still, expresses my
shame of inexplicable sorrows and self-criticism, and my shame of autoerotic scribbling.

Maugham used to say that certain old axioms did a great deal of
harm. Dinned into our ears, perhaps scarcely noticed, they are taken
for granted—and the reverse of the truth. For instance, "Absence makes
the heart grow fonder."

Another, which has been harmful to me, is *"Tout comprendre, c'est tout pardonner."* To understand all is to forgive all . . . Monroe often pronounces it when I indulge in extreme bitterness, resentment, recrimination. He forgets that the effect of that indulgence is precisely to lead to charitableness. It is a safety valve. I bark in order to keep from biting. In fact, and in practice, I forgive plenty; I even think that I have forgiven to excess.

A sentence with five terminal prepositions: Said a plaintive child to its mother at the hour of the bedtime story, "Why did you bring that book that I didn't want to be read to out of up for?"

Elizabeth asked to be invited to lunch yesterday. She is indeed desperately unhappy. I don't know why and she did not say. Nor did I relax into any particular emotion or frankness, or advice or admonishment. I did not even encourage her in her inclination to break with N. My *benign* insincerity . . .

Now it will be Nick's turn to be made to suffer, the poor devil. I shall be sorry for him, and he will have earned my compassion, my quite powerless compassion, for what it will be worth to him: not much. I do not garrote people, but I do outwit them. When things go badly, I do slip out of people's lives, worldly-wise as the serpent, and as slippery and cold-blooded . . .

Dog, that is, my type of dog, does not bite bitch; at all events tries not to . . .

The original form of my dedication of *Apartment in Athens.* I found it on a dog-eared manila folder, along with a great scribble of about thirty possible but not satisfactory titles. It must have been at the time I learned that it could not be entitled "A Change of Heart" (Miss Faith Baldwin having taken that for a magazine serial); some months before Monroe had his final inspiration . . .

> *To my dear Barbara, who houses*
> *me and gives me to eat, who*
> *advises me and gives me courage.*

At noon on the hottest day in the full blazing sunlight, on the sidewalk in front of 450 Park Avenue there lay, spread-eagled, flat on his back, face up, a fine young workman.

At first glance I thought him dead, but he was breathing heavily and there was some nervousness of his eyes and mouth: the extreme light perhaps penetrating his unconsciousness, or something in his dream or delirium disturbing him.

Quite golden he lay, wearing no shirt, only faded dungarees; his rough short blond hair and the coarse hair on his chest shining bright with perspiration.

And the many hastening New Yorkers bound somewhere had to step aside, around him, but none stopped or broke step. They cast down at him various looks of concern, or puzzlement, or amusement, or impersonal admiration; but they neither commented nor asked one another any question; neither did I.

But as I drew close near him, and went past him, and left him behind, I had decided that probably there was nothing to worry about: a little madness perhaps, but no injury or illness. Two observations reassured me: under him on the sidewalk he had his shirt spread out. And just around the corner of the building, in the side street, two other older workmen also lay, but as one would expect, close to the building, in the shade, and curled up, in positions somewhat reminiscent of the soldiers asleep at the open tomb in many a painting of the Resurrection . . .

But if it was only just siesta in the spread-eagled one's case also, what vanity or awkward, defiant spirit prompted him to lie so far out on the sidewalk, underfoot of everyone, at some real risk in the full dangerous sunlight risking sunstroke? No telling, no knowing.

The last line of *This Side of Paradise*: "I know myself," he cried, "but that is all." Which I think—whoever may cry it, whether or not it is a sincere cry—is never a true statement. *One never knows oneself*; and it is only a small part of the sentient being anyway.

Conclusion of a love story—Now the tooth is out, but still the tongue is infatuated with the hole.

When Dr. Lovell questioned me about my sense of phallic genital inferiority, the tininess of my genitals, I told him that J. and M. and B. had all referred to it at the time of withdrawing from sexual relations with me, citing it as one reason for their dissatisfaction with me; and that Nick warned me of it before he committed himself to love of me (a kind of saint; for in fact he did more than anyone to heal me of this shame and distress, which counted for a good deal in the anguish of losing him . . .).

Now certainly, whether or not it is psychoneurotic to feel dissatisfaction about genitals as small as mine, certainly it was psychoneurotic if not sadistic to mention it to me in connection with farewell. And I would have so recognized it and dismissed it accordingly, but for the fact that I too felt as my lovers did. I understood so well; how could I not forgive them? And every time, the nature of the forgiveness was like rubbing salt into each little scar . . .

A somewhat dismaying news item: Poor Katherine Anne is returning to the Eastern Seaboard to live, very soon. But where, how, on what? She hopes to find a house that she can afford to buy, with some money presumably still due her. She is as bad about her real estate as I have been about my love affairs; with some abler operator always coming along and foreclosing on us . . .

As for myself, I continue to do a good deal of work—evening hours as well as daytime just lately—some of it semi-secretarial; that is, tidying up and typing and retyping, cleaning and burnishing and varnishing, things that have been more or less done this long time—as one might say, constructive rather than creative. But also new bees swarm in the old honeycombs.

As it seems to me, the story or stories of my life are quite wonderful—but how rarely I get them written, as such. I've had occasion to read hundreds of my letters recently, and I've been dismayed to find how abstract they are—analytical or lyrical—*unnarrative*. And it's not only the rush of events or the slowness of my style or weightiness of my mind—it's something in my purpose, almost always wanting to accomplish something by writing, to teach my various dear correspondents something, worldly wisdom or the like, to build up their egos. Or often enough to benefit myself somehow: to calm and check my wild temperament, to doctor myself into some sufficient degree of reasonableness, healthy-mindedness; or perhaps just to persuade someone to go to bed with me . . . How ashamed I have been of this last maneuver, but not so bitterly now—for that at any rate is a reality, a known knowable, constant factor, and once in a while . . . As for the rest, the abstract altruism, minding other people's business—I seem to be coming around to the opinion that they are rather worthless except to provide bits of story, uninventable plot, passionate dialogue, to be written as such—and certainly that I am worthless except insofar as I do so write . . .

When the family relationships really went to pieces earlier this year, and I was in dangerous temper, I decided I'd better have some sexual intercourse—it was therapy, and indeed my psychiatrist more or less prescribed it—and taking a good look around, not at all sentimentally, there appeared to be only one in all New York the least bit responsive to me . . . One of Carl [Malouf]'s poor boys—he had planned it indeed, from the start, and informed me of it; his form of triangle, the furthest thing in the world from my form . . . Delectable in the one way, the main matter; otherwise pitiful.

This weekend I had to ask him to the country. Of course I understood him perfectly, but I fancied I could manage him; my usual bravery or conceit. He cracked up in the Navy, and a series of four or five Veterans' Administration psychoanalysts have been giving him the superficial treatment; meanwhile the Third Avenue bars, etc. Well, he cracked up on Saturday afternoon. (The sort of thing that I call slight paranoia, but I dare say that's a misnomer: I must remember to ask Dr. L.). I managed him, but it wasn't easy . . . I yelled at him like a sea captain, then made love to him quite a lot. He adores me.

Then yesterday morning I came back to town with him; and while I was around the town, my father suddenly lost the sight of his remaining eye; retina detachment again. So I must go to the hospital at 9. It may be possible for them to operate . . . Then at 11, back to the country, to the county fair—it is Lloyd's hospital [dedication] day, with a beauty contest, etc.

I spent the better part of yesterday with Father*—his little deathbed speeches were wonderful and I was able to cheer him up—and they performed the dread operation in the late afternoon. He came out of the anaesthetic all right.

All my friendships are under severe selfish scrutiny, perhaps in transition, just now. I don't mind solitude, whether or not it is good for me—I enjoy seeing strangers—I suppose I have grown selfish—I seem to have lost the moral vanity, the vain goodness, which made my "friendships" agreeable to all and sundry.

In particular, Tommy† has begun to be spoiled by me, and I have begun to be somewhat difficult with him. He has been a godsend, a godsend. But I am a triangular man, and I shall be much happier when Carl gets home, whatever else develops or fails to develop. On Tuesday evening, for example (before dining at Mrs. Potter's), I went to Third

---

* Bruce Wescott (1874–1953), unsuccessful farmer, talented taxidermist, had long ago made peace with his adult son.
† Tommy Sullivan. Mutual friend of G.W. and Carl Malouf, a war veteran, and a talented illustrator.

Avenue to pay Tommy a call; and it was perfectly delectable. Only I postponed my own final delectation—which is all right for me, if I have another rendezvous to look forward to, not too far forward. We had a rendezvous at dinnertime Wednesday evening.

Wednesday morning I woke at 6 a.m. (after about five hours' sleep, with dreams not all good); then wrote hard for three hours; and then had hell raised with me by the psychiatrist for one and a half hours; then went back to my office and wrote hard for another two hours; then went to the Authors League council, and during lunch and all afternoon, sat in continuous tense debate about copyright and closed-shop and Communism, etc., for five hours—with just time for a bath, etc., before the above-mentioned rendezvous; having had, yes indeed, little man, a busy day . . .

Tommy, after I departed to Mrs. Potter's, painted a bit of a picture, not a good one—(he has painted one that is more than half good, of his pigeons, in oil)—and started to bed with a sleeping pill; but instead teamed up with some girls who live on the floor above, and spent the rest of the night in Twelfth Avenue, until 6 a.m.; but then slept until noon.

I was so tired I wanted to cry. We had to hurry out to dinner, because he wanted to be taken to the theater (that musical with the Gladiola Girl number in it, whatever it's called . . .). After the theater he did not want to go home, to say nothing of going to bed. I suppose it made him restless, he was tired too, but in his case it seems to take the form of restlessness; whereas I just grow feeble and oversensitive. Anyway he got me to go to bars with him, first that Irish Eugene O'Neillish place, and then the place that belongs to a friend of Belle Livingstone's, Mrs. Shaw or some such thing. And I suppose I sulked . . . A drunken female came over to me and told me, "Hey, get the corners of your mouth up! That's what they always tell me, hey!" Mrs. Shaw's was quite crowded and very soused. I suffer just a little from agoraphobia, and after a while I begin to get weak in the knees, I tremble, I bristle, and I incline to kill somebody. Poor Tommy then said, "How extraordinary! All these people who come here every night and hang around for hours, and all they really want is to be at home in bed with someone!" And as this was my own case to a T, it made me feel a worse fool than ever; perhaps I lowered the corners of my mouth again. Tommy said that I made him so nervous that he didn't know what to do; but still he didn't want to go home. Finally I insisted; and we did get to bed at last, about two-thirty; and it was heavenly, heavenly. But next morning I was tired, tired.

* * *

Ll. and I agreed upon a plan of my finances for the present and near future, of which this is a memo:

I will draw fifty dollars a week for my personal expenditures (Stone-blossom bills to go to Eliz. via Anna as heretofore . . .).

Monroe has suggested that, as I am spendthrift and unarithmetical, I'd better have only fifty dollars at a time, give up my charge accounts, etc. This makes me blush, but it serves me right, and doubtless will help me . . .

I can only be happy when I am absorbed in really literary work—and even that wants to be some old manuscript, or at least subject matter of the past, which I can interpret as I see fit, with no one else caring, no committee work, no argument or appeasement.

Dr. Lovell has done me a world of good. He has served as a kind of lightning rod for my tragic bad temper, to catch it and carry it harmless into the ground. He has also confirmed for me with sufficient authority and objectivity the particular problem of Baba's state of mind at this stage of Horneyan analysis. In struggling this way and that, to get out of my painful circumstantial trap, I might have given her a bad setback. Lovell has plenty of respect for homosexuals; and on the other hand, his morality—particularly with regard to sex relationships of homosexuals with women—is quite close to my own. He was really sorry for me, in the circumstances, in the coincidences, which alleviated my self-pity. He would not have me psychoanalyzed for anything in the world. He is keenly, professionally interested in what he expects me to write, about homosexuality and so on—a contribution to psychiatry!—and that lifted up my ego a little. It made me less ashamed of certain considerations of self-interest: Stone-blossom for our old age, and security enough to write scandalously.

We must remember that there is in us all not only conscious and subconscious but also unconscious; not only mind and heart but also that terrible thing which psychologists call the Id (which I call human nature). God knows at any given moment what it wants. I often think that up to a certain time of life it wants just quantity of life, maximum pleasure and power and other mere experience, come what may; and then perhaps it just grows weary, and begins to want just death—which is not necessarily a tragic development, for it may give the mind and heart a better chance.

Having spent the night in New York, returning home—the only home of my entire lifetime, my birthplace was not one—suddenly I observe that great autumn has taken place again, in full panoply and full color, incomparable.

And to think that I have spent all this summer indoors, or with my eyes myopic or introverted; in physical indolence, letting my body loosen to its final paunchiness, puffiness; concentrating on only momentary human interests, attitudes of vain, irreconcilable minds including my own. Fool, fool.

As Thornton Wilder said to me in Villefranche, oh, perhaps twenty years ago, in his intense whisper, "We writers can tell each other all sorts of things, things we cannot and must not write." And, alas, he meant and believed in the negative clause, the *must not*—and he still does. I don't. I do not mean or believe any such thing. Only I suppose I ought not to give myself away too much, or foul my nest too badly, until I get around to writing things properly. Unless I hurry up, and somewhat hold my tongue the while, somebody else is going to get rich on the plot of my life. No copyright on one's fate . . .

Today, all by myself all day and all evening, I have read Henry Green's *Party Going*, and a second-rate detective story, and *The Cossacks*, and a little periodical journalism along with my lunch and my dinner on a tray, and the first few pages of another detective story, while waiting for my soporific pill to take effect . . . Also (let me be a little fair to myself) I wrote some. Now my eyes are pulled tight in their orbits and a little dolorous. Perhaps I need a change of my reading glasses, stronger.

Party Going shows a very decided gift for fiction; but what, more than anything else, it makes me think of is Miss Ruth Draper;* it is mostly mimicry. No very salient thoughts in the way of ethics, morals, or psychology; little or nothing of the cause and effect in the heads and hearts of his characters; only a little sociology, and something about the classes and the masses, that's about all.

Also the realism or surrealism of his reporting of passing moments as they pass seems to accumulate as a kind of crushing burden on the rest of his subject matter, and weigh it all down. The views of the crowd, the horde or mob of commuters jampacked in the railroad station, is exciting; but one is not allowed to keep one's mind on it, distracted every moment by the hallucinatingly true-to-life small talk of the protagonists of wealth and leisure. An aesthetic of fiction of

* Ruth Draper (1884–1956). American monologist.

which there appear to be more and more exponents: much ado about nothing.

A walk in the moody, dusty autumn. It pretends to rain but does not even settle the dust. It looks chilly, but the little swirling breeze is warm.

As much blossom in October as in May; only now the plants of which this is the sex life are half shattered, lowering leaves hanging loose, whispering. The background is exhaustion, mummification. The colors are as pretty as can be, purple and gold and white, and there are berries brighter than any blossom; not to mention the autumn foliage. It is like the final work of one of the octogenarian artists, Titian or Renoir.

From a letter to Bernard Perlin, returning after a year abroad

Just now the day is breaking, with a wash of colors: bright gold on the sycamore trunks, and pink on the stone house amid the shadows of the leaves—we still have had no frost.

Now to conclude: Of course I should love to have you bring me a little present—but rather something symbolic than something precious. No, not *La Querelle de Brest illustrée*. Others have provided me with all the earlier volumes of that horrid author [Genet]; and, come to think of it, my preference in erotica is lower-class, simpler. Instead, when you get to Paris, if you think of it when strolling on the boulevards, try one of those hole-in-the-wall bookshops near the Opéra for an ordinary dirty book—a lot cheaper than Genet-Cocteau, and easier to stuff away in your duffel bag—one of the perennials in outrageous English, only not *The Flea*, which I have.

Oh, this is something I would like: If you pass by Alinari's, see if they have a detail photograph of the head of blind Homer, Raphael's, in the Parnassus in the Stanza della Segnatura; just on the left of the Muses, next to Dante. But don't make it a nuisance to yourself; either the noble or the ignoble symbol.

Eliz. and I have not exchanged a single sentence of personal reference for about two months; we are like a couple of marionettes playing our parts in only the life of the farm, the hospital, the parents—with the right smiles and courtesies. She and Beulah are now holidaying in

Virginia, and I believe Nick is to spend the weekends with them; but I do not even know that for sure.

All along, Baba would not admit to anti-homosexuality (it is a sickness, that is all); and Eliz. surely thinks of herself as having the greatest possible insight and sympathy—but in the somewhat conceited, somewhat motherly, pitying, disrespecting way.

The moral is that one cannot war upon women, one cannot compete with them, one cannot make peace with them. Only in due course they change, for better or worse, and they forget—it is their way of forgiving— and if worst comes to worst, one leaves them high and dry, in their solitude of growing old; and very often in the end nothing matters to them, no one matters to them except their families, their sons, and indeed their brothers . . .

I went to Dr. Lovell as a kind of courtesy to Lloyd and labor-saving device for Monroe; as an act of good faith and to improve my manners— the effect and influence in my case has been mainly literary; and I have enjoyed every minute of it . . . In fact, I have been happier this past month or six weeks than at any time in two years and a half.

From a letter to Dr. Alfred C. Kinsey

First, please, will you accept my apology for not having replied in proper time to your courteous kind letter? Certain excuses for my delay I shall not trouble you with in detail: a little illness, and a project of traveling abroad, postponed from week to week, and now given up for this autumn.

Certainly, if you will ask me your great set of questions, I am at your service, sir.

As I declared to our little writers' conference at Bloomington, and as someone there may have reported, my admiration for your work is greater than for any project of our time that I know about; and with special reference to my own job of fiction writing. What a joy it has been! the example you have set us timid lagging ones, in a field of science so closely parallel to the narrative art; the frontier you have marked out for us.

I live in New Jersey but I can come to town almost any time. So if you will assign me an hour to give you my sex history, ask your secretary to telephone me, person-to-person collect: Clinton (New Jersey) 186 R. Our friend Monroe Wheeler tells me that he hopes to get you for dinner or other sociability, and he promises not to leave me out of the plan.

I had to measure my poor penis in its two states and both dimensions for Dr. K., and roughly speaking, in various connections I have got my sense of humor back. All in all I gave the good strange man the better part of a week: my simple history, then surprisingly, requested by him, a Sunday afternoon of my advice upon his attempting a special study of writers (I discouraged him a bit), and his advice upon my writing stories of homosexual love (he encouraged me). In his investigation of myself, there was very little effect of confessional, except in one particular: something I had not had occasion to tell a living soul, not even Monroe— and K. said, "What a good story that would make!" But by Sunday he had forgotten it—he says they've taught themselves to erase everything from their minds, in order not to embarrass people in subsequent conversations!

The night of the showing of indecent films at Oliver D.'s.

Mediocre films, intended to be rented out to businessmen's smokers, stag parties, etc. Badly done in the first place (why so much bad play-acting and so little fornication?), worn out, broken, cut, and patched together—overexposed and out of focus—all the modeling of the bodies, all the texture and detail of the sexual organs lost—a kind of wrestling match of paper dolls . . .

But the form of the sexual organs, even in silhouette, always seems to be beautiful—it is only the entirety of humans which becomes vulgar or ugly—the entirety including their minds . . . For the beauty of sexuality is in the physiology itself, in the actual working of the sexual organs together, and especially male and female organs—the contrast between the smallness and softness of the male organ in repose and its exaggerated state in excitement and in action, the contrast between the small female aperture (always relatively small) and the large form at work in it (always relatively large)—and above all the rhythm of increasing pleasure, the rhythm of the approach nearer and nearer to orgasm—communicating itself in glorious ripples to the buttocks, hips, thighs, bellies, fingers, toes—and the digging, thrusting, jabbing, probing, the rolling and the heaving and undulating, the female finally lifting in a kind of continuous kiss of the entire body from head to foot.

In this set of films, only one attractive couple—a slim and serpentinely graceful girl and a coarse sullen husky male, not very young but strong, heavy, ex-handsome rather than handsome, with rather pouting lips, slow but shining eyes—and with a singular penis—singular in a combination of strength and weakness. Bulky in its erection—never standing quite erect, drooping—as of its weight—but able to work where he aimed it, and to muster sufficient strength to thrust into the female organ at no matter what angle—even downward . . .

Oliver's young friend Frank attracted to T., and they lay in my arms until they could not resist one another; the triangle as in *Der Rosenkavalier*, and I as the Marschallin had to depart alone. Windy and cold Second Avenue, and my meeting a drunken Negro by whom I more or less expected to be mugged, and my leaping out into the avenue, risking being run over, screaming brakes, a taxicab to Carl's—Carl not there, so home alone—but Carl's the next morning—consolatory pleasure, and then to the country.

I never did contribute to the Goyen* fund as I intended, and indeed promised. But I am still on the Institute grants committee, though I have given the chairmanship back to Van Wyck B.; and I put Goyen's name on that list—so simultaneously did Christopher.

There are two categories of this love life: the great experience of *passion* which straightens out the subconscious which fires the cold or hard heart, which wakes up the intelligence, which perhaps can never be had for the asking (but only by the grace of God, and by the wisdom and goodness of friends who love one) because one can almost never imagine it for oneself in advance—mysterious or mystic, with something of a religious effect: *laudamus* and *magnificat*.

On the other hand, there is the lesser but naturally the more frequent experience, or indeed one may say exercise, of pleasure which puts the mind to sleep and then the body to sleep beside it: peacemaking between the two, until the next morning purified and rested.

Thanks to Carl and Tommy, I am not the discouraged austere submissive regimented abstemious "middle-aged" man I was a year ago. Even six months ago. I am an aroused reinvigorated rejuvenated promising ambitious even conceited man. And my happiness is really dependent on two, not on one . . .

Relations with my brother at this point are enchanting, in brief talks by the way. Really no formal peacemaking—one day he just began

---

* William Goyen (1915–83). Novelist, playwright, and editor.

telling me about his sex life, as of the present; and I had the courage to reply by just comparison and correlation with the equivalent in homosexual experience. Some more of my romanticism, poeticization, thus scaled down (doubtless a good thing): as to heterosexual pleasures—they don't always have the best of it. No one has the best of anything, here below—perhaps a good part of art is to provide a little necessary heaven on earth, if the artist has been lucky enough to acquire and to keep ingredients . . .

They say Elizabeth is unhappy—I see no certain manifestation of that. Certainly she is harder, rougher, more extrovert; perhaps healthier (or is it simply that she is the person on earth whom I understand least—my one untransposable romanticism?). She sometimes doesn't look well—but I myself think that she now drinks a little more than is good for her. She laughs in a new way, boisterously; and when she is pleased, she says "Gosh!" and when she is angry she curses, "God! God!" Oh, I am not self-assured about her, neither do I congratulate myself upon our past relationship . . .

In Richard Hughes's *In Hazard* (which I have read once more and which has greatly touched my emotions once more), old Mr. MacDonald, the chief engineer of the cargo vessel *Archimedes*, in direst peril of the storm, in irremediable weariness of the sea, thinking of his three children for whose upbringing and education he worked:
" 'I'm worth ten of those kids,' he suddenly remarked out loud, with feeling.
"Of course he was: there was so much more of him. For in the long run, if you want to say how much of a chap there is you can only measure his memory. The more he has in his memory the more of a chap there is. By that reckoning the old are often huge, and the young, for all their vanity, midgets. For surely somebody's person—well, it is the whole content of his mind. And there is very little in anybody's mind, at any time, except memory: the mind is nine parts memory, just as a jellyfish is nine parts water."

I have become relatively a cheerful kind of character and would like to spend one or another of the early evenings with Carl and Tommy, perhaps theater (but it seems that even Chadwick cannot get tickets to *Gentlemen Prefer Blondes* until sometime in January; it is what we New Yorkers are crazy about this year, with a great cow of a girl named Channing as "the new Beatrice Lillie.")

* * *

The other evening, at the end of a Sunday of perfect significance and enjoyment, joyousness, Carl and Tommy, had to return in the train with Nick. I was too happy to mind but I shivered quite a while; my body minded, like a touch of malaria.

This is also true, truer: I have been shedding the past; not the old friends as such, but the outworn patterns which are good now for nothing but literature.

What lessons I keep learning: of enthralling, pitiful, angering, thrilling life!

For instance:

Pleasure, mere pleasure, is not all that I strive for (though I *am* a most needful man). There is also human interest and the desire to be beneficial, curative, educative; as though I were at once a devoted, irritable elder brother—vis-à-vis Carl; and an austere, fierce, but soft-hearted father—vis-à-vis Tommy.

And I grow angry at the thought of Carl's becoming a victim of love, letting the world or art or even any length of time be lost for it. Strange, for I am the romantic theorist usually, the one-shot gambler, the wastrel and unrealist. But I want Carl never to fall into any of *my* pitfalls; the world is *never* well lost for love.

1 9 5 0

*I believe that there is a more precise, potent truth
in story than in philosophy. In a truthful account
of something which has happened, our minds
discover, almost without thinking, a kind of
knowledge of the world which lies deeper and is
less subject to perversion and change than all the
rules of ethics cut and dried.*

—"Fiction Writing in a Time of Troubles"

One day Dr. Kinsey said to me, "I have come to the conclusion that the worst thing that ever happened to Western humanity, the chief cause of its weakness and frustration, confusion and bitterness, was the conception of romantic love, about the beginning of the sixteenth century . . ."

"But, Dr. K.," I protested, "by your own account I have not been frustrated, and certainly I am not bitter; and you have never encountered a more romantic man than I . . ."

"Yes," he answered, "for whoever has a talent for it, stoicism and obstination and discipline enough, and good luck, and above all something besides personal relationships to live for, some great career or mission or vocation or art, romanticism is the best way, even perhaps the best means of maximum sexual pleasure in the long run . . . But the ones I am sorry for are those who fall between the two stools . . ."

Yesterday I wrote to Carl, in working hours, breaking that most necessary New Year's resolution, with painful conscience. Stamped for special delivery, Marty had it, to go past the post office; but I ran after him and took it back. Let that be a lesson to me: the New Year's resolution not only broken, but in vain . . . What it is to be a romantic!

The point of that letter was to suggest that perhaps I ought to withdraw for a while, to keep out of the way during this transition time, this ordeal between C. and T., trial or retrial marriage. For in the nature of the case now, it is for each of them to determine for himself, and the two of them for one another; a duality, not a triangle. And it has been evident that all I can do is excite, now one and now the other, now in preliminaries of great pleasure, now in the solemn realization of difficulty or despair—I cannot resolve anything.

In the desert there is one thing more dangerous than mirage, and that is sighting the reality, the real oasis and palm tree and well head and sweet water and thinking it a mirage, not believing it, and turning away.

I have been reading one of old Colette's extraordinary stories, *La Naissance du Jour*, her last great love affair, at about fifty. "At the age I have arrived at, there is only one virtue: not hurting or harming anyone." Her mother told her this, and she tried to live up to it. I try, too, of course, but we cannot entirely succeed, any of us, at anything.

Bernard is Don Juan—more than anyone I have known, and certainly I have learned from him something of that form of destiny which is not in Molière or Mozart or Byron—the sincere self-commiseration . . .

Of all the forms of cancer, this is probably to be wished for rather than any other. It is common, and often does not develop into the throat. The lip is the best place for it to start; the lower lip better than the upper. If it does not recur in five years, it usually is all over . . . Slow in any case, I gather—tedious little surgeries.
So now we can put all that aspect of it out of mind—no matter . . .
I was not surprised at the word of its seriousness, because of the expression on Dr. Solley's face when he first looked, and the tone of his voice: "Gosh! I wish I could get rid of that for you this very afternoon, but I just can't . . ." though afterward he told me not to worry, it probably wasn't . . .
Lovell was surprised and talked to me at length, in the way of reassurance—I must say, it didn't exactly reassure. He has been so discouraged at the changelessness of my life, slowness of my work, developments around Baba and Lloyd, etc., little or no development for me or news about me, except literature prizes and copyright negotiations—he will use this reality severely upon me, I expect.
Meantime everyone is impressed by my not smoking—(Bob Solley can scarcely believe it)—and not only by the efficacy of willpower, all

at one stroke, but by my taking it easy, at least not troubling others with manifestations about it, woes and tempers. I really have been good.

And now I think I can begin to school myself to work. The physical nervousness, the quivers and the jumps, wildness of little muscles, etc., abating now; better every day . . .

The strangest and most touching thing: Someone evidently has reported my news, or something of that kind, to [E.E.] Cummings—I cannot think who; no matter.

Anyway, he has sent me a penny postcard, typed, with no signature, as follows:

> sorry to hear you've been having a tough time; and hope that
> what Lachaise would call ting ("hell-lo, Cum-ming: how-is-
> ting?") goes very much better than well!

I have a new ornament which goes especially well with my new blue-black neo-sweatshirt, and that is a medal which my Monroe especially sought and had blessed for me, for present purposes, from Laghet, which is not far from the residence of our youth. It is the Madonna of Monte Carlo, and the medal commemorates something that happened just fifty years ago, that is, when Monroe was an infant and I a foetus . . . something—I've forgotten what—to do with crowns for both Madonna and Christ Child—and Monroe got himself motored up there by the Honorable Mrs. Reginald Fellowes, who is the daughter of a French duke and an American sewing-machine princess, who was the most notable female Don Juan in Europe in the twenties, who once tried her charms on me on a moonlit terrace over the Mediterranean, only once, and of course in vain . . .

Hypothesis:

Wescotts no good except to write about. No Wescott will ever write—too spoiled, too impracticable, too pleasure-mad—

Just now, opening the pleasant precious Simenon which Monroe has sent me from Villefranche, I turned on the radio for news, and there was the *St. Matthew Passion,* the great opening: "See him! Who? The Son of God"—and I remembered the rehearsal in Evanston twenty years ago; how I waited in the vast almost empty auditorium, and Monroe entered during that double chorus, "See him" on one side, "Who?" on the other, and he had a bandage round his neck, and he, the young undiscouraged all-expectant innocent non-Christian beautiful one, wept . . .

* * *

There is a humorous interest in dictionaries; especially implications of that collective mentality which must have caused the formation and acceptance of certain words. For instance, my old Funk & Wagnalls does not give the adjective *unperceptive*. On the other hand I note with a kind of mixed amusement, *unpervert* as a transitive verb!

In Valéry's *Tel Quel*, Volume II, this is the first entry in the section entitled Literature:

Châtiment.

. . . Et Pour La Punition, Tu Feras De Très Belles Choses.

Voilà ce qu'un dieu, qui n'est pas du tout Jehovah, dit *véritablement* à l'homme, après la faute.

Thrilling to me, as I look back upon a lifetime's luxuries, lusts, humorousnesses, and idlenesses—tragic also, of course, though it does not say *très nombreuses* or *très grandes* . . .

If I ever want this for a commonplace book, I'll have trouble translating: the overlapping words, *châtiment, punition*; also *péché*, which means original sin rather than fault, a little difficult in a Protestant culture. The distinction between the believable, philosophical God—or to be exact, the God of artists and aesthetes—and mere old Yahveh could not be put more clearly in an ample paragraph. The truth is, aphorism is a very extreme, even perverse form of expression—comparable to the strict versifications.

In these past twenty-four hours the springtime has happened—I do not remember ever having noted it so distinctly. Yesterday there were birds, a boisterous robin, a certain larklike sparrow, blackbirds with their sexual mutterings and swelling up of plumage, and the dear doves I mentioned—yesterday there were crocuses—but that was all. As a whole everything seemed unalive, or abnormally sleeping, somewhat like a patient after an operation, sodden, flat, putty-colored . . . But then it rained softly for hours. In the middle of the night the moon strengthened through the clouds in a great formless gleam, as in magic. This daybreak it is primavera: the patchwork bark of the plane trees, semiprecious green; some raindrops adamantine, glittering all the way across the wild acre; the springing lilies and clumps of the daffodils vivid green upon the varnish-brown of dead leaves; the lawn awakened, the sky alive as if it were a pausing wind, as if it were a visible fragrance . . .

* * *

Easter weekend ahead, the only holiday I delight in, the only holy day that seems to me holy, the rebirth of Adonis more than the resurrection of Christ—and I have decided to spend it alone.

Balmy yesterday, it turned cold at sunset, then windy when I went to bed (with the buffetings peculiar to our house, like little thunder), and this morning sunshiny again, but with a sprinkling of snow, like sugar on cakes . . . I woke sleepily, and read *Les Vrilles de la Vigne* to awaken my mind; and then, not until then, realized what day: Easter.

All my life, Good Friday and the Saturday in Hell have been awesome and nerve-racking in a peculiar way. A notion from my childhood, of Christ not really dead but in semblance of death; that is, buried alive, holding his breath, etc., as it might be someone in a circus or vaudeville show, or some yogi, and with anguished suggestion to me of claustrophobia and all that . . .

Reading Colette's *Mes Apprentissages*—pages about Willy's not being able to write, untalentedness or psychic impediment, I am reminded blushingly how much of that there must be in my cupboard: theory and example mixed. If I find time I shall strictly abridge all that sort of thing—or perhaps combine in a real diagnosis or at least case history (this however would be compounding the first offense, the unhappy egocentricity, bad conscience in vain . . .). Whoever my literary executor may be, let him *cut* a great deal.

Yesterday morning I had a most decisive talk about the future, the financing, etc., with Lloyd—perfectly sympathetic to all my needs, and perhaps to all or almost all my feelings. Baba will not, should not, cannot either make decisions about money or handle accounts (he says, dismissing Eliz.'s pronouncements without even homage of argument . . .). He wants me to have St.-bl. in my name at once, and thinks Baba will happily give it.

Jeff Keller arrived, without warning, and stayed the night: Do you remember the cow-tester writer, the Casanova-Shelley, the stammerer? Still wonderfully good-looking, devoted and grateful—still strangely uninteresting, and therefore perhaps no success as a writer, though he works so meritoriously. He has turned from cow testing to expert stonemasonry. He has a young mistress who is the daughter of a sailor-lover of Hart Crane's who married some money . . .

Bulletin on tobacco disintoxication

Two or three times I have had a siege of tickling of my throat which I take to be deviltry of my desire to smoke—otherwise in only three or four days my famous cough and most of the catarrhal effects ceased entirely. I must have had, underlying all my enjoyment, a real allergy.

The deviltry does not cease. Its latest form is a longing for just so and so many cigarettes a day, "like other people," at the formal hours: just after meals, before saying good night, just after lovemaking, etc. But I am not such a weak wit as to indulge.

But the painful moments about tobacco are no matter, anyway— What is wonderful and encouraging is the improvement of my general nervousness, the secondary effects—I am sleeping better, I can sit still without ants in pants, I am ceasing to be hungry between meals, etc.— so, little by little . . .

Somewhat unexpectedly, I enjoyed my birthday dinner party. K.A.P. canceled at the last minute—back in bed. Zosha K. brought me Horowitz Mozart; exchangeable?—Joe Campbell, Hennessy Cognac. (He is editing a *Portable Arabian Nights* for Viking; abridging and synopsizing the Lane translation . . .) George, a great quantity of enchanting small dark red tulips. Pauline, strange idea, Skira's book of Picasso's ceramics; and, if you please, one of the plates—the brown moon-face. Which shall be for Monroe—note that it impresses me far more in three-dimensional reality than in the facsimile—the glaze is wonderful to touch as well as see, like satin or, rather, like lacquer.

Last night Edna came for potluck dinner with me, and Lloyd joined us before we rose from the table—both free on short notice. Charming tales of lunatic females, inmates in or out. Eliz. rather favors the daffy ones, and never fears them. She has one now who believes that she is Truman's daughter (the spit and image of Margaret T., etc.); who is so pious a Roman Catholic that she refuses to believe that she could possibly be pregnant without the marriage rites . . . However in fact she is pregnant; it shows; and she has taken a hot flatiron to her swelling belly, to flatten it, and burned herself . . .

K.A.P. worries me: uneasy conscience, and at the same time ill will; no, not "ill," just hopeless, helpless, and therefore neglectful. She canceled my birthday dinner—and now her niece is getting married, and K.A. is giving a reception for fifty people this Friday . . . It will mean an extra two days in town; and I have a feeling that, daffy creature that she has become, it signifies or symbolizes more than anything. The Southern sociability—in Elinor Wylie,* in Nelson Lansdale, in her; as it were a kind of malaria . . .

Pauline praised my mood, my talk, etc., at my birthday party. Really flattering: she said I was like a diamond, a rare diamond, a *pink* diamond.

The most interesting bits of news are of the fuss about homosexuality in the State Dept.: Richard Rovere in *The New Yorker* very commendable . . . Government now really contemptible, nitwitted. The Democrats started it: "Oh no, those weren't Communists we had to dismiss! They were just queers . . ." The Republicans now have decided to sacrifice our votes: six million, according to Kinsey? Clifton Webb for President? Or a Wilde case, if someone perjures himself. But somehow I have a feeling that it will blow over—Americans are really frivolous about erotic things, for better as well as worse.

From a letter to Christopher Isherwood

I have been charmingly telephoned by W. Goyen, whom I shall see presently—thank you. Did I tell you how Miss [Elizabeth] Bowen stammered her praises of him, with the word "genius" almost truculently? When I said that Stephen [Spender] had called my attention to him, she stammered some more, to the effect that this was almost a *mis*fortune, that he was really better than Stephen understood, etc. . . .

I am profoundly struck by your mention of a worry about your continuing to write scenarios . . . You know, a good while ago, Thornton Wilder, speaking as your admirer to me, as both admirer and friend, harangued me about that. I asked whether he detected any falling off in the quality of your other writing, he said not; but argued that you could not stand Hollywood indefinitely, no one could, and therefore you should be discouraged from just going on in a sort of lifelong habit of earning a living there, you should be goaded to try to devise some other livelihood. (I know how to counterattack him, as to his own way of life and livelihood, but let that pass . . .)

I did look hard at your dyer's hand, at that time, and before that, and since then—and let me say to you, the color of it has not either

---

* Elinor Wylie (1885–1928). Poet, novelist, and the second of poet William Rose Benét's four wives.

displeased me or worried me. Indeed, you are the only Hollywood worker I have known whom I have *not* found demoralized—mainly because (I have supposed) you have seriously drudged. Whereas others, K.A.P. for example, have made or tried to make a racket of it; not honestly intending to give the employer his money's worth or anything like it . . . Humility or even humiliation about some part of one's production probably not so distressing as a vague general sense of oneself as a bad egg . . . I suppose there are courtesans like that, *priding* themselves on not having any orgasm!

It is thrilling to learn that your novel goes forward (mine has been dull and deflated . . .). Bless the new manners; I don't think you can go far wrong in that way. In fact, if I may be brusque and oversimple, I think you have only one general sort of shortcoming as a writer—not enough self-assurance, therefore not enough impulse to write. But that is so simplified that it must seem silly . . . Your mind in your work, as indeed in your talk, always seems to me well inspired; but in your work sometimes not altogether impelled or prompted . . . Sometimes I am hypercritical, and sometimes I find weaknesses of detail that seem of the same nature—reservedness, marginality, and a certain anti-dramatic or dedramatizing spirit.

But, dear Christopher, forgive this half-arsed commentary. My point is to refer back again to what you say of the dyer's hand, etc. I only worry about the things that make you uneasy about yourself, unproud, etc. One thing you and I have had in common, I think, which probably has cramped or slowed up our storytelling: In the matter of homosexuality we haven't been hypocrites like X, we haven't been show-offs like Y and Z; but in one way and another perhaps we have been appeasers.

Jainism (older than Buddhism) reveres a hierarchy of twenty-three saints, Tirthankaras, who have attained Nirvana, who care nothing for the world and exercise no influence on it, who nevertheless or therefore are worshipped as gods. (Thomas Sullivan thinks of his former lovers rather like this . . .)

As I went down a corridor on the second floor of the Hotel Roosevelt, I heard a clear strong voice behind one of the closed doors, giving an order, upon the telephone or into a dictaphone: "And then I want two dozen good-quality half-inch brass knuckles . . ."

Odd and interesting employments, briefly—which must cast a spell on the lives of the employed in question for years afterward. For instance, when Roosevelt flew abroad, a certain young swimming champion was taken along, to keep him afloat if the plane crashed, until rescuers got there.

Re Pavlik [Tchelitchew]'s new work:

The catalogue of the show in Rome has just arrived, with half a dozen half-tones. I said, several years ago, that his art had gone wrong, with the anatomies, heads, sinuses, *et seq*. It was not a question of his craziness—he has always been in a certain way insane, non-sane, psychopathological; but his art, even in pornography, even in the rendering of morbidity, has been sane.

I picked up in the wild acre, and carefully cut and tacked over the entrance to my part of the house, a catenary of ash, almost perfect (as in a geometry book); to bring me luck.

Upon the final funeral pyre of my life some of the brightest or some of the smokiest brands will still be my burning curiosity . . .

A strange weekend, pleasant but not good. Samuel and his friend Charles C.—a c.-t. to beat the band. And I did, in that way, somewhat allow them to make a fool of me; no, that is not putting it correctly—I made a fool of myself, but really only *by myself*, all by myself, in thought, in feeling, in mid-nocturnal solitude. But no one was obliged to notice it; and I bore Monroe's somber disapproving scrutiny peaceably. It seems to me that the time is coming when I shall not want anyone to visit me here.

The large friendly snake really seems to have emigrated, or met with disaster—I seem unable to induce the young one to let me come close . . . Instead I have the largest known velvety, African-black spiders; beautiful but not likable.

Jean Paul Richter's formula for romantic writing, cited by Harry Levin in his James Joyce: "warm baths of sentiment followed by cold showers of irony."

Odd, my knowing almost nothing about this great or semi-great German, so quotable and often quoted.

*From a letter to Mrs. William Rose Benét**

I have had it in mind, and in my heart, to report to you what Bill said to me at the Institute Council that last afternoon of his life. Felicia Geffen† has telephoned to tell me that you would welcome it.

My putting it off, my sense of its being a difficult or delicate theme, was not the usual fussiness of writers, as to the platitude of death, and condolence so overgrown with conventions. Nor was it my mere sorrow, as a friend of half a lifetime; for, as you shall hear, my anecdote really is non-sorrowful or anti-sorrowful. Only it has to be prefaced with a tale of myself, my own state of health, liability to die, etc.—vain and silly to go on about, in the circumstances of his death.

So forgive me the preface, as follows: About three months ago I had to have removed from my lower lip a little lump which proved to be as noxious as suspected: a little cancer. The removal was perfectly successful, painless, not extraordinary in any way.

Only the name of that illness is superstitious now, is it not? And in my case there was something about the presumed cause or causes, and certain coincidences, which appealed enormously to my imagination. Not in dread of death, believe me—my weakness is rather the opposite. Dread of time, lifetime running out, waste of time on my conscience—literary! It made a solemn bell in my mind. For obviously I have not fulfilled my promise, not in anyone's opinion; and all my life has been a unique wonderful opportunity to write greatly, and so on. My procrastination, my sociability, talkativeness, and activeness, my very love of life, and love of friends, all has grown a little dissipated, worrying. Especially since the war, with a certain point of conscience or *noblesse oblige* inspired by the war, I have got upon too many committees and councils and juries: Authors League, Commission for UNESCO, whatnot. And with the hypothesis of cancer, possibly somewhat curtailed life expectancy, all this spring I have been resigning, refusing, reneging, and evading.

At that Institute Council, the day of Bill's death, Douglas Moore‡ offered me a little new honor and responsibility; and I made my excuses as I have done in other recent connections, perhaps hinting, perhaps portentously. Then Douglas Moore challenged me: "What is all this? You worry us . . . What is wrong? Are you really ill?"

---

* Marjorie Flack, author of children's books, was the fourth wife of William Rose Benét.
† Felicia Geffen. Secretary of the National Institute of Arts and Letters and a longtime friend of G.W.
‡ Douglas Moore (1893–1969). American composer, organist, and teacher.

So I stated my case, as above; and of course confirmed the general thought that the chances of cancer's starting again are now, after successful operation, very much in favor. But, I added, I have scarcely wanted to be reassured, for the time being. I have been using the alarm as a pretext for changing my way of life in various particulars; using it not so much against others' importunities as against my own weakness of character. Having spent half my life already, and a great part of it in vain, I am now very willing to be whipped to work; in order not to be put to shame in the end.

Whereupon Bill spoke up: "But, Glenway, are you so puritan, so ill at ease? Do you mean to tell me that you have a sense of having wasted time in the course of your life, seriously? I have no such sense . . . Have you not enjoyed yourself? I have . . ."

And, do you know? as he said this he was laughing at me, because of my expression of willfulness and at the same time of insufficient willpower—but it was laughter so affectionate and indeed so respectful that it was good for me.

"My life has all been a pleasure," he continued, "and though indeed I have involved myself in needless activities and in causes less important than the literary art, and certainly devoted to various frivolities and vain devices weeks, days, hours that might have been spent at my desk, I do not remember any week or day or hour in vain or unavailing. I sincerely believe that if ever I have written anything worth reading, it has required all that previous indirect preparation, accumulation, investment—fallow season every so often, and involuntary cultivation, and scattered seemingly lost seed—to bring it about. It takes a great quantity and quality of living to furnish any little good work of art."

Oh, I think he expressed it in fewer words, simpler. My excitement, and my sense of discipline and education in what he said—not just now, in funereal retrospect, but at the time, with reference to my own ambition and fate—have given it a bigness and even coarseness of phrasing that seems not like him.

But the others will bear me out in the main matter, surely—Katherine Anne, Douglas, Cecil Howard, Isabel Bishop, Felicia, Philip James—they were as deeply touched as I. Bill himself seemed perhaps more amused than emotionally affected. There was a moment of our not saying anything, and we all looked at him, conscious of one reason for our fondness of so many years: that humor, and wisdom, and critical asperity, and lifting enthusiasm—and I think he felt our fondness. He and I wanted to continue the subject, philosophy in a way; but then Douglas and the others shushed us, to get through the agenda.

After the meeting Hannah Josephson gave Katherine Anne and me a lift across town and downtown, as we were in a hurry; and on our way we spoke of Bill's dear mood, and his happy nature; but we also remarked that he looked a little tired, flushed, heavy, delicate. How old was he? we wondered; and tried to figure it out by our memories of Elinor Wylie. If he was as young as we fancied, then, alas, perhaps he was ailing somehow; but on the other hand, perhaps he was older than we remembered, and in that case wonderfully healthy. Healthy indeed, though dead; and young and old indeterminedly; and dear and profound and valuable . . .

Bernard's mother died suddenly—about a fortnight ago. Poor devil, it will make or break him.

I still have some virginity about death, having lost only Frances Robbins *et al.* I scarcely suppose that the passing of Josephine G. Wescott,* that storybook or history-book character, that wearying elder statesman, will trouble me so much, as she is already seventy-four. What if Monroe or Lloyd? No, what if Baba?—and I sit brooding—

My sister Elizabeth is getting married a week from tomorrow, to Joseph Ladislas Baker, M.D., a local Hungarian-Jewish refugee physician whom we all like and respect. We do not know him very well— sudden.

And next Saturday we are to celebrate my parents' fiftieth wedding anniversary with all offspring present, plus all in-laws including Monroe and Nick, here on my lawn, with marquee and piano and accompanist . . .

"The corn was orient and immortal wheat . . ." V. Sackville-West quotes this without identification, and coming upon it with my first cup of black coffee this morning, for a moment I could not identify it, and felt ashamed of my raggedy mind, my magpie cultivation. The Bible? I asked myself sheepishly. Of course not, Traherne, I realized suddenly, Traherne—whom I have always admired as everyone else does, but scarcely ever read, only a bit at a time, because it is cloying, like the richest possible candies.

I have borne Carl Sandburg a grudge this long while, because, in about 1920–21, when I was a poor budding poet in Chicago, he spoke unkindly of me, as to the little scandal of my sexual proclivity. He has

* Josephine Gordon Wescott (1876–1960), G.W.'s mother, maintained a close and supportive friendship with her son.

much mellowed in his old age, and when we meet at the Institute or the museum he appreciates my politenesses; he is pleased to count me as one of his "boys" from the Middle West.

Not long ago Patrick O'Higgins made acquaintance with him down South and, seeking subject matter for conversation, mentioned me or quoted some opinion of mine. What S. said embarrassed and delighted Patrick: "Oh yes, I know him. I knew him when he was just a small kid. He's a fine fellow. Of course, you realize, he's a homosexual. That puzzles me, but you have to be tolerant. After all, you know, Shakespeare and Julius Caesar were homosexuals."

Woods Hole

It is the early morning; my bed faces a great bluish gleam of mingled ocean and island and sky, with swaying of sailboats, distant flashing of motorboats; and in the distance there is a routine crying of gulls rather like babies for their bottles, and downstairs the marvelous caged Venezuelan bird issues his several melodies extraordinarily reminiscent of Wagner.

In creature comfort and scenery and all that, this is surely earthly paradise—and yet I am not enjoying myself in the slightest.

Except for the presence of my Monroe, my great unpardoning undiscouraged consort. He is so beautiful—yesterday, for instance, naked but sitting up in a straight chair and the salt grass against the seascape writing something in his lap, or lying exactly half and half on the sand and in the waveless tide of Buzzards Bay, to keep cool.

I have had to help Monroe with his Soutine book, with one of those will-o'-the-wisp deadlines for weeks. Also, all month, I have had that (in my circumstances) disgraceful trouble known as writer's cramp. I must say it bothers my sleeping more than my writing, but especially sleeping after writing—it makes an unbeatable excuse, but so painful . . .

Turgenev's answer when asked what audience he wrote for: "For the sex unknown." This is truer to my own feeling than Stendhal's "happy few."

There is a sort of pretentiousness, no, glibness, in his assuming that they would be happy. Turgenev is never pretentious.

Stone-blossom

Anna puts up some tomato juice of our own tomatoes; wonderfully thick and vivid. Well, just now I overturned an entire large glass of it in my bed. It was as messy as a murder, and colder.

* * *

The Soutine opening on Tuesday night will be very grand, and (I think) fun, with various Astors, Sitwells, Maughams, etc., to spice the multitude . . . I am dining with Mrs. Astor, after all—her canceling, that is, pretending to cancel, her dinner party was just to punish Monroe for committing infidelity with Mrs. Rockefeller.

Patrick, poor devil, has got the flu, and thus far refuses to go to a doctor, and is feeling acutely sorry for himself. He was to have come to Stone-blossom this Saturday, but had fallen so behind on his work that he had to stay and catch up . . .

Night before last at the jail, we showed *Caged* to the entire multitude of the jailees. Both Edna and I made speeches; to prevent a dangerous mood to riot, etc. Two of Edna's matrons made her terrible scenes, said she was crazy, etc.; frightened to death. But of course all went well . . . Nice contrasts in my life—the Morgan Library multimillionaires one night and that the next.

The autumn destroying itself now, though with some pink and gold still, and I still have two bouquets of ghostly-scented fleabane, and the honeysuckle persisted until last week. Anna's old mother is dead at last, the burial early tomorrow morning; which has inspired Marty to get drunker and drunker. Anna ruined by the long hospitalization, and seven hundred and fifty dollars for the funeral . . . It has been generally agreed that I cannot afford her anymore; but still I have not learned to drive, handicapped by my painful neck all summer, and indolent as always, and afraid.

Tommy sold his first drawing last week, a Bergdorf Goodman advt.—and he should be blissful; but he isn't, because charming little Jerome Sutter is also here and we talk too much French, and Tommy feels left out and therefore, in the neurotic way, a little nonexistent— but blissful in bed.

E. Sitwell is giving a recital of scenes from *Macbeth* at the M. of M.A., with me as her leading man, that is, as Macbeth—and I am almost word-perfect except in the Banquet Scene, which I must make Tommy or Monroe, or both, hear me in, this afternoon. To town all this week, for that, and to give Anna a bit of a holiday, and for farewell to William Maugham.

Strange contrasts in the minds of low-class homosexuals, the cruelty, the hypocrisy, the fateful obstination, the silly humorousness, inscribed in the five-cent pay toilet of the bus terminal. "I'd like to shove my 8″ down your throat and choke you to death with it, you degenerative [sic] cock-eater."

And underneath this, in larger plainer handwriting, "What a lovely death!"

For almost two months I have had a very painful right arm and clumsy hand and numb forefinger. Three doctors disagreed about it; and I, for my part, in the beginning, called it writer's cramp and was embarrassed by the psychosomatic aspect and therefore put off going to a doctor for almost three weeks. By that time it hurt so, especially at night sometimes, lying on that side, I would wake up crying . . . Then one of the doctors put me in a kind of high collar of impregnated bandage, which relieved the pain, which made me look like one of those stout-faced Scottish gents by Raeburn, *et al.*

It appears to have been two things at the same time: a little herniation of a spinal disk, a little arthritis. The former, perhaps, from pruning my sycamore trees stretching up beyond my reach, very well healed; the latter not bad . . . If it recurs badly, says Solley, I may have to stop drinking, even my modest martinis. I shall be a sort of paragon.

In my youth, it was believed in New York that I had danced naked at a cowboys' ball in New Mexico, and later that I was smoking opium with Cocteau, and therefore had ceased to write . . . A little legend-prone . . .

The main thing I discovered in that course of psychiatry (which I ceased by the end of the summer) was how conciliatory, appeasing, overadjusting I have been all my life in the particulars of my sex life— and when the women of my family clamored nevertheless—I felt more independent in a strange way, even solitary; and also perhaps more secretive . . . perhaps I shall never argue morality with anyone again, seriously.

Sometimes I think my fond friends wish I were a eunuch, and no wonder, perhaps—as I make (or have made in the past) such a fuss . . . Someone very dear to me once said it in so many words. But enjoyment *is* the great thing, and it is one of the very great virtues to be able to enjoy what one can get, modestly—and the next best thing is a continued, no matter how anguished, pursuit of the enjoyable. Such is life, until one begins to deteriorate in old age . . .

* * *

The lesson of my life, perhaps too late for me: gather ye, *not* rosebuds, but laurel leaves, while ye may . . .

Janet Flanner has been the most personal and precise journalist we have; the least propagandizing, least prophetic, least opinionated and opinion-molding. Her readers can and do depend on her—not for the dope, but for the data, and everything human. Speaking for myself, she has set my standards of journalism.

The second misfortune of my life (the first was tripping my brother against the hot stove, and burning his hands): I was nine or ten, just before puberty; and Father took me along into the woods, in the late winter, maple-syrup time. We had a farmboy with us, and also my cousin Clyde, a very grown-up and very male boy, my first desire, never enjoyed . . . Up in one of the leafless maple trees I spied a birds' nest, but on a heavy branch, beyond my reach—and I wanted one of the men to get it down for me. My father ordered me to climb up the tree and to help myself to it. I was afraid, and desperately ashamed to be observed in a state of cowardice by the others, especially by Clyde. I suppose Father was ashamed, too—he always wanted me to show off, to my advantage, and creditably to him (oh, he still does). He bullied me until I did climb up the tree trunk, and out on the limb. The limb was rotten; it broke; I fell, onto a stump and the frozen ground; and at first it seemed that my back was broken. For many months I was absolutely convinced that my father had known that the branch was rotten—and had urged me out on it with malice aforethought—after all, he knew everything about the outdoors in general, everything about trees and tree branches in particular. Fateful months, for all that first phase of my life—and of course when my father and mother found out my suspicion, my absolute mistrust, it seemed to them wicked.

Bernard's letter of the twentieth was delivered during a little hurricane. One of our neighbors, owner and occupant of a nationally advertised prefab, lost the entire roof of same, etc. Stone-blossom lost only one old expendable scrub apple tree. But no water, no heat—which will hamper me a bit at my small urgent job for today.

To wit, assembling certain papers and preparing my cards, etc., for a full-length lecture tomorrow at C.C.N.Y. on (principally) Ernest Hemingway, that least popular best-seller; defending him on a good number of the current charges—with a general theme, autobiographical or pseudo-autobiographical elements in contemporary fiction, with (I think) a nice title: "Oneself as Hero or Villain." That old fool Prof. Leffert has misannounced it as: "*My*self as Hero *and* Villain"; and devilish Monroe vexes me by pretending not to see much difference between the two.

George Lynes has taken a photograph of Edith Sitwell as Lady Macbeth—wearing a crown of gilt paper (cut in sharpnesses), looking down her famous nose, and frowning, with both her incomparable hands held up before his, all ten fingers pointing—which seems to me to characterize Lady Macbeth better than most of her reading (except the sleepwalking scene). "Restless, somber, and desolate vanity underlying the Shakespearean ambition . . ."

This last phrase is quoted from my own conversation at George's. Marianne Moore commended me for the three adjectives. Therefore I have remembered to note them.

"As a general rule the most significant period in the life of an individual is that of his development. Later begins his conflict with the world, and this is interesting only insofar as something comes of it" (Goethe).

Conflict with the world, yes—though it be only the pitting of one's willpower against temptations; the maintaining of one's plan against diversion and dissipation and weariness.

Strange to think how luckily my life has gone: I have known scarcely any other conflict. Yet I have a tragic sense. Or, perhaps, only a great awareness of the pathetic . . .

At the same time I am happy in myself, in my potential, in mysticism. Other people trouble me; other people sometimes frustrate me, etc. World politics fill me with horror. I have very grave problems, as to the latter years of my life with Monroe, Stone-blossom or else; and money, like everyone else, more spoiled than almost anyone. And yet I am blissfully happy so often . . .

1 9 5 1

Very great men as a rule seem incapable of any
very satisfactory self-love. They tire themselves
out incessantly, and a great part of their work is
inward, another part is self-expression and acting
out the role of self. Naturally they weary of
themselves to the point of surfeit, of dangerous
revulsion. The mind of the ideal friend provides a
holiday from their drudgery, a shield against
their self-criticism and self-bedevilment, a hidden
pool in which to wash away whatever has put
them to shame, a cool pillow for the hot cheek.
—"Talks with Thornton Wilder"

The only news here at Stone-blossom is the springtime. I have been
rescuing an uncommon variety of white violet naturalized around the
ruin of an old house, where one of my neighbors has determined to
pasture cows, deadly to violets. The most authoritative harbingers of
good weather here are the water snakes in my brook—I counted six
yesterday. They hibernate all in a heap in (I think) a woodpile, and now
they will choose one another and, in pairs, divide up the territory. Two
of them have a manner of hammock of dried grasses caught up in a dead
branch over the water, and there they lie in one another's arms and
make monograms all day long . . .

Item: I was fifty years old last week, and I seem the healthiest
extant creature; a huge, coarse, tough-faced, gray-haired child. At the
same time, Lovell has taken alcohol away from me, for at least two
months. Not because of drunkenness, but to be kept from too much
fluctuation in my blood-sugar count . . . then, once a week I get two
shots in the behind. Whether one of them is the famous adrenal-cortex

mixture I've no notion; probably. I feel fine. I delight in pitchers of ice water, quarts of milk, cans of vegetable juice, and orange and grape and all; as much as I want in the gluttonousness of my mouth.

Baba, panacea-minded, despairing of everything and everyone except the Horneyan elite—"few are called and few are chosen"— prophesies that my drinking friends will not be able to forgive this emancipation; rebelliousness and vengefulness are to be expected. And she adds, if I refrain from preaching, if I underwrite the flowing bowl for them, they will blame me for their hangovers.

This month I am writing an essay on Colette—oddly enough, the first very serious consideration she has had in either language—to serve as the introduction to an omnibus volume. Then back to my own lifelong multivoluminous manuscript . . . In July I shall give six lectures at Kinsey's university.

Last January, we nominated Osbert Sitwell, along with Braque and Henri Sauguet, for the honorary associate membership of the Institute. Bertrand Russell also had some backers, reminded by the Nobel Prize, and this is what Katherine Anne said, to knock him out: "Philosophy is an ephemeral form of literature. Osbert Sitwell, as a pure literary artist, concerned with everlasting aspects of the world and of human nature, will be read with delight and benefit long after Bertrand Russell has grown incomprehensible."

The same evening, I nominated poor Carson McCullers. She is such a proud devil; I think our homely pale-purple and yellow rosette will add some years to her life, which always need adding . . . Katherine Anne does not approve, but kindly restrains herself from opposing. I shall ask Mr. Faulkner to second. I understand that he is a curmudgeon, but I shall say that this is his duty; as 'twere parental duty.

Sense of guilt; more exactly, sense of transgression—and my mal-formation of the chest. I must reread Longfellow's poetic drama of the New Salem sorcerer who was executed by the heaping of a weight of stone on his chest, more and more until it collapsed and he was dead. I remember associating this with my homosexuality—

This was not, however, my first observation and awareness of the hollowness of my chest—that was during my love affair with E.R.K. One effect of it is to force my stomach and abdomen in general a little farther down in the torso than it should be—making an effect even in boyhood of a little round potbelly; and as I passionately desired to have a baby by my young lover, and prayed passionately for this miraculous outcome, I remember looking down at my paunch and asking myself: "Is it possible? Can this be it?"

Charles Williams* points out one of the advantages of ceremony or formality: "It gives a place to self-consciousness, and a means whereby self-consciousness may be lost in the consciousness of the office filled or the ritual carried out."

In its context, in *The English Poetic Mind* (pages 116–17), this refers to Milton's verse style. But of course it is applicable to a wide range of human interests—as, for example, religion on the one hand, fashion on the other, and psychotherapy on the one hand, etiquette on the other—and I think he wanted to suggest all that.

The thought of an artist has to be running water; one can't be exactly true to oneself.

X, for all the consequential years of his young life, has lived with Y in a homosexual relationship certainly more respectable and more intense than the average. Now Y, a veteran of World War II, has been called back into the service, which is hard for X.

Last night he said, in his slow boyish way, moderate but emphatic, "Oh, it has been hard to accustom myself to being alone at night."

For a moment no one said anything. What indeed was the thing to say?—A facetious impropriety on the one hand; some softness of sentiment on the other . . .

Then he continued: "Night before last, in the middle of the night, I was wakened by a voice calling from the street under my window, 'Help me! Please help me. Somebody, come down here and help me!'

"I sprang out of bed and rushed to the window. There is a streetlight just here, but I couldn't see anyone. I didn't hear anything more. I didn't know whether it was a reality or a nightmare."

"Was it a male or a female voice," I asked, in a not facetious tone.

"It sounded like a very young boy," he said.

Bard College gave a doctorate to Wallace Stevens, who said, "An honor done to a poet is a poetic act . . ." It was their ninety-somethingeth anniversary, and Kenneth Burke and I gave lectures. His subject was the Orestes trilogy of Aeschylus . . . He is a friend of many years, but

* Charles Williams (1886–1945). British novelist and poet.

I have never been able to understand one word of his philosophy books. Even in the course of his lecture, when he took up a manuscript and read a few paragraphs, I blacked out. But when he simply talked, in an ardent roughish Greenwich Village–Irish way, it was like that scene in Wagner where someone puts on a different sort of hat (is that right?), which enables him to understand birds; delightful. My subject was the poetical novel: *Mrs. Dalloway* and Mrs. Woolf, the poetical as a form of secretiveness, the postponement of suicide as a sort of morality, even sainthood.

The Duchess of W.!—"I have superseded Mona Williams.* I am the Queen of the pederasts now."

Edna Ferber, with her somewhat buffalo-like face, and her long, stiff upper lip (like my grandfather's) pressed down thinly on the lower, holding her head not only up but back, at a sort of combative angle, with hair well coiffed and dressed to kill. She has no charm, but a sort of brilliance, especially at lampooning people.

For instance, one evening she went to confer with Arthur Hays Sulzberger† upon some matter of policy to do with Zionism. "And I must frankly confess to you," said Edna, reporting on the conference in her harsh, overaudible, but not really loud voice, "I must admit, I had no notion what an old and aristocratic family the Sulzbergers are. They are unique. The Pilgrim Fathers came a good deal later. Arthur told me all about it, and I was edified, not to say spellbound. I was, as they say at Sardi's, riveted . . . Why, it appears that when Columbus discovered America, there was a particular Indian who was the first to welcome him. He came running down the shore with outstretched arms, bearing gifts, of fruit, flowers, feathers, beads, wampum, and that Indian's name was Sulzberger!"

Fear and Trembling: my least successful book, by whatever criterion of success; written very rapidly and emotionally, with a great sense of its importance and utility, in anticipation of World War II. It sold somewhat less than a thousand copies, my friends and usual readers saw no sense in it, and the press despised it. After a while I realized that, in spite of its foresight, and good passages of poetical and witty

---

* Mona Harrison Williams, a wealthy socialite and a friend of Lady Emerald Cunard, the London literary hostess and patron.

† Arthur Hays Sulzberger (1889–1968). Publisher of *The New York Times* from 1935 to 1961.

writing, it was not a good book. My sense of its failure had a depressing effect on my talent, never very well assured anyway.

People who oversimplify their sex lives are much inclined to pontificate, I have found; Turkish baths are especially conducive to smugness . . .

Absurdity of Auden's authoritarianism—or his bossiness . . . Taking his own several little emancipations as a model, he orders other people to become, as promptly as possible, like unto himself:

> *Thou shalt not be on friendly terms*
> *With guys in advertising firms,*
> *Nor speak with such*
> *As read the Bible for its prose,*
> *Nor, above all, make love to those*
> *Who wash too much.*

What a hue and cry he would howl if anyone had ever suggested that, "above all," Auden himself might wash somewhat more . . .

As I sat on Lovell's sofa waiting for him to look at the canker sore, there took place just within earshot a terrible little dialogue—a terrible-looking, husky youngish man, gangsterish perhaps, was pleading to see Lovell, pleading and pleading in a low murmuring voice, shaking his head back and forth, pleading and being refused—the little front-desk nurse, perhaps afraid of him, standing well back behind her desk in a doorway softly repeating, "No, Dr. Lovell has discharged you, don't you understand? No, not even ten minutes. He is sure that he cannot do anything for you. Don't you understand, you are not his patient anymore, no, no . . ." It was a soul being damned to hell, and it broke my heart, because the conclusion of love is sometimes so much like that.

Bach's soprano trumpet, in the major Brandenburg concertos, sounds like a Baltimore oriole, a male, or, to be precise, two males, when they are amorously competing, truculent and blissful.

Katherine Anne is romancing with W. Goyen—passion for some weeks at Yaddo. Now he has gone back to the desert, and she talks of the future. She is penniless. Her health is better just now—she has given up cigarettes—but no one takes a very bright view—

I am inclined to envy anyone whose beloved is healthy and happy and strong, so that one may lose one's temper without doing any real harm. Even heave ho! out of one's life, one fine day, if one feels like it—no bones broken . . .

Dr. Kinsey has asked me for a list of the top-ranking contemporary authors, with some indication of sexual subject matter in their work, and of their use of autobiographical material . . . I am a great promiser. I attempted to fulfill as soon as I got home; but I bogged down, I began to question the worthwhileness of any such thing, I procrastinated. I am not really slothful; only I undertake too many little things—Paul Cadmus says that this is a form of sloth—and whatever the undertaking, big or little, I am apt to conceive more than I can chew. I am a great elaborator.

When Richard Hudson engaged me for this year's Writers' Conference—and I received Dr. Kinsey's welcoming letter, I began listing again. It has been my pastime and my trouble, my secret and my bad conscience, all this month, in the intervals of my Colette introduction. On the one hand it is a great piece of presumption; on the other hand it is only a lick and a promise. I have not dared to ask Monroe's opinion; he caught a glimpse, and (I think) looked down his nose.

As for my evening lecture at the Writers' Conference, I have decided on the Virginia Woolf. It is not minutely critical, it is rather narrational; that is, it does not call for any great familiarity with the detail of the novels in question. It is also constructed better than the Hemingway lecture, therefore easier to deliver, which is important, when I have to work all day long that same day. Then too, I shall be specially conscious of a New Critic or two, and a New Journalist or two, in the evening audience—and my Hemingway discourse is too indiscreet for them.

A rather dim emerald morning. I refrain from waking Monroe, who came out on the bus late last night, sickish and pseudo-furious . . . He has had a bad bronchial cold all week, and I bullied him into going to the doctor, who forced a typhoid shot on him, into him, which made him sick. (The doctor has had bad reports from Italy about typhoid . . .) All this because he is about to fly abroad; next Tuesday, that is, the sixth. He will travel southward to pay a call on Maugham if he is then in residence.

Last year Monroe and I promised each other to manage so that I could accompany him next trip. Alas. For one thing I have not succeeded in getting Stone-blossom deeded to me, though it has been promised in good faith—insofar as the absentminded can be faithful. Now Baba's father, paralyzed, in a wheelchair, and with wife number six, the wild little Spanish creature, is flying back from the Philippines, with no house to move into; and I do believe that if Stone-blossom were unoccupied, Baba might not know how to keep them out of it, but possession would appear to be, indeed, nine points of the law. Wescotts, both of the blood and of alliance, are a lawless lot. It would break Monroe's heart to lose Stone-blossom.

Very strange, and in a way thrilling; Monroe let me read Willie's last letter. Perhaps he wouldn't have, if he had stopped to think what was in it. Comment on my having given up fiction writing: "Wonderful!" Willie always the judge, never the physician . . . but compassionate. I'll always remember one bitter afternoon (I was then in my forties; a bit late to change vocation!) when he bluntly but not unkindly asked me, "Whatever gave you the idea, whatever made you think, that you had the talent to be a novelist?"

Oh, how ill I have planned it all; what a fool's life! But let me state something that I am usually, I suppose, too puritanical to admit: I fancy that I have enjoyed life more than anyone. Feeling that I have not deserved my good fortune and happy nature, I must have seemed ungrateful . . . And now, with my senses keyed up a little further by the deprivation of tobacco and alcohol, I am in a way blissful—my chastity, enforced just now by misfortune, turns to a mystic notion; my particular sorrows seem to me at worst a fascinating spectacle.

I have scribbled a good bit about Colette, from daybreak on, about the utility of fine style, what is the purpose of it: to clarify and enlighten, to distinguish and discriminate, to keep the blessed present moment (Faust's *Augenblick*) from passing; to presume from mortality, a sort of embalming fluid—the sweet body odor of Marguerite Moreno, especially a place on her neck, under her ear—ditto of Alexander the Great, in Plutarch. But is there any likelihood of my being able to find a place for these two pages in my essay, in its final construction? I'm afraid not.

What a grave lesson I have learned about myself in the course of this year's love affair! Certainly I spoil my young lovers, so that it is no wonder they use me ungenerously, and they derive from me nothing but a development of ego—no discipline, no therapy, no wisdom. Lovell has suggested that it is a sense of guilt in my own psychology which makes me so weak. But I don't understand it so . . .

My weakness is imagination, with perhaps a kind of vanity. Thus: it has seemed to me that the difference between T.'s just managing to keep going and, on the other hand, breaking down altogether, has been my loving kindness, palliation, good cheer. At every moment I can imagine breakdown, and I am racked by my compassion.

My other weakness is horror of chastity, dread of being left absolutely to my own devices. I don't approve of being by myself in the non-working hours; I don't approve of the kind of passive happiness, by the non-stimulation of desire, which I have begun to develop in the country . . .

But the worst inconvenience brought about in my character by chastity—the form of melancholy which I chiefly dread—is the vacillation, indecision, planning to plan and not succeeding in planning; just sitting in contemplation of the fact that I have no optimism . . .

Later: Disapproving of the vacillation above all, I called Jojo; and offered to cook dinner Monday night; and sure enough, he did ask to bring his guy, and I demurred, but I couldn't stick to it. Then I said, "Shall I not ask a fourth? Who? Bill?" And he replied, strongly, "No. Let us just be three."

Thus, for whatever reasons, every sort of intimacy is very expensive for me. Except for my spoiling, everyone would leave me all alone. No one at all pleasant makes any sort of approach to me—except those who foolishly expect me to get them Institute grants for their novels, or to buy their abstract pictures, or whatever . . . But I don't approve of thinking any of this; it is misanthropy, cynicism.

Monroe writes that Willie is being unkind to Alan. Of course the remainder of his life, and all the fair world he travels around to look at so fondly, is but a death cell. He feels condemned. And any sense of not having his own way in the interval fills him with self-commiseration and indignation. It is strange, when he has studied so earnestly . . . The success-seeking life does *not* lead to philosophy, because it goes counter to the grain and pattern of existence, which is tragic. Further, his principles have been so far inferior to his practice. He has seemed almost to cheapen his lifework by his foolish account of what he has worked for—foolish and, in a way, affected. Cynicism in avoidance of pretentiousness . . .

One of our new roses has blossomed, thrilling—the darkest red (beet-red plus lampblack)—with petals curled back tight, flattened back, to show stamens.

I think I am the best bouquet-maker I know. Pink alsike and purple vetch trailing out of a goblet. A compotierful of elder flowers and roses—this last makes me laugh aloud; it is for a wedding—

The young orioles outside the window are voracious. Both parent birds are kept busy. The male doesn't mind my watching; the female suffers, chatters.

Could I not be content without any accomplishment of art; making a sort of art of spectatorship, as multitudes today do with their spectator sports . . . ? I should think so, except that the frequentation of certain men of great character has made me ashamed to . . . Just now, for example, Kinsey; and indeed, in a way, Lovell—and all my life, Monroe, who seems unflagging as the weariness of middle age touches him . . .

My essay still hasn't got going. I haven't failed to work at it, but in my damned way, scribbling new thoughts, not perfecting anything, not quite conceiving the form, the order, the dimensions, the proportion— Now I have begun to be desperate, and I assume or presume that I shall be able to buckle down—

The cold and wet spell has ended; it is bright and hot all day, with round silvery clouds, and very cool with the moonlight. Fantastic fragrance—these are the weeks of most multitudinous small blossom: the gleaming white daisies still, and dead white campion, and buttercups; and honeysuckle in its overripeness, like a fruit; and all the clovers in their simplicity and glory, the green-white and the pink-brown and the rosy purple and the yellow; and elder and milkweed starting. Over the field, the blue distance—thus, three dimensions, a perspective.

Which reminds me: K. Clark's *Piero* has disappointed me. Wonderful passages about mathematics of composition, about color schemes as such, etc., but an odd dearth of the poetical and narrational, indeed the iconographical.

A postcard from [Nelson] Lansdale in England, to tell me that at a performance of *Oklahoma!* he wept in memory of me. Oh well, some part of everyone's life is intended to turn out idiotic—it prevents the sin of pride . . .

This is the season of the graveyard lilies and of black-eyed Susans and milfoil and water hemlock and—this is the season of wild black raspberries—just enough juice in them to convey the musky taste to one's tongue and seeds very pleasant to catch between one's teeth . . .

Excitement today: a young copperhead in the brook; so Bernard and I identified it, and he killed it with a whip scythe—worrisome and sad.

It seems certain now that I am not getting my Colette essay done on time. It makes me so angry at myself, so injured in point of pride, that some of my time, some of my energy, goes to waste. So perhaps tomorrow I'd better notify Helen [Straus] and George Joel. It would not be serious if I were not committed to Indiana—what I do not produce before the seventh having to be put off until the seventeenth or eighteenth.

Nothing is wrong with it, or indeed with me—except that I haven't been able to increase my working schedule to any effect beyond six or seven hours—only this morning is well inspired, forceful, and cheerful . . . Shall I buy Benzedrine today?

Nothing wrong except the faults of my character—indulging too long in the general study, the expansive and discursive notes, seeking to discover what to say. It is true that when I accepted the job, I really had nothing in mind. I stalled too long, expecting a miracle of myself when the time came, cutting it too close. Perhaps my worst fault: a sort of optimism, refusing to take a dark view of circumstances . . . therefore always, in spite of knowledge, surprised, dismayed . . .

Dinner with Marco and Harold and G.P.L. The meal was a wonder, especially the cream of sweet pepper soup. And the young man of G.'s whom he brought this time, Weslow, is not only the most beautiful but the funniest, in an obstreperous roughhousing and camping way, grade-school level plus Alaska plus Broadway . . .

Tommy was to have come out last evening, but after tergiversations he felt too ill. Diarrhea and nausea and dizziness; solitary-confining himself in that deadly little room again, etc. He won't go to a doctor; he won't even take his annual VA physical examination, though he is afraid they may take his disability payment away from him; and he is letting the rest of his G.I. money go by not enrolling at the League. I begin to be afraid that it is one of the psychopathologies which can only get worse.

Javanese weather—torrential warm rain at least once a day . . .

Yesterday I did a wonderful lot of work (with, let me confess, one half of a Benzedrine). Optimistic again; or is that just some more of my melodrama?

There was an hour-long, insufferably sentimentalized dramatization of "Noon Wine" on WNBC last night. I only listened to a few minutes but I telephoned Porter and pretended. She sounded fairly energetic; choked a bit, but specified that it was only getting a swallow of her new tipple, namely, grenadine, down her Sunday throat . . . She has under way four magazine pieces, amounting to two thousand dollars. One of

them is one of her attacks—against the twenties—for Russell Lynes*—
and when she bogged down, he came and spread her manuscript out on
the floor and selected some fifteen of the disjoined pages and will do
the joining himself. "Honey, you should have an editor like that, ha
ha!"

According to the orator Lysias, Alabrades and his friend Axiochus
married a girl in common, whom they enjoyed turn and turn about. They
had a daughter thus of uncertain paternity and, when she grew up, also
enjoyed her, each one declaring upon these occasions that she was the
other's child—

Oh, my love life would be so happy if it were only spectatorship,
but it is in fact only envy.

In my list of calamities the other day I forgot to say that the snake
Bernard and I so overexcitedly destroyed was not a copperhead; and I
have really suffered remorse.

The velvety leaves of the peppermint geraniums catch so much dew
in such fine particles that from across the lawn they appear silver-gray.
While dusting Monroe's rosebushes with what's-its-name—the chemical
compound that supposedly will save them from insect voracity—I catch
sight of five large spiderwebs drawn across the brook, and I dust them
also. As pretty as a picture!

Americana

Someone has named his little summer residence on Fire Island
"Psy-cottage."

Nationwide advertisement: "Levi's Dungarees guaranteed to fade
and *shrink*." (My italics.)

Bloomington, Indiana

Friday the 13th, and my big day, and I am weary—I have given
four one-hour lectures to my group of twenty-five; I have perused fifteen
manuscripts, and given three-quarter-hour talks to each of the fifteen
inditers; and eaten my three meals a day with my colleagues *et al.*
(except three meals with Alfred [Kinsey]); not to mention cocktail parties

* Russell Lynes (1910–   ). Editor, writer, brother of George Platt Lynes, and friend of the
Wescott family.

before dinner and nightcaps after lectures—with maximum celebration and maximum *cabotinage*— Three of my students are psychopathic, three are subnormally stupid, one is a vain hideous Communist professor, two are talented—

Just now I heard someone below on the campus (I have a beautiful room in a tower) whistling *"Warum willst du den kein Jages."* I teach under a tree (in spite of chiggers)—I did not say it was like Plato, but one of my students did—and a pair of cardinal birds like the noise I make, and they keep swooping and perching about.

I haven't had any fun at the Institute for Sex Research thus far. No time . . . Mrs. K. is one of the greatest of cooks—if Alfred were not the hardest-working of men he would be the fattest. They have a new $1,000 phonograph—I've never heard anything to equal it—he plays Palestrina, Sam Barber, Beethoven—which is reposeful.

The Institute has been on an emergency assignment almost all week in the field of humane citizenship—eight of them, including an endocrinologist and a lawyer from other departments of the university. There having been two or three rape-murders in California, both houses of the legislature have passed a terrifying bill, with long prison sentences, in some cases as much as lifelong, for sex offenders, including ordinary homosexuality—with the specification that you can be let out if you voluntarily get yourself castrated. Praise heaven, the governor, [Earl] Warren, has refused to sign it until he has had the advice of medicos, psychiatrists, and Kinsey and Co.— He is hopeful.

Ah, now I must get to work on my Virginia Woolf cards for tonight.

Caroline Gordon (Tate)* has just harangued me for twenty minutes on the telephone about the greatness of Ford's Roman Catholic historical novels . . .

Day before yesterday, I finished with my poor writers, including an oldish woman who boasted of a demand for her work, especially in Canada, also in Ohio—"Only *I hate Ohio*. You see, my first husband was murdered there, and, oh boy, that burned me up. I made up my mind I'd never contribute to that state."

My Virginia Woolf lecture was a success—the length perfectly adjusted now—I didn't have to skip over any of my cards; I ran only five minutes over the hour— The audience, as you might say, "tickled . . ." Allen Tate in a fury: "It was brilliant but, Glenway, I

---

* Caroline Gordon (1895–1981). Novelist and poet, wife of Allen Tate (1899–1979), poet, critic, and biographer of Stonewall Jackson and Jefferson Davis.

don't think you said two true things from beginning to end." Especially certain epigrams against Henry James outraged him . . . "Why, Glenway, you can read and write, can't you?" —"Well, Allen, I'm not sure; I think you'll have to define your terms."

In the afternoon I skimmed a couple of shelf-fuls of terrible fiction—one good odd coarse truthful Henry Miller—and I saw the porcupines, and some youngsters. The former are weird, in a way more human than monkeys—slower, moodier, soberer—in their great overcoats, only shining eyes and occasionally bared teeth showing through their all-over beards; like nineteenth-century men of genius, Tennyson, Ibsen, Whitman—

One thing I have learned from Kinsey and Company—not of course from the Writers' Conference—is the advantage of absolute recreation—ten hours' work—four hours' home life or sociability—then another four hours' work—but in the rest interval almost no exercise of the main part of the mind—the smallest small talk, mostly about gardening and phonograph records, etc.

Newport

One excursion worthwhile: not the robber-baronial palaces (I have no sense of humor about things not intended to be funny) but the eighteenth century, of which I had not been told. Prettiest of all, the syn agogue, the oldest in this country: pure Louis XVI—with teenage Orthodox boys obliging you to put on black crepe-paper skull caps. "Certainly not!" said Monroe, dismaying them—but then whipped out his own beret. And Katherine Warren has the most beautiful beech tree in the world, half copper—and half water—in a sort of open-air salon—And Nin Ryan has Canada geese, which do corps-de-ballet runs across the paddock . . .

First sentences of possible, very short stories, all conversational:
1. Pauline said, "The only man who ever beat me was one of my mother's lovers, and I slipped away from him, under the bed."
2. Monroe said, "Geordie, now tell us again how you set fire to Mount Lamentation."
3. I was in the bathtub with the door open and I heard Monroe as he came in from the garden:
"I don't approve of it, but I wish to perpetuate it."

I could not for the life of me have guessed what he was talking about. (*Geordie's mustache—!*)

One should not ask, of a youth like R., whether or not he really loves one; how much; is it worth whatever the cost may be? He is too immature; too unskilled in verbal formulation; too male; too proud and uneasy, anxious and unrelaxed. Also, don't forget, love is not a merit, not always a good thing, *per se*. Especially quantitative love, muchness of love, is as likely to do harm as good. It is expressive only of the force of the lover, not exactly of his goodwill or good intention—for the very simple reason that so much of it is not under his conscious control, so much of it is subject to the limitations of male potency, and to the natural male dread of impotency.

Oh, blessed right-minded Tom Brown! I do not refer to the boy-hero of Aldous Huxley's great-grandfather's silly novel, but to Dr. Johnson's first schoolteacher, who compiled a spelling book and boldly dedicated it—to the Universe!

As for my dear Doctor and fellow-Thespian Edith: I had a dream of reading this sentence in a newspaper: "Dr. Edith Sitwell has gone to Scotland, where she will be visited by the symbolic wild boar." Charmed by this, rash fool that I am, I wrote her a little letter about it, since which time—six months!—she has suspended our correspondence.

I think it is immoral to determine one's circumstances in terms of love *alone*. Love is to be judged by its results, its fruits; therefore in relation to work, health, duty, art, education, family, even citizenship.
Furthermore, for my part, I no longer believe in the pattern of two-part lifelong relationship, the imitation of matrimony. Even male and female matrimony is not, as a rule, for the most part, in the long term, really a sex relationship. In the honeymoon period, yes!—and afterward when sexual energy has abated, or hardship of life requires it to be subordinated, yes, but as a mere convenience . . . Otherwise matrimony is parental; social; financial or ambitional; residential; sometimes just friendly, and by way of insurance against the loneliness of old age.

Last night, while sorting magazines, throwing away most of them, I came upon the issue of *Harper's* containing Katherine Anne's portrait of Elsa [Maxwell], which I kept. With no intention of reading, rereading, just then, my eye lit upon a chance paragraph, and it gave me gooseflesh

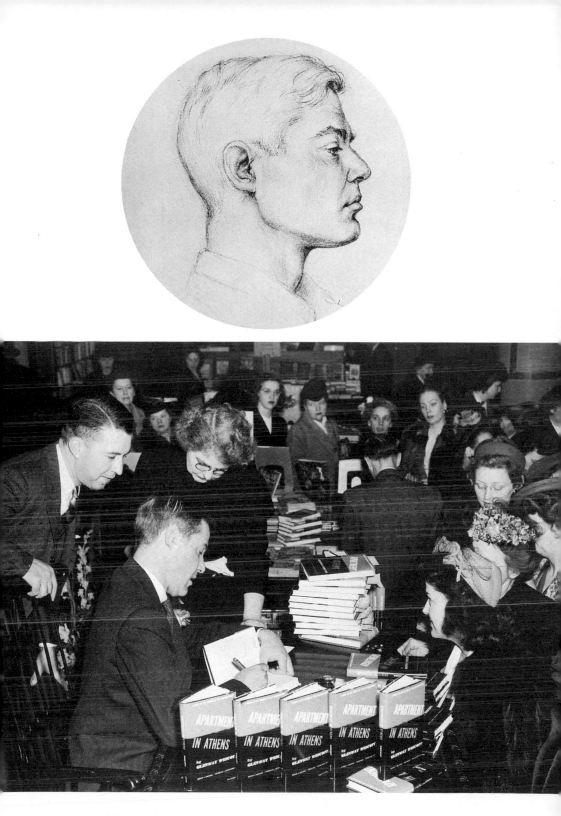

(*Above*) Sketch by Paul Cadmus, 1943. (*Below*) Signing copies of *Apartment in Athens* at a Chicago bookstore

(Right, top to bottom) At Stone-blossom with Louise Bogan; with Pauline Potter, May 1951; Wescott, with Wheeler *(standing)* and a visitor. The pictures above the mantel are silverpoints by Bernard Perlin of Lloyd Wescott, Somerset Maugham, and E. M. Forster

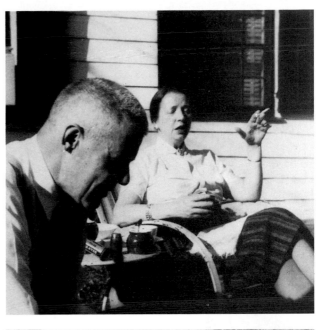

(Opposite, top) Stone-blossom, home to Wescott and Wheeler from 1937 to 1957. *(Bottom)* Sketch by Paul Cadmus for a portrait of Wheeler, Wescott, and Lynes

(Above, left) Portrait by George Platt Lynes: *"My notion of myself, fairly constant from year to year."* *(Above, right)* Portrait by Charles Caron, 1952. *(Left)* At home. *(Opposite, top)* At his desk. The painting, by Tchelitchew, shows George Platt Lynes. *(Bottom)* Writers' conference at the first Congress of Cultural Freedom, May 1952: Cyril Connolly (far left), Stephen Spender, and Czeslaw Milosz (second from right) can be identified in the back row; in the third row from the back, James Farrell (with chin in hand), Robert Lowell, Wescott, and Katherine Anne Porter; at the table, André Malraux, Salvador de Madariaga, Denis de Rougemont, William Faulkner, and W. H. Auden

(Opposite) At Stone-blossom. The painting, *Washing the Blood from Daniel Boone*, is by Jared French. (Above, from top) Gathering before Truman Capote's black-and-white ball, November 1961: Monica Stirling, Virgil Thomson, Natalia Murray, Wescott, Janet Flanner, Anita Loos, Wheeler; with Philippe de Rothschild and Stephen Spender at Mouton-Rothschild, Christmas 1969. (Right) *"In 1971, when I thought that I could trust myself to complete and publish the intricate little book entitled* The Odor of Rosemary, *this was the likeness that I wanted on the jacket"*

Wescott and Wheeler in their eighties

immediately. As if it were a bit of Byzantine mosaic suitable for a ring or brooch.

If I were her publisher I think I'd pay her by the page, with perhaps a slight bonus for pages that connected in some way, but no insistence on any preconception of her form.

Said I explanatorily to Lou S., passingly, with no improper or even intimate detail: "I lost my virginity in a bed with two other boys. One of them was, indeed, asleep; but he was there, and perhaps it was then that the pattern of my life first appeared . . ."

Leonardo in his youth had not enough facility to do the work there was a market for, so when he went to the court of Milan, it was not as a painter but as a flute player, and after he got there, he undertook the hairdressing for the Sforza ladies upon state occasions, and then presently, irrigation, and later on, the inventing of horrendous weapons of war.

The morning is my best noticing time; my senses freshened by sleep, even by little sleep, and my blood-sugar level wonderfully responsive to black coffee.

Looking toward the daybreak through slight mist, rectangularity of the neighbor's cattle; indeed oblongness. They seem not to like to face the sun; I suppose their eyes dazzle.

Perhaps I might not notice any such thing if I had not, at one stage in my life, greatly enjoyed Cuyp and Potter.

The working methods of Matthew Fontaine Maury, the nineteenth-century sailor who founded the science of oceanography:

"He laboured assiduously to obtain observations as to the winds and currents by distributing to captains of vessels specially prepared log-books; and in the course of the nine years he had collected a sufficient number of logs to make two hundred manuscript volumes, each with about two thousand five hundred days' observations. One result was to show the necessity for combined action on the part of maritime nations in regard to ocean meteorology. This led to an inter-national conference at Brussels in 1853 . . . which produced the greatest benefit to navigation as well as indirectly to meteorology." (*Encyclopaedia Britannica*, eleventh edition, Volume XVII, page 916.)

This makes me think of Kinsey, and the work of his Institute for Sex Research.

* * *

An intelligent, reasonable, and self-respecting man can indeed learn *not* to be ashamed of masturbating, yes indeed—I have learned; in fact at this age I am sometimes inclined to feel that I ought to masturbate more than I do.

I find in a notebook in which there appears the label of a stationer named Schroeder in the Invalidenstrasse in Berlin, and in one of the mannerist stages of my handwriting—I suppose it must be 1922 or 1923—this sentence from Leigh Hunt's *Autobiography*, which still strikes me with its perfection: "The walls of the room seemed to spin round with the waltz, as though it would never leave off—the whirling faces all looking grave, hot, and astonished at one another."

Probably Hunt was as talented as the men of genius to whom he attached himself; only perhaps weaker-minded and less lucky. Almost all his writing was hackwork.

There was some wittiness at Monroe's dinner party for Josephine Crane—Katherine Anne, acknowledging the infelicity of Eleanor Clark's novel *The Bitter Box*: "Yes, it was a poor, strained, weakened little thing, with marks of forceps all over its head."

Mrs. Crane quoted a lady named Mrs. Bell of Boston, who, having forbidden herself to eat meat all one winter, made up for it by excesses of seafood. "I ate so many oysters that my bosom rose and fell with the tide."

Then suddenly there was an outburst of anger between Katherine Anne and myself; beginning with one of her tirades against Truman Capote. She said that he was "a pimple on the face of the literature of the day and age, nothing very serious, but symptomatic, indicative of what ails it."

I think she should never speak her mind of people she dislikes or of whom she feels resentful. Then her malice is not for fun; it is an expression of self-pity. Her attitude toward homosexual writers—Gide, Maugham, even Forster—becomes an expression of her (deadly) lonesomeness . . .

The physical life, certainly the sexual life, is miracle as much as it is routine. Miracle cannot be managed but it can be prepared for. For instance, just before any sociability of festivity, indeed during it, I withdraw to the bathroom from time to time, not only to urinate but to clean my fingernails, to whisk a little soap and water upon the very sebaceous place just before my lower lip, in case someone should care to kiss me; and my genitals and my fundament likewise . . . in case . . .

One of the strangest things in my case is that I happened not to read Forster's work in my early years, not until circa 1930. It was Katherine Anne who directed me. I can still hear the scorn and zeal in her little breathy New Orleans voice: "What? You've not read Forster?"

And nothing that he has written is better value than *Two Cheers for Democracy*. In its small shapes, its independency of component parts, it is like a great flower bed, and with flowers not only aesthetic and conceptual but also some medicinal.

News item: Christopher Isherwood is in town, for rehearsals of Van Druten's Sally Bowles play [*I Am a Camera*]. In good looks and lovely mood and mind—though he has just given up living with [William] Caskey. He says, he thinks, he feels that resigning themselves to their incompatibility, impracticability, at least for the time being, has only consolidated and clarified their devotion. Caskey has sailed away in the Merchant Marine for a while.

There is a new little highbrow book club called the Reader's Subscription; judges, Messrs. [Lionel] Trilling and Barzun and Auden. Their first selection is Forster's *Two Cheers for Democracy*, and their second, Colette introduced by Wescott. "There is not a fool can call me friend/ And I shall dine at journey's end . . ."

Auden had to fight for it, he told Isherwood. Of course it was for Colette, not for me; but I choose to feel flattered and honored by it. It is time that I abated my vexations against him: so great a poet! What if he is pompous, fatuous, and a bit hypocritical . . . What if his poetical gift should be failing . . . Posterity will require no more of him than he has already produced . . .

To town tomorrow for almost a week of even more than my usual activity. While hammering out the prose for the Reader's Subscription, I have also to harangue the Institute tomorrow night in behalf of Porter for the Gold Medal, against advocates of Faulkner and Hemingway and Wilder; to lunch with Kinsey on Tuesday, and to cook dinner for him and my young man that night; to confer with Helen [Straus] Wednesday

afternoon; to take Tommy to the premiere of Balanchine's *Tyl Ulenspiegel*
Wednesday; to take Kinsey to the premiere performance of Balanchine's
Apollo; to talk very seriously to G.P.L., who insists on photographing
me. Funny, my feeling that I wish to stand over him and tell him exactly
what to do, and what not to do, for example, real furniture, no painted
backdrop or other bogus effect; and the more inclined to be bossy in
that, this time, I shall have to pay him quite a lot.

Having received this brief message from Carl, dated November 26
a.m., 1951: "Glenway: Instead of monkey—have a lovely penis for you."
I composed the following answer, November 28, 1951:

My dear Carl—

I am charmed, touched, amused, impressed by your two-
line missive of Monday morning; promissory.

It is true that I suffer from a foible of being afraid of
monkeys, exacerbated just lately by having to spend a whole
evening with one, a beautiful half-grown rhesus belonging to
the friend of a friend. We all felt obliged to pretend that we
were not terrorized, for friendship's sake. A kind of pretense
often necessary . . .

Odd, about the fear of monkeys. Of course it is not just
their plucking fingers and needle teeth. Nor do I think of them
as the ancestors of the human race (although the rhesus of the
other evening did resemble Mrs. L. . . .). They seem rather
like our children, unsuccessful children. So often fatherly, I
have never wanted to beget in reality, of my own undependable
loins . . .

Christopher has seemed to expect me to feel fear of Anubis, the wild carrion-dog, or some other morbid responsiveness; he said it worried him. Oh no, I worship it, in
fearlessness, in anti-fearfulness—there is reassurance about
it for me in more ways than one.

Yes, sir, certainly, when the time comes, it will carry
away my indecipherable scribbled pages, my unpayable debts,
my unkeepable promises, etc.—no hurry about that. And
meanwhile he symbolizes the discarding and the transcending
of all sorts of odds and ends of past life, in order to have more
facility and felicity in the present and future—vain ideals,
inappropriate enterprises, obstinate bereavements, unservice-
able loves, unavailing powers, points of pride, etc. Anubis
the untrammeler, the emancipator.

And of course the phallus is the greatest emblem of all;
that is, the happiest . . . But I have explained to you, haven't

I?—I could never say "happiest" until I have emancipated myself in that respect also, from vanity, pretension, and inferiority as to my own physique. Not thinking of myself as a eunuch, no, indeed, but enjoying something of a eunuch-like life along with other enjoyments.

How fantastic, my letter writing for letter writing's sake! Is this all a riddle, or as it were a kind of surrealist poetry? No matter—it's just fun and affection; and not just doodling, perhaps a kind of sketching, useful somehow.

George, with a retinue of good-looking young men, arriving at Jimmie Daniels's nightclub one night when it was crowded; Jimmie and waiters taking great trouble, inserting the necessary extra chairs in little or no floor space . . .

Vincent O'D. was there, with a clever elderly female friend. "Who in the world is that?" she asked.

"George Platt Lynes, the fashion photographer," he answered.

"Oh! It's like the *Queen Elizabeth* docking."

And now this same poor George has finally been seized—the income tax people have padlocked the studio, and will auction the cameras, etc., and in some way this will lead into, or substitute for, bankruptcy proceedings. And of course it is costing everyone money—and it seems no one has hope in any way.

Yesterday I arose and went to work at 3½ a.m.; worked until train time, and continued in the train; lectured to the "Monday Class" two hours for fifty bucks; returned by bus without a proper meal, dined out of the icebox, then knocked myself out with a pill . . . And today and tomorrow I must prepare a very different lecture, to be delivered in Haverford Thursday for two hundred and fifty bucks. Not pretentious—but, yes, a bit boastful . . .

The sin of pride in eroticism—

I expect that my soulfulness and optimism about sex will irritate some people to whom my immorality as such might not give offense. Kierkegaard, gruesome little man of genius, formulated it, did he not? in the essay on *Don Juan*, which I read long ago and do not care to reread. —Don Juan "dared" to make of his sensuality an intellectual, indeed a spiritual, matter; therefore deserved punishment.

Am I not right in the following observation? —Whereas it may well be that throughout our civilization romantic love has caused more unhappiness than any other factor, as our authoritative friend suggests, the other attitude, natural non-romantic pleasurable sex activity, does not immunize or mithridatize . . . Sometimes it seems that happy promiscuity, perhaps because of the capriciousness, and the easy excitability, and a certain egocentricity, and a habit of not taking counsel, etc., only softens one up for liebestod of some sort.

One day I said to Bill, "Really, dear dope, you have as uneasy a conscience about sex as anyone I know."

"What, what?" he protested laughingly. "After all the trouble I've taken to paganize myself?"

My only rule about parties is not to fall between two stools in any way—which means, generally, not combining opposites: *not* males with females; *not* intellectuals with children of nature; *not* ambitious ones with ne'er-do-wells; *not* the decidedly sexy with the relatively pure, and so forth. A selfish rule in a way . . . For if there are two or three sides to any question, two or three stools, I always find myself compassionately cushioning someone's fall between, or picking up broken pieces. A mission in life like another; but I'm getting old and lazy.

I don't mean to suggest that I regard females, or heterosexual couples, as just hard work. Only, when they are around, I really devote myself, I pay tribute, I concentrate. It's in the way of home life away from home. I repress myself a bit, and neglect or mistreat anyone around who seems to me at all like myself . . . After all, I have four sisters and five half-sisters-in-law, and four nieces, to say nothing of ex-sweethearts.

A memory of the discipline in Indiana:

I was writing in the outer office, and Alfred sent for me, for just a few minutes' conversation; and as I began to gather up my papers his remarkable secretary said, "You can leave your work here. No one will disturb it."

"Thank you, no," I said. "It is one lesson I hope to learn in this place: to keep private and confidential matters out of the way, out of sight."

She replied: "It is hard at first. It took me quite a while to get used to it; especially here, where everyone passes my desk, coming and going. But after a while I hit upon a system. You see, I know German well; my parents are German. So when I have to make a note of anything confidential, I translate it in my own mind into German; then I say it to myself in English phonetics, and I take that down in shorthand. It works quite well."

Night before last was the opening of Christopher I.'s play, that is, Van Druten's play: Julie Harris as Sally Bowles. Wonderful fun, though just an extended character sketch, and a vehicle for a new matinee idol—scarcely drama . . . Faithful to Chr.'s text, insofar as J.V.D. could manage—and yet what a sea change! Two sea changes; and that of the passage of time in Chr.'s mind seems to me very great, very ennobling and complicating, Glory be to God. For certainly he no longer is just a camera. Oh, I longed to deliver a discourse on that to him, a criticism of all his work of the Berlin period; but I didn't. One afternoon Thornton Wilder and he and I took a long taxi ride and had a drink. T.W., with characteristic strange profound whimsicality, offered to write a page of Chr.'s journal, to be inserted; declaring that he could make it indistinguishable, perfect pastiche. His *Ides of March* was all composed like that, in mimicries of his characters' writings—a method somewhat derived from drama. All the stage is a bit crazy, I feel: even playwrights . . . I fancy Chr. will not become one. They'll scare him off.

After their meeting T.W. wrote me as follows: "A great pleasure meeting Isherwood. You may tell him from me that I am not taken in by that wide-eyed childlike manner, wandering about among us as though we were big, unpredictable, capable at any moment of the monstrous or the delightful or the brilliant. Tell him it's he who is formidable and that the lamb's fleece is very engaging, but that I saw the *fauve* beneath."

For my part I felt no fleece, saw no *fauve*. But we did not see a great deal of one another, prevented by my country residence, Chr.'s wearying dramaturgy, weeks of it out of town, and so on. We dined together alone the second or third night after his arrival. Then I gave him a welcoming party at G.P.L.'s at which he was heard to cite approvingly "Glenway and Dr. Kinsey, those two saints of sex . . ." which of course entranced the young hearers. I introduced him to said doctor. For him to give his history was an act of allegiance in a sense; for, in the circles in which we move, no one is more notably opposed to the research than Auden. He said that he liked the doctor, but somehow, I got an impression that he did not enjoy him much. What I have wanted is for Chr. to visit Bloomington. The history giving is not much, for candid men like ourselves. Whereas, out there, one gets a certain vision; a new objectivity, with implications in morals and philosophy.

* * *

Speaking of Kinsey, he has sent me a set of flashbulb photographs of himself and me taken while I was lecturing to the entire staff on the E[rotic] books—so funny; I laugh aloud at the thought of them. A real morsel for posterity if it cares for us at all.

Roughly speaking, my mind rejects the premise of the life after death, although it is in my nature, almost in my physiology, to *feel* immortal. And as I grow older I increasingly long to live again, the same life over again, and with the same me and the same others if possible, in the certainty of being able to improve on it, by increased understanding and better practice. A great part of my philosophy is nothing but Faust's cry to the passing moment: *Du holde Augenblick, verweile doch, du bist so schön*—Blessed present, wait awhile, you are too beautiful, I cannot bear to let you pass.

As for my inner secret life: I have been feeling unwell for days and days: blood-sugar levels dropping precipitously, jitters and anxieties, wonderful bad dreams, etc. It is absurd: I am to have a session with Dr. Parks on Thursday but he will not be able to help me because I will not reveal the psychological factor to him. Dr. Lovell would be entirely understanding, and give me hell on the one hand, Escotin on the other; but I am ashamed to bother him. Christmas is the worst season for all his alcoholics . . . I'd enjoy telling Dr. Kinsey the entire tale; but what a sardonic eye he would cast upon me! It would confirm him in a good bit of his hypothesis about romantic love. I dare say that "Dr." Malouf will fire me up all right in a few days, with his petty but profound Levantine wisdom, and with palliatives of pleasure, or at least humor.

The fact is, I have been suffering pangs of love; not bad pangs but the real thing, and made to measure for my discomfiture—in a triangle; a real nutcracker, testicle-twister. What a long story! But I dare say it will do me good to try to tell it briefly—therapeutic, eradicative, anti-toxic . . .

He is from Texas, his name is Michael Mikshe, and he lives with a somewhat older young man named R.D., who befriended him, taught him to be homosexual, taught him to be a successful commercial artist; who has dominated him in every way until just now, and now the balance is shifting. He hasn't half Michael's sexual faculty and desire, but he is delectable in bed. They also share a fine studio, etc., and are used to working together. R.D. is very jealous, and very wily and troublesome about it.

Michael is determined to preserve this matrimony at all costs *without* sacrificing either his main friendships or his freedom of sexual action. I dare say he makes R.D. suffer, but he is a good creature, and yields to R.D. often enough. He has said and done all he could to keep R.D. out of our circle, that is, apart from Carl and me. Nevertheless, R.D. and Carl have made friends, perhaps deliberate seductiveness on R.D.'s part, to make future trouble—this is what Michael thinks, and he is a little resentful of Carl's loose friendliness. Carl always the same, with his genius for the present pleasure, and his lack of future strategic sense in every way (in fact, in the way of sex, etc., he rather disapproves of future considerations . . .). I have encountered R.D. only twice: at a cocktail party a good while ago, before I met Michael, and last week, at a wildish party without Michael . . . (I have a feeling that I ought to copy all this for Michael himself—) It's what he likes me for, anyway: my mind is the greatest mirror he has ever looked into—only now it has begun to cloud up.

One horrid thing about being "in love" in the romantic way is that one's sufferings are at once so picayune and so complex. We romanticize partly because we are ashamed to tell the little things that have hurt us.

I am going into town Christmas night to spend an hour with Michael. Perhaps will keep it a secret from R.D. (my idea); or will join R.D. afterward for a friendly chat and Christmassy drink (Michael's idea). But I shall not quarrel with him, and with all this under my belt (this kind of journal writing makes me think of those tubs of cold water that medieval Irish monks and nuns kept by their bedsides . . .), I shall not dread the weekend tête-à-tête. I shall be able to act my age, and to preserve detachment, and perhaps to love sufficiently without being "in" love.

For the thing I feel most strongly is that being "in love," even writing about it, is boring, or at any rate unpleasant; and it wants to be tragical or it is nothing at all. Perhaps it is one reason that tragedy has lasted better than comedy, from century to century.

As to my not being greatly troubled by Michael sexually: he is certainly a splendid enough creature, as powerful in the flesh as he is impressive in his young talent; as he is interesting and pleasing in his dear youthful mind. No doubt he could bend my sexual nature to his, if he chose to, if I gave him occasion. The weekend is rather more of an occasion than I bargained for . . . In any case, all my life I have been a very moderate creature; at any age his particular passionateness would have seemed to me too much of a good thing. At my present age it would make me feel inferior, feeble, even in a way lazy.

Also, there is a psychological factor concerning the first intimate or very personal thing Michael ever said to me. We were in bed with two other persons, and a few minutes after his first orgasm, he turned to me and said, his voice almost breaking with erotic enthusiasm, "How wonderful, how wonderful! I think these are the two most sexual men in the world, don't you think they are?" and he hugged them. He said it to me, not *of* me—it did not even occur to him to say anything *of* me and he did not hug me (though for my part, I was perfectly happy).

Alfred Kinsey has said that perhaps the samurai tales are the best homosexual fiction ever written, the simplest, the least guilt-stricken, least perverse . . .

Now, isn't the above a samurai tale; as of our time and place? But here is the trouble: it is all a little boring to me, thus a little unwritable. I have forced myself through it, but the only part that seems to me worth working over enough to make literature of it is the little indecent scene in bed. (After all, as Gerald Brenan says, referring to Unamuno: "A man who is more interested in what people have in common than what divides them can scarcely be a good novelist or dramatist.")

Meantime, I reaffirm my new neo-platonism: love not of any beloved, except Monroe, true love of my youth, dearest companion of the aging years ahead—love of no one in particular, love of lovers, love of Love.

1 9 5 2

Life is almost all perch. There is no nest; and no
one is with you, on exactly the same rock or out
on the same limb. The circumstances of passion
are all too petty to be companionable. So there
you sit, and you try to sit still, and doze and
dream to save trouble. It is the kind of thing you
have to keep quiet about for others' sake, polite-
ness's sake: itching palm and ugly tongue and
unsighted eye and empty flatulent physiology as
a whole; and your cry of desire, ache, ache,
ringing in your own ears. No one else hears it;
and you get so tired of it yourself that you can't
wait to grow old . . .
—The Pilgrim Hawk

January 1

The only holiday that is at all distinctly holy, to my mind: the day
sacred to Time. Such other gods as I care for—Memory, Sex, Language—
have no particular season or fixed feast.

January 3

On Friday evening, December 28, 1951, with Michael and Carl,
mood and circumstance could not conceivably have been happier, not
within human potentiality. It was a reunion after several weeks. It was
a peace-making after certain misunderstandings and mistakes. Physically as well, or perhaps I should say, nervously, each one of us in his
way was at concert pitch. M. took C. in his most male fashion, with
animal force but no deliberate or playful brutality, with unbroken rhythm;
never more beautiful.

I was on my knees beside the bed, and spent upon the instant of

M.'s spending, falling forward, with my face pressed to the edge of the bed, my eyes blotted out.

Scarcely waiting for his orgasm to abate, M. drew back, stooped down, and took C. in his mouth, with animal voracity or, rather, bird voracity—(even that of the eagle upon Prometheus)—but swifter than any bird. And I remember how hard it was for me to force myself up straight, bracing myself with both arms, upon the edge of the bed, in order to observe C.'s final ecstasy, which was more powerful than any I have ever seen him possessed by, and quite different: a flinging of his head and neck from side to side, in a half circle from shoulder to shoulder, with a jerk or a crack as of a whip . . .

To Nick—upon His Gift of a Gilded Metal Dolphin

January 7

I need not remind you: I am a sort of Scrooge—only submissive to others' Christmas interests when they confront me. Therefore my thanks are always awkward, blushing, but sincere. Thank you.

Also you know how I am a symbolist in my way, and so I ponder the significance of dolphins, according to Yeats mainly: emblematic of the complexities of human physiology, "the fury and the mire of human veins"—which, surprisingly, in a poem of old age, with deliberately repeated key words, bear the innocent dead to a kind of paradise which is full of sensuality, but sensuality without fury . . .

Bernard, coming back from Rome, has found me changed, for the better; he said, "You have ceased to be romantic. You have grown poetical instead." With no assurance that it is for the better—for the happier, yes, certainly, but I am of an age to realize that this is not the same thing—I understand the two words very clearly.

Never forget, when I feel too much duty-bound to my young friends—or it may be sympathy-bound—that the influence I have on them is not a good influence, the example I set them is not a good example. Therefore if I resist them or refuse them, I shall not be wronging them . . . Never forget how my weaknesses masquerade as goodnesses.

January 25

First meeting with Ronald Neil.* One of my little dinners at Carl Malouf's. Ronald's blithe friendly talk in the kitchen while I cooked.

---

* Ronald Neil (pseudonym). A major, longtime lover of G.W.

After M. M. departed, angry, perhaps jealous—perhaps taking C.S. with him—R. and I knelt at the foot of C.M. and W.R.'s bed, watching conjointly, turning to gaze into each other's eyes, afire, with more love than lust. I must express my gratitude to Michael for introducing me to R. I want to see him again, no matter how; on his terms—for lunch or whatever. I love him for a particular reason: In some ways he is more like me when I was young than anyone I have ever met! Also, last night, he seemed to me the most beautiful because he was the happiest, as it happened. With his mouth like the opening of a trumpet, passionate upon empty air—with those blue eyes as round as a falcon's, with that look of the inexpressible—then the sudden radiance of his smiling at me, because he was not alone even in the strange lonely role of spying, because of that little likeness between us . . .

As for Marianne's latest folly: Morton Dawen Zabel, the University of Chicago professor and distinguished obscurantist critic, with a sick sister to support, finds himself obliged to reduce his standard of living, to take a smaller apartment, where oh where will he put his books, and to sell his grand piano. Marianne is planning to give him her Bryn Mawr earnings, and also wants Institute money, but it would hurt his feelings to have to accept it in the form of "relief." She talked to me about it on the telephone for a full half hour, and it made me so angry that I couldn't really argue with her . . . So I wrote her a perhaps well-calculated note.

Beware of letter writing, the unworthiest of the categories of writing; given over to seductiveness and apology, diplomacy and didactics. Where there is so much purpose there cannot be much sincerity.

I love Kinsey, and I aspire to his particular virtues: laboriousness, secretiveness, and neatness.

In writing about love relationships and the sex play of males with males, we have trouble with our vocabulary. To begin with, *virile* and *effete* won't do; *manly* and *effeminate* won't do; even *bitch* and *sissy* are only a little better. And yet one needs some such contrasting terms even when the partners are very similar.

Active and *passive* are just a mystification, unless the usage has been agreed on by convention . . . (Is the rapid insatiable laborious cocksucker passive . . . ?) As for *sadist* and *masochist*, it seems to be a disgrace to have named so mighty and universal and multifarious a characteristic aspect of humanity after a French lunatic and a pornographer. Furthermore, too great an emphasis on the one factor of physical pain, infliction of—so often not felt as such, nor even thought of as such either by inflicter or the inflicted. Certainly *coercive* and *submissive*, or something of that sort, would serve better and deter our minds (both scientific and literary minds) from oversimplification. Even *exhibitionistic* and *voyeuristic* are ugly and linguistically somewhat objectionable—and also at this point too, restricted petty and pejorative implications.

February 5

As to this matter of critical writing, it seems that I cannot truly resign myself to it—because I seem to require some hope of making some money by what I undertake to write. It is not a wish for more money (I give up Europe without bitterness); it is a dread of finding myself with much less . . . Bird in gilded cage, from whom even the cage may be taken away— It is the female-inspired anxiety neurosis— for example, Baba, day before yesterday, worrying the hell out of poor Tommy by questioning *him* about my writing: Does he not think that my psychopathology prevents my working, etc.— Therefore, a novel—? The simple fact about that is that, all these months, I have been trying to discover, to conceive, to respond with the necessary excitement and optimism, to some sort of plot—the missing incident for *The Ocean Liner*, for example . . . Now, is that because W.S.M. is right: no talent for fiction? Or is it only because I, psychoneurotically, have exposed myself to, and overresponded to, and alibied myself by, destructive critical attitudes—others' also; even Baba's?

Oh, it is a horror to be a talker: Johnson without Boswell! Or, to be more exact, it is a horror to have been told, to have come to believe or half believe, that one is a Johnson; to await or half await a Boswell! Even the scribbling of this journal is (for me) the same as talk . . . As soon as I try to put it in good order, all the difficulties of my non-creativity set in all over again—whatever they may be: inhibition, indecision, wrong circumstance, wrong influence, or actual lack of writing ability—down again I go, between the stools . . . This is the real point and force of my wishing I had a secretary. Oh, I don't suppose it would help me to be creative—to write novels, etc. A secretary would be a sort of substitute Boswell—

Tonight Michael is bringing my new interest, young Ronald Neil . . . Empathy to a new degree: he is like myself, young in these present circumstances of myself-old. Does that make sense?—a contemplater like myself. Though still in the vigor of youth, the warmth of infatuation . . .

My lecture for Bryn Mawr has been fixed for April 15: at the Deanery, not at Lina's—"Characterization of the Feminine in the Fiction of Colette"—isn't that a truly academic title?

From a letter to Alfred Kinsey

February 20

Did I mention a young man named Ronald N., whom Michael brought to a party at Carl's the week before your visit? He is the assistant editor of Alcoholics Anonymous's little periodical, the *Grapevine*. He is not a reformed alcoholic, indeed has never taken drink, nor smoked. He has made obscure allusion to some aspect of his sex life as, in some sense, vice. I expect him to confide all that to me before long.

Only twice in his life, he says, has he found lovers who have suited him in both spiritual and physical ways at once. One of these is a recent acquaintance, a Marine stationed in Washington, D.C., whom he wants me to meet. He also has been a Marine. Miami is home. He has been in New York three years and, except for sexual opportunity, seems not to have liked it much.

There is something slight and boyish about his physique, but he has developed himself impressively, by gymnastics and swimming. He has a very Irish face, with a homely sharp nose; clear blue eyes; quick thin expressive lips, quickly smiling. I have never known a face so prompt in the expression of sexual interest. His body also quickly manifests excitement. Often at the mere thought of pleasure he instantly moves, little fluencies of his arms, shoulders, neck, like a cat, like a baby.

That night at Carl's, January 25, Michael brought another as well, a good-looking easygoing Italian. He and Ronald had not met, and Michael did not know either of them well, except for his sudden impulsive brusque concentrated enjoyments of them upon several occasions. Michael in his high-strung temper, with a combination of his natural virile selfishness and his good-natured moral vanity, wanting to give me pleasure and to prepare for your visit. I had been rather beating the bushes, seeking especially a friend for David Q. All the first part of the evening was a sort of fiasco. Carl and I did not respond to Michael's cues as we should have done; Michael did not cue us cleverly. He and Tim Lowe were plainly *not* compatible. Michael spent too soon, and then did not recover powers quickly. You know his temper; he was rude to me, and then really offensive to Carl. I could see us suddenly without a roof over our heads; or I might have had to serve up the head of Michael on a salver . . . So I sprang to Carl's defense in my top-sergeant style. Away Michael, with the good-natured Italian, in mixed emotion; and wrote me a dramatic letter before he went to bed.

Then Carl and Tim and Ronald and I had pleasure; and instantly there developed between Ronald and me a certain fellow feeling which we have not yet explicitly considered together—for one thing, a specific phallus worship, with that overevaluation which may come naturally to men who think of their own genitals as small (in Ronald's case, compensated by uncommon potency, and relieved by his athleticism and pride of appearance); and natural spectatorship, only more youthful than mine, only more excited and less truth-seeking. Also, something that perhaps throws light on my own case, my lifelong inclination to a triangular pattern of love: as to the third person's presence, this youngster's feeling seems not just complacency, not just erotic playfulness, but a positive desire, a feeling of need, more urgent as his climax approaches. He calls out to the extra one, "Where are you? Come close to me . . ."

The reason we did not introduce him to you was simply because he told Michael that he did not want to give you his history. We still do not understand why not; and we think that probably you can persuade him. He is eager to have a chance to meet you, and ardently believes in all the purposes of the research; indeed we haven't found in his conversation any inkling of the difficulty . . . Something he is ashamed of, I suppose. Some close friend of his has been cooperative with the research for some time, and has visited Bloomington. I shall not press him for the time being, to ascertain any of these little mysteries, but lull him as best I know how.

The afternoon that we matched Michael with Chuckles, Michael and I especially regretted your not knowing Ronald, because he also clenches his fists and strikes his partner during his orgasm. No sadistic gestures or histrionics along that line in the earlier lovemaking; just at the end his caresses turn to clawing, and then little blows—every time, by which I mean seven times, to my knowledge. A very strong orgasm, with marvels of the muscles, though not as wild as Chuckles's; none of those leaps like a back bass on the hook.

Michael at first worried over my enthusiasm about Ronald. In a letter to him I said that in some ways I found Ronald more like myself in my twenties than any other young man of our acquaintance; allowing for circumstances that never presented themselves in my youth. I described Ronald's way of opening his lips in excitement, "round, like a trumpet, passionate upon the empty air; and the round stare of his blue eyes, as round as a falcon's," with the look of a desire that fancies itself infinite; and his way of turning toward me every two minutes and radiantly smiling, and holding hands with me, glad to be not alone in the strange lonely role of watching.

All this Michael misread and objected to, until I had occasion to retell it in four-letter words. It is the great difficulty of writing about erotic experience: what may be called the threshold of clarity is so finicky and so variable. When is enough said? With colloquialism and plenty of realism in detail, one may lose realism. Likewise, or worse, with the scientific language. On the other hand, with poetical utterance, this or that reader is apt to miss all the matters of fact . . .

February 23

The anger and sorrowfulness of Katherine Anne derives from the fact that men have ceased to love her, and want her to continue loving them, thus depriving her of the sense of their ever having loved her.

Georges Bernie and I protested that this was not to be regarded as the character of males, but simply the badness of certain men. Pauline declared that men simply do not and cannot understand women, and therefore the poor devils always conclude with some devilish misinterpretation and hurtful injurious statement.

Georges Bernie contended that no two human beings, even male and male, female and female, ever understand each other. Life is compartmentalized; each individual is in his own pigeonhole, his own death cell; and their communications, even of greatest love, are, first, a maneuver for pleasure's sake, and then an illusion, in the tradition of love, while it lasts.

I spoke against them all: "Certainly love is a reality; absolute understandings and communications do take place; indeed, sexual attraction itself is a kind of understanding, orgasm a form of communication, a pantomime . . . but perhaps only for a few minutes, an hour, a few days, a month, a year. It comes about by chance, and it is a miracle."

Oh, for two cents I'd fly out to our father in Bloomington and weep on his shoulder, and perhaps shout at him: facts of life that he wots not of, psychosomatics of sex, etc.; certain difficulties that the human animal finds when he tries to rise to the dignity of the other animals, at least the homosexual human animal, and certain ways in which the homosexual, at least the literary homosexual, wastes his emotion and his willpower and his talent. When Kinsey inveighs against the patterns of romantic love as rather conducive to unhappiness and frustration, does

he observe something like a disapproving look on my middle-aged face!
It is only a look of skepticism, of discouragement. How the hell does
one keep out of romanticism? Wouldn't one think that, at my time of
life, in the best of health, with an exceptionally fortunate amount of
pocket money, with the good influence of Lloyd as well as of Kinsey,
with a number of protagonists most distinguished and dissimilar, notably
Carl and Michael and Ronald. Wouldn't you think that I could find some
way of having sexual intercourse once a week without having to move
so much heaven and earth about it, so many mysteries and misunderstandings, and shyness of a sixteen-year-old and shamefacedness of an
old man, and hurt feelings, and dreams and sleeplessness and long letter
writing . . . Oh, I am angry with myself. But it isn't all my fault. The
romantic pattern is something that one falls back on when one's sexual
endeavor has miscarried or failed . . . I can put it a little more plainly:
it is a kind of convention in which the weak man cloaks his weakness,
when the strong have tired of him or have fooled him, to dignify his
emotions, to save his face. Romance is also sometimes just a matter of
semantics; and indeed nothing is harder to express than the overlappings
of love relationship and sex relationship.

As between R. and me, for instance, just at present . . . He troubles
me most of all now, not only as he enters into my fantasy of hope and
desire, perhaps beyond his power to fulfill, but by getting me to commit
myself in the way of the spirit little by little, more than I can afford,
more than I can continue. If it were not for him, I believe that I should
cut my losses, abate my pretensions, take my medicine—and go back
to Carl and the raffish comradeship, or perhaps just give up love and
sex altogether.

But R. persuades me that he does need me somehow; that if I grow
disillusioned about our relationship, if I turn away from him, it will be
a great sadness for him, bad for him— I don't understand this but I
believe him. It touches me and it attaches me. If he is making a fool
of me, why? He wants nothing of me. If he were fooling, wouldn't he
promise me this and that; wouldn't he flatter me? Not a word, not even
about sex— Nothing but ardor, tenderness, eagerness, and the feeling
that he needs me . . .

March 2

I have an exceptional aptitude for old-fashioned love relationships
in binary form, for co-residence, for fidelity, etc. Nevertheless, I have
come to the conclusion that for most males the two-person pattern is
just an ideal, an imposed discipline, a convention, a hypocrisy, a phase

or episode; and that especially in homosexuality, that is, in double maleness, everything that may come under the heading of an imitation of male and female romanticism is rather short-lived, one-sided, anguished, laborious, wearisome. Promiscuity has certain obvious advantages, but many men find it not good enough in the details of the physiology of intercourse; and others find it fatiguing in the pursuit, boring or unpleasant in the psychological, conducive to a sort of loneliness . . . The most impressive love lives, or perhaps I should say the love lives of the most impressive men, the happiest, the most forceful in their environment, the most productive in the arts, etc., do show predominantly some strongly romantic attachment, long-term commitment. But, as a rule, if you look close, not in simple duality . . .

Nor can I really see the point of any absolute or final morality except work morality—certainly nothing absolute about sex except does it help or hinder, is it holiday, etc.? Perhaps *nothing* is too big a word—I guess I'm against rape . . .

Further, I believe that everything may work, in some case; nothing works, if one insists on the romantic expectations and irrationalities; and nothing matters anyway—except the main things. Which are: (1) work; (2) love, true love, friendly love, caritas; and (3) sexual pleasure, which is a good thing *per se*.

March 11

Pace, pace . . . Not just the words the Mozart tune: which, in our early days, after any altercation or overstimulation, M.W. and I used to whistle to one another instead of apologizing.

The sentence of criticism of me which has, all these years, amused me most is by Kenneth Burke, writing in 1924: "Mr. Wescott is determined to leave nothing offensive unsaid, but at the same time is anxious not to give offense; therefore his style necessarily is unctuous."

Hemingway's last novel [*Across the River and into the Trees*] is the self-portrait of a deteriorating, deliquescent, dying man, executed in a quite appropriate overblown decadent technique. As such, it is of intense interest; work of genius. Only the middlebrow reading public rejected it—American everyman, on the one hand, and Wilder and Isherwood and I, on the other hand, were fascinated.

We have lived in the time of Yeats, greater than Catullus, greater than Donne; the time of Valéry, greater than Pascal; the time of Proust, almost as great as Balzac; the time of Colette, incomparable—not to mention Forster and Maugham and Mann and Hemingway and Lorca and Apollinaire and Rilke and Eliot and Auden; not to mention the philosophers and the like: Freud, as great as Marx and less maleficent; Santayana, perhaps as deleterious as Nietzsche; not to mention those I personally disregard or forget (I do not admire Mr. Faulkner, I do not love Kafka . . .). To me it all seems glorious and dazzling.

March 15

Crocuses and snowflakes in bloom, though it hasn't been warm; just sunny. Last week there were patches of snow—Ronald N. and I followed a stag, perhaps two males, fresh treads in the muddy road, then in the snow along the Black Brook; and we found one of his antlers, four-pointed, very pretty, just shed, with a drop of blood on it—

Strange how our little young fast international set has suddenly got in a tantrum against gossip! You'd think they all suddenly had hopes of getting favorably inserted into some puritanical old rich relative's will. Even Bill M. rages against the entire Rome–New York axis, thus of course amplifying and restimulating every report— I said to him, "It's best not to fight back; but if you feel you must, if you can't help it, then for pity's sake, fight dirty!"—but he didn't understand—

March 22

How I detest the chopping down of trees for the direct-mail advertising to me of this and that organizational, governmental ideology, etc.—into the wastebasket, unopened; the fatter the envelope the faster. On Sunday M.W. fished out an especially fat one: Nicholas Nabokov's* invitation to represent literature (along with Auden, James Farrell, Robert Penn Warren, etc.) at the culture festival (along with Lincoln's ballet, Virgil T.'s opera, Mr. Forster's opus, etc.)—expenses paid for two weeks . . . Then how authoritatively everyone here—M.W., Pauline, Ll., Baba—made plans for me; and how rebelliously I thundered back at them! I was tempted to decline, for I'll have to work hard, in the way of conferences, forums, perhaps a lecture or two. The culture bureaucrats have sent over some themes of discussion: "The twentieth century has increased the isolation of the creative artist." Matisse and Picasso isolated? Strauss and Stravinsky isolated? Hemingway isolated? My objection to all that organized whining is going to involve me in giving them their money's worth—

---

* Nicholas Nabokov (1903–78). Composer and musicologist, cousin of the novelist.

On the other hand I shall have a droll agenda of my own, literary for the most part, energetic, eccentric, independent, expensive fortnight: one-night stands to see pictures, perhaps tea at the Villa Mauresque between planes, if invited; and hours and hours and hours shopping, book-shopping for one thing—I want all the travel books of Paul Morand . . .

This was interrupted and now it is fifty hours later. That night at dinner Lloyd suddenly made a hideous face, withdrew to his bedroom, presently began groaning—fortunately! A bit more of his show-off stoicism, inspired by his father's histrionics (and perhaps mine), and he'd have been a goner— It was a perforated duodenal ulcer: perhaps the worst pain in all pathology, doctors said—the stomach acids dripping upon the other organs— Nightmarish hours: the subintelligent and stone-deaf American Legion volunteer ambulance men couldn't find the Mill— the famous squirrel-cage stairway wouldn't take a stretcher— Baba's challenge to Debo to be stoic, Debo's stoicism, in fact, were heartbreaking. Baba and Monroe rode in the ambulance. The number 1 stoic groaned all the way. No analgesic would work. Operation at Harkness Pavillion at 1 a.m.—successful.

Ronald and I spent that night at the Mill for Debo's sake; and most of Sunday— Monday morning by the earliest train I went into New York, not good for my bronchae—lectured on Hemingway to the "Monday Class," by means of analysis—then called on Lloyd for three minutes— he is progressing wonderfully. He made me a little speech, as follows: "It's like a menopause. Because now I know I can't do everything. I can't have any more babies, I can just do certain things." To which I replied: "I have found that changes of the rules do not take away the pleasure of the game. You will soon learn the new rules." He thought it a good answer—

I wonder if Nicky Nabokov has tried to get Thornton Wilder for his twentieth-century forum in Paris? He is the real Chrysostom or Golden Mouth among us . . . I shall never forget his Blashfield Address to the National Institute and the American Academy in 1948, against the defeatism of writers and artists—"In a Time of Troubles."

"Gottes Zeit ist die allerbeste Zeit."—"God's time is the best time of all . . ."

March 28

I think Monroe will be here this weekend. I can't discourage him, as he has been absent more than usual, the spring is developing, and

I am heading Europeward so soon . . . There is a little disadvantage for me in his company when there may be any mysteriousness in the amorous way—he makes me self-conscious, as to my untimeliness, undignified-ness, etc.

But what does matter this weekend, with Ronald and Will* here, is the allocation of beds in the not large enough house . . . What embarrasses me is that I am going to want to leave Monroe in his room, to put Will in the little guestroom, and to put Ronald in the library on the tapestry bed. Then I can change places with Ronald—give him my room, where he can invite Will to join him. Of course, this may be very hard on me: but not as hard as my old Monroe's ruthless disapprobation, and little whip-like remarks all the rest of the spring, if I were to with-draw upstairs and yield my part of the house to Will and Ronald, and he has right on his side—right enough. It is true that a great part of my life has been a waste and a torment in certain triangular rela-tionships unconsummated for my part, in my angle; and it is true that I have taken the distress and complication of all that as an excuse now that my lifetime is shortening, with my promise as a writer only half fulfilled.

Therefore now he does not even let me invite those couples of my friends who mean nothing to me in the amorous way, if he can dissuade me . . . with no sort of abode in town, St.-bl., says he, is my one and only allurement, etc., and if I turn it into just hospitality, it makes me lonelier and lonelier . . . And if he observes me in any involvement of emotion or fixation of my five senses upon any person, and then catches me facilitating that person's intimacy with another person or other per-sons: hospitality with complicity and subservience and abnegation—then hell breaks loose. In his opinion it is not just weakness and stu-pidity—it is wickedness and craziness, which it is the duty of a friend to interfere with as relentlessly as possible. Worst of all, after any such misdemeanor or mismanagement, for quite a while I get no sympathy from him, in any lonesomeness or privation or frustration—it serves me right, no matter what . . .

No moralistic prejudice in any of this. The other sort of triangle, when consummated, seems to him lovely. Only with due skepticism, as it seems to him I have just happened to be terribly spoiled this past year; and I have complicated my life when perhaps it was time to simplify it. And in this spirit, when there is anything in my life that may mean—

---

* Will Chandlee III (1928–   ). An intimate of G.W. for several years and a devoted friend for the rest of G.W.'s life.

not happiness, but probably just embarrassment and frustration, he asks me categorical questions.

From a letter to Ronald Neil

April 6—3 p.m.

Let me try to tell you my story of the Bach cantatas; if I can't tell it properly, perhaps you will remember to ask about it another time. You know I love music, and Bach most of all. It is very important how one conceives heaven, whether or not there really is a heaven. For years and years my thought has been that only two things would please me throughout eternity—to make love in my own particular strange way, eternally: to sing polyphonic Bach, eternally . . . The greatest of Bach is the series of cantatas, about forty or fifty of which are absolute masterpieces. I know perhaps fifteen; they are not often performed except in Germany, and when I lived there I was ignorant of them. All these years, perhaps twenty years, I have just taken it for granted that sooner or later I could hear the other thirty or thirty-five—the U.S. would grow Bach-conscious, or I could return to Germany—I was young enough, there would be time enough, time enough for everything . . . So I said to myself. Then, you know, I had a little cancer—no great matter, but naturally inspiring some solemnity and poignant feeling of shortened life expectancy. One day I happened to look at a big record catalogue, and observed what Bach cantatas had been recorded—only ten or eleven. I went out for a walk, down the road toward Baba's. Suddenly I realized that in all probability I was going to die without ever hearing the rest of those cantatas. Bach had been born in circa 1700, the most beautiful composer who ever lived; and I had been born in circa 1900, with a most passionate ear for music, especially for Bach—all in vain, all in vain! I burst into tears there on the twilit country road. I shook from head to foot. The earth shook under me. The sky shook over my head. It was the most powerful experience of the horror of death that I have ever had. Tragic, yes, but not pathetic . . . By such a vision of what death will take away from us, we learn what we have to live for.

April 11

Moral of my fifty-first birthday: Unless one has learned to work when one is happy, one is no worker. Unless one has learned to work in spite of extreme unhappiness, one will never accomplish much. One's lifetime will not be long enough.

On my fifty-first birthday, I worked a little, off and on all day long:

the new Colette lecture for Bryn Mawr. I am afraid that I could not have done so well if the work in question had been more important, creative.

I have got into an enthrallment (a compulsion, if you like, though that has come to seem to me an ugly word . . .) to write letters, especially to write Ronald letters. I find them in my mind when I wake up, half-composed; I seem unable to think of anything else until I unburden myself of them a little, to make room for (perhaps) literature; I tell myself that it will only take a half hour, with my thermos bottleful and my winter-withered apple and my nibble of cheese . . . It takes hours and hours, I get carried away, I attempt the inexpressible—nothing so interesting and challenging as the inexpressible—and above all, I meditate; sometimes half an hour passes between sentence and sentence, all in a sort of prayerfulness and profundity and athleticism of mind, like Jacob wrestling with his angel . . .

"Everything can be acquired in solitude, except character" (Stendhal).

At the beginning of my fifty-second year I seem on the verge of a sort of desert. Forward march . . . with no knowledge of oasis, no incentive of mirages. Glare and heat of my intelligence, and like clockwork the end of every day, blackest nocturn, loneliness, *Te Deum* of myself alone. It is not a tragedy, it is only a vacuity. It is an accidental effect of a certain depopulatedness of my life just in the last month or two, the last week or two, the last few hours. Carl's in despair on his own account, as to his talent, his livelihood, his physique, etc.; therefore no more fondness, no more fun. Michael has ceased to charm me. Insoluble pity of the poverty-stricken life and the psychology of Tommy. Disillusionment in dearest Ronald, as he succumbs now to the meretricious and inauspicious love of S.S. A feeling of not knowing anyone except all these persons whom I know far too well. Seeming inability to conceive of there being, anywhere within my range of acquaintance, any very different personnel . . .

And does Monroe provide no palliation for this forlornless? He does not. Why not? We are too much at one. Little by little, decade by decade, a double being, without polarity; only sometimes divided against itself. My worthlessness makes him ashamed; his anxiety about me is insulting, etc.

And is there no pleasure in the fragmentation of my fellow writers and such? Not much. Conversing with, let us say, Wilder or Raymond Mortimer or Mr. Maugham is like one of my little lectures, only delivered to an audience of only two persons, one of whom is myself.

Sometimes one of them lectures to me, but as a rule they just keep interrupting. For my part I think I prefer real lecturing, since the choice of what to lecture on is then left to me, and I can prepare a bit, and get paid a little. When I take so dull a view of life and of myself, it is not possible for me to believe that I have any true vocation for literature or any sort of genius or valuable talent whatever.

April 18

I have wanted to voyage by small or smallish ship instead of airplane, hoping that might reactivate one of my little lifelong dormant works of fiction. But it has seemed impossible to get passage—until yesterday, when I was assigned a berth in a cabin with unknown persons on the *Westerdam* leaving Saturday, April 26, and arriving in Amsterdam May 5. Never having seen the Rembrandts there or the Halses in Haarlem or the *Adoration of the Lamb* in Ghent or the canals of Bruges, I shall enjoy all that, probably alone, and plan to get to Paris May the 12th, or the 11th, or the 13th—my first engagement for the congress is the 15th . . . The *per diem* they provide is modest, for the present Paris cost of living—and also, I am greatly concerned to get away from my fellow authors, Katherine Anne and Auden and Tate and Farrell, and worst of all, Faulkner—indeed also from the grand foreigners, Mr. Forster, [André] Malraux, [Ignazio] Silone, Huxley, [Salvador de] Madariaga, gosh! Therefore I shall stay with François Reischenbach, at 17 place des Etats-Unis. How strange! I cannot remember ever having stayed with anyone as long as two weeks . . .

April 26

Three in a cabin . . . One of my cabinmates has a mistrustful stare, a hideous little mustache, a bursting paunch, and a mephitic pipe. At intervals in the night he snores liquidly, drowningly.

April 30

Good weather. Unperturbedly, at our snail's pace, we creep ahead upon a vast block—a disk rather—of intensely blue sapphire.

Though the Dutch are famous readers, famous publishers, famous booksellers, the library of this *Westerdam* amounts to only a few shelves; American detective stories for the most part, though I was delighted to find Paul Morand's *Rien que la Terre*. Some of the most interesting, certainly the most poetical, journalism ever written was the sort of hackwork written by poets and fiction writers of the twenties—Colette, Cocteau, Montherlant. Their mere reportage was often much more literary, and fundamentally more serious, than the Germanized philosophizing of today.

I wonder what has become of Morand. I feel a real friendliness and sympathy for him. A Vichy diplomat, perhaps now in more or less voluntary exile, he once asked me to a luncheon party at his apartment just in the shadow of the Eiffel Tower. It must have been my first fashionable luncheon party in France, and I had to play second fiddle to another American writer, Willie Seabrook, who wore an iron ring on his thumb and regaled the ladies, including a duchess, with stories of sadomasochism and voodoo. A little later, when we were neighbors and Morand had the Orangerie in Villefranche, I called on him. Up from the harbor that Hercules built, there wafted a fragrance of seaweed, a tartness of shellfish, a muskiness of *oursin*, a little rankness. In a low, cushioned chair sat blue-blooded bluestocking Mme Morand, who was an exceedingly cultivated Balkan lady of high degree, with books in several languages piled elbow-high on either side of her, working away at them with her paper knife, as we carelessly chatted. I remember a tale of Cocteau's, of an evening party of writers in the happy time of the Boeuf sur le Toit at which there was a renowned fortune-teller who glanced a bit into everyone's palm and promulgated a bit. In Paul Morand's case, the promulgation was that he lacked a proper fate line. It was an excited party and somewhat bibulous. Morand had drunk a good deal, and presently he vanished into the kitchen and was heard to cry out in pain. He was found in a state of mingled despair and clown-ishness, all dabbled with blood, having tried to carve himself a fate line with a vegetable knife.

How humbly I read Fromentin's *Maîtres d'Autrefois*! (which so very evidently influenced Valéry, even as the travel—North African travel journals—influenced Gide). But the obvious reason that I could never hope to write this kind of book is that I am not humble enough.

We are under a large, softly lit cloud. But in the distance southeast of us there are two great apertures of direct sunlight; two great concourses of waves composed of broken crystal, melted silver.

Oh, my dear great Monroe—perhaps I ought to be kept from com-munication with him *except* by the printed or printable word— For hasn't that been the great motive power, motor power, in my life always: the need to express myself to him? That, and sexuality . . .

* * *

Perhaps the most enchanting utterance of one of the reasons for
voyaging abroad is in Shakespeare's *Cymbeline*:

> *we, poor unfledged,*
> *Have never wing'd from view o' the nest, nor know not*
> *What air's from home . . .*
>   *What should we speak of*
> *When we are old as you? when we shall hear*
> *The rain and wind beat dark December, how*
> *In this our pinching cave shall we discourse*
> *The freezing hours away? We have seen nothing . . .*

May 5

Suddenly, yesterday, off the coast of England, there came the
warmest, softest springtime, and in the night under the broken moon,
we made up for the lost time, more than an hour— Therefore this morning
they have been bossing us and rushing us unmercifully— I am writing
this standing up, in line, for the passport inspection, and in charge of
a sprite of a five-year-old, child of an Irishman and a Dutch woman,
who insisted on having her own U.S. passport . . .

Oh, it is beautiful, and I am ecstatic. I must say a new prayer: "O
Almighty! O Inexorable!" (to use Colette's great word)— "Keep me from
too much pride. Keep me from too much joy!"

Yesterday was Holland's Liberation Day, so there was nothing to
do all afternoon. American Express closed; shops closed; still no guidebook. Museum closed—perhaps just as well. After the ecstasy of the
morning, I was rather insensitive and deflated.

Pauline had left a message for me at the Hotel Atlanta in Rotterdam.
I telephoned her, and we took the round trip of the canals in a beautiful
new boat, with information barked at us by a handsome man, hideous-
voiced, amplified. We do not admire the architecture of Amsterdam—
Pauline has got a crush on Constantinople, anyway. I don't mind a bit,
so blissful otherwise. Is the male population here in general more attractive than any other, or is it just the rosy spectacles I seem to have
got on? A very great percentage of them are flagrant flirts.

Mon's letters are a marvel. I am deeply moved by bad news of
K.A.P.—with almost a feeling of guilt, because of my lack of liking,
my inability to enjoy her. Her relations with young men make as wonderful a tragic story as Kierkegaard's hatred of his father and love of

Regina—only the latter led to God and overproduction, the former to the devil and to silence . . .

May 7

The Dutch are the most high-strung nation on earth—Amsterdam the most nerve-racking city on earth—and I respond with wildest atavism—the blood of my great-grandmother Wescott, born Condeback, roused to awareness in my veins . . .

Extremest insomnia: three and three-quarters hours last night, and my high-strung pretty little room waiter forgot to fill my thermos bottle, so that I have had to spend two and a half hours in limbo—but now here he is—bliss of caffeine!

Pauline's energy is sublime and diabolical— How have her men stood it? But, I guess, in a way, my energy ditto, and my men ditto question mark . . . Of course they haven't stood it, more than a certain length of time—except my Monroe. And in her case, no Monroe—how brave she is about that . . . her morale a matter of the hard work and the much money—

No rest from morning to night— I don't, can't, count the hours of laborious eating and talking . . . Insomnia. It seems to take me longer to bathe than she—perhaps she doesn't bathe. She takes a nap and is back up again fresh as a daisy, in the time it takes me to decipher something in Dutch, to look up something in the guidebook. For this kind of forced accelerated, hungry, gluttonous culture travel, she is the perfect traveling companion . . .

I adore the *Fiancée Juive* [Rembrandt], as I expected, as I remembered—I must write something about the two pairs of hands. I adore the *Night Watch* even more than I expected; it is unexpectable, unimaginable, indescribable (of course I imagine that I could describe it if I tried hard enough, long enough . . .).

I also adore the group portraits of Hals—the Mozartean ones of 1627 almost more than the Beethoven-like or Bach-like ones of his eighty-fourth year . . . Remember the red tablecloth in the *Regentesses*, so dark that it is almost imperceptible—what I perceived first was how it made the surrounding blacks a little greenish—absolute mystery of blood-red darkness . . . It is the pool of sacrificial blood in Book XI of the *Odyssey*, poured by Odysseus when he was lost on the dark Cimmerian shore in order to attract the ghost of Tiresias, who could show him the way to go home; and it also attracted the ghost of his aged mother, who gave him news of his aged father . . .

I have a theory of how the greatest painters' minds work—metaphor or by cultural reference . . . They paint something they think *of*, as well as what they see and what they feel . . . Certainly when we look at paintings we respond to the similitudes and allusions in some measure, if we have any education or cultivation at all— But in most modern art there is so little—it will always prove a little boring to the knowledgeable, thoughtful person—Klee is the exception; that is his importance.

Now it is time to dress, shave, and run . . . Soft constant sunshine for four successive days (cold moonlight nights)—it never happens, they say. It hasn't happened since the death of Hobbema, in 1709.

Sometimes in my little rooftop room with two flags just outside, and a great vista of chimney pots—in the twilight while Pauline is putting herself to rights for dinner—I whisper Ronald's name.

May 10

On the way to The Hague—when was that? only day before yesterday—in the comfortable train I told Pauline that I had to write to Ronald, therefore to hush, which she did very nicely, in simili-serenity— But then a young plump Fulbright American in the seat beside me piped up, to ask, "Pardon me, sir, are you not Glenway Wescott?" and he peered over my shoulder to see what I was writing— I took Pauline all the way back to Rotterdam to see just one picture: a Chardin still life—plums with their blue skins broken and brown juice running, and a jar full of light, and a loaf of bread composed of fourteen-carat gold. At one moment Pauline left me alone in the room with Rodin's *Man of Calais* and quick as a flash I kissed his hand.

Lucian has a story of someone who tried to have intercourse with a sculpture of Venus . . . I don't try anything impossible.

Just now the tall intellectual-looking boy who brings me breakfast, waiting for his tip, inquired, "Did you went home yesterday?" meaning, Are you going home today?—and it gave me a twinge of homesickness. Oh, far from home, this afternoon at 4 I shall be in Paris. Meantime I must get the hell up and pack, and change money and tip, and rush to the municipal museum for Monroe, once more; and then for an hour, one last hour, the National Museum: the Rembrandt with the four amorous hands, and the *Night Watch*, which is as glorious as the Sistine Chapel, as glorious as *The School of Athens*—

The moment of flight, my first flight in Europe, the moment of slight peril, when I always rededicate myself to my love of Monroe, commit my future, in the event of death, to his remembrance . . .

Nearing Paris—A beautiful cubism of grain and perfectly tilled earth and mustard— All that as expected, but now I have just seen a dream woodland and, exactly in the heart of it, a dream château—and it brought tears to my eyes—
One has only one life—I want it over again—

Oh, it was strange! After fourteen years away, I arrived in Paris from Holland at about five o'clock. I had time only to take a French bath and to unpack amid French luxury, that is, eighteenth-century rosewood but no coat hangers, incomparable gloxinias but no wastebasket, etc., and to eat huge white asparagus and strawberry tart—then up and away to the Opéra. *"Et qu'est-ce qu'on y donnait ce soir-là? Le ballet américain!"*

And as I am here as, so to speak, a propagandist, I was as nervous as a cat. The press has been wildly unfavorable to the festival as a whole: partly because the festival secretariat has mistreated everyone in the matter of tickets; partly infiltration of Communist standpoints, and/ or desire to appease Communists . . . I met Lucia Chase* in the street yesterday, and she said that Balanchine was dead tired, a bit melancholy and perfectionist . . . But the first night was a triumph.

---

* Lucia Chase (1897–1986). American dancer and choreographer, she directed the American Ballet Theatre.

1 9 5 3

But worst of all, for me, is the loss of nerve
about A Year of Love *because it leaves me with-*
out any particular and immediate justification for
my privileged way of life . . .
—Journals

April 4

All day long I associated the perfect weather with Monroe's flight equatorward, awe-inspiring . . . By this time he is in Oaxaca, I hope.

Will came for lunch with his strange, stuffy, blushing, heavy-drinking, good-natured friend. Will has the brightest eyes on earth. He kept referring to the past. "This is the anniversary of my first visit, isn't it? When I first came, with Ronald, do you remember? Please let me come again soon, please write to me . . ."

After lunch we walked up along the Black Brook. I showed them one of the places where black snakes hibernate, and sure enough, there were two, dreaming in the sun together like Cadmus and Harmonia. Will took the largest in his hands, a four-footer all shoeshine-black with a white face, and played with it. I turned away and refused to look, lest my mind be furnished with the image of it for this or that nightmare. It made his fingertips fishy, and he seemed to mind my not being willing to sniff them.

All the slope down to the brook, close-stream with last year's colorless leaves, was starred with great bloodroot. The hepaticas at their best, bluer than usual; and the dogtooth violets beginning . . .

I listened to my broadcast, the one with Marianne and Wystan. They were even more tongue-tied than I thought, and I indefatigably proficient, filling in their gaps, wheeling around through double-talk to something that I could put to them in question form . . . My voice more disagreeable than ever, and I stutter, but one can understand every word I say—indeed one can't *not* understand, which is perhaps a part of the disagreeableness. It disillusioned me as to my ever being able to earn my living like that, if and if and if . . .

Last night I dined with Edna and Lloyd, and heard wonderful stories of inmates. There is a murderess who is somewhat hermaphroditical, and who is troubling other girls a good deal. "You haven't lived, none of you," she tells them. "Do you know about me? Do you realize that I sired a son, and then I had the operation, and then I delivered a daughter?"

Old Dr. Beatty, the female resident physician who has been there for years, has had a heart attack, and Ray Germain is pinch-hitting. He is dismayed at the number of girls who come to him with make-believe ailments, especially gynecological ailments. The other day one came with good-sized arrows painstakingly drawn on her thighs and belly in indelible ink, all pointing to her vagina.

Though I went to bed dog-tired last night, I woke irremediably at four-thirty. The sky was snowy-blue, and the demi-moon was pale apple-yellow.

I haven't any great strength of character even for art's sake; only a certain persistent subtlety. I haven't great inspiration; only a lifetime's know-how, and accumulated subjects.

My principal objection to Genet: within the framework of his works of fiction, he makes too many references to their being fictitious.

With my new amplifier, I can have music while weeding the petunia bed. Last night, I had the *St. Matthew Passion*, with the male catbird even approaching the open door in his ardor, and singing fortissimo.

Responsiveness to other males is an aspect of maleness in all mammals. Circumstances like imprisonment are of course greatly conducive; a part of it is just habit—and for the rest it is a great mystery, connected with the power of sexual fantasy, very male, and with educability, and having to do with economics much more than is generally thought, and with psychoneurosis much less—no one can generalize as yet; not even Kinsey has tried to.

Then what is the significance of the traits by which I seem to recognize Blake as homosexual? Certainly nothing causative—just *ex post facto* . . . The more or less actively homosexual person will tend to develop social characteristics, habits of mind, etc., according to his self-conscious differentiation from others in his country and class, etc.—roughly speaking, minority-mindedness.

Of great consequence, as discernible in "Blake's" text, the sado-masochistic, coercive-submissive factor, often disguising itself as something to do specifically with elements of maleness or femaleness in greater or lesser degree— There is also the dread of impotence, than which, I think, nothing is deeper-seated in the psychology of the male—

What I tried to write yesterday was a basic statement of the nature of homosexuality—thinking of it as a sort of necessity for *100 Affections* or any such book; half a page, or a page and a half, of dialogue with someone naïve . . . With perhaps what Thornton advocated in Venice: hortatory iterativeness. After all, think how subjective my own morality was a few years ago: before Malouf, etc., before Kinsey— And one has no right to expect one's readers to understand anything, in the way of general principle. Perhaps if I can get it into words of one syllable, five-word sentences, three-sentence paragraphs—something like the catechism: Responsiveness to the same sex, enjoyment of sexual play with the same sex, is potential in most humans (as in other species of mammals) for reasons unknown—though greatly subject to effects of circumstance, as in prisons, schools, etc.; also to factors in the society, the nation, the class: religion, education, economics much more than is generally thought, psychoneurosis much less.

But all this is a bore, in these abstract terms, as if it were sociology . . .

I have a sense of humor about my sex life, though perhaps not about my love life.

I am a little prejudiced against the higher education; at least present American education. Fine for the sciences, its concept of and effect on the arts and the humanities are beginning to be questionable. While billions are spent on the millions, television develops, publishing declines, photography flourishes, vocabulary shrinks (except perhaps for humorists). Even great writers express themselves in baby talk or booby talk—to which I see no objection in aesthetics, but a grave danger in the general culture: inarticulateness, for lack of language. Even what our great highbrows utter often is not exactly what I call language—so much of the time it is remote from the dictionary, slack in syntax, careless of pitch, neglectful of cadence, non-clear and unbrief . . . That great frame of reference, vocabulary of thinking as well as talking and writing, which is Mediterranean mythology—perhaps the greatest single treasure in the custody of the schools and colleges—is vanishing from the general mind . . . Oedipus is a word, thanks to psychoanalysis; Orpheus has his ballet—but Antigone? Penelope? Dionysus?

* * *

I borrowed $100 from Lloyd at the beginning of the month and have not repaid it. With pleasant timeliness there came the last six months' royalty on the Colette omnibus: $120. This made it possible to delay the great showdown, the confession and submission to my family . . .

Ll. does not want the responsibility; I must approach Baba directly about it. Oh, I am afraid. My hand is not strong enough. If only the book were further advanced—she is anxious to see some of it—

From a memo to Dr. Alfred Kinsey

I may tell you that I have rather wanted to come along with my Ronald, and some playmate of his, or mutual playmate—and not just pleasurable wanting; also with a concept of my getting certain results for you . . .* As though I were the accustomed handler of some rare high-strung monkey or other wonderful small beast—knowing how to calm its fears and tempers, what to give it to eat, and what medicines, etc. Not essential now, I think—perhaps not desirable . . . Anyway we haven't at present any playmate whom I could confidently send to Bloomington without your acquaintance and familiarization in New York beforehand. Our dear one of last year, Will Chandlee, excellent—but we have lost him; he ceased to respect Ronald, and Ronald ceased to desire him . . .

As to my reasons for thinking myself so important to Ronald or with him upon his visit to Bloomington: for the record, as follows: Do you remember that Sunday afternoon, how I stepped out of my role or, more exactly, crept out of it suddenly, along the floor to the foot of the bed, and took him in my mouth? Did you suppose that it was spontaneous passionateness or possessiveness on my part? No, he was about to fail to have an orgasm, and beckoned to me. As of last year that was the one infelicity or non-facility in his extraordinary range of pleasures: no one or almost no one could make him spend in the oragenital way. He taught me, with impassioned intolerance—once or twice his extreme rudeness and bossiness suddenly during intercourse aroused my extreme resentment and despair—and that was often my role in our triangular intimacies, with Michael, with Will, and some others. Not being brought to his climax would infuriate him, with histrionics verging on hysterics

---

* The Institute for Sex Research, with strict secrecy and a coding system, interviewed large numbers of people about their sexual experiences and acquired and created films of sexual activity. A number of G.W.'s acquaintances were volunteers, as was G.W. on two occasions.

. . . In those days he was ashamed to be seen masturbating—I got him over that, with some more little intimate drama—and now he often concludes with that. Indeed now, except for his operative anal fornication when he has the right young pretty responsive even submissive partner, his favorite position is up on the balls of his feet, astride of the fornicating male, with his own penis in his hand (to be exact, in his own fingers, just three fingers . . .).

If his coming to Bloomington works out well, I think you may want him more than once with a change of partners. What seems to me extraordinary about him is his intensity and strength in the several roles, the different patterns: the extremely romantic (and indeed neurotic) gerontophily, with me particularly but not exclusively; the regular auto-eroticism; the powerful and enamored maleness with youngsters some-what less male; the ecstatic submission to maximum maleness—all seemingly necessary in his temperament and nature and character—no real predominance of any one function over any other, or inhibiting or enfeebling or even moderating or disciplining effect . . . all very spon-taneous and self-prompting—very different from Michael's sort of desire to be all things to all men, and to be loved by almost all; very different from Tim's dear courtesan-like disposition . . . Ronald doesn't want to be loved—except by me, the gerontocrat, and by certain un-attainable beauties, dreams come true, for the moment. And he is most egocentric in his pursuit of whatever pleasure, though as good as gold, and a sufficient pleasure-giver—but unless he is at concert pitch him-self, with fine erection, he can't stand it, he wants to jump out of the window . . .

For your records, his masturbation of course, especially the second or third bout, for the most pronounced physiological effects—and as I have said, I thought he might be shy or shamefaced about that without me; it was his delight in my admiration, my shamelessness—in the autoerotic way, and above all, his ability to narrate previous sexual experiences to me, which got him over his sense of inferiority about that . . . He is irresistibly responsive to pictures and books—and I think he will work for you in that way like a charm . . .

My earnings by my pen for the first six months of the year, to wit: 51 copies of *The Grandmothers* at 7 cents, $3.57, and my share of the omnibus royalties for *The Pilgrim Hawk*, $3.31. Total, $6.88: just the price of an LP record, I said to myself—but as I have a lovely new one, the Ravel and Debussy quartets, I'll pass the checks on to Ronald.

* * *

Great literary inspiration as a rule has been fanatical, monomaniacal if not megalomaniacal. Good influence has never seemed to moderate it much.

The truth is, I am suffering more than can serve my constructive purposes. I can only weep. Too many knocks at the same time—too many shames, too many changes: love life, sex life, Stone-blossom, literature, budget . . .

I must try to break up the problem—and the consideration of my strange unsuccessful destiny—into its several immediate issues, and try to assign them priority:

Stone-blossom—Europe, no? New York, no?—where? My parents—etc.

Anna—no?—

Willing to try to write for money, willing to write *100 Affections* and *A Year of Love*, but not for publication—not in disgrace—

Sex life—willing to give up what I call *gang bangs*—willing to keep all my life out of 410 Park Ave.—

Willing to narrow down my life, but not to forswear it or renounce it—not to dismember myself—not to renounce the triangularity.

Ronald, withering away—

But worst of all, for me, is the loss of nerve about *A Year of Love* because it leaves me without any particular and immediate justification for my privileged way of life—

And then the thought of Mon's going away for almost all the winter when our minds are so divided, or at least so confused—our prospects so obscure—just makes me cry, and cry out; and my head aches so.

Pauline Potter is departing from the U.S. to reside in France, and marry Philippe de Rothschild. He has been ill, and must stay quiet in the château this winter—and he is one of those spoiled fidgety over-vigorous nobles. But he is a gifted amateur poet and she has got him interested in the sixteenth- and seventeenth-century British poets whom the French don't know. She has been making an anthology for him to translate—a pleasant sort of *dot*. She is arriving today with a carful of books, and a stenographer-typist, to pick my brains as well as to bid me farewell, until her flight Wednesday noon.

In the darkness, just before daybreak, there comes a little unsteady wind, coming and going every now and then, for a few minutes, and each time removing some more leaves from the sycamores. It sounds something like rain, something like hail, something like tinfoil.

* * *

I have read some P. G. Wodehouse for the first time in my life, with an appreciation that surprises me. Of course he repeats his effects too much. That seems to be one trouble with laughter as an objective—it is not self-limiting. When the writer sets out to amuse, what is to stop him? The more the merrier, he thinks.

October 10

How can I ever thank Ronald enough for the warmth and strength of his love when he and Will arrived last night and found me in tragical frame of mind?

I felt like a house lately flooded, or unroofed by a bad wind, dark and haunted—in the fireplace of which R. lit a fire. He made me *habitable* by myself once more, with his characteristic loving blue glances all evening, full of sympathy, humor, forgiveness, and slight kindly but disciplining words once in a while, which kept me functioning. In the circumstances, anxious and haunted and extravagant, I couldn't have behaved at all without his concern for me, unselfishness.

And when bedtime came at last—all three of us scared, each in the way of his particular fate and weakness—R. showed me nothing but kindness, and perfect performance.

The other day he gently, almost blushingly, expressed pride in his oragenital lovemaking, as much improved of late; or at least more consciously enacted, for his love-partner's sake. As his admirer this long while, I couldn't imagine what improvement. I took it to mean just something in his thinking and feeling—subjective.

But last night I saw, with blissful admiration all over again. Nothing subjective about it. It was virtuosity—like some great musical performer making music, inaudible music, on the great instrument of Will's body, like young David with his harp in the Rembrandt painting that has meant so much to me all my life, old Saul wiping the tear out of his eye, but a mystic tear, not a tear of self-pity or sadness . . .

Some sadness of course there was last night, but it was common to us, it pertained to both youth and age, it was in the nature of love and sex . . . Oh, I am not complaining. I had my only complete pleasure in weeks and weeks—with certain impressions that I shall not confuse with any other experience, or ever forget.

Ennoblement of Will's body especially, in complete arousal and in orgasm—as though he had died and gone to heaven; all his fleshiness vanished, and the small of his back and his buttocks like an angel's. Furthermore, in spite of my regret and anxiety at R. not himself coming to climax—my orgasm was powerful and profound, instantaneously synchronized with Will's. It was R.'s great kindness to us both—and I slept as I have not been able to sleep for weeks and weeks . . .

The chief lesson of the half century for me has been simply the old platitude: The years bring distresses and destruction inevitably—but oh, surprise, surprise! pleasures as well, that youth couldn't have conceived . . .

Mrs. Crane has engaged me to discourse to the "Monday Class" on November 25, and proposes my doing so regularly, once a month. Can I think of subjects enough? This time I shall talk about Forster, especially Forster's India. A good theme, perhaps too extensive . . .

Forster had just published, with explanations and commentaries, the letters he wrote home from India in 1912 and 1921—raw material of *A Passage to India* (1924). He specifies that he had already commenced it prior to 1921. On the other hand some passages of the 1921 letters reappear in the novel, just paraphrases, expanded. Why did he never write another novel after that? "Physical debility! Physical debility!" says Edith Sitwell, but I am inclined to think he did himself an inner injury by not publishing the homosexual novel, *Maurice*. Of course no particular subject matter is essential; and even secretiveness or hypocrisy is all right, if the writer really believes in the moral or theological taboo or the convention of society to which he conforms—(Proust did believe . . .). But if he just vaguely suspects himself of cowardice . . . I guess I must not go into all that with the "Monday Class."

My aged father is apparently dying. He is in the wonderful new Hunterdon Medical Center, and on Tuesday they have scheduled a bold terrible operation that may save his life, but the chances are against him.

At the same time, Mr. [Nelson] Rockefeller is sending Monroe all around South America upon a mission, or two or three missions overlapping—beginning next Sunday; and I have promised to help him with a lecture which he has to give here and there, and to help him get off. Therefore I must be in N.Y. next Friday night and Saturday.

The main preoccupation this week has been my strange wonderful old father's deathly illness, and responsibility for my mother the while. They prepared him, with intravenous feeding, Terramycin, etc., for a big risky hopeful operation—but found cancer through and through.

Colostomy, and maximum narcotics from now on, have helped, as to his pain. How long, they can't tell . . . days, I guess. I stay with him a good deal. When he gets restless he reaches out his hand—when he feels that I am clasping it, pressing it against my chest, he falls back into the Demerol-induced sleep . . . Mother is not only courageous but exquisite: amorous and philosophical at the same time. She must not get too tired, that is all . . .

The new hospital, which has been my brother's lifework for two or three years, is a wonder . . .

Just after I woke this morning, at 6 a.m.—with my first coffee, I was reading *Time*'s account of the trouble about homosexuality in England—the telephone rang: I fancied it was the final word from the deathbed. No, it was my dear R., saying good night, telling me that he had had a good time . . .

Thus death and love, and indeed sometimes frustrated love and sometimes meaningless sex and youth and age, and disease and health, are all interspersed in our existence—therefore some tragedy all the while, some tragedy in everything. And shrinking from the consideration of this, or refusing to act upon one's recognition of it, is just silly; it is wasting one's intelligence, compounding the peril—like not going to the doctor in time.

Father
A sort of Don Juan, but monogamous and polyphiloprogenitive, trying to behave like a sort of King Lear.

November 18—evening
My father died this morning at 2:15 a.m. I had spent the last three nights, and most of the days, there in the hospital—on account of my mother's health, and indeed my brother's—(she has a perilous heart, he has a stomach ulcer)—and at the end, the nurse happened to go down the corridor for a cup of coffee, I alone with him for two minutes, when it happened: the sound of a high-pitched bubble once or twice, then the welling out of blood; the head falling forward, then lifted up high and flung back on the pillow. It was wonderful—afterward he looked like a drawing by David, one of the assassinated revolutionists.

For almost an hour I have been staring at the blank paper, gazing into the eyes of the *Lion-Boy* across the room, looking back at 1953, peering into 1954 fearfully but (I believe) not weakly . . .

The death of my father was three days after Monroe's departure—a news item so great, with consequences so fateful: I scarcely know what report I gave him. The South American air-mail service is slow and uncertain; M.'s mission has amounted to incessant sociability, and he has written me less than ever; and all just a listing of activities, a naming of diplomats, artists, plutocrats, connoisseurs, never *replying* to my letters, never commenting on my life, or almost never. It has made an odd solitude . . .

My mother could not endure her solitude in Leigh Street, with only a little old local lady-housekeeper; and needless to say, she and Baba are too much for each other; and my sisters are wage earners. Meanwhile the necessity of some showdown about my monthly borrowings from Baba, and monthly deficit even for Stone-blossom, not to mention my spending money in town, pressed harder and harder. At last I got Lloyd to sit down and listen. I proposed dismissing Anna and her brother and sister-in-law, cooking myself, etc. He then asked me whether I would take Mother to live with me, as long as she lives—I instantly said yes.

That night was nightmarish, especially the ordeal of settling everything without consulting Monroe—not only the mysterious commitment itself, but a hundred small questions of the shifting of the rooms of Stone-blossom, and rules and regulations. Never before, nothing of such impact and import, nothing so ultimate for him as for me, if her life should prolong itself, nothing comparable in the thirty-three years of our relationship—certainly very maturing. My bedroom becomes Mother's sitting room; my study her bedroom. My desk is in the library, a little cross-wise in the corner where the tapestry bed stood. I sit with my back to the corner, looking over the desk toward the front door.

My new room, which is being soundproofed between me and Anna, provided with bookshelves in place of the bogus fireplace, and other comforts. When we have guests I'll descend to the library. Once a month or so, I'll weekend in N.Y. with Monroe—it will give him an opportunity to re-establish a little joint worldliness with me, which should please and perhaps reassure him—and then Mother will play hostess to her daughters and their beaux and such.

The worst of it has been, still is, cupboards, closets, attics, archives. In no time at all, it all vomited itself forth on the floor: fifteen years of scribble, and all the manuscript and typescript versions of my books (property of Monroe Wheeler), and periodical publications, and mountains of art catalogues and pamphlets, three years of letter files never really filed . . . Of course I would have liked a real installation of mouse-proof cabinets; shelves on attics, economy or at least solvency

. . . I need a hundred little things: a paper rack, an overhead lamp, a carrier for firewood, a tiny chest of drawers, etc.—absurdities . . .

Though exhausted, I am exhilarated. This may do good: a refurbishment of the rut; a shining up of the gilded cage; and, if I find my character at all strengthened (as I hope), perhaps opportunity to impose on my near and dear ones a little better planning in some respects—even on my dearest Monroe, and lesser darlings, if this high wind doesn't blow them out of my life once and for all.

Of course it may all be in vain, for better or worse. Mother may die of the move. She has had two little strokes—or to be exact, comas, from insufficient circulation of the blood into the brain: arteriosclerosis. Her euphoria and then exhaustion is dismaying, and certainly her faculties are on the wane: eyesight and motor reflexes especially. If she dies, all this will be like one of those chancy surgical operations—the patient hopeful and happy, the surgeon chopping himself just a bit, along with the surgeree—but of course we'll not begrudge the expense and effort. In fact I think she may continue a good while, even perhaps blind or paralyzed or with enfeebled mind.

She said, one of the early days of the planning, "Now, Glenway, we must remember that I am not going to live more than about ten years; so we must not spend too much money on changes just for me."

She said, Christmas night, "I have never been able to understand how grief-stricken persons could use certain phrases, such as 'Merry Christmas.' Tonight I understand. I've been *merry*."

The worst of it, for me, may be, in the event of her death presently, having to refinance Stone-blossom all over again; with or without servants. I try to think with alternatives in mind, either way. But now I seem unable to think of giving Stone-blossom up, or going abroad, or taking employment on a magazine or in a publishing company, etc. The coincidence of all this with Monroe's anxiety about my morals, ambiguity about my work, is fantastic.

What work comes next; which book, moral or immoral, for posterity or for money, etc., I shall not even ponder or discuss, until the dust dies down—in perhaps a month. Meantime "he-festivals," as Whitman called them—(had he the experience, or only the desire and daydream?—one can scarcely tell about poets)—"he-festivals, with blackguard gibes, ironical license, bull-dances, drinking, laughter . . ." Forbidden me until Monroe's morale is restored, his pessimism alleviated . . .

Oh, surely the strangest part of morals is the economic . . .

1 9 5 4

As you may gather, I am a believer in style.
Often, I think, a writer's handling of language,
vocabulary and diction and syntax, irony and
imitation and colloquialism and rhetorical effects
and figures of speech, and some degree of cour-
teousness and ceremony in his writing according
to his love of literature, express his knowledge of
the world and his feeling about his life and his
responsiveness to the environing world more origi-
nally and fundamentally than what he thinks of
as his subject matter, his learnedness or cogita-
tion or experience, as the case may be.
—"Talks with Thornton Wilder"

I am having a time of anguish with Monroe still. Of course he loves me, always—but with so much less confidence in me, less approbation, less optimism, that it is almost a tragedy. For the present, nothing is so important, nothing, nothing— Not even literature, not even devotion to Ronald, not even pleasure—as to try to restore his faith in me. He doesn't blame me; he just despairs of me. It seems to him that my need of money is so great, the sense of duty imposed on me by my family is so laborious, and my sexual pattern so difficult and unlucky, that I *can't* now be expected to fulfill my promise as a writer. As it was Monroe who perceived my talent and promise in the beginning of my life—(I didn't)— it is bad for me to resign myself to his misunderstanding and his discouragement even for an hour.

The first robin rendered his first aubade on the last day of winter. Daily now . . . Strange, the effects of my mother's failures of circulation, droughts in the brain— For example, I read aloud to her Santha Rama

Rau's *Holiday* article on India when it first came out. She has not the remotest memory of it—picked it up, attracted by the color photographs, and asked me to read it, which I have done, redone. Not like ordinary forgetfulness—this is erasure, haphazard.

I have had illusions of having lost my talent in the past, haven't I? This time it has taken the horrid form of not seeming able to remember enough about any of the things I had to write about. Illusion, delusion— probably . . . Due to the upheaval and disorder in great measure, of course—just never seeing ms. of work-in-progress, for one thing. Work habits broken, and not yet re-formed. My desk in the library still in- convenient, uncomfortable, unpeaceful. The day all fractioned; and more persons to and fro than ever before. But all this is conquerable by me somehow, I do believe—a matter of the technology of myself. I do not feel too old for it, though probably I shall be before long. It is only when, for example, Ll. tells me that they are going to fire Marty early in the summer, and then he'll teach me to drive, so that I can take Anna shopping and Mother calling, that I get panic-stricken and, indeed, indignant. A prospect of learning and learning, and never being allowed to be habit-bound in any way, never settling down—as though self- discipline or self-development, for its own sake, were the purpose of life. Of course the women of my family do believe that . . .

What I feel is a kind of brokenness—not brokenheartedness: many a time in my life I have been unhappier than I ever am these days. But instead of thinking, too much of the time I just brood and wonder, *vague à l'âme*—

As for Ronald, I begin to think that perhaps it would be better if he left me to my own devices for a while—let me sulk, let me try to write, let me rest, let me have my little nervous breakdown if I must, let me fight it out with my family, let me economize, let me grow older and wiser . . .

So be it—the only virtues are work and friendship; the only absolute is orgasm; nothing is long-lasting except art—literature and sculpture the longest. I seem to be ceasing to believe in love.

April 28

At breakfast time this morning Mother informed me that she didn't feel up to going to New York. Her cough troubled her a little—(she had decided last night that she could get along without her cough pills)— and the weather depressed her. Furthermore suggestions about it—the bus ride by herself and Beulah's flights of stairs instead of Elizabeth's elevator, etc.—intimidated her.

It took me an hour, more than an hour, to get this straightened out. She likes to pay for any telephone calls that I may make in her behalf, and it seemed to her extravagant to telephone about this. She could not see why a letter to Elizabeth, about her cough, etc., would not serve the purpose as well. Furthermore she disapproves of my telephoning Elizabeth in her working hours. I remarked that, from my standpoint, my working hours are as sacrosanct as anyone's. But on the whole we behaved well—neither of us shed tears (both of us did, last week . . .), and all's well that ends well. She has gone off to her Angela Thirkell records in tranquillized mood, ever the old-fashioned, enamored type of female, tyrannous over the male, overreliant upon the male, etc. And why shouldn't she be? I sometimes wonder if there is any such thing as psychology. Certainly her shortcomings of morale at this point are as physiological as all the rest; a matter of senescence.

May 1

Religious old American lady, reminiscing: "I am so grateful to Dr. Bachman. He introduced me to Jesus Christ, and also to the Queen of Rumania."

May 22—4½ a.m.

It hasn't been hard to do what I resolved, that is, to keep my distance from the amorousness of my weekend guests.

But I suppose their presence has troubled me, kept me from sleeping. Only three hours, with dreams. Now here I sit, longing, pondering, and the hours pass, yes, hours. The birds sing in the dark; the wind wears away the darkness; the first bits of sunshine in the crab-apple leaves really glitter, like gilt.

Upon my arrival last night I found my blond flesh-colored iris blown over. I am afraid this restless dawn will have toppled the gray one also. Too tall. I should have staked them.

The hours pass, and all the while I have wanted to masturbate. But my heart is too full of love to entertain any sort of cheap or unreal or forced fantasy; and as it happens just now, all the evocations of any of my dear ones or playmates are fraught with extreme sense of regret, unsuccessfulness, self-reproach—and the sadness makes me impotent.

June 9

Recently I went to a fashionable wedding and had a conversation with an old friend, a half-imperial Russian princess, now a rather broken-down dressmaker. "At our age, dee-ur Glenway," she said, "we must not ever complain. Only let us get angry. My dentist yesterday hurt me. Very angered, I gave him a slap; it was a good thing. But not complaining . . ."

I'm going to have to have a quarrel with my brother, about money, etc. Last evening after sunset I went with him to his woodlot, the abode of deer: twenty acres densely wooded but narrow, so that from the center of it we could still see the golden evening light, intensified by a field of wheat on the one side and of barley on the other side.

He also made me look at his corn, without one sprig of any weed, and smell his perfect hay, some in green swathes, some cured and raked, some in bales. Because I always have to forgive him for thinking his farming more important than my literature, now and then he likes me to see his ecstatic pleasure in hill and dale, in the crops and the beasts, etc. He knows that I believe in ecstatic pleasure more than in anything else on earth. A sort of observation of it is my religion.

Now I must take a trayful of breakfast to my mother—which makes me, so to speak, lonesome.

Alas, I must admit, perhaps plainness is not my way. Ronald and I have a rendezvous for Saturday. Only for the early part of the evening, R. having plainly specified that in the summertime, Saturday nights are as important and unsacrificeable as his Friday nights. And so I have planned to give him dinner—between 6 and 9 or 9½—either cooked by me there at 363 or in some restaurant. And naturally I hope that he may ask a playmate, old or new, to dine with us, if possible. If not, I'd like to be just by ourselves, peaceful and voluptuous, to be told his adventures and pleasures of the week, etc. I am like a sort of desert plant: when it doesn't rain I feed upon the evening breeze and the dew.

I never mean to be a lover, though little by little my gratitude for blissfulness and peacefulness accumulates, and is a form of love, and can be counted on, and indeed sometimes taken advantage of . . . If I could have my life as I should like, I'd scarcely want any passion of my own—I'd be nothing but a spectator of the lives and loves of my dear ones and I'd prefer the animal aspect of their humanity to the psychological or the moral or immoral—and I'd rather have domestic animals than wild beasts, for the simplicity's sake.

June 14

Every day or so it happens that my mother, weary, resting, looks the way she is going to look when dead.

She is, I think, like one of the great queens. Which one? perhaps Catherine the Great. The simplicity, the subtlety, the amorousness, the autocracy. I wonder if others who know her, even her other children, think or feel any such thing.

The last time I really clamored for a reconsideration of my budget, etc., was March 20—and when Lloyd expressed an opinion that I passionately disbelieve: as to the effect of Barbara's financing of my life and vocation. At her expense I have produced two or three good books, some other publishable writing, and a good deal of work in progress, not yet publishable. It is insufficient and unsatisfactory—evidently I have limited talent, certainly I have a weak character—but, I believe, the principle of the thing between us was right. Even if it seems a failure now, or if it can no longer be afforded, I cannot neglect to testify to the happiness of my life in the essentials, thanks to her.

August 4

In the subway: a young mulatto or octoroon with a nose worthy of a cameo, a sensual and sullen mouth, and bad bright eyes, wearing a visored cap, a dirty sport shirt, loose dungarees, and ruined shoes, swinging upon his wrist a tight-rolled umbrella with a curved wooden handle studded with rhinestones.

August 6

I haven't been anywhere this summer, except to Bloomington for ten days, where I did fascinating hard work with Paul Gebhard.* Kinsey himself is coming here next month upon his return from Peru.

Otherwise my becalmed life is as is. In my weak but stubborn way I continue with my improper novel. My mother is failing but still has great strength and good character. The family life often makes me think of iris rhizomes that haven't been reset for years—my rhizome gets heaved up from the earth, my roots stretch and strain for moisture and nutrition. But I'm all right.

We have been afflicted by drought for the third successive summer, the worst. The meadows are withered, as they used to be in Wisconsin when I was a boy—the crops are tragic, the flowers dwarfish. But the skies are glorious, azure, with vain immaculate clouds; the swimming holes are clean and deep, full of boys.

* Paul Gebhard. Assistant to Dr. Kinsey and a senior staff member at the Institute for Sex Research.

Ronald spent a fortnight in Florida, where the boys are happier-natured than anywhere else, he says. And now he has begun his new job: managing a do-it-yourself decorating shop.

The police in New York are arresting all the improper younger generation around town night after night. Thus far, knock on wood!— in spite of dungarees and T-shirts, none of my youngsters has been mistaken for a mugger or a hustler or anything else illegal. Very strange, when you read further than the headlines: The city needs seven thousand more policemen, and they must have increased pay; and by this crusade the mayor and the commissioner intend maximum publicity, until something is voted.

The McCarthy business still festers in everyone's mind, and somewhat in the newspapers, though they seem bored, perhaps because they can't print what is talked about more and more: the possibility that there are rival bands of ferocious queens blackmailing one another to a standstill. The reason the Army had to give up without substantiation its first set of charges against McCarthy and Cohn and Schine, we are told, is that heads would have rolled on its side of the fence as well; and the weakness of the chief of state is explained by his having a romantic secret of his own—*not*, goodness knows, an h. secret! For my part I have been extremely skeptical of all this; but in any event the suspicion and whispering campaign are serious, and bound to bring about a certain anti-homosexuality. Likewise a certain anti-Semitism—the testimonial dinner to Cohn after his resignation was presided over by a silly rabbi . . . My personal theory is that Cohn and his mentor Sokolsky are crypto-Communists, squeezing and maneuvering McC. The Hiss affair worked so well to poison the atmosphere of our government, like a dead rat behind the State Department wainscoting, that they might quite plausibly have decided to give us another dose . . .

Now to work . . . Somehow Mother is angry at me—or at least keeping a secret from me. I must smoke her out, I guess. Sometimes I feel a sort of horror and panic at the possibility of her senescence taking that sort of form, psychopathological.

Anna, in the early morning: "Did you read in the newspaper how some girl got electrocuted in the bathtub in Germany, daughter of some high colonel or palooka? It's the truth, and I saw how it happened at the Jewish people's where I worked; it happened to me."

I suppose that listening to talk like this must be one of the main inspirations of playwrights. Save for the one strange word, *palooka*, I might scarcely have listened this morning; the music of familiar syntax . . .

* * *

This week I'm going to try to write those damned fables Monroe has maneuvered me into.

Woods Hole
August 16

A great meteor streaked across the sky. What is it called, the meteoric shower through which we pass every August, as if it were the exhaust of some cosmic engine, or the wake of infinite invisible boat—the Leonids? No, the Andromeids.

How numerous the deaths in our circle of friends this year! A sort of Andromeids in reverse: streaks of blackness instead of incandescence; bits of nullification every so often amid our bold little ideas and bright talk; brevities of grief and dread.

August 17

There were two or three blues in the daybreak, sapphire, aquamarine, fused by the breezes.

Then I masturbated, with more blissfulness than usual. I found a few sentences of eroticism in one of my scribble books, and I scribbled a few more; and when my eyes shifted too much, when my pencil wouldn't stay in my hand, I thought of a youngster Jamie told me about night before last—a small boy with a homely mouth and a big uncircumcised penis, who licked him all over his body, tirelessly, as a cat licks her kitten, whose ejaculation was bitter.

Then I went back to sleep, and dreamed of home. I dreamed that I was walking in my sleep (which I have never done, as a matter of fact) and I found myself in my mother's bedroom, and whispered an apology for disturbing her, to which she made no reply, and afterward could not be sure whether she had heard me or not, whether she was alive or not.

Then I woke up again, with an altercation of gulls just outside my window, all in their high rubbery tone of voice.

Toward midnight we went for a walk with old Padraic [Colum], spry, gay, earnest, and unelderly. It is amazing, always, to think of his actual age. Did he not have a play produced at the Abbey Theatre the year I was born?

Very low in the sky lay the last of this month's moon, empty-looking and sinking.

Until a few years ago I was innocent, ignorant, of death—it almost embarrassed me, upon occasions of others' bereavement, and even in the planning of certain works of fiction. (Remember Hemingway's rather

thrilling though stupid avowal of this: based in his case upon the notion
that those who die of bullets or bull horns, etc., are somehow deader
than the cancerous, *et al.*)

Naturally I have been thinking of Lloyd Morris* a great deal these
days. With the horror of illness, the horror of war, the horror of poverty,
I never mind people's dying very much, not on *their* account, unless
they still have work to do.

The great theme of his life, I suppose, was having so strong a
creative urge and, in the early days, so little talent—devoting himself
then to others who were, or who seemed, more talented, with the heart-
break and vexation attendant upon that course, invariably, inevitably,
I guess. (The talented *envy* the untalented, don't they?— Every sort of
small Prometheus looking askance at everyone who seems free from
eagles . . .)

Then, of course, Lloyd found the form of work that suited him, and
developed talent, surprising everyone. He was quite conscious of all
that— I remember once, when I congratulated him on the first New York
book, a look of a kind of laughter fleeting across his face—it made me
think of Abraham's wife in the Old Testament . . .

But what I understand least about him was our own relationship
. . . I wonder if he ever talked to anyone about that, revealingly; never
to me, or me to him . . . First, the admiring one (influential professor,
doting critic, volunteer agent)—but no, surely that was not the point;
there was something hidden under it. Then the loving one, and indeed
he was overstimulated by me, hypersensitive, possessive—but no, that
was not the point either, something hidden, hidden. What I revolted
against was the parental character in him, powerful, power-loving—and
perhaps the artistic character, wishing to implement his creativity with
my talentedness . . . I wonder if he kept my letters, and if any of this
was expressed in them. I wonder if I have kept his letters . . .

And, strangest of all, I never had as much talent as he believed I
had, nor as much as Monroe Wheeler believed. And I too have been
finding my own peculiar aesthetic and unique or individual vision and
message, and (I guess) developing talent—too late? —Perhaps not.

September 1

In the meadow I noticed an uncommon-looking middle-sized boulder, and it moved! Needless to say, it was not a boulder, it was a turtle,
but for an instant, it made my flesh creep, just under my ears, and on

* Lloyd Morris (1893–1954). American biographer (notably of Hawthorne) and essayist.

my chest, around my nipples—and I wonder what it really was that made me so emotional: supernaturalness of the rock, and willingness to believe it? or just weak human nature, herpetophobia and all that?

Early Friday morning a telegram from François, Tim, and Will. I had written R. a sharp missive, with a sort of fierce plaintiveness which the French in any romantic connection understand—complaining especially of Will's not having answered my letter inviting him here for this Kinsey weekend . . . "All faithful to you stop letter probably lost everyone happy but missing you."

As read by the Western Union operator, the male one with the soulful young-sounding voice, I swear that I heard, "*lover* probably lost." So I said to him, "Well, that is double-talk, but I guess I can figure it out." Whereupon he reread it slowly: *letter*, etc. . . .

Can my poor ears, always lovelorn in the strangest ways, have misled me? Or did young Western Union misspeak? At any rate, his tone was extremely respectful, even unctuous.

I am tired, dog-tired. Ronald's anguish of trying to detach himself from me occurs so untimely. And as he is so afraid of perhaps injuring me in my self-esteem, or in my will to live, he keeps repeating that the only important thing is for me to write, write, write—"for all our sakes. So that the world will understand us better." And of course I am always inclined to reply that he has no right to ask this, unless he will help— which isn't very fair to him or indeed wholesome for me. But what would I not give for the helpfulness and restfulness in question just now, for an hour or two at the foot of someone's felicitous bed, forgetful of my own very existence, of my damned stubborn willpower, and my dire indefatigable criticism and self-criticism, and my weary little sense of duty, noblesse oblige or mere submissiveness, and tedious pathetic sense in every sort of petty connection—then, naturally, for the subsequent hour or two, or day or two, to have something else to express in my writing, something blithe and peaceful, disinterested and authoritative and general. Yea-saying in some way; not a nay-saying that is suspect, to me at least, when it seems to arise out of my own little frustrations, feeblenesses, mismanagements.

Twenty years ago, Monroe used to be afraid of my writing about homosexuality, lest the dark view that I seemed to take of it should prove too discouraging to the younger generation thus inclined? Likewise, those who urge me now, Write, write! certainly expect me to say yea, don't they? Certainly they want a book or books expressive of love—*not* indictment, either according to my individual plight and grievance or according to scientific averages or general sociological considerations. I am to be the opposite of the scapegoat, *not* bearing their sins away into the wilderness, but, instead, conveying their justification and their virtue and indeed their bliss to the marketplace . . .

But let me not ascribe to Ronald and the others more influence than is due. The main great difficult premise is my own—and if anyone greatly swayed me to it, it must have been Mon: I don't really want to write negatively, complainingly, compensatorily, vindictively. I don't want to give support in any sense to old tenets of occult religion and repressive ethics that, I think, have disproved themselves in every other respect all over the world . . .

It always embarrasses me to use the word *tragic* with reference to troubles of love life and sex life. Unhappiness is *not* tragic. Most of the ideas and ideals of romantic love seem to me as false as religion. Frustration and impotence and misunderstanding and jealousy and unfairness and unkindness—so often by-products of romanticism—are only mistakes and discomforts. I never seem to want to write about them, except in letters ever striving to get my own way. In literature I should like to express only naturalness on the one hand, aesthetics on the other; ecstasies of the senses and the arts, nothing really sorrowful except old age and death, seasons in human existence corresponding to other heat and cold and ebb and flow of earthly reality under the moon and the sun.

September 7

I am writing in Baba's red car, in fierce heat and windiness, on our way to Princeton.

Kinsey did not arrive, after all my nervous preparations, removing my mother to this or that sister's in town, and various secretarial responsibilities for him there, in and out, and waiting around the Statler . . . I called Paul Gebhard. They expect A.C.K. to pull through all right, but he was in bad condition. Some Peruvian bug, culminating in a "pelvic infection"—twelve days in bed, in a Lima hospital?

It did not occur to me not to, in making his excuses to people who had expected to have their histories taken, etc., not to specify the nature of illness until someone said, "Pelvic infection? Oh yes, of course, llamas . . ."

September 14

Monroe has been in Illinois and Wisconsin with his extremely aged but lively parents, and with some museum-minded millionaires. He returned to New York yesterday, in much better health than last year.

On the other hand, Mother keeps failing of course, though no one can, or no one will, prognosticate what sort of failure. I do so hope she will die all at once, and not get foundered in paralysis, etc. (which is a selfish as well as an unselfish thought). Then I shall take to the lecture platform for my living. I am resuming work on *A Year of Love*, as I please, as best I can, for presumably posthumous publication. My brother has been good about this, enabling me to avoid discussing it with my sister-in-law, who is still in the process of psychoanalysis—(and that school of analysts proposes to "cure" homosexuality).

Hurricane Carol went through Josephine's house, taking the furniture out to sea. No great loss *per se*, but of course bad for her, nightmarish, traumatic, and uprooting.

September 22

It was Lord Milbourne who said, "I wish I was as cocksure about anything as Macaulay is about everything." Lovell, the psychiatrist, said it to me, but naturally not about Macaulay—about psychoanalysts.

I am reading Virginia Woolf's journal, and I love it! If the rest is as I imagine, it will surely outweigh the novels. That is a great part of the horror of death for me—never having a chance to read things like this . . .

September 28

Termination of daylight-saving dramatizes the autumn. The change of course is in me, that is, in my clocks, but seems external. I go for a walk after tea, as usual, but it has become a stroll in the evening. Like the sort of illness that ages one, or indeed, the sort of sorrow . . .

The sun ethereal but blinding: it has descended far enough to get into my eyes at right angles.

The great hedgerow along the shooting grounds massive with honeysuckle, extremely sweet: its autumn flowering has started. Five-leaf ivy flaming up over it here and there, and soft little fruit of guelder rose sprinkling it like blood, translucent young-looking blood.

October 3

A panhandler after my heart

He spotted me from afar, halfway down the block, or a third of the way, and I felt my usual compassion, anxiety, anger, and acquiescence.

"Say, Mac, just a minute, listen—I've got a buddy, and we're winos.

I'm on my way to his place now, he's waiting for me, and I haven't got a bottle. Can you help us out?"

He looked me straight in the eye, a little fatuously, seeming to understand me, willing to be understood by me, determined not to be ashamed in the event of my refusing him, glad to ask, and indeed to risk refusal, because it was his heart's desire, enjoying desire as such, and whetting it.

I helped out to the extent of fifty cents. Only some shyness and perhaps self-mockery kept me from giving him the entire bottle.

Can he have recognized my extreme altruism, my life of empathy, love of lovers?

Now I regret not having given him the bottle.

October 9

I have never really liked Mr. Robert Frost. He has the appearance of a small man enlarged and coarsened, and he seems damp somehow. His manner is fatherly to everyone, perhaps not an affectation, but certainly a habit. I sense (or I fancy) unkindness. The work also suggests this, particularly references to his sexual puritanism, as though it were something to be proud of.

But how agreeably he expresses everything, even wrongness and eccentricity, with an effect of wealth and sparkle!

For example, in this Thoreau broadcast: "A great civilization in its greatness can afford to indulge in all sorts of deviations and aberrations"—which a utopia can never do. And what sorts do you suppose he craves indulgence for? The negative and the pecuniary; miserliness and secrecy; not carrying fire insurance or life insurance, not letting one's heirs know how much money one has for them to inherit, etc. In all this it is hard to distinguish the sense of humor from the self-indulgence.

A number of our important American men are poseurs, aren't they? (Whitman was . . .) Perhaps it is the way to command respect in our provincial places and on our campuses.

When Kinsey has not yet interviewed friends of mine, I enjoy talking to him about them, tell him their stories, speculating upon the motivations and the mysteries; and in return he sometimes makes general commentary and teaches me things. But *not* after a history-taking! He has trained himself not even to *look* interested or interesting about any researchee. He turns upon me a perfect poker face, and pretends not to know what in the world I am alluding to . . .

November 27

Some species of insects have eight times as many muscles as man.

The European maybug (Melolontha) smells with forty thousand infinitesimal nostrils. Little tiny noses.

How entrancing are the details of natural history! I gladly read through an entire issue of *Scientific American*, which with my poor education is almost incomprehensible, understanding almost nothing, nothing, just to glean a few such facts as these.

November 28

There is in our neighboring prison a remarkable, indeed now admirable Negress named Anne Brown. She came to Clinton as an accomplice in a murder for which her brother and another young man were executed.

Note that I say, *now* admirable. In the early years she made a nuisance of herself, excessively energetic in every way, in sexuality, and fights, and moods of grief and mystery. Once she bolted out of the hospital stark naked, streaked across the prison lawn, and pounded with her fists on Miss Mahan's door.

But all is well. She has grown up, and keeps peace with people, and has learned a sufficient means of livelihood as a beautician, and is soon to be released into the free world with everyone's blessing and good prognostication.

She is a big powerful dark creature with a man's speaking voice, rather like Ezio Pinza's voice.

When A.C.K. visited the institution the other day, she said to him, "I think I ought to read your book, Doctor. I'm going out now, and I'll need to know about the behavior in the world. You know, I've been here since I was sixteen years of age, so I'm not very experienced."

The book is being made available to her.

November 30

Anna, when she came in with my orange juice, protested: "Oh, Mr. Wescott, what a terrible singing you had last night! Was it on the record, or was it on the radio? What a terrible high note that kept going and going, just like a whistle!"

After a moment's irritation and effort to remember, I was able to tell her what it was: one of WQXR's rather intellectual programs contrasting how emotions are expressed by classical and sophisticated composers, on the one hand, and by (so to speak) native music-makers, on the other hand, including a realistic recording of a North African *muezzin*, and a Turkish love song, loud and catlike, and other such primitive pieces.

"Oh, primitive," Anna exclaimed, "that must've been it. Oh yes, I've seen it in the cartoons in the newspaper. There stands the primitive man, with a great big club with stickers out of the end of it, and there stands the woman waiting to be loved. Only instead of reaching out to her personally"—and she extended her own strong little arms as far as they were able—"he just knocks her on the head! And her eyes are twinkling all around, she is so overjoyed, because now she knows he loves her."

And away she went, back to the kitchen; then through the room again and up the stairs to make the beds, still gesturing, throwing up her hands as in consternation and perhaps admiration, and laughing.

Of course Katherine Anne's despairing letters are superior to any novel she could have written. Her concentration on fiction, fiction, fiction has been not only because it seemed to offer greatest remuneration but because she always wants to disseminate *un*truth, which seems easiest to do in the novel form. She doesn't stop to consider the fact that her letters are fictitious.

Once or twice when Alfred Kinsey was here last month, and I had to bring together certain difficult researchees for him, he would change his plans without telling me, or say something that he had instructed me not to say. Of course he isn't old, nevertheless is nearing his end, with a terrible cardiac deterioration. Perhaps the circulation of his blood in his brain is irregular, causing lapses of memory, or mechanistic recurrences of little old patterns, devices, prejudices, fears—it is so in Mother's case . . .

But also the aged develop a new and particular ruthlessness, because they are in such a hurry, with so little time left, with no more of the luck of life—they expect us to forgive them, afterward, when we look back and conceive what they were feeling; and so we shall do, no doubt.

One of the loveliest types of winter day, with sunshine refracted from fog.

In the northern sky a scattering of long feathers of jet planes; horrible egrets . . .

And then there appeared three of them close abreast, and a fourth as an outrider, racing obliquely up from the horizon toward the zenith.

Like Marianne Moore's "Garden of Eden": where "there was no smoke and color was fine . . ." and "obliqueness was a variation of the perpendicular . . . with nothing to modify it but the mist that went up . . ."

I believe that in entire human history no man has ever influenced his civilization so promptly and profoundly as Whitman has influenced us: our patriotism, our love life and sex life, our education and sport— not all good influence, but almost all.

1 9 5 5

It shall be an age of telling the truth. A worldly
age, if you like, a carnal age, all infatuated
with mere man . . . An age of confessions and
curiosities: yes, it must shock some people.
—Fear and Trembling

Embarrassed by a resolve not to write letters for a while; working, though never assiduously enough for career or conscience; writing something secret, also writing something publishable; naturally too contemplative and talkative and amorous and affectionate; involved in that great portion of fate which is family; neglecting friends but not forgetting or disowning any; aging and yet healthy; frustrated and yet happy—I wish you happiness in the holiday season and in everyday life.

Glenway W.

Christmas Day 1954 and New Year's Day, 1955
Stone-blossom, Hampton, New Jersey
(Written and printed to be sent to all my friends, but then not sent—it suddenly seemed indiscreet or [perhaps I should say] in bad taste.)

I am a bird in a golden cage—note that I say golden, not just gilded—and it is composed of love as well as of security and creature comfort. The three or four persons who love me want love in return, indeed require it and get it—whereas a good deal of the time what I want, what I need, what I lack, is just a little pleasure. And in that way I am not very free; and doubtless perverse and unfortunate, or let me say, rather, ineffectual; and of course less and less young. One of the disadvantageous effects of celibacy is that it induces lonesomeness; and a part of the wear and tear when one is lonesome is the temptation to write letters; and doubtless letters—long subjective introspective letters, with vainglory and penitence intermingled—are a dissipation of the literary energy.

"Mr. Wescott, did you read where tears cured human cancer in a mouse?"

"No, Anna. In what paper was it?"

"That I don't know. I didn't read it myself. Our laundryman was telling me yesterday."

She took a turn around the room, then came back and stood facing me.

"Anyway, you know, Mr. Wescott, someday they will just stumble on something stupid, like that Fleming. He left his food on his plate, and it moldered, and so he just stumbled on penicillin (penny-sillian)."

The Gold Tooth

The greatest of blessings—or shall I say, with a philosophical implication—the greatest of virtues—is staying power.

For instance, Strauss's song writing: "Zueignung" at twenty, "In Abendrot" (with the larks in the twilight) at eighty-four.

His wife was a lieder singer; and Opus 27, including "Cäcilie" and "Morgen," was his wedding present to her.

In musical society, when we were young, his little objectionable traits—avariciousness, for one thing—were often complained of and joked about.

Upon his tour of this country after World War I, he happened to leave a movable gold tooth behind in his hotel bathroom; various persons bespoke each other transatlantically about it, and in due course Monroe had the honor of returning it to him.

*From a letter to James Charlton**

. . . perhaps I'd better put off answering your questions about myself until another letter—or answer tersely, even obscurely. When did you last hear of me? My father died in November 1953, and I had to take my mother to live with me. That is the main fact . . . I have had a hard time in that, seemingly, for months and months at a time, I have lost my creative ability. But I have not admitted that it was final or definitive, or that it was all my own fault; therefore I have been able to keep trying. And no matter how much I attribute to circumstances or hold others responsible for, I always discipline myself somehow; as soon as I see a way in which I have failed, I devise some new discipline; I experiment with my mind in the creative sense—so I may achieve something, in the end.

* James Charlton. A California friend of G.W.

In fact I have done better in recent weeks. I suspended work on my big novel, *A Year of Love*, for circumstantial reasons that still seem to me valid and undestructive. I have a good manuscript entitled *A Dust-Basket*, which needs only one more revision—it is a sort of journal, but not real, not chronological—composed with a beginning and middle and end, and quite extensive subject matter. Now I am occupied with a reminiscence entitled "The Yellow Fog"; and up ahead I have, half-planned, with some serviceable notes and documents, a nouvelle, or very long story, or short novel, entitled *The Lieder Singer*.

What every man knows best about himself is how to masturbate.

As of a few years ago, W. S. Maugham, in ingratitude—and in divided mind about homosexuality, fundamental disbelief in it—had decided not to bequeath Alan enough to live on. (The superfluity all to go to his daughter, Lady John Hope.)

But think what a happy, humorous life Alan could look forward to, with a sufficient income. How hard it will be for him to shift for himself, accustomed to luxury and sexuality, growing old, losing all his looks, and burning, burning! W.S.M. ought to be able to imagine all that . . .

In this connection, I told Monroe that for my part, if I were a rich man, I would immediately settle an income on my Ronald.

"Even if he gave you no more pleasure? Even if you were to have nothing more to do with him? Even if you were not there to share his life?"

"Certainly."

"Isn't that buying oats for a dead horse?"

"This horse is not dead. My no longer being able to ride it, or for that matter, its balking and not transporting me where I want to go, is not death. I see no sign of its dying . . ."

For the sake of that part of the future which is in the present; and to have things right and happy in my imagination after death; and to take the cruelty out of the present moment . . .

January 13

The beauty of heavy snowfall does not give me quite the pleasure I hear others express—a world all of one substance, with structure hidden almost as by obesity.

Daybreak, today, rather my ideal. A small amount of snow fell, and when it ceased, there was not a breath of wind. The sky was white, still full of the snow clouds; and wherever one looked, the meadows, the road, was blue-white. But all the forms in the landscape, the meanings in the landscape, the tree trunks and branches and twigs of the trees, the dormant plants and the remaining leaves, had kept their dark lineaments and colors just mantled with the gleamingness and purity.

Mother is at the medical center, for a basal-metabolism-rate test, having to do with the enlargement of her goiter. I cannot remember having spent a night here by myself all year. Her visits to New York are all ponderously prearranged, with a list of my friends waiting to be invited; also for invitations, or departures of my own correspondingly scheduled.

I find myself somewhat shocked, almost frightened, by what I feel: no delight—just abnormality, loneliness.

But of course I could not feel joy—delight is out of the question, as it would entail a death wish—

From a letter to Cyril Connolly

January 23

If I am a good narrative writer, if you are a first-rate critic and diarist, if the present is an important chapter of literary history—if any or all of these premises is valid—then what I am about to do is worthwhile: The explanatory statement of a little out-of-date grievance or two. The acknowledgment of my feeling about your first-rateness as follows . . .

When you were in this country assembling the special American issue of *Horizon*, you consulted persons whom I do not respect, you did not consult me, and you did not ask me for any contribution of my own writing. As my vanity is moderate, and as my work-in-progress just then was not flourishing or convenient, I only minded this; I did not resent it. But in due course, when you were back in England, you wrote me a letter of reproof for not sending you something that (said you) I had promised—which did vex me, and occasioned a malicious attitude for a while.

In the spring of 1952 we met at Pauline de Rothschild's, do you recall it?—and you demurred at my attempting to write about Paris again when (said you) I had already done so adequately; and you made me recite the titles of my books, pretending that one had slipped my mind; and finally, to keep from losing my temper, to change the subject as the convivial, fashionable circumstance required, I let you conclude that what you were vaguely thinking of was *Fear and Trembling*, and that it comported not only impressions of *la ville lumière* but a chapter about

Plato. Whereupon in my own inner jurisdiction, and in talking to Pauline and perhaps others, I declared a little war on you . . .

Have I made humorous reading matter of this? I hope so. For, certainly, it is small and nonsensical. For, meanwhile, you have been writing and writing, perhaps more than ever, certainly as well as ever, perhaps better than ever; and I have been reading it all with a constant rejoicing and cumulative gratitude . . .

What you do better than anyone is the evaluation of the literature as such, especially contemporary literature; taking examples of it, practitioners of it, and general problems, one by one, or in natural connections and sequences, and telling us what to think, in such a way that we participate in the thinking ourselves.

Sometimes, for me, it is like a dream of greater cultivation and intelligence than I have in fact, and of taking things more seriously— as though I had decided to devote an afternoon to making up my mind about something, and went for a walk, and sat under a tree—until suddenly my ideas, I mean your ideas, come clear, with emotion as well as order and plausibility, like a sort of vision; all that in the few minutes it takes to read a book review, and I wake refreshed as well as edified.

January 28
I should be writing other things, my ultimatum to the University of Wisconsin, my agenda for Harper's, etc.—but I can't think of anything except my anxiety about Ronald, my disbelief in his course of life as it is at present, my self-contempt because I have so far failed to exercise any essential good influence; worse still, because I believe I have exercised bad influence.

Of course I am referring to his unwillingness to work for a living. The other troubles in our two lives (and in our relationship) I can face. The recklessness of certain of his pleasures, and the recurrent obscure problem of health—these are possibly tragic prospects, but acceptable in the fatalistic way; not ignoble; presumably not his fault, certainly not my fault; and balanced by beauties and virtue in his life as in no one else's—lovable.

I'm like Coleridge . . . More like Coleridge than anyone else— allowing for the fact that I have neither the poetical talent nor the philosophical brain—with neurosis, in my entangled family relations, and obstinate though weak sexuality instead of opium.

A cold snap—

I brought in two old fenceposts of locust, and burned them at an angle, sticking out into the room. The little flames curled up passionately through the rail holes. Then I heard the ghost of a bird that must have nested in one of those rail holes, cheeping and warbling.

With thanks for the weekend, Bill C. and Mike L. have sent me the recording of Carl Orff's *Carmina Burana*, which I enjoy and admire far more than I expected. Certainly it's not quite first-rate musical composition but, for the medieval texts, as effective and insoluble as a great translation—pastiche, for this purpose, I take to be better than mere neoclassicism.

Especially the first of the tavern songs, "Estuans interius," touches me, seems important to me.

Nothing that I can think of expresses so well the mind and morals of certain of my playmates at our wild parties: Merrill H. and Johnny G. and Jack F. and perhaps Jimmy A. and Howard What's-his-name— the shameless and intrepid and/or desperate ones:

> *No fetters, no locks . . .*
> *I am looking for my lie*
> *And I join the depressed.*
> *Testing is lovely*
> *And sweeter than the honeycomb.*
> *A fool I am, like a gliding river . . .*
> *Greedy more for lust than for welfare,*
> *Dead in soul, I care only for my body.*

Oro pro nobis, Tolstoy

"What would you do," Tolstoy inquired of the plowman, "if the end of the world was announced for tomorrow?"

"Plow," the plowman answered.

When Tolstoy lay in his grave, and his peasants filed by, one of them (could it have been that same plowman?) commented, "With too much book learning, you often lose the way."

Great Flaubert! I think of him in a more loving way than other writers; and often, with regard to a given sentence or set of sentences, at his best, it is a fresh and fanatic feeling, like love at first sight— Glorious little things seem altogether new to me:

> *"Notre vie est du vent tissu."*

"Our life is but a wind, woven."

"Nous employons aux passions l'étoffe que nous a été donnée pour le bonheur."

"We use up in our passions substance that was given us to be happy with."

"Le soir de la vie apporte avec lui sa lampe."

"The evening of life brings along its own lamp with it."

"La sagesse, c'est le repos dans la lumière."

"Wisdom is being [to be] at rest in the midst of light."

In the crowded subway at 9:15, as I was on my way going to Wall Street, one businessman type said to another, a seat having been vacated at Fourteenth Street, "You sit down. I sat down yesterday." And the other accepted and sat. Perhaps they were friends. In any case, I observed them all the way downtown, and they neither exchanged any further words nor glanced at one another.

February 13

Surely [Ralph] Vaughan Williams's *Pastoral Symphony*, from beginning to end, means exactly what the title proposes, subdividing the word: in the first movement, just love of countryside in a sort of paean, with soft interpolations of his feeling at home in the country, warblings as of a nesting bird; in the second movement, rural melancholy, voiced with the strange valveless trumpet; in the third, rustic enjoyments; and in the fourth, mysteriousness of nature, (even the simplest) nature, verging on religiosity.

But though I have labored at this statement more than it is worth, how unsatisfying it is! how categorical and flat!

In music there are pages and pages consisting, as you might say, of just one word, with its definitions and derivations; nothing else. Love of nature in this symphony is entirely sensuous and descriptive, not in the least abstract; but it is more merged and continuous than any corresponding effect in literature. The variations upon short haunting melodies are not for the sake of variousness; they are to show us how everything in landscape, the light and the twilight and the wind, and the wings of birds, and running water and ocean surges, and cloud and foliage, all move in the same manner, partake of one design.

February 16

"He doth, as if your journey should be through a fair vineyard, at the first give you a cluster of grapes, that, full of that taste, you may long to pass further."

—Philip Sidney, from the *Defence of Poesie*

I cannot resist taking this as an epigraph to the sampling of sample pages of my notebook that I am giving Monroe for his birthday, though it is too grand for them. I am often or always pretentious, I'm afraid.

Alas, Monroe doubtless would prefer to all my magpie cultivatedness, commonplaces with comment, analects with glosses, no matter how small a narrative text, a piece of fiction or reminiscence, anything to which the more famous Sidney sentence could be prefixed: *"With a tale forsooth, he cometh to you, with a tale, which holdeth children from play, and old men from the chimney corner."*

Or perhaps he does not care so much, one way or another, since he knows now that I am no Philip Sidney. In my strong anxiety about writing pages like this, and feeling of impotence because I seem not to have the talent to write novels, is it self-indulgence of my own that I transfer to him, inferiority—the everlasting childish pattern: forever and ever the unsatisfactory, untalented, weary son and the insatiable righteously indignant father or elder brother who flatters my talent in order to demand more than I have it in me to produce?

More probably, from Monroe's sincere point of view, anything that I may write—anything completed, corrected, assembled, legible, printable—will seem to him better than mere scribble and unfulfilled agenda and futile letter writing.

To think that those two above-quoted sentences of Sidney occur in the same essay, on the same page, in the same paragraph! Such was the genius for writing of that prodigious and mysterious youth, who never learned to write either prose or poetry very well. Too busy; too busy making friends and frequenting authors; and playing politics and making a career of diplomacy and hesitating between religions; and toying with the possibility of being crowned King of Poland; and having his portrait painted by Veronese; and learning horsemanship in Vienna from John Pietro Pugliano, whom he praises by name in the opening of the *Defence of Poesie*; too busy with his pretty sister at Wilton, watching the breeding of the stallions and mares from the balcony with her, and writing the *Arcadia* for her, but incompletely, "in loose sheets of paper"; too busy tiring himself out, and never very healthy, but up, and away to the war! and dying of a heroic gesture and a little wound and probably of accumulated exhaustion at thirty-two years of age.

There are so many things I should like to know! For instance, did they already have, in Vienna, in John Pietro Pugliano's time, the pallid Lippizaners with nose-blood-pink nostrils, which Marianne Moore so intensely fancies? And were the horses that Sir Philip and Pembroke watched in intercourse like my brother's and my brother's wife's Suffolks,

Eclipse of Morston, and old Beauboy with sagging crest, whom Sir Victor Sassoon, the great Bagdad and Shanghai millionaire, sent her for a wedding present? (I once wasted weeks trying to describe them, heavy and dreamy and consequently clumsy in their lust.)

Fame? certainly not. I should hate it. (I have hated what little I have had of it in the way of brief best-sellerdom and publisher promotion.) As for fortune, that is to say, a lot of money—money for wages of a secretary, foreign travel, a large library and record collection . . . fine. But note, please, that I am not under the illusion that, at this time of my life, greater affluence would appreciably ameliorate my love life or sex life. It would only expose me more than ever to the unfairness which is rife in relationships between older men and younger persons, with my middle-aged choler ever on tap in consequence.

It has been my dream—at least one of my dreams—for many years: to write prose bit by bit, as though it were lyric poetry—it is one of the habits of mind that have most handicapped me as a fiction writer. Sometimes one has to make a specialty of one's handicap.

March 11

Now I must humbly apologize to Lloyd for my sad and perhaps angry talk yesterday.

As to the particular issue of whether or not to go to Utah, I still haven't made up my mind, though Lloyd and Monroe, and indeed Mother, jumped at it for me while I was still in the stage of just thinking out loud about it. To be sure, I have been hoping to manage some sort of holiday or journey this summer, without being away too long and without having to ask for extra money.

But for the record, let me specify that Utah is far from perfect, in my opinion. They will work the hell out of me, and my enjoyment of the two or three lectures I shall be scheduled to deliver will be counterbalanced by the pseudo-creative work on half a dozen manuscript novels, which I have always found embarrassing and unhappy.

As I feared, Monroe also gave me hell about Utah. He is always unsympathetic if not merciless in this kind of connection because he believes (he says) that everyone would do what I want done if I asked for it politely and made myself clear. As it seems to him I prefer to make a martyr of myself, and I refuse to let him intervene in my behalf, etc. I have this to face every week or so about something, and alas, he has in hand the letter I wrote him in December '54, when he was in Peru, in which I detailed my agreement with Lloyd about Mother as I then understood it.

And, naturally, when I get woebegone or listless about anything, he raises the ante. This time, he says that obviously I need a couple of days a week away from Mother, and proposes that I spend three weekends a month with him in town, and that each of our three Eastern Seaboard sisters visit St.-bl. with their friends—he cannot believe that they would be unwilling. "Have you ever proposed it to them?" Upon which he concludes that I really prefer my life with Mother and don't really want to get away . . .

Everybody should have either a friend or a psychiatrist—by which I mean someone with no stake in one's life; no undertaking or point of pride or conscience as to the troublesome circumstances; no very personal opinion of, or relationship with, the other persons in my life. It is no position to put a brother or consort or lover in . . .

April 1

Shall I recommence *A Year of Love?*

Yesterday, up the Black Brook, tawniness of the winter enlivened by only one small hepatica, blue and pink, which I gave to Ronald while we quarreled.

"It has a lucky number of petals," he pointed out. "Seven."

"I must follow up the continual lessons of the air, water, earth; I perceive I have no time to love."

—Whitman

April 7

Anna picked up a press photograph of Monroe at an art exhibition, in front of a Degas, gesturing for the benefit of pretty Mrs. Richard Rodgers, and looked at it long and ponderingly.

"He's smart, our Mr. Wheeler, very smart. He's what you would call a real gentleman. Everybody's not like that, it's either in your nature or it isn't. He's like Clara Bow"—(she pronounced it Bough)—"he's *it*.

"What I mean is, you can see it just in the way he stands, every minute, as if you were going to photograph him or draw him."

April 14

I am an aging man now. I am willing now to give up sex life, more and more austerely—to live for my work, and for love, even sexless love, little by little; to express my love in my work . . . But I must keep from overstimulation, tantalization, hopefulness, etc.—I must have more solitude, more self-indulgence in other ways, leisure, sleep, society, etc.

I am still anxious about Ronald's summer with François, on his account—but it will be good for me, in spite of my loneliness.

What Ronald seems unwilling to understand is that I don't compare our relationship with the loves of my youth, or even of my middle age— but only this year with last year, last year with year before last.

By the time he gets back I shall have learned to shift for myself a little better; aged a little more, as I must; established better working habits—or possibly committed myself to that monastery I keep dreaming of; where can it be?

Breakfast, and dear Mother, who enjoys eating, thank goodness, but whose appetite is capricious, and whose willpower often expresses itself along this line, sent me to the kitchen for some change of menu, I forget what—perhaps soda biscuit instead of toasted raisin bread, or an egg instead of cereal.

Anna sympathized with me a little maliciously, shaking her head like some old actress: "Oh, Mr. Wescott, my mother was a doll compared to yours. Even my brother, who's nothing but an old souse, he isn't hard to feed. I can give him any old junk, he eats it."

April 17

Lloyd always speaks of self-pity as the worst of the vices of the mind.

R., whether it is to console me in my fits of sorrow or to defend himself against me when I try to get him to treat me better, scolds me for it.

I believe in both pity and self-pity—but not in self-indulgence . . .

April 19

At the end of the afternoon, suddenly a gleam of lightning and murmur of thunder caused me to look up from my desk, and the contents of my window, especially the colors, took my breath away: the wild virgin green of the lawn that Marty has not yet found time to mow; and a scarlet handkerchief on Anna's head; and the violent gold of a bonfire in the kitchen garden . . .

April 27

Someday I will live in or near a university town and read Emerson's *Journal* in its entirety, and other such immense vast and expansive works.

Dangerous—I seem to be diminishing into a bookworm; my creative power in a torpor or a coma—so long unpracticed that I scarcely know what it is, what it was, what it felt like, how it felt, how to start it.

Rather like sexual impotence . . .

But as Anatole France said of St. Denis, the patron saint of France, who was beheaded on the Île-St.-Louis, whose headless body then miraculously arose, picked up his head, and walked to the suburb of Paris named after him, *"C'est le premier pas qui coûte."*

May 7

François cannot put off his departure any longer. When he last applied for an extension of his visa, they asked him what for, and he said, with his innate persuasiveness, "I want to see the dogwood in full bloom." They gave him an extra week. But now his passport itself is about to expire.

From a letter to Christopher Isherwood

May 24

Reading Marianne Moore's Bryn Mawr lecture on Wystan, encrusted with his beautiful lines, I say to myself that he is the only admirable creative man whom I might have admired more—sustained and expressed my admiration better—if I had not known him personally. When I say "personal," I don't mean self-concerned; he has never harmed or hurt or even hindered me. Just a matter of untruthfulnesses, pretensions, hypocrisies—and all of them, I believe, doctrinal in his mind . . . self-righteous.

And these thoughts have made me furiously lonely to talk to you. All week I have had a little sense of duty to inform you of very bad news: so here you have a really mixed bag.

George Lynes is hopelessly ill, in New York Hospital, but probably to be removed to his brother's house soon. After all sorts of tests they located a tumor in his lung, and attempted an operation on it last Friday, which was unsuccessful. The doctor has told him, or will tell him, that they removed what they could but are afraid that they may not have been thorough enough; therefore will follow it with some deep X-ray treatments. I think he will accept, or at least give lip service to, whatever hopefulness this may imply. Poor creature, in these nightmarish years of his insolvency he has learned to turn his mind away from irremediable or worsening situations, which will stand him in good stead now. The fact is that nothing could be removed; it was not only malignant but already diffused into the other lung. So it will be a matter of months . . . His brother has already dismantled the apartment. Do I seem harsh, or somewhat too sure of what I say? No matter. I understand him better than others do, and certainly in the present circumstance I am the spokesman for him, not against him. For my part these days I am not really sorry for anyone except those who feel compelled to commit homicide or suicide; and except for the prolongation of physical pain—which is the doctor's fault, in a sort of jurisdictional overlap and no-man's-land between our new religion of medicine and our old. George will not be very much unhappier than he has been. I spent an hour with him on the eve of the operation, and the expression on his face was almost obvious: the relaxed, relieved look of one asking for sympathy in a disaster that indeed now everyone does understand and believe. He will feel extraordinarily loved in the time remaining. All of us feel contrite about various bitter reactions to his inertness, unfairness, arrogance, last-ditch self-indulgence, all year—and now we interpret it otherwise, thinking of the mysterious physical causation, etc.

Do you remember my own tiny cancer of five years ago? Do you remember the very noble and appropriate advice you gave me, against using the shortened life expectancy as a means of coercing my environing dear ones? I am not sure it was good advice, given my weak psychology and strange parasitic situation. Something for us to talk about someday . . . Also my present, I mean recent, love life will interest you: wonderfully pure, though amid scandal, and almost entirely pessimistic—Dante inarticulate, Beatrice alive—but let me not try to be funny.

May 26

The last few hours of Ronald's departure went so fast—I think of him as in France already—in fact, I began composing a letter on my way to the bus, in French: *"Mon petit cher R., ton départ finalement m'a semblé . . ."* etc.

The new disciplines of the summer began at once, amusingly and (I feel) propitiously. Q.L. really didn't want to stay until R. got under way and downstream—he felt too much in love, bereft, and nervous; he said so. I thought R. would fret if he just disappeared, so I engaged him to lunch with me, and kept talking and making him talk: meanwhile R.'s handkerchief appeared wonderfully white and large, like a dinner napkin or a pillowcase.

Then we strolled eastward, looking for a restaurant, found none— so in my spoiled way I suggested the Astor Bar, because of the air conditioning; and not until we had menus in hand did I recall having given R. almost all my money, all except taxi and busfare.

In consequence of this I walked from 410 to the subway, with my carryall, suitcase; and all the way, at intervals, the last-mentioned kept opening, whereupon I'd have to squat and begin all over again . . .

Now homeward-bound—to my air conditioning, my irises, my half-written or three-quarters-written pages, some erotic, some aesthetic, etc.

I have no plans of returning to N.Y.—no wish or desire—but of course I shall have to visit G.P.L.

June 14

François has now packed Ronald off in a Thunderbird with Mlle Violette Leduc* for a fortnight—to Spain, as R. understood it to be, when he wrote. No, Philippe tells me on the telephone, to Italy . . . François will not be back here this month—he expects his new visa in July. And Monroe is departing this week: an emergency in the Museum of Modern Art publications program—Milan, Venice, Munich, Brussels, Amsterdam, London—and back, as of museum necessity again, within the month. As it appears now, he will not have time to go to Paris or to see his many friends, grand and creative. He tried hard to take me with him, springing it on me by surprise one evening, in Mother's presence as well as Ll. and Baba's.

June 17

Ronald's letters are perfect—so unpetty, and intimate, and yet objective. Two today, from Biarritz; and I kept them in my pocket unopened, until I couldn't be interrupted or hurried—which was in the bus, on my way to Easton; and they might have brought tears to my eyes, except that I was too closely packed in with young persons. Behind me, a soldier rather like a Polish and skinny Lefrieri; beside me, another soldier, a great brutish but gentle blond one, with heavy-boned round-fleshed fingers—the speeding vibrating old bus gave him an erection, which he pinched from time to time, but with no consciousness of me.

---

* Violette Leduc (1907–72). French novelist and critic.

François's brother, who spent Tuesday here, lunched with Baba yesterday and half persuaded her to buy a not very expensive, not very valuable Bonnard. He also offered her various sums for certain pictures; less than she thinks they are worth . . . wanting to talk and talk and talk about all this, she met my bus from Easton. But she misread her watch by one hour; and my bus was forty minutes late . . .

Just before dinnertime my new irises arrived—oh, I am glad that most of the heavy work of preparing the beds for them has been done. Then Monroe, so tired that he looked like a charcoal caricature of himself, but not black—in sunburn sepia—and more and more pessimistic about his mission in Europe—now emergency has developed also in Brussels . . . The printer's wages in Holland for the *Masters of Modern Art* have gone up so that the French edition is hanging in the balance, and the Germans and Italians have not yet signed up—and unless he can bring them around, and get the unit cost down, even the Spanish edition, which he got the University of Puerto Rico to underwrite, will have to be given up. So he had to reverse his itinerary: Belgium first— fortunately that gives him a palace, Hansi Lambert's, for first stop (he hasn't hotel reservations anywhere) . . .

This is the first day of summer, but not Midsummer Day (last night was not Midsummer Night), that is the 23rd–24th—I have never understood why . . . and meanwhile I have got Monroe off; finished my dentistry, until July 9; and set out all my new irises; and commenced *The Lieder Singer!* I talked to George this morning, which was heartbreaking—so I am going to town this afternoon, just to dine with him. But he can't dine, only soup—fever and nausea at the end of the day He thinks that will cease after this week, when the X-ray therapy halts.

Yes, I'll stand a better chance with *The Lieder Singer*. Over beyond it, in perhaps the same form, "The Wander-Bird" and "A Proustian Tale"—as well as, someday, God willing, *The Little Ocean Liner* once more. Thinking of the latter reminds me to try to avoid overdeveloping, extending, enlarging my little story materials. It seems to me that, if I aim at brevity, first-person storytelling (as it were, *viva voce*), instead of form and meaning, it will enrich itself as it goes along; rich enough. Also, briefness and colloquialism, spokenness, will relieve my worst anxiety about these European stories: the possibility or probability of my having forgotten too much of the atmosphere . . .

I began *The Lieder Singer* Tuesday morning, strangely, with a sentence that came to me in a dream. On page 2, I will (I think) quote what Daniel Boone said when he finally got back to civilization. "Did you get lost?" someone asked. "No, not lost—but I was bewildered once, for three days."

June 23

Detail, not humorous: At the hospital yesterday there was a beautiful though fat girl, nocturne-eyed and voluptuously smiling, and a corresponding baby in her lap. They both looked like the Caravaggio *Bacchus* in the Uffizi; and both of course perfectly exemplified those theories of the Harvard professor that Paul Cadmus and Jerry French used to delight in: the viscerotonic type. But the baby's legs were twisted outward in a fantastic triangle, in plaster casts with a cross bar; and the expression on its face was of an almost occult immunity to pain, concentrated tranquillity, as though it were a saint or yogi or Buddha . . .

George speaks often of having to earn a living, but not of anything that he might be capable of doing or that he might enjoy, except—guess what!—sculpture . . .

Apropos of K.A.P.'s planning to store her furniture, he informed me that in this instance it had not proved very expensive: only a couple of hundred dollars for the packing and moving, then $17.50 a month. "I got the bill just the other day. Russell took it, and I hope to hell he means to pay it—he didn't *say* he would! You know," he added, "I sometimes think he wishes I'd just die . . ."

"Oh no, surely not," I answered, "though I do believe he'd like to have, not just you, but all of us do public penance for our entire way of life, especially our economics—perhaps a procession, with sackcloth, or with dunce cap, and just a few touches of flagellation."

François gave me Rossini's *Messe Solennelle*, which he wrote when he was seventy-four—after thirty years' idleness, gluttony, self-contempt.

A memory of Michael: Three years ago, after the cocktail party for Isherwood. On a couch facing another couch across the room he sat or lay with Jojo; and I likewise with young String. His eyes and mine kept meeting, and with dreamy gaze embracing.

Jojo's face turned pale and he shut his eyes tight, making of his voluptuousness a kind of sleep, so that he could escape from his intense little morality in it.

Young String, in easy absorption in his stupid young physiology, let his eyelids flutter halfway down over his eyeballs, not focusing on anything.

Meanwhile my eyes delighted in Michael's eyes, and his eyes welcomed mine, and two or three times he winked. Thus, I fancied, one of Leonardo da Vinci's creatures would have winked; one of the Apostles on the ruined wall, or one of the great anatomies.

There followed a little fiasco, Jojo's fault; also my fault, my optimism, my mismanagement. But let that pass uncommemorated.

Come to think of it, sexuality is the only thing I am ever optimistic about.

Anna, at the end of menu-making, with the usual little issue between us of fattening or non-fattening foods:

"Just have what you like, and what goes good, that's it. After all, Mr. Wescott, when we disappear, we're not going to come back and eat, are we?"

June 26

Friday I had to telephone Harper's about the inclusion of my Villefranche story, "The Sailor," in a 25-cent anthology to be called— can you imagine?—*Crazy, Mixed-up Kids*; taking advantage of the very questionable present excitement in the newspapers, etc., I gave permission, with the hope that it will be (so to speak) honestly on the pornographic side—not pretending to be moralistic . . .

While waiting for Beulah to find out something about this, I spoke to Russell Lynes: George did not have to go back to the hospital. The strange fever he ran all last week (104 degrees, the evening I spent with him) evidently resulted from this or that antibiotic—a new prescription reduced it . . . R.N. said that he had received a letter from François, and that it had changed all the prospect of his going abroad, etc., he was not willing to tell me what change; George would inform me . . .). I record this—what my mother calls "dee-tail"—as, alas, typical of my life, and characteristic of all concerned. Half the time one is misinformed, or left like a goalkeeper in a corner of the field, while the game moves elsewhere . . .

June 28

The fact is that when I come to N.Y. so infrequently, it seems to me a waste to spend time in theaters, to say nothing of money.

The only thing I *need*, but let me not use that verb, it is immoral— the only thing I at all desperately desire is pleasure, pleasure, pleasure.

I've never had to traverse so much desert, and my camel's hump of remembrances and imaginings shrinks away to nothing.

Oh, am I never going to grow old? I grow more patient, less ugly-tempered, etc. I suppose that is age.

Another excuse for my fussing just now is the moodiness of my several deathbeds, especially G.'s. The answer to death is *not* love, in which the suicidal spirit enters too frequently; it is sex: the all-forgetting sensation, the paroxysm of present tense, and relief from willpower.

From a letter to Ronald Neil

July 1

When you get back to Paris and revisit the Louvre, look at the big Poussin: Apollo, the god of poetry, and the poet, and the muse—and give a good wish, that is, or to all intents and purposes, a prayer for your old Gl. (man of letters), in front of it. It may seem to you a little formed or academic, but it has perpetual power to my way of thinking; like religion. And remember for me any other Poussins that they may have got around to cleaning.

Also, find the large Le Nain which is the seventeenth-century French equivalent of *The Grandmothers*. Also, the little Watteau called *Le Faux-Pas*, in which you see a calm concentrated good-looking long-nosed French-looking boy down on his knees about to possess an elegant shadowy female—he is tipping her down on the evening grass, with his hard excited hand on her back.

Meanwhile, in the Prado, especially find the homosexual Veláz-quezes: the dwarfs, the Mars, the Bacchus—but that will have to be with me. Indeed, come to think of it, perhaps no one except me knows that they are homosexual—(except Jim Lord* and his French friend— I told them . . .).

Remember things, to describe them for me—and of course people as well as things; for example, Pop, the friend of June 25, and the French serviceman or service boy who had parents but who gave you a rain check for June 27 . . .

July 4–6

We are having furnace heat, and it is beginning to look like destructive drought.

Now I must begin to press Anna about her taking a little more

---

* James Lord. An American art critic living in France.

vacation— She has been ill, that is, half-ill, and woebegone all this week and perhaps will consult Dr. Goger today—ophthalmic migraine followed by delusory hypochondriacal preoccupation, or perhaps just liverishness, heat, and fatigue . . . She has no place to go on vacation now—I shall propose Atlantic City, and Ll. will make a contribution of money.

Always the Fourth of July is the hardest day of the year for me— and there is some mystery about it, anniversary feeling—the farewell to E.R.K.* in dread of homosexuality in 1915; and the fit of anger against Ll. for speaking to me as Baba and Elizabeth's spokesman, and my yelling and kicking in Monroe's arms because he sided with him, or seemed to, in 1949 . . . There has been some deep underlying connection in my mind or (perhaps I should say) my psychology, between the two scenes—

Ll. and Baba are still in trouble about the state office. "Wescott Mum about Agriculture Post," says the *Democrat* headline. A Wescott *mum?*—that'll be the day.

We dined on the porch at Ryland's last night, Ll. and Baba and I, with only Debo, who presently withdrew indoors for the television; whereupon to my amazement he brought the subject up again. I may say that in recent talks (without her) he had met my objections so well that I was getting quite reconciled to it. He had said that Baba seemed somehow ambiguously in favor of it; but she had spoken otherwise to me and to Mother. Last night to my dismay she came out strongly, almost violently in favor, for two immediately stated, terse, and categorical reasons: her old anxiety about his health and the analyst's great consideration of money, $18,000 a year indeed (but tax deductible). His activities in the public service thus far have been neurotically impelled, self-destructive, and he cannot and will not curtail them; and nine to five-thirty in Trenton will be easier for him. And this is something that he "could have had" by his own endeavors, without her fortune. "You have been married to money long enough, and it is too painful for you." Poor wonderful man, he leaned forward in his chair and wrinkled up his face as though caught in a hailstorm . . . He does not really want the job, now that he has looked into it: too much nursery business, as important in the state economy as milk; and too much egg business and, worst of all, pig business.

Of course it may facilitate his arguing with Baba, to have brought

---

* E.R.K. Carl, G.W.'s boyhood lover in Wisconsin.

her thoughts out into the open. As a rule he has power of resistance enough, when he gets set.

As to the thesis about money: "For whom the bell tolls . . ." etc., I said to myself, naturally. But perhaps it is significant that my thought immediately following that great tag was to hie me to Donald Klopfer* and ask for a record-breaking advance on that Harrison-Wescott saga he used to proposition me about . . .

No sagas in present circumstances, God knows. But by the same token there is no future in the circumstantial setup. Good aged Louise Bogan made a very odd suggestion, speaking as one "professional" to another: that if I cannot have specific regular hours per day, I ought to demand one or two days per week, and then work around the clock. But of course poets know nothing about saga writing. And she, poor stoic creature, has become just a *New Yorker* staff writer, settled into regular critical writing: her poetic inspiration has entirely lapsed.

A burnt-out volcano: love and madness! which is not my case, nor am I uninspired. Sex need or lovers greatly complicate my existence, except insofar as they enter into my overresponsiveness to R., with economic consequences along that line. Boredom is of course a problem as never before. But the fundamental difficulties are of time and place: the hours in the day, the rooms in the house; and of course dollars and cents.

Monroe got his job in Milan done, and felt tired and homesick, so gave up his weekend in St.-Jean-Cap-Ferrat, and flew straight back home—and made all tragic here, because I had not worked enough in his absence. At every turn of the conversation these days he takes, as it were, a whip to me, even in others' presence, in a way that is surely the worst way in the world to get any artist's temperament going—indeed it seems to injure me in the organs of the creativity that he is demanding of me. It is terrifying. I can't think of any way to stop him, any other way than creation—but every possible circumstance is wrong, even the lovely Stone-blossom circumstances that I have to be grateful for. I think that perhaps I shall destroy myself trying, or at least wanting to try, trying to try. Those who love me seem to have devoured me. Naturally the fate of Geo. makes Monroe more illogical than ever—and only adds heaviness to the impact he intends to have on me.

Apart from him (I try to keep him unaware of it) Geo.'s illness has another bad effect on me—it makes me feel like a sort of sheep whose

---

* Donald Klopfer. A cofounder of Random House publishers.

instinct it might be to follow the scapegoat instead of the bellwether—
entire morbidity, I'm afraid.

By the way, the day George departed to the Berkshires, he gave
me the two hundred nudes: wonderful . . . his selection of his two
hundred best nudes, his own selection, requested by Kinsey and I
suppose to some extent paid for by the Institute for Sex Research,
Bloomington.

July 23

We had a thunderstorm this morning, at about 5 a.m. All our lawn
cushions got soaked.

I said to Anna, "You know how my mother sometimes talks to me
as though I were fifteen years old."

"Yes, I know, you poor thing."

"Last night, just at bedtime, she ordered me to bring in the cushions, just in case it should rain. I said, 'Pooh, leave them there, to tempt
Providence.' "

"Thank goodness you did," said Anna, as though in earnest. "That
caused the rain, all right."

"It's one of my problems, Anna," I went on, warning her also
not to be too motherly. "I'm fifty-four years old, but everyone seems to
think I'm young and can still be taught and disciplined. Even Mr.
Wheeler . . ."

"That's because you *seem* young, you're so jolly, and nothing worries
you."

"That's what the nurses at the hospital said: 'Oh, what a jolly man!
Is he always like that?' —'Yes,' I told them, 'he's always jolly, because
he's a writer, he can work just when he feels like it; he hasn't got
anything to worry about.' "

July 24

It has been a bad weekend, perhaps destructive in my relationship
with Chuck. I seem to be liquidating a good many friendships in one
way or another, perhaps the thing to do; in any case, a compulsion.

Strangely: to my view, neither Chuck nor Ted has any great beauty
with clothes on; but both their bodies are beautiful, sprawling naked
and half-embraced, with the bedroom door open in the fierce heat. But
I pass without a pause. Probably they wouldn't want me to watch them
make love, in any case; perhaps they haven't been making love; I haven't
desired to watch them; I have kept my door shut.

July 25

Wagner's widow, in her very old age, listened to *Tristan and Isolde* without a tremor; but Offenbach made her cry like a child. In my case too, I guess—it will not be the greatest music, not even Vaughan Williams, but rather, for example, *Puritani*, which doesn't mean much. It will always mean to me these months of Ronald's absence, this month of his not writing to me.

Poor Anna! already the coons have started on her poor desiccated sweet corn . . .

Baba reports that she will have to lie still for about a month; which must mean the major removal.

Now I must thank Pavlik T. for the drawing—not easy, after so many years of silence, with so much on my mind, and my heart overflowing . . .

July 26

The express buses, Clinton to New York, bypass Newark when they haven't any passengers for it.

Today I heard the driver say roughly to a small elderly man, gray-haired, gray-skinned, "Are you going to make me go all the way into Newark on a hot day? You're the only Newark passenger I've got."

"Oh dear, oh dear," said the man. "Don't you see, I've got to get home somehow. But it's too bad, it's silly, I'm sorry. I just went to Clinton for the ride, round trip, to cool off!"

July 27

Country life: The Dalrymples butcher a pig, and its great terminal squealing, almost shouting, excites the heifers in the pasture behind the pigpen. They gambol about, they kick up their heels, over the withered grass, along the weak brook. And the young ducks, also excited and alarmed, rise on tiptoe and arch out their wings.

City life: George's last day in his studio; I helped him. Katherine Anne's last day in her apartment; George and Monroe and I went down there for whatever is the opposite of a housewarming, rather bibulous, affectionate, and humorous. Her nephew Paul was there, whom George passingly seduced years ago. I fancy that may have been the start of her anti-homosexuality. It was when she was living with George for three or four months in Hollywood, and felt some inclination to marry him. There are more plots in our lives than in our books.

George's preparations for his fate are all as though he were going on a long journey, emigrating to Australia or enlisting in the Marines;

packing, storing, sorting, discarding, listing, bequeathing. It is a god-send for him to have the real journey to Paris to refer it all to.

"Think what a strange situation I'm in," he said yesterday. "No apartment, no studio, no money, no plans, no ambition. Thank God I don't have to face the facts of life until I get back from Paris. I'm dead against the facts of life."

New York tired me out. The heat is tiring Mother out—she is beginning to feel like something that should have been kept in the icebox and hasn't been.

Waiting, waiting, all afternoon and evening, for news of Baba's operation. At last Hella told me: no malignancy.

Later, Monroe and I saw the Italian film about South America, excellent, except for mediocre color photography: voodoo dancing; Inca wedding ceremonial; serpent devouring serpent; sacrifice of a young steer to the piranha in the Paraguay River, so that the rest of the herd could pass over uneaten . . .

Nightmarish off and on, all week. As for myself in the main aspects or issues of my life I am nightmarish—I feel like an automobile wheel that has come off, en route; and the automobile in question (as a whole) and the other three wheels do not know it yet, and are speeding along the highway with other traffic; and I am madly propelling myself after the dear vehicle, trying to catch up and reattach myself to my old axle where I belong, before there is a wreck . . .

August 3

It seems François sent Ronald up north with someone named Jean Fontaine, a radio broadcaster or announcer (why? Scandinavian-speaking?). As it turned out, Fontaine drove execrably. They got within sight of the Arctic Circle and, up there, R. got nervous and gave him a piece of his mind; then went for a walk, perhaps to quiet himself down or perhaps to cruise the Arctic Laplanders. Whereupon Fontaine *drove off* and left him high and dry, taking all the money François had given them. R. had enough to take the train via Oslo; caught up with Fontaine in a bar in Copenhagen, and, with those bony Irish fists and Sansone-conditioned muscles, got his half of the money back . . .

Yesterday I went to see Baba—in the bus; it took all p.m. She is recovering amazingly and either is, or pretends to be, happy.

* * *

Katherine Anne to Monroe one day: "Do you know why I have lost my husbands and lovers, and now have to conclude my life all soul alone?

"Because I have always talked too much at breakfast time."

I spent almost all day with George. To begin with, we brought his two Cadmus paintings and two Tchelitchew paintings down from his brother's; the idea being that perhaps their hanging at 410 will enhance their value, so they can be sold. I myself have another idea, not out-spoken—perhaps George has, too, as it is his wont.

"Moore wants to buy *The Golden Leaf*," he told Monroe, "but I won't let him have it."

"Why not?"

"Well, if you must know, I owe him $1,000, and if I sold it to him, I'd have to pay him back."

I can imagine the look on poor Monroe's face—!

For almost four hours George tagged after me like a child.

"You know what I'm going to have to do," he said, "if I'm to be an entirely useless, ornamental, recreational personage from now on, which is what I intend—I'm going to have to organize myself, and make all my friends pay me about five dollars a month."

"But you'd have to find about two hundred friends, wouldn't you?" I asked, rapidly calculating, but in a tentative tone of voice.

"Just about, I suppose," he answered. "Although probably I could get Moore to keep me supplied with booze, on account of he gets it from his government so cheap . . . But how right you are! I'd be damned lucky to *find* one hundred; I'd have to charge them ten a month."

And yesterday he ordered a dinner jacket. Crazy . . . Nevertheless (how extraordinary!) I enjoyed him more than I have in five or six years. He told me many things that fascinated me—about the Frenches; about Gustave; about Ralph McWilliams and himself. We talked of our young manhood; he questioned me about the earlier years, with Monroe in Germany, etc.; he listened to me about my literature, etc., with that perfect, rather feminine responsiveness which used to be characteristic of him, perfectly sympathetic and seemingly thrilled . . .

This morning I experienced a little explosion of creativity; or do I mean fecundation? It felt explosive: twenty minutes of incandescent thought, seeing as in a vision solutions not only of problems of *The*

Lieder Singer but also of *The Refugee* (that is, *The Little Ocean Liner*) and "The Wander-Bird" . . . twenty minutes of the bliss of creative power, feeling sufficiently sure of my talent, with exact sense of the necessities, etc., pertaining to it. If my two or three or four nearest and dearest will help, in just the particular ways that they can, and for the rest, for what can't be helped, if they will withdraw from me just a little, without bitterness or faithlessness, without suffering too much—I believe I can make them proud of me . . .

All this in the shabby old Hotel Taft, where I haven't been since the autumn of 1940 (or 1941)—Nelson Lansdale brought me here for an Ethel Merman opening, and drank eighteen Scotch-and-sodas in a row, I counted them; and about 1 a.m. went off his rocker for a few hours . . .

Woods Hole
August 12

Monroe also woke up early, anxious about having to drive in the rain, and we started promptly. But it did not rain, it was only a little foggy, and by midmorning we arrived in good spirits in this almost nightmarishly familiar place. Even the hurricanes do not change it.

Josephine had had her downstairs windows boarded up, and the wicker furniture from our private boardwalk all piled up in the big sitting room. By early afternoon the radio had announced our reprieve—this particular hurricane, called Connie, veered into North Carolina or Delaware. Another, called Diane, has started.

The latter part of the afternoon we had hot sunshine, better late than never; we went for a walk, and got caught in a sudden downpour.

As we set out, I made my usual complaint of Woods Hole: no homosexual society (or almost none), and all the young scientists notably unhandsome. Whereupon there appeared, down the side street from the beach, in a sort of bikini, accompanied by unhandsome older friend, the ideal twenty-year-old, with pectorals faultlessly related to collarbone.

Woods Hole
August 13

My plan for this early morning was to write half a page descriptive of someone's erotic action once upon a time, with perhaps ensuing autoeroticism, then ensuingly to indulge in autoeroticism if so moved; and then to go right to work on the outline and chronology of "The Yellow Fog."

But first I always have to read something, with my initial cup of coffee, to get my eyes in focus, easy in their sockets; and I took an English book review, something about translating poetry, and there the reviewer had quoted the earliest, shortest, perhaps greatest love poem in our language, a thousand years old—*"O western wind, when wilt thou blow,/ That the small rain down can rain?/ Christ, that my love were in my arms/ And I in my bed again!"* That's all; and it has made me feel my love for R. so strongly and poignantly, forcefully and pathetically, that I ached.

Nothing small about our rains here, by-product of Connie . . . At daybreak, looking down from my window on the Vineyard Haven side, I couldn't distinguish between the downpour and the ocean flattened out beneath it; and the gulls, flying along heavily, soddenly, looked like drowned bodies afloat in the air . . .

Woods Hole
August 14

I suppose it must be my stubbornest "neurotic" characteristic as a writer: whatever I plan to write in the early morning, I am apt to find myself suddenly writing something else instead. Of course if I were very great and productive and self-assured, I should call it *inspiration*. It is like the drunkenness of the sibyl, the prophetess-priestess of Apollo, crouching over some opening in the earth out of which fumes, vapors, gases arose (as in Yosemite Valley), speaking under their influence. This morning, instead of describing London in a Vaughan Williams fog, I scribbled pages and pages about Elena Gerhardt's* fatness, which brought to my mind various other surprising, creatively serviceable things: vaporousness of the past . . .

Under my window a man in a blackish rubber garment, medieval-Japanese-looking, almost breast-deep in the Haven water, agitates a sort of long-handled dustpan up and down, to and fro, every now and then bringing up quahogs. When the gulls get one, unable to open it, they fly up over the driveway and drop it and break it on the asphalt; then feed joyously.

Now among other little tasks, I shall decipher and copy (to be quoted in my London piece) the letter of Cunninghame Graham† upon my having dedicated *The Apple of the Eye* to him. It shocked him, and his moralistic attitude shocked me.

---

* Elena Gerhardt (1883–1961). A renowned German mezzo-soprano whose family hired G.W. as a traveling companion and secretary in 1923.
† Robert Bontine Cunninghame Graham (1852–1936). British travel and story writer and historian.

Woods Hole
August 16

Last night for the second time Padraic Colum came and read aloud to us from his manuscript of remembrances of James Joyce, very brilliant and delicate; and this morning I woke tormented about it, and spent an hour noting down some things he told us that he may not have the power to write, and trying to draft a letter to his publisher, that is, Ken McCormick of Doubleday's, with a suggestion of the way to influence him—especially how to bypass his broken-spirited and bad-natured old wife, who is holding him back.

I must remember, though, that if I do draw away from younger men, to avoid sexual excitement and frustration, this will be a part of the nemesis: I shall be sucked into too much preoccupation with the creativity of other writers, too much editorial and critical influence and helpfulness.

Woods Hole
August 17

Dawn, in the thickest gray veiling; a warm gray. It is one reason the Cape is recommended to very old people: night and day have almost the same temperature. Which does not suit me; I am like certain bulbs that need a special dormancy; you chill them just before their flowering. I miss my air-conditioned room. Also, the soft pillows here give me backaches.

I have spent an hour drafting the little narration of a certain perfect, unforgettable orgasm. I still seem to keep peaceable, with my renunciatory thought, for love's sake and literature's sake, and with no teasing by Messrs. X, Y, and Z. But, oh, I have sexual energy still, subject to infatuation, prone to horrible melancholy.

Mrs. Bruce Crane, who is beautiful—like a wild French boy, blond, with very wide-open blue eyes—goes fishing in a fast green boat, and last night brought us a large bass, silver, with a design of dark chains from end to end. The great old cook has retired—we no longer eat very well, unless we have these local goodies.

Woods Hole
August 19

A scientific morning: Newton Harvey took us all over the Marine Biological Laboratory, wonderful, almost comical. There are ice-cold rooms, furnace-hot rooms, pitch-black rooms (for the television microscope), as well as vast witches' kitchens for combinations of researchers.

There is one great warehouse for everything out of the sea alive and kicking; another for ditto dead, pickled in barrels, stinking. There is a great library, four floors of fireproof stacks in which we caught sight of nothing readable by us except *Who's Who*. Ten times more little magazines in every known language than there are for literature anywhere. We had this and that demonstrated to us; for example, the minutest observation in all biology—measurement of the amount of oxygen consumed by a single cell—it is confined in a sector of glass filament with a cork like the pricker of a thistle, handled by a plump little girl with long pointed fingernails . . . Mrs. Harvey is the authority on the fecundation and gestation of sea urchins. With a touch of electricity she caused a male and a female to ejaculate a little for us, then brought sperm and egg together under the microscope; and showed us the first two minutes of life.

The human research*ers* are almost as diverse and bizarre as the marine research*ees*: lovely-looking nuns, tiny tottering old men, bad-tempered Turks . . . The worst Turk was in charge of the roomful of poisons. In one mysterious room that Newton Harvey flung open for us, there was an extreme hunchback, his face situated at just about the juncture of his collarbones, with a husky helper, and, mysteriously seated on the floor, a little golden-haired child. In the subbasement storeroom we found the most beautiful youth in minimum shorts up on a stepladder working along the shelves: waistline as slender as the stalk of something, muscles of his back rippling, legs stretching—and sprawled down below, underneath the shelves, another not so beautiful, taking a rest, reading *Life* magazine.

Woods Hole
August 20

We had a northeaster yesterday in the late afternoon and evening, which I enjoyed. It blew itself out in the night, and all is exquisite this morning: the Haven like a great loom incessantly and softly weaving itself with gray-blue threads and blue-white threads; and empty masts turning to gold; and something made of metal in a small boat far out toward the lighthouse striking great sparks as the sun rises and reaches it—and far more silence than usual; even the gulls sound half-asleep, unhungry.

We shall be glad to have fair weather for the drive back to New York. Newport tomorrow.

During the northeaster we took the Colums to the Landfall, to cheer Molly up. But instead of cheering, on just two cocktails, she flew into one of her wild Irish rages. Then along came Jim Lord and his red-headed museum official, Mr. Greer, unexpectedly, on their way to Nantucket, and she insulted them. Afterward Monroe got the huge Buick wedged amid other cars, and I had to stand out in the downpour to direct his maneuvers, barefoot on rather painful stones. Except that the Colums had nothing in their pantry, and intended to buy a bluefish, and the fish market was closed by the time we got there; and we couldn't take them to Josephine's because she is beginning to be unable to stand Molly, and in fact, unless I am a worse fool than I take myself for, Molly is beginning to go crazy . . . All this I found exhilarating: I have a feeling for slapstick, even tragic slapstick.

New Haven
August 21

Back in the Taft, the shabbiest hotel in the country. When I was here with Lansdale, years ago, after the football game a great many university boys congregated here and got drunk and had fights and spilled drink and broke glasses and fell asleep in armchairs, and indeed on the floor; and older men from New York, also, come to think of it, an older woman, with a lorgnette, hovered around over them, etc.

The last day on the Cape we had the Goltzows to lunch: lovely old pink and blue Russians, authoritative on the oyster pearl and the albatross; and we drove to Cotuit, the most aristocratic of the towns on the Cape, with white porticos and large lawns and clipped hedges; and then we had another Joyce evening with Padraic, all about the madness of Joyce's daughter, brought to the fatal pitch at last by the marriage of Joyce and Nora, which advertised to the world that the children were illegitimate.

Ridiculous personal news item, for completeness of the record— (I sometimes think I aggrandize or ennoble things too much)—I have broken out with a strange extreme rash in my crotch, with mingled itch and soreness. Drugstore remedies have not taken effect; I shall have to put it up to Dr. Fidellow. Is it psychosomatic? Have I been conceited about my not simply howling with my sexual sorrows? Neglect. Do I just twine myself round with imaginary poison ivy instead?

New York
August 22

There was no one I wanted to see except Michael, and I wanted to see him either alone, to hear his troubles, or with some playmate—not with Elaine and/or George. No one (to the best of my knowledge) wanted to see me, except George, who tagged after me all afternoon, wild, provocative, changeable.

"Isn't it fantastic how I've changed? For one thing I talk and talk, and it's a great success. I'm more popular than ever. Why didn't I think of this earlier? But the change that is important, I suppose, is my truculence. What causes that, do you think?"

"I think you always have been truculent," I said. And in fact he has been, for about ten or twelve years.

"But nothing like this. I seem especially to attack my nearest and dearest. G.T., for example, I have insulted him really unforgivably, especially about his new love, which is so boring. But no matter, I can do no wrong, he adores me!

"Then I wrote a letter to Katherine Anne, pure poison, a kind of thing that nobody should ever write to anybody, and resigned myself to never seeing her again. But she didn't mind a bit.

"And what do you suppose I took it into my head to do next? I picked a quarrel with the only female on earth that I can stand: that really saintly old character, my mother. And she just thought it was funny. She laughed at me. And she gave me seventy-five dollars to buy a suit of clothes. It paid off!"

All this gave me gooseflesh, because, if he knew and reflected upon his fate, everyone's indulgence would seem understandable enough.

Stone-blossom
August 23

Let me not dwell lengthily on my impressions of Stone-blossom in miserable state, due to the flash floods from Hurricane Diane last Thursday and Friday. Depressing. It has been a historic calamity, with billion-dollar damage, especially in central Connecticut, in the Poconos, and along the Delaware. The Frenchtown motion picture theater is ruined, broken, clogged with mud; walls contaminated, bridges gone.

No real harm done here. We can't take baths. The cellar is still knee-deep, with firewood and corrugated-cardboard boxes and Anna's various poor little properties floating. She looks ill, and of course having Beulah and Eugenia and three babes here from Thursday to Monday would have been hardship enough. Mother also shaken up . . . but virtuous, courageous.

August 24

Wallace Stevens has died. The first modern poet that I loved and memorized.

. . . there never was a world for her
Except the one she sang and, singing, made.

If you substitute "him" for "her" it makes a good epitaph; it suits him. Will it ever suit me? Am I really determined now to have it suit me? It seems that I am.

August 25

Yesterday I worked for eight hours with two Reformatory girls, one blond, one black, emptying and cleansing the basement, with brooms and Lysol and the hose, and throwing away ruined things. Now I am waiting for Fidellow to give us typhoid shots.

Dalrymple's ducks have learned about poor Anna's tomatoes—Marty chased them, threatening to shoot them, a little hysterical, and fell down flat on the overflowing edges of the brook . . .

Nothing seems to touch my heart except the second movement of the Vaughan Williams two-piano concerto—and to think that it too was lent to me by Ronald. Now perhaps I shall take a nap, or perhaps weed my irises, in the romantic sunshine traversed by white clouds, in the strange wet air not sweet except along the phlox bed.

August 26

There is a young Englishman clamoring to see me, with a letter of introduction from David Posner; but in his second communication he proclaimed his pennilessness, friendlessness, etc., in an alarming way, so I think I shall avoid the relationship. David Posner has always brought me bad luck, in a small tedious bogus way.

Monroe gave me money to buy a gray Dacron-and-wool suit; but, alas, I had to let Anna have it for household expenses. I am still several hundred dollars behind in the general budget, to say nothing of my dentistry.

August 27

Mother has failed very much this month. Anna, without the least prompting, surprised me by saying that it was not the noisiness of the great-grandchildren, nor the scare of the flood—"it was just not having you there night and day, to hitch her life on to."

All I really do is to keep her amused, distracted, thinking of this and that—so that she can avoid contemplating the solemn alternative: increasing infirmities of old age, of which she has a horror, or the nothingness of the beyond, which, passionate about so many things in life, enrages her. Do I sound very morbid? I am not, really. For all this is just vision, and as such, writable; and writing, if the subject matter is humanity and animality and nature—not just theory and argument, vanity and propaganda—is life, at least my life, remainder of life.

August 29

Oh, the Stone-blossom mornings! The moral, about not coming downstairs at all in the morning, not answering the telephone, etc., more terribly pointed than ever, since I got back, with the added unavoidable commotion of plumbers, electricians, handymen, etc. We still have no heat, for which somebody or other seems to have been to blame. Lloyd in a most unusual towering temper . . . I suppose my mother complained inopportunely or inexpediently in my absence. Poor Santa Claus, furious when the children are not satisfied with what they find in their stockings.

And what do you suppose George told me the other day? The reason that myrrh and frankincense were so much appreciated when brought by the Wise Men to Bethlehem was that they are powerful insecticides. Presumably the babe in the manger, and indeed everyone then and there, suffered from fleas, etc.

When I went for a walk yesterday, I found a cushion of wild thyme still in bloom, and stooped over suddenly for a fistful of it, for the delectation of my ever sensual nose, and took no notice of the stiff broken dried stalk of some weed, and got it in my eye—which is very bloodshot and sensitive today.

August 31

Mother had been unhappy all day, so I read aloud to her rather longer than usual—fortunately, we still have a few chapters of a book that I love, *Out of Africa* [Isak Dinesen]—and then for an hour she confided her troubles to me, in the indirect feminine way: feeling her lifetime waning, lonely and bored, though hating to have to admit it, wanting more sociability with ladies—and she too shed tears.

One of the great troubles with Stone-blossom is its almost epidemic emotion. Not just the issues of my own temperament and sex and age, but others' impact on my mind and spirit, almost incessant. I never have found out how to protect myself from it or to render myself indifferent to it or even moderate about it.

September 6

Anna is in one of her slumps again, looking ill, and morose in her histrionic way: flashes of temper out of incomprehensible cloud.

One of her African violets took a chill and has been drooping its outer leaves, as to which I expressed sympathy. "Oh well," she said, casting up her little eyes, "I don't care, and I guess the violet knows it."

September 8

To the Maryland State Fair at Timonium with Baba and Debo, a four or five hours' drive each way, mostly after dark, averaging about fifty miles an hour—hard work but all enjoyable.

What we went for was to watch and take notes on the Guernsey judging, from nine-thirty until four-thirty, with less than three-quarters of an hour for lunch. But once in a while we spelled each other and took a turn around with Debo. It's a marvel of a fair: Hundreds of species of pigeon, some unimaginable, implausible, thrilling. Hundreds of pigs, with teenagers maneuvering them with walking sticks, as is traditional (Irish), with movement rather like a hockey game, this way and that, to and fro, to and fro, over the golden straw of the judging area. A great showing of Shetland ponies; they have revolutionized the breed: no longer tranquil and clumsy and dwarfy as they used to be: wild fairy-tale creatures, as slender as greyhounds, and not much bigger; with an exaggeratedly long cut of hoof like ballet shoes, and long profuse ring-letted seventeenth-century hair . . . to be watched and judged made the mares weep and gave the stallions erections.

September 13

I worked on my phlox beds awhile, and two baby boys came with their mother, Sis McMichaels, who used to work in the dairy by way of war work; and I gave them rides in the wheelbarrow.

The last few days a golden kitten has been hanging around Anna's back door. Now it lies dead in the hedgerow, upside down, with its white lips parted; and I wonder about it.

The extreme drought in July appeared to put a great many plants to death: estivation like hibernation. The flood last month was a springtime to them. Violets are in bloom again; so is the bush honeysuckle; so are someone's lilacs in the village. The sweet-leaf geraniums and the spearmint and peppermint are more aromatic than ever.

Baba tells of a visit to a lady orchid fancier near Morristown, to whom every one of her orchids was an individual with a history, a temperament, a morality, like, as it were, a child. Some, she said, were inclined to be "sulky"—that is, not to flourish, not to blossom, no matter what care she gave them. "Look, here under my worktable," and she pointed down to a darkish corner where there lay a pot on its side, a stem at an awkward angle, a leaf in the dust . . . "That's what I do when one really sulks. Often an orchid will only bloom when it thinks it's going to die."

I wonder if I am like that.

September 14

Amid the morning's petty disturbances—the sound box out of order, Mother needing a seamstress, Baba finding the sale of the Delacroix to François all very difficult, though gratifying, etc.—in comes Anna, to tell me her dream of Ronald last night. And apparently I have not mentioned his homecoming to her, so that it makes a fine occult effect. "Oh, Mr. Wescott, I dreamed about Ronald Neil last night, that he was back, and he was so happy, dancing all around, and he was just exactly like himself, nice, and pretty, and jolly. And then it rained and rained, and there got to be hundreds and hundreds of puddles all around, until I woke up."

Monroe has called me on the telephone and invited me to (a) dinner with Jos. Campbell, just back from India, and (b) Sadlers Wells and (c) *Henry IV* Part 1 at the City Center and (d) a reception for Miss Machiko Kyo, the leading lady of *Gate of Hell* and of *Ugetsu*. I accepted only (a).

From a letter to James Charlton

September 16

I wish you were here—I have been lonelier than usual this summer, especially lacking an objective sort of friend who might listen to some of my difficulties without minding too much or hitting back too hard. How much easier it is to talk interestingly than to write truly!—a difficulty in itself.

Give Bernadine my love, with a little injunction to her not to mind my writing to you instead of her. One's oldest friendships, with roots entangled all the way back, often are the least articulate. I am touched by your having heard the bad news of George from her, instead of Christopher or someone else. She brought him into our lives, did she tell you? He was a rather sensational teenager, seemingly rich, a Gertrude Stein fan, also fancying himself in love with someone in a musical comedy in London (could it have been Dennis King in *The Student Prince*?). I remember Bernadine's writing from Paris with the thought of his coming to see me in Villefranche, and of my perhaps having a good influence on him—oh, alas, alas! He didn't get to Villefranche that year; perhaps he went to London instead. I first met him in the old Hotel Lafayette in New York: a schoolboy with a waistline like a Gibson girl's, and a not very good complexion, wearing a bowler hat.

I make him sound older than he is, by these reminiscent glimpses, don't I? In fact his life has been running out, very worryingly in the last year or two. Until this happened, we all wondered how it could possibly develop or conclude. As I have implied over the page, he influenced me more than I influenced him, especially in the way of an unjustifiably high standard of living, too much sociability, etc. But I have got away with it this far, partly because I go on dedicating myself to literature with a kind of fanaticism; or to be exact, because Monroe Wheeler ever fanatically dedicates me . . . Whereas George lost interest in photography, except for nudes once in a while—or so it seemed; in fact he made some ostentation of not being interested. He never got back any of his commercial success after he returned from Hollywood. This spring it appeared that he would have to go bankrupt for the second time. While he was in the hospital his brother found that he had not been paying his rent for some months, and vacated and gave up both his apartment and his studio.

At the time of the operation his morale was wonderful. Not only that lion-like courage and sense of comedy, but a pacification and simplification and deflation . . . All of us who had lost patience with him were naturally contrite, not knowing how long the illness had been in effect. He felt loved, and for a while, it seemed, it was a relief to him to have a kind of misfortune that he could be sure of everyone's sympathy about.

His recovery from the operation as such was wonderful, though it was not a success. Then of course, all the confusion and misrule of his life began again, demoralizing to him as well as to everyone else involved. It is hard to tell exactly what concept or understanding of the future he has himself. He speaks of it in first one way and then another, according to his schemes and fantasies. He seems resolved not to alter his habit of life very much, and that, by his own admission, calls for about a thousand dollars a month. All is well at present, as he is enjoying the hospitality of a couple of our affluent French friends; but we expect him back in October, unless his or their plans change.

You see, it all still manifests that self-determination and defiance of the commonplace which you mention as characteristic of him in other circumstances; "perverse and patrician"—yes. A great many of his friends speak of this in almost the same terms; and others who did not admire it nevertheless found it exciting and enjoyable—so that we cannot help thinking of him as a sort of scapegoat.

September 18

Something I often remember: One day a Puerto Rican friend of mine (a friend of Bernard's) came out here, and was pleased to see my various wisteria on the garage, up on one corner of the house, and in the wild acre. "Oh, my mother in Puerto Rico loves wisteria, she has many vines and bushes."

"Alas, mine almost never blossoms. Does your mother know what to do about that?"

"Yes, she does. But if I tell you what, will you please promise not to laugh at her? She is a very old-fashioned woman.

"She has the Negro boys whip it!"

Monroe has tried something like this in the past, I mean just conversationally, to no avail.

From a letter to Will Chandlee III

October 6

. . . I am enthusiastic about your writing about the Camargue. Let me say prefatorily—but I have said it before, haven't I?—I do not think that you have the specifically literary talent that we once supposed. And indeed, as you say, college education does not count for much in this respect . . . But you have the creative or at least constructive stubbornness; and certain disciplines, the power to work hard, modestly, and faithfully—and now a wonderful opportunity . . .

But be wary of the thought that writing gives access to the most enjoyable way of life. The intention to become a writer, the premise and the preparation, serves very well as a pretext for living enjoyably, when one is young. But later there is a dilemma: as soon as it begins to be one's profession or vocation, either one has to let enjoyments go for the sake of it—or hedonism will hinder one's development. And if one fails, it is one of the most self-conscious and saddest forms of parasitism. Even in my case . . .

But the more I think of the Camargue possibility, the better I like it. Only make a fairly big thing of it; take plenty of time—go about it the hard way. Even as it may seem roundabout. Note that I recommend your taking the large view, the Camargue as a whole—situating the gypsy camp meeting and convention, when the time comes, in a general background of the history and the other picturesqueness of the area, make a research project of it, to begin with. Find out about the European gypsies in general, as well as this particular assembly. I wonder how one goes about research in Europe: the Bibliothèque Nationale? the Sorbonne? I seem never to have known a researcher there . . .

Look up the hagiography, for maximum oddity and mythical effect of the lives of the saints who landed there: not only Sarah (was she a saint? only to the gypsies, I guess) but Mary Salome, and Mary Magdalen, on her way to the cave in Les Baumes where she organized her hair in a sort of fur coat, and (I think) Martha, with that extra-long garter which she used as a leash and a tether for the dragon of Tarascon, and Lazarus . . .

Find out about the Levis Mirepois family, descended from which of the group? The Virgin was born Levy, was she not? It used to be related of certain devout old L.-M. ladies that in their prayers they addressed Nôtre-Dame as a relative: *Ave Marie ma cousine gratie plene,* etc.

Don't forget Aigues-Mortes, one of the most beautiful bits of architecture in France (for Jerome to photograph)—from which St. Louis launched one of the Crusades, I seem to remember; in which heretics were imprisoned. Did not a heretic incise in the stone some strange saying? Half-memory makes me feel like a sort of fool . . .

Did you see the much-admired short movie about the white horse and the bullfighting bulls? Did François not say that he knows some bull breeders, or perhaps that Gustave knows them?

Did you know the arena in Nîmes? Perhaps the prettiest of all . . . And in the little museum there (I think), look at a sculpture of the toreador god, Mithra . . . Montherlant's *Les Bestiaires,* the first book about tauromachy that I ever read, is worth reading . . .

You see my thought: If you will assemble and record very simply a great amount of the knowledge of that corner of France, none richer, none more haunted, and by the liveliest and most educational type of ghosts, you can't lose. If it isn't written the way they want it, they'll be tempted anyway—they'll instruct you, or rewrite for you, or come back for more . . . If not *Holiday,* perhaps *The New Yorker*—common glamour on the one hand, spit and polish on the other . . .

Perhaps I'll haunt you myself—perhaps especially on the beach at Palavas les-Flots; there is a place where someone's vineyard comes (or came) right down to the sand—one of the places where Jean Bourgoint frustrated me. When Ralph Pomeroy* was putting some letters of 1927

* Ralph Pomeroy. Poet, lover of Monroe Wheeler, friend of G.W.

in order—(I thought I might let that professor in Wisconsin have two or three, about *The Grandmothers*)—he found a quite readable poem, inspired by my dolorous concupiscence, Jean Bourgoint inspired . . . He is a Trappist monk; is or was. Howard Sturges is dead. Whatever became of Roland Tontain . . . ? He did acrobatics from the wing of an airplane for a living, and had a renowned penis—

October 13

My life has been more agitated than usual: Pauline de Rothschild has been in N.Y. for a week, A. C. Kinsey for half a week—they overlapped. He is about to go abroad for a couple of months, with Mrs. K.—Paris only one day, there to give a lecture to doctors . . .

I am going to give a poetry recital in the next month—jointly with Louise Bogan. I am practicing Stevens's *Monocle de Mon Oncle*—equivalent to the mad scene from *Lucia di Lammermoor* for the bel canto and the coloratura.

October 15

Human nature, or at all events, Ronald's: Early in the morning I was unkind to him about his intolerance of Monroe's old Buick, and about Monroe's disapprobation of his getting fined for speeding in Baba's Thunderbird. Down the stairs he streaked, to devour three large chocolate creams! Descending blood-sugar level, due to feelings of transgression and/or insecurity.

From a letter to Deborah Wescott, aged 14

October 21

Do you know, I sometimes quite frequently get melancholy—as a slow-poke author, an old bachelor aging, a world traveler immobilized, etc.—and perhaps the best remedy or palliative is a sense of humor. I have found this limerick (by Edward Lear) helpful:

There was an old man whose despair
Induced him to purchase a hare,
Whereon one fine day
He rode wholly away,
Which partly assuaged his despair.

Isn't it good? Stop and think: He intended it only to be an entertaining pet, but it turned out to be the temptation of temptations. And his departure, or alienation from himself, was total, whereas the assuagement only partial . . .

I have been lazy and stingy about buying sheets and (even more urgent) pillowcases. Yesterday Anna returned from Phillipsburg with half a dozen of the latter. "I can't wait until you get rich. See! they're good quality. Now I'm going to charge you for them in the household book, and you'll never know anything about it. You'll just think it's something you ate."

October 27

Alas, October is drawing to a close, and I haven't redug and divided and replanted my old phlox bed, weeks late. Both Monroe and I have been hampered by backaches—his serious, the sacroiliac kind; mine perhaps just a fatigue.

I am reading poems to select my program for my joint recital with Louise Bogan at the Academy. Old Ezra Pound, who lately wrote me an angry lonely letter from his insane asylum, is a problem, because his best poems have streaks of craziness, and phrases of old languages unpronounceable by me, Chinese, Greek, etc. Young Anthony Hecht is a problem, too—his poems are too long.

November 9

News grave and gay: Poor G.P.L. has had to go back to the hospital today; explosions of pain in his head requiring diagnosis. I am without a phonograph; I need a new record-changer belt and a new needle, about $40 worth. Craftily I thought I could wheedle François into this expenditure for me. But just as the gold-digging words were on the tip of my tongue, he presented me with $30 worth of new records, including some that I don't really want.

November 16

Anna says, "Now, if you're going to be home sick with your cold, will you eat two old thighs of broiled chicken and one half breast? We're going to have hot dogs. All of a sudden I got a yawn for hot dogs." Yes, *yawn*.

George is asking to see me. The great mortal ebb tide seemingly is beginning to be perceptible under him. I wish he knew Gabriel Fauré songs, *"L'Horizon Chimérique."*

Very wet and dim today—rather like the bottom of an aquarium that needs to have its water changed. Little Anna enters, with all the manner and tone of a big tragedienne: "Hah, what a sa-a-a-d morning!" I am reminded of the story of Mrs. Siddons, the greatest eighteenth-century English actress, famous for sepulchral voice. She went to a dry-goods store for a dress and asked the young salesman behind the counter, "Will it wash?"—so powerfully and sorrowfully that he fainted away behind the counter.

New York
November 21

I went to a party of a lot of middle-aged youngish men, all of the rather successful type, no threat to each other's peace of mind or reputation or pocketbook or anything. All wore pullovers, etc., but elegant Italian imports for the most part; and work trousers, but beautifully tailored. There were some "exceptional" persons: I myself for example, yes, and Bill, and Thornton Wilder, *et al.*, but as the midnight hour passed I'm afraid we all got to looking alike—the terrible pull of American collectivity.

I also went to see poor George, in the hospital with his unimaginably bad headache, with a great ice pack on his head, two heat pads under him, and a needle every so often. "They say it's just the same as a hangover," he murmured in his strange lipless voice, "only worse, much worse!" Hangover from life . . .

November 27

One of my difficulties as a writer, or perhaps I should say, one of my vices, is susceptibility to sudden untimely inspiration, which often seems better than what I am doing, what I have promised or contracted to do; quickness on the trigger; all my faculties set on fire by a chance spark—as you might say, promiscuity of the creative mind. Sometimes I think of it as especially a homosexual fault.

For example, this morning—with the Ford Madox Ford lecture still to prepare, at least eight or ten hours' methodical work—the El Greco Apostle postcards that Ronald brought me from Toledo happened to be on my desk; one of them aroused my curiosity—why has Bartholomew a little chained monkey or marmoset? Not irrelevant curiosity; he is in my Frick lecture . . .

So while breakfasting with Mother I looked him up in my *Calendar* and in Lucy Menzies; then looked up St. James the Great also . . . And suddenly, like fireworks, like a dream, I invented a form of story, a kind of connecting plot, that I have been tormenting myself to invent for years—to use the wonderful experience of the automobile accident in Spain with Russell Lynes and Akin, and something about miscarriage of justice, etc., particularly referring to homosexuality, and other unused material, hitherto wasted, hitherto useless material. An hour and a half's work to make a note of this, to remind me someday . . .

November 30

I feel punk. At 5 a.m. I awoke with stomach cramps and other such symptoms; somewhat abated tonight, but I still feel as though kicked from head to foot. Is it what Anna calls "wy-rus"?

December 3

What makes Gothic architecture so beautiful where it belongs, and in Soutine and sometimes in Utrillo—and altogether ugly (though picturesque) here in New York: like the skeleton of some shellfish, magnified.

Yesterday we (the National Institute and Academy of Arts and Letters) inaugurated our exhibition of poetry manuscripts, etc.—I was proud to be included. Also I had a good talk up there with John Hersey, perhaps affectionate, in any case unembarrassed, for the first time in many years—and I think he will take the presidency of the Institute; my nomination.

December 6

My horoscope, in Carroll Righter's column in the *Daily Mirror*, which came to my attention too late: "Finding ways to increase efficiency . . . requires you to pay more attention to consistent course regarding details and to go dashing off less frequently to tempting sites at a distance."

What a day! I intended to stay at the air terminal, to finish my tiny story entitled "The Mouse." But, alas, I still had not rediscovered or replaced my fountain pens—so I wandered back to 410, and I was so overexcited that various little things that happened on the way seemed to me strange and wonderful, and I tried to write them too. Then it was time to fetch Mother down from 168th Street, and I decided to economize and go by subway, and with the preoccupation of the writing added to my usual lack of subway talent, I landed to hell and gone, away over in the Bronx. Then I took Mother to Merian's, where she bought new shoes, and to Bloomingdale's, where she bought handkerchiefs and a nightgown, and to Schrafft's, where she ate turkey hash.

When I got back to 410, Hannah J. had telephoned: WEVD also wants me to broadcast poetry—and Alfred Kinsey had telephoned, wanting me for breakfast. So I took Mother home to Stone-blossom, ate dinner with her, read the newspaper to her, and came back on the nine o'clock train.

December 7

It was one of the hardest days ever, and manifestly there are to be ditto ditto ahead. I am writing this on my way to meet Mother at Dr. Selesnic's, who is to do the little surgery on her jaw; and before that I shall have my hair cut in Flemington—which rejuvenation I postponed yesterday in order to see George. He was in a deep sleep, with his face nestled down sideways in the pillow like a child. I stayed some minutes, looking at him and whispering to his nurse. I wrote him a loving little note, promising to come back on Friday, etc. He looked better, handsomer, than I have seen him all year, but something told me it was not health; also the politeness of the nurse was compassionate. When I got downstairs I went into the chapel and said a prayer and shed tears. Perhaps my praying is superstition or auto-suggestion rather than religion, but not just a false habit. In this case, in George's behalf, I asked for the obvious things, relief and release, and for something more personal, for all of us to be enabled to understand the story and the moral of his life rightly—without spite, without mistaken moralistic judgments, without quarrelsomeness, without self-indulgence . . .

Then I hastened to two bookstores in search of Walter De la Mare's poems for a Christmas Eve broadcast on WEVD (to be taped). Then Monroe and Ralph and I went to *The Matchmaker* by Plautus and Wilder, a good farce, perfectly performed by Ruth Gordon . . . (The philosophizing or moralizing soliloquies are excellent Wilder—the play as a whole seems a mistake. He might better have devoted the time and energy to his *Alkestis*. I especially mind a complacent effect: the suggestion that, in the theater, a kind of trashiness has to be respected by us, just because it has gone on like that for centuries. Even Mr. Eliot, holier than thou in many ways, has joined in this thesis somewhat, as it were for the profit.)

It was after we had come back to 410 that Russell Lynes got us on the telephone. Monroe kept saying, "Oh dear, oh dear . . ." He said, "Now I have a lot to think about." This morning he said, "Oh, I am glad you are still alive."

I tend to keep my sense of the ironic, indeed the comic, even in sincere solemnity. Russell had given obituary notices to the *Times* and the *Tribune* before we got back from the theater, and boasted a little to the effect that he has friends in the necrological department of both papers, therefore all would be well. But the *Times* gave him a mean

little notice (which Monroe minded), and the *Tribune* did him proud—
only they illustrated it with an old photograph of Joseph B. Platt mis-
labeled as George P. Lynes.

From a letter to Deborah Wescott

December 8

Our poor George died in his sleep Tuesday night, and yesterday
we all went to his funeral in St. George's Chapel in Stuyvesant Square.
After which Russell and Andrew Jackson and Bernard P. and Monroe
and I took the body to Woodlawn, where his father and grandfather also
are buried. We are all profoundly moved—he had the gift of keeping
friends, no matter what grievances developed. Also, in a way which I
may try to explain someday, he was our scapegoat. Of course we are
grateful for the fact that his suffering did not go on and on. He slept
almost all the last week.

INDEX

"Adolescence" (GW), ix

Adrian, 180

Agee, James, 4, 213–14

Allington, Lord, 91

American Academy–Institute of Arts and Letters, *see also* National Institute of Arts and Letters, xvi, xvii

Ames, Elizabeth, 232, 233–34, 235

Anderson, Sherwood, 73

Anglesey, Lady, 92

Anglesey, Lord, 92

Anton, Nick, 177–78, 186, 190, 191, 203–4, 227, 241, 249–50, 253–56, 257, 265, 269, 281, 312

Apartment in Athens (GW), xvi, 123, 125–26, 128, 139, 142, 148, 154, 189, 252, 257

Apollinaire, Guillaume, 320

Apple of the Eye, The (GW), xii, 57, 382

Askew, Kirk, 222

Aswell, Edward C., 150n, 151, 152

Auden, Wystan Hugh, 4, 49, 51–52, 56, 73, 75, 79, 216, 230, 291, 303, 307, 320, 325, 331, 368; GW correspondence with, 64, 137–38

Aurevilly, Barbey d', 174

Authors' Guild, 156

Authors League, 261, 279

Babe's Red, The (GW), xiv, 150, 195n

Bach, J. S., 187, 247, 291, 323

"Bad Han" (GW), xii

Baker, Joseph Ladislas, 281

Baker, Josephine, 6, 38

Balanchine, George, 330

Baldwin, Faith, 257

Balzac, Honoré de, 29, 81, 157, 174, 223, 320

Barber, Samuel, 64

Baring, Maurice, 67

Barnes, Caska, 6

Barnes, Djuna, 206–9, 249

Barnes, Howard, 196

Barrymore, John, 93

Barzun, Jacques, 143, 210–11, 303

Barzun, Marianna, 143

Baudelaire, Charles, 25, 27

Beaton, Cecil, 3, 38, 39, 73

Benét, William Rose, 102, 216, 279–81

Benét, Mrs. William Rose (Marjorie Flack), 279–81

Benga, Feral, 6, 7

Bérard, Christian, xii, 36

Bernie, Georges, 317

Berthelot, Mme Philippe, 30

Bishop, Isabel, 280

Bishop, John, 73

Bishop, John Peale, 75, 80, 122

Bitterns, The (GW), x

Blake, William, 217, 223, 332–33

Bloom, Hyman, 159

Bodenheim, Maxwell, xi

Bogan, Louise, xvii, 214, 376, 394, 395

Born, Cecil, 44

Boulanger, Nadia, 247

Bourdet, Edouard, 38

Bourgoint, Jean, 39, 393, 394

Bowen, Elizabeth, 224, 238, 240–41, 276

Bowles, Sally, 303, 307

Boy, Jean, 29, 30
Brakke, Anna (GW housekeeper), 40, 189,
    192, 196, 201, 205, 262, 282, 283,
    340, 343, 347, 354–55, 358, 366,
    367, 368, 373, 377, 378, 387, 390,
    395, 397; illness, 374–75, 386,
    388–89
Braque, Georges, 234–35, 288
Brecht, Stefan, 229
Breit, Harvey, 233
Brenan, Gerald, 310
Bromfield, Louis, xiii
Brooks, Van Wyck, 178, 182, 267
Brown, Anne, 354
Brown, Tom, 300
Brundage, Robert, 172
Bryson, Lyman, 145n, 236, 237
Buck, Pearl, 68
Buckingham, Bob, 238, 245, 246, 250
Burke, Kenneth, 289–90, 319
Burns, John Horne, 214
Butts, Mary, xii, 38–39

Cabell, Ury, 4n, 56
Cadmus, Paul, 4, 8–9, 10–12, 42, 52n, 60,
    65, 69–70, 81, 87, 165, 172, 292, 372,
    380
Calendar of Saints for Unbelievers, A (GW),
    xiv, 4n
Campbell, Joseph, 213, 222, 243, 245, 275,
    390; GW correspondence with, 237–38
Canby, Henry Seidel, 217
Capote, Truman, 186, 200, 248, 302
Carré, Marguerite, 36
Caskey, William, 220, 228, 303
Cendrars, Blaise, 37
Chagall, Marc, xiv
Chandlee, Will, III, 322, 331, 334, 337–38,
    350, 392–94
Chanel, Coco, 224
Channing, Carol, 268
Charlton, James, 358, 390–91
Chase, Lucia, 330
Clark, Eleanor, 173, 181, 182–83, 195n,
    214, 232, 233, 302
Clark, Kenneth, 70, 295
Cocteau, Jean, v, xii, xv, xvii, 3, 6, 31, 36,
    37, 38, 39, 39n, 78, 211, 213, 224, 235,

248, 284, 325–26; GW relationship with,
    36, 37
Cohn, Roy, 347
Colette, xvii, xviii, 174, 271, 274, 320, 325–
    26, 327; GW introductory essay for omni-
    bus edition of, 288, 292, 295–96, 303,
    334; GW lecture on, 324
Collier, John, 56
Colum, Molly, 63, 384–85
Colum, Padraic, 63, 143, 246, 348, 383,
    384–85
Connolly, Cyril, 59, 196, 360–61
Cooper, Lady Diana, 91
Coward, Noël, 215
Cowles, Fleur, 248
Crane, Hart, 274
Crane, Josephine, 156, 172, 173, 302, 338,
    352, 381, 385
Crane, Louise, 139–40
Crouse, Russel, 46
Csere, John, 133–34, 135
Cukor, George, 140
Cummings, E. E., 183, 216, 217, 272
Cunard, Nancy, 32, 35
Cunninghame Graham, Robert Bontine, xi,
    382
Curtiss, Mina, 123

Dalí, Salvador, 40, 54
Damrosch, Walter J., 188
Daniels, Jimmie, 6, 7, 12, 17, 305
"Dare, The" (GW), ix
Davenport, Russell, 16
Davis, Ellabelle, 139–40
Davis, George, 63, 74, 248
Deadly Friend, The (GW), xvi
"Death of Isadora, The" (GW), 96
de la Celle, Henri, 239–40, 242, 244, 247–
    48, 249–50
Desbordes, Jean, 38
Desti, Marie, 62
Dietrich, Marlene, xvii, 17, 235
Dinesen, Isak, xviii, 388
Dolin, Anton, 38–39
Dorval, Marie, 14
Dos Passos, John, 232
Doubleday, Nelson, Sr., 95, 98, 99, 100
Doubleday, Nelson, Jr., 95

"Doughboy Penitante, The" (GW), 96
Douglas, Lauri, 154
Draper, Ruth, 263
"Dream of Audubon, The" (GW), xv, 69, 72, 75, 80
Dream of Mrs. Cleveland, The (GW), xvi, 63
Drew, Robert, 181, 187, 188, 191, 196–97, 205
Dudley, Katherine, 39
Duncan, Isadora, xii, 62, 78, 222, 224
Dunn, Blanche, 6
Dust-Basket, A (GW), 359

Eden, Mrs. Anthony, 224
Edman, Irwin, 236
Ehrenburg, Ilya, 168
Ekstrom, Parmenia, 66, 80
Elder, Donald, 73
Eliot, T. S., 4, 207–9, 320, 398
Ellis, Walker, 86
Erskine, Albert, 235

"Farmer in the Dell" (GW), 96
Farrell, James, 320, 325
Faulkner, William, 54n, 288, 303, 320, 325
Fear and Trembling (GW), xiv, xvi, 57, 290–91, 360–61
Fellowes, Mrs. Reginald, 272
Ferber, Edna, 159, 186, 290
Fitzgerald, F. Scott, xii, xvi, 80, 89, 139, 211
Flanner, Janet, v, xvi, 31–32, 35, 112–13, 141, 145, 285
Flaubert, Gustave, xvi, 362–63
Fontaine, Jean, 379
Ford, Charles Henri, 54
Ford, Ford Madox, xi, xii, 57, 78, 204, 241, 248, 298, 396
Ford, Hugh, xix
Ford, Ruth, 54
Forster, E. M., xvii, xviii, 46, 52, 65, 79, 204, 221, 230, 238–39, 242, 244–45, 250, 302, 303, 320, 325, 338
Fortune in Jewels, A (GW), xvi, 87
Fouts, Denham, 59, 211, 212
Frank, Jean-Michel, 32
Frasconi, Antonio, xvii

French, Jared, 8, 11–12, 52, 60, 65, 172, 221, 242, 372, 380
French, Margaret, 60–61, 65, 70–71, 380
"Frenchman Six Foot Three, The" (GW), xvi
Freud, Sigmund, 168, 210, 238, 320
Frost, Robert, xi, xvii–xviii, 352

García Lorca, Federico, 320
Gaynor, Janet, 180
Gebhard, Paul, 346, 351
Gebhardt, Edna, 171
Geffen, Felicia, 216, 279, 280
Genet, Jean, 185, 213, 264, 332
Gerhardt, Elena, xi, 382
Germain, Ray, 332
Gershwin, George, 15
Gide, André, vi, vii, 35, 36, 46, 74, 85, 174, 234, 302, 326
Girard, Michel, 30, 31, 37
Goff, Lloyd, 8–9
Gogh, Vincent van, 48
Goldman, Henry, xi, 110–11
Goodbye, Wisconsin (GW), xiii
Goodspeed, Bobbie, 143
Gordon, Caroline, xii, 298
Gordon, Ruth, 398
Gorky, Arshile, 131–32
Guyen, William, 267, 276, 291
Grandmothers, The (GW), xiii, xix, 39n, 79, 103, 147n, 249n, 394; royalties, 335
Grant, Jane, 186
Graves, Robert, 152
Green, Henry, 263
Green, Julien, xiii
Green, Paul, 126
Gregory, Alyse, 147
Grigson, Geoffrey, 56
Guérin, Jacques, xiv, 14, 29, 30, 36–37, 132, 150, 151, 258
Guggenheim Foundation, 206–7, 208
Guitry, Sacha, 7

Halicka, Alice, 16
Hamilton, Nancy, 44
Harcourt, Sir William, 162
Harris, Jed, 236
Harris, Roy, 70

Harrison, Barbara, *see* Wescott, Barbara Harrison (Baba)

Harrison, Dora Maxwell, 115–20, 121–22

Harrison, Francis B., 84*n*, 86

Harrison, Frederico (Kiko) (Francis), 116–20, 122

Harrison of Paris, xiii, 12*n*, 13

Hart, Moss, 193–94

Harvey, Newton, 383–84

Haymeadows (farm), xvii, xviii, xix

Haywood, Billy, 56

H.D. (Hilda Doolittle), x

Heard, Gerald, 56

Hecht, Anthony, 395

Hellman, Lillian, 182, 216, 241

Hemingway, Ernest, xii–xiii, 249, 285–86, 292, 303, 319, 320, 348–49; GW lecture on, 321

Herrick, Fred, 63

Herrmann, Bernard, 69

Hersey, John, 397

Hobson, Laura Z., 210

Hope, Lady John, 359

Hopkins, Harry L., 134, 148, 156, 164

Hopkins, Louise, 148, 164

Hopper, Edward, 210

Horney, Karen, 195, 210, 215, 217, 218, 219

Hotchkiss, Bruce (nephew of GW), 195

Hotchkiss, Elizabeth, *see* Wescott, Elizabeth (sister of GW)

Housman, A. E., 75

Howard, Cecil, 280

Hoyningen-Huene, George, 229

Hudson, Richard, 292

Hughes, Richard, 66, 268

Hugnet, Georges, xii

Hunt, Leigh, 302

Hunter, Sam, 235

Huxley, Aldous, 56, 99–100, 230, 325

Huxley, Julian, 216

Images of Truth (GW), xviii, 3*n*, 160*n*

"In a Thicket" (GW), xii

Institute for Sex Research, xvi, 241*n*, 288, 298, 301, 334*n*, 377

Invitation to Learning (radio symposium), 145, 191, 236, 237

Isherwood, Christopher, xvii, 51–52, 56, 154–55, 173, 210, 211, 212, 225–26, 234, 235, 241, 267, 303, 319, 372; GW correspondence with, 220, 276–77, 368–69; in Hollywood, 228–30; journal, 229; and Van Druten's play, 304, 307

Istrati, Panait, 211

Jackson, Andrew, 399

James, Edward, 54, 162

James, Henry, xiv, 169, 241, 299

James, Philip, 280

Jennings, Oliver, 56

Jessup, Eunice, 195

Joel, George, 296

Jones, Ernest, 168

Josephson, Hannah, 280

Jouhandeau, Marcel, vii

Joyce, James, 241, 278, 383, 385

Kafka, Franz, 181, 241, 320

Kallen, Horace, 156

Kallman, Chester, 64

Kavanagh, Mrs. George Washington, 65–66

Keller, Helen, 187–88

Keller, Jeff, 152–53, 274

Kelly, Gerald, 160

Khill, Marcel, 3, 31, 37, 38, 39

Kierkegaard, Sören, 305, 327–28

"King David and His Court" (GW), ix

Kingsley, Sydney, 235

Kinsey, Alfred C., v, xvi, 241, 245–46, 270, 276, 292, 295, 297, 298, 299, 301, 303, 304, 306, 307, 308, 310, 313, 317–18, 332, 333, 334–35, 346, 350, 351, 353, 354, 355, 377, 394, 397; GW correspondence with, 265–66, 315–17

Kirstein, Lincoln, 52, 80, 320

Klee, Paul, 329

Klopfer, Donald, 376

Kochno, Boris, 185

Kriendler, Jack, 235

Kronenberger, Louis, 222, 241

Lambert, Hansi, 145, 371

Lansdale, Henry Nelson, 52, 60, 65, 67, 69, 70, 74, 81, 82, 85, 87–90, 91–92, 113–

14, 126, 205, 235–36, 276, 295, 381, 385
Lavery, Sir John and Lady, xi
Lawrence, D. H., xii, 28
Lawrence, T. E., 46, 129
Leavis, F. R., 216
Leavis, Q. D. (Queenie), 216
Leduc, Violette, 370
Levin, Harry, 278
Levy, Julien, 21
Lewis, Janet, x, 231n
Lewis, Sinclair, xii
Lieder Singer, The (GW), 359, 371, 381
Lindsay, Vachel, x, 49
Little Ocean Liner, The (GW), xvi, 371, 381
Livingstone, Belle, 261
Loeb, Jane, 147
Long, Herbert, 58–59
Lord, James, 374, 385
Loring, Eugene, 15
Lowe, Tim, 315, 316, 335, 350
Lowell, Robert, 232, 234
Loy, Mina, x, xi, 248
Lynes, George Platt, xiv, xv, 4, 6, 7, 9, 10, 11, 12–13, 15, 17, 20, 22, 23–25, 31, 34, 36, 52, 53, 54–55, 56, 58, 59–60, 62, 63, 65, 66, 67, 71, 73, 84, 86, 87, 97, 107–10, 113, 115, 117, 118–19, 145–46, 151, 154, 155, 165, 167, 173, 192, 196, 200–1, 205, 209, 215, 221, 232, 233, 249, 275, 286, 296, 304, 305, 307, 372, 388; death of, xvii, 398–99; GW correspondence with, 108–9; and GW writing, 64; illness, 368–69, 370f, 371, 373, 374, 376–77, 378–79, 380, 385–86, 390–92, 395, 396, 398; photographs of N. Lansdale, 69, 70; photograph of E. Sitwell, 286
Lynes, Russell, 297, 373, 396, 398, 399

McCarthy, Desmond, 222
McCarthy, Joseph, 347
McCormick, Anne O'Hare, 142–43, 188
McCormick, Ken, 383
McCullers, Carson, 288
MacDowell Colony, xi, xviii
MacGregor, Frank S., 150, 172, 187
McIlhenny, Henry, 235

MacLeish, Archibald, 214, 221
McMichaels, Sis, 389
MacNeice, Louis, 51
McPherson, Kenneth, 6
Madariaga, Salvador de, 325
Mallarmé, Stéphane, 27
Malouf, Carl, 210–11, 224, 244, 260, 267, 268, 269, 270–71, 304–5, 308, 309, 311–12, 313, 315–16, 318, 324, 333
Malraux, André, 325
Mann, Klaus, xv, 56, 73–74, 80
Mann, Thomas, xiii, xviii, 47, 63, 173, 241, 320
Marin, John Cheri, 217
Martin, John, 75
Masters, Edgar Lee, x
Maugham, Lisa, 91
Maugham, Robin Cecil Romer, 90
Maugham, William Somerset, v, xvi, xvii, xviii, 69, 77, 79, 84, 89, 102, 117, 129, 136, 140, 151, 164, 166, 186, 191, 204, 230, 232, 234, 283, 320; advisory work, 140; GW on, 57, 103; and GW homosexuality, 209–10; on GW writing, 293, 314; omnibus edition, 160; K. A. Porter's attitude toward, 302; portraits of, 168; relationship with A. Searle, 292, 294, 359; relationship with GW, xiii, xv, 86, 87, 90, 93, 94, 96, 97, 98, 99, 153, 154, 155, 161–62, 163, 165, 187, 324; M. Wheeler and, 160; works, 223
Maury, Matthew Fontaine, 301
Maxwell, Dora, *see* Harrison, Dora Maxwell
Maxwell, Elsa, 300
Merrick, Gordon, 239
Meyer, Arthur, 14
Mikshe, Michael, 308–10, 311–12, 313, 314, 315–17, 318, 324, 334, 335, 372–73, 385
Miller, Henry, 299
Miller, William, 132, 149, 249, 306, 320
"Mr. Auerbach in Paris" (GW), xvi
Mistinguett, 33, 36
Moe, Henry Allen, 208
"Monday Classes," 156n, 305, 321, 338
Monk, Jules, 29
Monroe, Harriet, xi
Montherlant, Henry de, 325–26

Moody, Mrs. William Vaughan, xi
Moore, Douglas, 216, 279, 280
Moore, Marianne, x, xi, 68–69, 164, 188,
    211, 214, 216, 222, 223, 233, 286, 313,
    324, 331, 356, 364, 368; GW correspon-
    dence with, 190; GW essay on, xix
"Moral of F. Scott Fitzgerald, The" (GW), xvi
Morand, Paul, 321, 325, 326
Morris, Lloyd, 349
Mortimer, Raymond, xi, 222–23, 324
Moseley, Henry, 141
Moss, Howard, xviii
"Mouse, The" (GW), 397
Mulhocaway (farm), *see* Stone-blossom
Museum of Modern Art, xv, xvi, xviii, xix,
    283, 370

Nabokov, Nicholas, 320, 321
"Naked Man, A" (GW), 96
National Institute of Arts and Letters, 207,
    217, 221, 223, 238–39, 245, 279, 288,
    313, 321, 397; anti-censorship effort, 232;
    grantees, 232–33; grants committee, 213–
    14, 267; GW activities with, 210, 303; GW
    formal institution, 180–81
Natives of Rock (GW), xii
Neil, Ronald (pseud.), 312–13, 314, 315–
    17, 318, 320, 322, 324, 329, 334–35,
    336, 337–38, 339, 342, 343, 345, 347,
    351, 359, 367, 373, 376, 387, 390, 394,
    396; break with GW, 350, 366; in Europe,
    369–70, 378, 379; GW correspondence
    with, 323, 324, 374; letters to GW, 370;
    relationship with GW, 361, 382
Neumann, Teresa, 175
Ney, Elly, 70, 78
Nicolson, Harold, 238
Noguchi, Isamu, 44
Nouilly, Lecomte de, 156

O'Faolain, Sean, 236
O'Hara, John, 210
O'Higgins, Patrick, 183–84, 186, 210, 216,
    223–24, 242, 282, 283
O'Keeffe, Georgia, 210, 217
Oswald, Marianne, 38
Ouspenskaya, Maria, 63

Pagano, Mark, vii
Parker, Dorothy, 84, 194
Parker, Maude, 216
Paulhan, René, 29
Perkins, Maxwell, xii, 178n
Perlin, Bernard, 160, 168, 172, 181, 186,
    187, 188, 191, 196–97, 205, 211, 212,
    214, 227, 250, 258, 264, 271, 281, 285,
    297, 312, 392, 399
Petin, Jean, 30–31, 37
Phelps, Robert, xviii
Picasso, Pablo, xii, xiv, 150, 238, 275, 320
Pilgrim Hawk, The (GW), xv, xviii, 63, 64,
    69, 72, 73, 74, 76–77, 154, 173, 335;
    critical reception, 128, 196
Poe, Edgar Allan, 25, 26–27
Pomeroy, Ralph, 393–94, 398
Porter, Charles, 230
Porter, Cole, 11
Porter, Katherine Anne, v, xiii, xvi, xviii, 3–
    4, 12n, 15, 18, 20, 69–70, 72, 73, 74n,
    138, 151, 173, 205, 225, 235, 236, 259,
    275–76, 277, 300–1, 302, 317, 325, 327–
    28, 372, 378, 380, 386; GW correspon-
    dence with, 112–13, 181; GW essay on,
    xv; GW on, 79, 86; GW reviewing works
    of, 123; health/illness, 275, 291; and Na-
    tional Institute, 181, 182, 280–81, 288,
    303; nephew Paul, 378; relationship with
    GW, xiv, xix, 83, 209, 231–32, 302, 303;
    and Yaddo affair, 233
Posner, David, 129, 131, 146, 157, 163,
    387
Potter, Pauline (Pauline de Rothschild), 134–
    35, 148, 153, 157–58, 170, 195, 222,
    224, 234, 235, 275, 317, 320, 327, 328,
    329, 360, 361, 394; on GW work, 276;
    marriage to P. de Rothschild, 336
Pound, Ezra, xi, 395
Prescott, Orville, 222
Preston, Stuart, 235
Printemps, Yvonne, 7
Prokosch, Frederic, xvii
Proust, Marcel, 29, 319–20, 338
"Proustian Tale, A" (GW), 371

Rain, Charles, 4, 8, 21–23
Rau, Santha Rama, 342–43

"Refugee, The" (i.e., *The Little Ocean Liner*), (GW), 96, 381

Reischenbach, François, 246–47, 325, 350, 367, 368, 370, 371n, 372, 373, 390, 393, 395

Reischenbach, Philippe, 246n, 371

Renoir, Pierre Auguste, xiv, xvii, 11, 140, 142, 156, 164

Richter, Jean Paul, 278

Righter, Carroll, 397

Rilke, Rainer, 320

Ripper, Jack von, 235

Rixkuelthau, Carl (E.R.K.), ix, 13–14, 288, 375

Robbins, Frances, xii, 149, 281

Roberts, Elizabeth Madox, x

Rodgers, Mrs. Richard, 366

Rops, Felicien, 27

Rose, Sir Francis, xii

Ross, Harold, 186

Ross, Nancy, 179

Rothschild, Pauline de, *see* Potter, Pauline

Rothschild, Philippe de, 134n, 336, 370

Rovere, Richard, 276

Rubinstein, Helena, 16–17

"Runaways, The" (GW), 4

Russell, Bertrand, 288

Ryan, Nin, 299

Sahl, Ethel, 133

"Sailor, The" (GW), 373

Saint-Léger, Alexis (St.-John Perse), 123, 167, 170

Sandburg, Carl, x, 281–82

Santayana, George, 195, 320

Saroyan, William, 210

Sassoon, Sir Victor, 365

Sauguet, Henri, 288

Saxton, Eugene, 74; Saxton Fund, 150–51, 152, 153

Sayão, Bidú, 66

Schine, David, 347

Schorer, Mark, 196

Schwartz, Delmore, 213

Seabrook, Willie, 326

Searle, Alan, 161, 162, 165, 187, 209–10, 294, 359

Shannon, Charles, 232

Shaw, George Bernard, 46, 222

Sheean, Diana, 32

Sheen, Fulton J., 243, 246

Sheldon, Edward, 92–93

Sherwood, Robert, 235

Sidney, Philip, 94, 157, 364

Silone, Ignazio, 325

Sitwell, Edith, xvii, 202, 204, 210, 216–17, 222, 223, 283, 338; GW correspondence with, 300; Lynes photograph of, 286

Sitwell, Osbert, xi, 202n, 204, 210, 216, 222, 223, 283, 288

Smedley, Agnes, 232n, 234

Solano, Solita, 32

Solley, Bob, 251, 255, 271, 284

"Somerset Maugham and Posterity" (GW), 160n

Spender, Stephen, 59, 66, 75, 230, 276

Spies, Heinrich, 111

Spriggs, Sylvia, 153

"Stallions, The" (GW), 160n

Stein, Gertrude, xiv, 38, 75n, 241, 248, 390

Stendhal, v, 150, 282, 324

Stevens, Wallace, x–xi, 289, 386

Stewart, Katie, 86

Stone-blossom (country house), xv, xvii, xviii, 32, 53, 60, 86, 101, 107, 109, 125, 151, 156, 163, 168–69, 172, 196, 240, 251, 262, 285, 286, 287, 322, 336, 376; flood damage to, 386, 388; GW finances and, 340; GW tenancy of, 192, 255, 274, 292–93, 341

Straus, Helen, 145, 172, 235, 296, 303

Stravinsky, Igor, xii, 6

Sturges, Howard, 192, 394

Sullivan, Tommy, 260–61, 267, 268, 269, 271, 277, 283, 293, 296, 304, 314, 324

Sulzberger, Arthur Hays, 290

"Summer Ending" (GW), xv

Sutter, Jerome, 283

"Swamp Garden, The" (GW), 96

Szold, Bernadine, 16, 169, 229, 236, 390–91

Tanguy, Yves, 214

Tate, Allen, xii, 298–99, 325

Taylor, Peter, 213

Tchelitchew, Pavlik (Pavel), xiv, 4, 6, 16,
22, 54, 66, 72, 149, 151, 153, 155, 188,
235, 278, 339, 378, 380
Tennant, Robina, 216
Thayer, Alonzo, 6
Thomas, Edna, 6, 7
Thompson, Dorothy, 194
Thomson, Virgil, 75–76, 84, 223, 247n, 320
Tichnor, Jonathan, 107, 108, 145–47
Trenet, Charles, 39
Trilling, Lionel, 303
Turgenev, Ivan, 152, 157, 282
Twelve Fables of Aesop (GW), xvii
Twysden, Duff, xiii

UNESCO, xvi, 279
Untermeyer, Louis, 182

Valdez, Tito, 30, 31, 32, 33–36, 37, 38
Valéry, Paul, 27, 167, 247, 273, 319, 326
"Valley Submerged, The" (GW), xviii
Van Doren, Carl, 216
Van Doren, Mark, 213, 214, 216
Van Druten, John, 56, 303, 307
Vaughan Williams, Ralph, 363, 378, 382,
387
Viertel, Peter, 229
Viertel, Salka, 229
Vigny, Alfred de, 14
Villefranche, xii, xiii, 30, 390–91
Vilmorin, André de, 170
"Visit to Priapus, A" (GW), xv
Vreeland, Diana and Reed, 188

Wagner, Richard, 63
"Wander-Bird, The" (GW), 96, 371, 381
Wanger, Beatrice, 38
Warburg, Mary, 224
Warren, Katherine, 299
Warren, Robert Penn, 173n, 235, 320
Washburn, Gordon, 141
"Wastebasket, The" (GW), 96
Watson, Peter, 59
Waugh, Evelyn, 137
Welch, Elizabeth, 44
Welty, Eudora, xvi
Wescott, Barbara Harrison (Baba) (sister-in-
law of GW), xiii–xiv, xv, xvii, 3n, 4n, 12–

13, 16, 32, 51, 60, 63, 67, 85–86, 100,
101, 102, 113, 115, 116, 117, 128–29,
132, 135–37, 139, 148, 150, 152–53,
153n, 155, 159, 188, 190, 197, 201, 202,
203, 210, 215, 217–18, 219, 233, 236,
240, 253, 255, 265, 271, 288, 320, 321,
351, 370, 389, 394; activities with GW,
168, 169, 216, 241; art collection, 142,
156, 164, 371, 375–76, 390; death of, xix;
father of, 151–52; GW correspondence
with, 97–98, 107–8; and GW finances,
274, 334, 340; GW financial dependence
on, 187, 189, 346; and GW tenancy of
Stone-blossom, 243; and GW writing, 314;
illness, 378, 379; psychotherapy, 181,
184, 191–92, 251–52, 262, 352; relationship with GW, 145, 196, 252, 256
Wescott, Beulah (sister of GW), 41, 86–87,
101, 113, 186, 237, 242, 264–65, 344,
373, 386
Wescott, Bruce (father of GW), ix, 52, 56,
77, 101, 140, 157, 215, 281; death of,
xvii, 339–40, 358; illness, 232, 260,
338–39; relationship with GW, 285
Wescott, Deborah (Debo) (niece of GW), 122,
135–36, 141, 169, 181, 189, 321, 375,
389; birth of, 100; GW letters to, 171,
394, 399; relationship with GW, 178
Wescott, Elizabeth (sister of GW), 13, 25,
41, 56, 113, 147, 163, 165, 171, 178,
181, 184, 188, 189, 192, 196, 201, 203,
205, 212, 215, 233, 243, 245, 249, 251,
253–54, 257, 262, 268, 275, 281, 344,
375; activities with GW, 247; GW correspondence with, 100–2; relationship with
GW, 256, 264–65
Wescott, Glenway: advice to young writers,
149–50, 199–200, 218–19; aesthetics, vi,
40, 75; agoraphobia, 261; and American
Academy–Institute of Arts and Letters, xvi,
xvii; anxiety neurosis, 131, 163, 178, 314,
382; on art, 48–49, 114; autobiographical
note, 78–79; awards, honors, xiii, xviii;
childhood, early life, ix–x; correspondence,
xiv, 64, 95, 97–98, 100–2, 107–10, 112–
13, 137–38, 165–66, 171, 181, 190,
199–200, 204–5, 206–9, 218–19, 220,
222–23, 237–38, 241, 246–47, 265–66,

Wescott, Glenway (*cont.*)
276–77, 279–81, 300, 304–5, 315–17,
323, 324, 358, 360–61, 368–69, 374,
390–91, 392–94, 399; on death, 348–49;
death of, xix; education of, ix–x, 78; as expatriate, xiii, xviii; family affairs/relation-
ships, v, 55, 133, 191, 192, 259–60, 361;
financial affairs, 55, 63, 83, 110, 125,
128, 129–30, 152, 189, 192, 251–52,
262, 274, 334, 335, 342, 345, 346, 365,
376, 387; French nouvelles omnibus edition, 173–74; friends, friendships, v, xi,
52, 68, 134n, 202n, 231n, 246n, 260–61,
312; health/illness, xix, 35, 65, 114, 205–
6, 225, 275, 282, 285, 287–88, 308, 385,
394, 397; health/illness: lip cancer, 271–
72, 279–80, 323, 369; on his homosexuality, 9, 52, 252, 284, 297, 301, 367; on his
life, 220–21, 235, 293, 324, 336, 345; on
his literary talent, 20, 98, 178, 209, 243–
44, 252–53, 279, 291, 325, 332, 343,
346, 349, 381; on his psychoneurosis,
252–53; on his writing/working, 58, 63,
96, 103, 184, 225, 314, 343, 364, 365,
376, 380–81, 382, 396–97; homes, resi-
dences, xi, xii, xiv, xv, xvi–xvii, xviii, 71–
72, 107, 262 (*see also* Stone-blossom
[country house]); homosexuality, x, 4, 10,
13–15, 17, 18–26, 42, 102–3, 105–6,
121, 159, 176, 205, 209–10, 240, 256,
259–60, 267, 268, 281–82, 288, 293–
94, 342, 344, 348, 376, 383; on homosexuals, homosexuality, 8–9, 10–11, 196,
197, 198, 249, 283–84, 317, 318–19,
332–33; on immortality, 308; journals, v,
xiii, xv, xviii–xix, 25–26, 47, 65, 66–67;
lectures, speeches, xviii, 73, 126–28, 198,
241, 285–86, 288, 297–98, 305, 315,
321, 324, 352, 365–66, 396; literary career, 79; loneliness, 28, 32, 72, 121, 131,
155, 159, 176, 178, 222, 236, 357, 360,
367, 390; on love/sex, 53, 58, 85, 88,
89–90, 103, 121, 122, 132, 189, 238,
302–3, 305–6, 313–14, 317–18, 339,
343, 357, 373; lovers, xiv, 4, 15, 22–23,
34, 35–37, 38n, 74, 82–83, 85, 87–90,
91, 102, 125, 177–78, 196–97, 225–26,
227, 229, 230–31, 236, 254, 258, 260–

61, 269, 283, 288–89, 293–94, 308–10,
311–13, 337–38, 350–51, 359, 376; on
male beauty, 43–44; on masturbation, 302;
ménage à trois, v, 9, 20, 54, 107–10; morality of, 191, 319; narrative voice of, xiii;
pacifism, 72–73; personal characteristics,
ix, 29–30, 292, 296; physical appearance,
156–57; on pleasure, 267, 269, 373–74;
psychotherapy, 255, 258–59, 261, 262,
265, 284; public speaking, 77–78 (*see also*
under his lectures, speeches); reverence/
love for nature, v, 53, 54, 55, 95–96,
106–7, 111–12, 140, 152, 273, 294–95,
349–50, 354, 359–60; travel, xi, xiv,
xvii, xix, 325–30; on women, 265; on
work, 323–24; writing/working, xii, xvi,
xvii, 9, 17, 131, 152, 153–54, 159, 175,
179, 186, 214, 357; works, ix–x, xi–xii,
xiv, xviii, 96; aborted, xvi, 87, 160n; critical reception, xi, xii, xiii, xiv, xv, xvi,
xvii, xviii, xix, 124, 128, 196; novels, xii,
xiii, 148, 162–63, 242; popular success
of, xvi; in progress, 129, 359, 371; republished, xviii

Wescott, Josephine Gordon (mother of GW),
41, 55, 56, 101, 140, 178, 254, 281;
death of, xvii; ill health, 360, 398; and
illness/death of Bruce Wescott, 338,
339, 340; living with GW at Stone-
blossom, 340–41, 342–44, 345–46,
347, 352, 355, 360, 365, 366, 367,
370, 373, 377, 379, 387–88, 390,
397–98

Wescott, Katherine (Kate) (sister of GW),
225

Wescott, Lloyd (brother of GW), xv, xvii,
12–13, 32, 41, 51, 56, 59, 63, 67, 85–
86, 97, 101, 115, 121, 128–29, 131,
134, 135–37, 153, 155, 159, 178,
184, 196, 197, 201, 203, 210, 215, 239,
241, 255, 260, 265, 271, 275, 318, 320,
332, 343, 365–66, 367, 370, 388;
farming, 129, 133, 163, 172, 191, 239–
40, 252; GW correspondence with, 107–8,
252–53; and GW finances, 262, 274,
334, 340, 345, 346, 352; illness, 321;
relationship with GW, 192, 256, 267–
68

Wescott, Marjorie (sister of GW), 232, 243
Wescott family, 78, 249–51
West, Rebecca, xii, 124, 135, 186
Wetmore, Maude, 61
Wheeler, Monroe, vii, xix, 3–4, 12–13, 14n,
  17, 28, 29, 39, 40, 55, 57, 58, 62, 66,
  107–10, 113, 117, 118–19, 123, 129,
  131, 138, 139–40, 144, 145–46, 147,
  149, 150, 151, 153, 154, 155, 157, 159,
  163, 164, 167–68, 172, 179–80, 191,
  202, 204, 216, 220, 221, 243, 244, 245,
  247, 250, 251, 252, 257, 265, 272, 275,
  281, 286, 297, 299, 302, 319, 320, 329,
  331, 338, 340, 341, 359, 365–66, 375,
  377, 378, 379, 380, 381, 385, 390, 392,
  394, 398–99; books published by, xii,
  xiii–xiv; career in arts, xiv–xv, xvi, xvii,
  148, 242, 248, 282, 283; death of, xix;
  and GW, x, xi, xiv, 3n, 4, 9, 17, 21, 22,
  64, 67, 69, 95, 111, 176, 178, 187, 188,
  195, 215, 239, 240, 258, 278, 282, 295,
  310, 321–22, 324, 326, 328, 330, 336,
  370, 371; GW correspondence with, 232,
  327; and GW financial affairs, 262, 387;
  and/on GW literary talent, 183, 342, 349;
  and GW ménage à trois, 20; GW on, 49–
  51, 238; and GW writing, 348, 350–51,
  364, 376, 391; ill health, 395; and Kinsey,
  265–66; and L. Wescott, 136, 321; and
  Maugham, 160, 292–93, 294

Whitman, Walt, 217, 223, 299, 341, 352,
  356
Wilder, Thornton, xiii, xvii, xviii, 92n, 198,
  236, 239, 241, 263, 276, 303, 307, 319,
  321, 324, 333, 396, 398
Williams, Charles, 289
Williams, Mona Harrison, 290
Wilson, Edmund, xvi, xvii, 80, 222
Wind, Edgar, 202
Windham, Donald, 190
Winters, Yvor, x, 231
Wodehouse, P. G., 337
Wolfe, Thomas, 151, 169, 214
Woolf, Virginia, vii, 290, 292, 298–99, 352
World War II, 73, 80–81, 84, 90, 122, 127–
  28, 141–42, 144, 149
Wrentmore, Norvil, 84, 85
Wylie, Elinor, 276, 281

Yaddo artists colony, 232, 233–34, 235, 291
Year of Love, A (GW), xvi, 336, 352, 359,
  366
Yeats, William Butler, 17, 49, 66, 79, 142,
  232, 312, 319
"Yellow Fog, The" (GW), 359, 381
Yeon, John, 121, 153, 225–26, 230–31

Zabel, Morton Dawen, 313
Zayas, Virginia de, 86
Zilbourg, Gregory, 15–16